Masking Selves, Making Subjects

Masking Selves, Making Subjects

Japanese American Women, Identity, and the Body

Traise Yamamoto

UNIVERSITY OF CALIFORNIA PRESS

Berkeley / Los Angeles / London

Part of chapter 1 was previously published as " 'As Natural as the Partnership of Sun and Moon': The Logic of Sexualized Metonymy in *Pictures from the Water Trade* and *The Lady and the Monk*," *positions* 4, no. 2 (summer 1996): 321–41.

Mitsuye Yamada's poems are reprinted from *Camp Notes* (Latham, N.Y.: Kitchen Table / Women of Color Press, 1992) and *Desert Run: Poems and Stories* (Latham, N.Y.: Kitchen Table / Women of Color Press, 1988), all by permission of the poet. Copyright © 1992 and 1988 by Mitsuye Yamada.

Janice Mirikitani's poems are reprinted from *Awake in the River* (San Francisco: Isthmus Press, 1978), *Shedding Silence* (Berkeley: Celestial Arts, 1987), and *We, the Dangerous* (London: Virago Press, 1995), all by permission of the poet. Copyright © 1978, 1987, and 1995 by Janice Mirikitani.

Kimiko Hahn's poems are reprinted from *Air Pocket* (Brooklyn: Hanging Loose Press, 1989), *Earshot* (Brooklyn: Hanging Loose Press, 1992), and *The Unbearable Heart* (New York: Kaya Production, 1995), all by permission of the poet and the respective publishers. Copyright © 1989, 1992, and 1995 by Kimiko Hahn.

University of California Press
Berkeley and Los Angeles, California

University of California Press, Ltd.
London, England

© 1999 by
The Regents of the University of California

Library of Congress Cataloging-in-Publication Data

Yamamoto, Traise, 1961–
    Masking selves, making subjects : Japanese American women, identity, and the body / Traise Yamamoto.
        p.   cm.
    Includes bibliographic references and index.
    ISBN 0-520-21033-6 (alk. paper).—ISBN 0-520-21034-4—(pbk.: alk. paper)
        1. American literature—Japanese American authors—History and criticism.   2. American literature—Women authors—History and criticism.   3. American literature—20th century—History and criticism.   4. Japanese American women—Intellectual life.
    5. Japanese Americans—Ethnic identity.   6. Japanese Americans in literature.   7. Group identity in literature.   8. Body, Human, in literature.   I. Title.
PS153.J34Y36   1999
810.9'9287'089956—DC21   98-14154
                                                                                      CIP

Printed in the United States of America
9 8 7 6 5 4 3 2 1

The paper used in this publication is both acid-free and totally chlorine-free (TCF). It meets the minimum requirements of American Standard for Information Sciences—Permanence of Paper for Printed Library Materials, ANSI Z39.48-1984.

For Paul A. Simon and
Kiyoshi Roger Simon—
my best love to you both,
my best loves.

And for my mother,
Jane Toshiko,
with respect and love.

Contents

Acknowledgments

Through the years the thinking and writing of this book have taken, I have often thought of the many people who enabled me to undertake this task. I want to begin by thanking some of those who helped prepare me for the work I now find myself lucky enough to do. Thanks to Carolyn Radar, Bernard Jeffries, Suzanne Babinski and Denise DeRose. During my years as an undergraduate at San Jose State University, I benefited greatly from the many professors there whose intellectual rigor, enthusiasm and excellence in teaching gave me many of the academic tools that have informed my life as a scholar: Virginia deAraújo, Hans Guth, Donald Keesey, Joan Todd, Katherine Blecki, Robert Hass and the late Naomi Clark. I feel an especially deep respect and affection for Nils Peterson, in whose classes I first began to realize the possibilities for bringing one's engagement with life into the classroom.

At the University of Washington, where this book began as a dissertation, I would like to thank Joycelyn Moody, Shirley J. Yee and Susan Jeffords, three of the readers on my committee. Many thanks and affectionate appreciation to Shawn Wong for guiding me through the field of Asian American literature, for generously loaning or giving me needed books and articles and for providing professional opportunities that were essential to the completion of my graduate degree. And my heartfelt thanks to Carolyn Allen, without whom I would never have undertaken this study or engaged with its issues in the first place. Though she would protest in embarrassment, I owe her a great deal and will never forget her patience with my resisting self in seminar. She has taught me how one can be both critical and compassionate within, as well as outside, the academy. A teacher in the highest and best sense, her courage and high personal and academic standards will always remain for me a guiding model.

For leading me through the often confusing labyrinth of graduate requirements, I thank Kathy Mork, at the University of Washington, for being so incredibly good at what she does. Many of the opportunities I benefited from were a direct result of her attentiveness. I acknowledge here the many fellowships I received from University of Washington's Minority Graduate Division, and I gratefully acknowledge Richard Dunn and Míceál Vaughan for extending departmental support at a critical point in my graduate career.

Thank you to all those who volunteered the cheerful and loving child care that enabled me to concentrate on the completion of my degree: Harry Neal, Jody Segal, George Howland Jr., Kandice Chuh, Kim Johnson-Bogart and Victoria Schoenburg. And for other kinds of care, I thank Marla Herbig and, with special fondness, Paul David.

At the University of California, Riverside, I have been blessed with the best colleagues one could hope for. The excellence of their own work has acted as a spur and inspiration to my own, and all have welcomed me without reservation. I am grateful to the members of my writing group, Katherine Kinney, Joseph P. Childers and George Haggerty, for their insightful and demanding readings of key sections of this book. My conversations with my colleagues and friends have been both informative and supportive: thanks to Jennifer DeVere Brody, Tiffany Ana López, Sue-Ellen Case, Carole-Anne Tyler, Parama Roy, Steven Axelrod and, in History, Devra Webber. I also want to thank my colleagues Edward Chang, Piya Chatterjee, Rodney Ogawa and Deborah Wong, at the Center for Asian Pacific America at the University of California, Riverside, for their enthusiastic and informed readings of parts of this book, as well as for their rousing friendship. I acknowledge the Center for Ideas and Society at the University of California, Riverside, for a research fellowship in fall 1995. No list of thanks due would be complete without expressing my appreciation for Nancy E. Rettig, whose professionalism and humor keep us all on-track in the English Department.

To all my students, both undergraduate and graduate, here and elsewhere, I give many thanks for the ways in which my own work has been forwarded by their often difficult questions and their insights. My appreciation to James Ka Chi Mok for library research. My very appreciative thanks to my graduate research assistants Thao Xuan Lam and Hanna Nguyen for help with sources, references and other tasks; and many thanks to Shani Bergen and Jeff Rhyne, without whose help I could not have finished this book in a timely manner.

For her support, integrity and friendship, I thank my colleague at the University of Washington, Caroline Chung Simpson. From its inception as a dissertation, this study has benefited from her advice and research, which she has shared unstintingly. Similarly, Shelli Booth Fowler at Washington State University has lent me her ear on numerous occasions and shared helpful professional advice. Thanks to my friends and colleagues Gregory Choy and Catherine Ceniza Choy for their readiness to fire up the barbecue and talk (and talk and talk) shop, and my special thanks to Greg for his bibliophilia, from which I have benefited outrageously, and for reading through this manuscript with a keen eye. Also, gratitude and appreciation to Alan Chong Lau and to John M. Liu, for everything they do; and to Elaine Kim, Shirley Lim, Amy Ling, Lisa Lowe and Sau-ling Wong, whose work and presence in the academy have meant a great deal to me.

At the University of California Press, I want to thank William Murphy, who first saw the potential in my book and enthusiastically supported it through the approval process. I couldn't have asked for a better or more conscientious advocate. I also thank Naomi Schneider, Rachel Berchten, Jeanne Park and Edith Gladstone, who all helped bring the project to completion. I gratefully acknowledge Debbie Henderson at the Japanese American National Museum in Los Angeles for helping me secure permission for the painting that graces the cover of this book.

Any endeavor like this one is never accomplished alone, nor is it only the result of professional and academic support. Throughout my graduate studies and the writing of this book, my family has been wonderful. None of my work would be possible had not my grandparents, both maternal and paternal, imagined a life different from theirs for their children and grandchildren—an imagining whose cost was hard, long and ill-paid physical labor. I dedicate the spirit of this study to my paternal grandfather, Kenzo Yamamoto—who could not have the life of the scholar he would have so loved but who spent ten years researching and writing a book published near the end of his life—and to my maternal grandmother, Hisami Morimitsu Tanigawa, who passed on to me her love of reading and, I hope, her determination and pride.

My parents have each unstintingly given encouragement and support—emotional, spiritual and, frequently, material. Love and many thanks to my father, David Hiroshi Yamamoto, who still surprises me with his sense of adventure and the possibilities of change, and to whom I happily claim my many likenesses. His support, in all kinds of ways, has been terrific and so appreciated. Love to Mary Steichen Yamamoto, and a gaggle of far-away kisses to my little brother and sister, Ryan Ryota Yamamoto and Kathryn Akane Yamamoto.

I hardly know how to begin thanking my mother, Jane Toshiko Miller. Buying my first computer, listening to me hour after hour on long-distance, she has shown in ways great and small her belief in me. To her I owe both the dark and the light that make a person whole: she is a woman of great inner strength and fierce love, and I am proud to be her daughter. My loving thanks to Richard Miller, for being there through everything.

Much love to my brother, Todd Yamamoto, a wonderful, laughing man whose generosity to those around him is a pleasure and to my languages-whiz sister-in-law Sydney Gaoiran Yamamoto. Love and thanks to my cousin and sister of the heart, Maile Vanderford, for laughter and the courage of longing, as well as to Ty, Tei and Haley; to my other sister of the heart, Coleen Higa Gulbraa, who keeps alive the sense of possibility and the necessary connection to one's inner life; and to Tony, Matthew and Rachel for always making space when we descend on your home. Love to Ron and Mary China, the Okamura and Sakamoto families, Mark and Cathy Simon, and Julie, Dave and Adam Ruark.

Finally, my deep love, appreciation and abiding friendship to my husband, Paul A. Simon, who has seen me through every doubt, enthusiasm, depression, challenge and accomplishment for over fifteen years. From reading and critiquing drafts to cooking meals, from listening to my half-formed ideas to making sure I have some downtime, he has never failed to put my needs before his own and has done so with grace and few complaints. Somehow he has managed to continue his work as an artist, as well as to become a patient and tender father. This book is in so many ways the result of your faith in me and belief in my work. Thank you for everything, and more. We did it.

And to the light of my heart, our lovely boy-chan, Kiyoshi Roger Simon—who has lived with this project all of his life and among whose first multisyllabic words were "dissertation" and "chapter"—my love beyond all language and reason. You make everything, past and present, remembered and forgotten, shining and whole.

Note on Terms

Issei, Nisei, Sansei and Yonsei are terms that denote persons of the immigrant and first, second, and third American-born generations, respectively. Thus, though "Nisei" means "second-generation," the term refers to the first American-born generation. "Kibei" describes a Nisei (a Japanese American born in the United States) who has returned to the States after being educated in Japan. "Nikkei" refers to anyone of Japanese ancestry, irrespective of country of birth or citizenship.

Readers will also find the shorthand terms "Japanese/American" and "Asian/American" throughout, which refer equally to Japanese nationals and Japanese Americans, and to Asian nationals and Asian Americans. I use such terms to call attention to those constructions, structures of domination or identifications that similarly affect Japanese and Japanese Americans, and Asians and Asian Americans, as well as to the ways in which the terms are often conflated by the dominant culture.

The term Asian American is a political, coalitional identification that refers to a wide range of Asian and Pacific Islander ethnic groups. Many prefer the term Asian and Pacific Islander American (API) or Asian Pacific American (APA). However, I have chosen to retain "Asian American," even as I recognize that it collapses distinct immigration histories, periods and circumstances and flattens significant differences in relation to citizenship and national identity formation.

Kazuo, Hisami and Ayako Tanigawa (1938)

Introduction

Oakland 1938: my maternal grandmother, Hisami Morimitsu Tanigawa, stands rigidly behind the chair in which her husband is seated. Her firstborn, two-year-old Ayako, stands in front, posed beside her seated doll. In a few short days Ayako is scheduled to sail to Japan, where she has never been. My grandfather's parents will accompany her, raise her as their child and, in return, expect to be cared for in their old age. My grandmother has had no say in the matter. She is pregnant with her second child.

Even in the formal order of the studio portrait, my grandmother's face is exceptionally closed. Some quality of the way she holds her face catches my attention, and it is difficult to tell whose face is more impassive, the doll's or my grandmother's. Her face is neither set hard in resignation nor slack with grief. It is a face that understands its own readability, one that uses the conventions of photographic portraiture to contain what must be feelings of chaotic desperation. Its surface is absolutely smooth, and in its almost studied blankness I think I can divine her anguish, the certainty of losing her child. In four years my grandmother will find herself and two young children interned at the Tanforan horse-racing track, my grandfather having been sent elsewhere. She will not see Ayako, raised to believe her mother did not want her, for almost forty years. For an Issei who was exceptional in her willingness to talk about the internment camps, my grandmother's almost total and lifelong silence about that day in 1938 is a notable anomaly.

None of this future, of course, registers in my grandmother's face, but little of the present does either. It is a mask of impassivity, a surface whose increasing hardness through the years meant survival. To have identified with the hardships and humiliations of her life as a Japanese woman immigrant in the United States, where non-Asians took one look at her and relegated her to the gibberish-speaking "oriental" masses, would have been to erase the distinction between what others thought of her and what she knew herself to be. She was a strong woman who had no use for anyone who assumed her quiescent passivity, and she never let anyone treat her with a level of respect not befitting her sense of her own dignity. My grandmother preferred to express only those emotions that maintained the exterior toughness that had helped her get through life's hardships and disappointments: anger, frustration, resistant stubbornness, pride.

Which made her choice of an American name all the more interesting. When she decided it was time to take on a name that non-Japanese could pronounce, she refused to go with the usual choices: Mary, Sue, Ann. My grandmother sat herself down in front of a mirror, looked long and hard at her own face and named what she saw: Rose. No matter that she could only with difficulty pronounce the first letter. No matter that the name evoked a whole range of softnesses and a kind of traditional femininity my grandmother's life as a working-class immigrant denied her. That was what and *who* she saw when she allowed her own gaze past the surface she'd created to protect herself from the indignities of everyday life: Rose.

I think of my grandmother not as Rose, but as the woman who named herself Rose, and that act of self-naming has become a paradigm for the contradictions and strengths of her life. In the photograph of that awful day in 1938, I see something within closing itself off: the two daughters born after Ayako was taken away rarely, if ever, saw whatever it was that had prompted their mother to take on a name so at odds with what they knew of her. But I also see something deciding to live, far below the surface and fiercely protected.

I begin with these stories because they map out what is at the heart of this book, *Masking Selves, Making Subjects,* and because it is vitally important to remember what grounds the scholarly and theoretical forays we make. Like my grandmother, other Japanese immigrant and Japanese American women have often lived difficult lives, laboring under harsh, frequently humiliating, conditions of poverty and subject to the authority of their fathers and husbands. Nevertheless, many of those women managed to find within themselves a dignity and emotional strength that they protected and that, in turn, protected them. In addition, Nikkei women have long been perceived by dominant culture as either perpetual foreigners or exotic others, both masks of "oriental" difference. In response, they have deployed the very surface whose opacity has denied them particularity and humanity in order to claim and preserve both.

The grammatical doubleness of the first part of the title, *Masking Selves,* is deliberate: it suggests both a process enacted by an agency separate from the socially defined self as well as a self whose agency is enacted in the process of masking. The language of surface and depth in my opening no doubt evokes for many notions of humanist interiority, the assumption that beneath social roles, there is a locatable "real" self. Thus, I should point out that this study grounds itself in the awkward juncture between two claims: that identity is a highly contingent and constructed category, one that for marginalized subjects must necessarily reference the ways in which the individual body is marked and circulates in the social and discursive arenas; and the somewhat contradictory assertion that for all the language of postmodern subjectivity, there remains a place for the self, that which is often rather condescendingly referred to as the product of a backwards humanism. I retain the language of the self in conjunction with that of the subject, conjoined in what one might call a critical humanism, in order to discuss modes of agency that disrupt and cannot be causally or directly traced to the social or discursive constructs that would seem to determine the subject in all its modalities.

Therefore, while much of what follows in this book relies on a concept of the subject constructed by various sign systems of race and gender that do not and never have corresponded to any inherent characteristics indexed by the body's supposedly visible difference from racial and gender norms, I also insist on creating a space for the self understood as conscious of its own complexity, contradictions and internal differences. In many ways my own theoretical stance is similar to that articulated by Dorinne Kondo. Thus, I too find myself

in the paradoxical position of deploying what is conventionally known as an antihumanist discourse for humanist ends. That is, my emphasis on complexity, power, contradiction, discursive production, and ambiguity is invoked in part to demonstrate complexity and irony in the lives of the people I knew, in order to complicate and dismantle the ready stereotypes that erase complexity in favor of simple, unitary images. (Kondo, 301–2)

While I argue for the multiplicity and complexity of Japanese American women, I do not propose that those characteristics carry value in and of themselves. As Kondo points out, her arguments for "the complex humanity" of the Japanese with whom she worked are ultimately "an argument for my own humanity" (302). Inasmuch as arguments for one's own humanity might be taken as nostalgic gestures, I suggest that the notion of a nostalgic return is irrelevant for those who have not been accorded the status of coherent subject in the first place.

One of the implicit arguments that informs this entire study, then, is that Japanese immigrant and Japanese American women assume a self-hood that has often been denied them. It is an argument that recognizes the necessity of claiming the self as a functional totality when it is frag-mented into identificatory categories defined less by an underlying hu-manity and more by a taxonomy of difference. My purpose is to inter-rogate issues of representation, essentialism and subjectivity as they relate to Japanese American women. How do they construct the self as subject within a society that constructs them as objects without agency? How do the intersections of race, gender and national identity frame, affect and modify the ways in which Japanese American women position themselves? What difference does difference make? These questions not only enable my discussion of the literature written by Japanese American women to engage issues beyond the scope of textual analysis but call attention to these texts as directly issuing from the writers' self-conscious concerns with questions of subjectivity.

This study seeks to contribute to the increasing, but still relatively small, body of Asian American literary theory by focusing on a specific ethnic and gender group.[1] Although some of my observations are ap-plicable to other Asian American ethnic groups, and to the women within those groups, I have tried as much as possible to limit my dis-cussion to the historical and cultural specifics of Japanese Americans.[2] One of my purposes in writing this study has been to provide a full-length discussion of Japanese American women writers and their work, a project that has not been previously undertaken. My premise is that this body of work has been misread, when it has been read at all, by a critical tradition based on either sociohistorical or formalist categories that marginalizes the Japanese American female literary tradition, a sit-uation that parallels the overall marginalization of the Asian American literary tradition.

Masking Selves, Making Subjects examines the ways in which Japanese American women's textual narratives employ discursive strategies that are ethnic-specific and that respond to the ways in which Japanese American women have been subject to orientalist constructions — manifested in textual narratives as well as filmic representation — whose underlying economy of visibility invests their racially and gender-marked bodies as sites of both difference and desire. Thus, Japanese American women writers find themselves in a highly problematic relationship to their own bodies. Through an examination of autobiographical writings, fiction and poetry, I argue that these writers have employed the trope of masking — which, at its most literal level, is directly connected to the construction of the Japanese face as the mask of difference — for their own ends. Through psychological, narrative and metaphoric forms of masking, Japanese American women writers enact a mode of discursive agency that allows them to claim a viable and resistant subjectivity. What emerges is a poetics of Japanese American female subjectivity inflected through the complex specificities of, as Jeanne Wakatsuki Houston puts it, "that other, private self."

In order to contextualize my discussion of the literature written by Japanese American women, chapters one and two focus on the representations and constructions of Japanese and Japanese American women by dominant white American culture. Because a primary element in the construction of Japanese American women as racial and sexual others involves their conflation with Japanese women, the first chapter examines the gender-marked relationship between the West (particularly Britain and the United States) and Japan. From 1853 to the present, the Western imagination has consistently infantilized and feminized Japan, constructing the Japanese woman as a metonym for Japanese national, racial, and cultural identity. Through the paradigm of heterosexual mastery, as suggested in my analyses of the films *Teahouse of the August Moon* and *Sayonara,* as well as in close readings of two contemporary travel narratives, the Japanese woman becomes the embodied site of both difference and desire. The logic of sexual reciprocity recuperates the West's flagging sense of national ascendancy and coherence, a process that is fetishistically enacted upon the "geisha-ized" Japanese woman.

Building on the discussion of the social politics of orientalism, chapter two examines how the combination of the geisha stereotype and the visually based racial economy of the United States results in the invisibility of the Japanese American female subject. Ironically, as I demonstrate through a reading of the film *Come See the Paradise,* her invisibility as a subject is paired with her hypervisibility as a sexualized, racially marked body. Through the work of theorists Trinh T. Minh-ha and

Frantz Fanon, I contest notions of subjectivity that both valorize indeterminacy and fragmentation as the privileged hallmarks of the postmodern subject and conflate difference with identity in a manner that
essentializes difference as ontology. I focus this discussion around two
Sansei autobiographical narratives in which the status of the Japanese
American subject in Japan puts pressure on the "readability" of body.
Finally, it is in this chapter that I introduce the trope of masking, its
connection to the construction of the Japanese face, and its implications
for any discussion of Japanese American female subjectivity.

The third chapter develops the trope of masking through a reading
of Nisei autobiographies by Monica Sone, Yoshiko Uchida and Jeanne
Wakatsuki Houston. The historical and social conditions out of which
these texts emerge provide a crucial contextualizing framework through
which these writers contest traditional theories of autobiography. Further, the tropical deployment of masking constructs encoded narratives
that resist and criticize the dominant ideology that erases Nisei women
as subjects. These autobiographies attest to a crisis of raced subjectivity
wherein the impulses of disavowal and abjection compete with the
equally strong necessity of identifying with the raced self associated with
the Japanese mother. The sense of a split or bifurcated subjectivity that
results from these contestatory impulses suggests that ambivalence is
one mechanism through which racial and gendered identities are constructed.

Chapter four examines the mother-daughter relationship and the
trope of maternal absence in the fiction and plays of several Japanese
American women writers, both Nisei and Sansei. Instead of following
a psychoanalytic model that presupposes the necessity of a break between the mother and daughter in order for the latter to individuate, a
model whose implicit and assumed point of view is that of the daughter,
these narratives fundamentally resist such a model. The mother-
daughter intersubjectivity in these works calls for a critical and theoretical recognition of the necessity for the daughter to both differentiate
from and identify with the mother, who models survival as a simultaneously raced and gendered subject. The trope of absence subtly foregrounds interpretive strategies that privilege the daughter's subjectivity
and suggests the need to read simultaneously from the mother's point
of view. Such a move recuperates absence from the lack to which it is
consigned in even feminist psychoanalytic frameworks and aligns it with
what King-Kok Cheung calls "articulate silence" and maternal agency.

In the final chapter I turn to the work of three contemporary Japanese

American women poets as extending and commenting on many of the issues raised in the preceding chapters. Writing in and after an era marked by feminist and ethnic protest, these writers overtly struggle with their often competing identifications as Japanese Americans and as women; with issues of sexuality and nationalism; and with the problematics of discursivity and essentialism. Perhaps most strikingly, in their efforts to claim a viable Japanese American female poetic voice, they reappropriate and identify with the figure of the Japanese woman as a source of their own agency. The three poets I discuss, Mitsuye Yamada, Janice Mirikitani and Kimiko Hahn, explore what it means to be an embodied subject and what that suggests about the role of and relationship to language.

The generic categories within which I explore thematic concerns allow me to discuss Japanese American women's autobiography, fiction and poetry against traditional theorizations of each respective genre, but the classificatory schematic I adopt, or impose, does not imply that similarities of genre override or are more significant than thematic resonances or generational similarities. However, just as African American slave narratives have recast formulations about the function of autobiography and its representations of the autobiographical self, just as early twentieth-century women's poetry complicates understandings about literary modernism, so does the literature written by Japanese American women necessarily and fruitfully revise our understanding of American literary expression. The autobiographies I examine, for instance, call into question the characterization of American autobiography as a tradition based on the experiential singularity of the individual subject, as well as one in which the implicit narrative traces the movement from "outsider" to "citizen." The poetry of Yamada, Mirikitani and Hahn often intentionally blurs the line between writer and speaker, thus problematizing the insistence on formal analysis that strictly marks explication off from the autobiographical.

Wherever possible, I seek to draw thematic connections between chapters in an attempt to counteract the artificial boundaries of genre and in the hope that by so doing, the issues I address in one chapter may be deepened by their discussion in other chapters. Thus, there is a necessary overlapping and reiteration of themes from one chapter to the next. In one sense, the resistance of these texts to being bound within discrete categories suggests an intriguing analogue for the models of subjectivity that emerge within them.

"As natural as the partnership of sun and moon"

Western Masculinity, Japanese Women and the Feminization of Japan

---

In the years since World War II, Japan and the United States have become perhaps the world's oddest couple—totally dissimilar in their ethnic and cultural heritages, yet deeply involved with each other in ways both obvious and not so obvious.

Robert C. Christopher, *The Japanese Mind*

The West thinks of itself as masculine—big guns, big industry, big money—so the East is feminine, weak, delicate, poor . . . but good at art, and full of inscrutable wisdom—the feminine mystique. . . . You expect Oriental countries to submit to your guns, and you expect Oriental women to be submissive to your men. That's why you say they make the best wives.

David Henry Hwang, *M. Butterfly*

If the East now has the power, it has long emitted potent metaphorical odors: the spiritual mystery, the sexual kink.

Richard Corliss, "Pacific Overtures"

One afternoon my third-grade teacher, Mr. Strieper, announced that we would begin our section on "foreign lands" with the geography and history of Japan. "It's far, far away on the other side of the world," he said, pulling down a large wall map. "Maybe you," he looked toward me, "could say the names of the islands for us."

"I don't know them," I mumbled.

"Sure you do." Mr. Strieper's supremely confident, if somewhat annoyed, tone assumed his rightness and suggested that I was being perversely forgetful. "All right," he finally said, "repeat after me," and he began to intone the names of Japan's islands in that particular inflection of the elementary-school teacher, "Hoe-kay-doe, Kee-yoo-shew, Hon-shew, Shee-kow-koo."

The next day's lesson concerned how "we" made friends with the Japanese, an unfriendly and humorless lot. Commodore Perry, realizing an icebreaker was needed, decided to give the Japanese court a gift, a technological novelty in 1854: a small-scale steam engine. As the train chuffs its way around the circular track, the heretofore silent court begins to exclaim excitedly. Soon, each small boxcar holds a court dignitary, the sleeves of his robes fluttering in the breeze.

I remember feeling simultaneously charmed and embarrassed by the image of a bunch of Japanese court officials riding around in what was essentially a toy train, while the commodore and his men stand and watch. It is largely, I think, because of that embarrassment that I can still clearly recall what I assumed for many years was the happy invention of a textbook company trying to attract the interest of eight-year-olds.

As it happens, there is historical documentation that corroborates this narrative of what was otherwise a minor element in the "opening of Japan."[1] However fancifully embellished, I nevertheless find this textbook lesson's account useful for the ways in which it emblematizes the dominant attitude of the West toward Japan. It is significant that the Japanese are constructed in terms immediately understandable to and synonymous with young children: namely, the lure of the steam engine reduces the Japanese court to the level of children whose curiosity renders them instantly malleable. Thus, the veneer of dignified gravity — which functions here to establish the otherness of the Japanese — gives way to childlike glee. And while their reaction makes the Japanese seem more like "us," that similarity is marked by the infantile, whose confirmation is secured through the body. As Perry and his men look paternally on, the Japanese court ministers are able to somehow fit themselves into the dimensions of a miniaturized train. The image of robe sleeves fluttering in the breeze further emasculates the Japanese, conflating the images of womanliness and childishness.

History Lessons: Making Difference

Japan has long occupied a problematic position in the Western imaginary. In the mid-sixteenth century the Jesuits proclaimed the Japanese to be "the most promising and accomplished of the heathen" (Dower, 94), but also frustratingly impossible to understand, inscrutable. The perceived paradox presented by Japan and the many projections and conclusions following from it have been, as John Dower has pointed out, "perpetuated virtually unchanged by succeeding centuries of Western observers" (94). Since Commodore Perry's unwelcome landing on the closed shores of Tokyo Bay in 1853, Japan has increasingly served as one of the many mirrors in whose reflection the West represents and constructs itself. Alternately figured as the absolute Other whose difference signifies the necessity to conquer, either militarily or economically, and as the mysterious and seductive Other whose exoticism is the come-on for Western cultural penetration, Japan has been consistently "Japanized" by the West.[2] One particular move of this process of Japanization has been to reduce Japan to a country of childlike women.

The continual reification of Japan as absolute other must be understood within the context of its perceived threat to the West. In tandem with the images of the feudally loyal samurai, the fanatically nationalist kamikaze, and the aggressively acquisitional corporate executive, the historical episodes of the Sino-Japanese war, Japan's colonialist aggression in the Philippines and Korea, Pearl Harbor and the "economic miracle" of the 1970s and 1980s have reinforced the idea of Japan as hostilely antithetical to the interests of the West. In response, the discourse of the West has served to assert its potency and erase the threatening figure of the calculating, cold and bestially cruel instrument of the Japanese empire (either soldier or salaryman) with the comic figure of the wimpy, buck-toothed, four-eyed, perennially badly suited, camera-toting tourist. While the West has acted with its own forms of military and economic aggression, such maneuvers have been constructed as essentially reactive and defensive, a corollary to its sense of enlightened decency. In the overlap of the geopolitical and the geocultural, the Japanese and Japan constitute a crucial site at which racial differentiation is played out, a site at which white Western masculinity (re)establishes its superiority, dominance and, increasingly, innocence.

While Japan has not been literally colonized by the West, it has been consistently subjected to the West's colonialist and imperialist attitudes—which became abundantly evident during the American Occupation following World War II.[3] I do not wish to elide important differences between Japan and those Third World countries that have labored under the oppressions of "classic" colonialism: what I am tracing here is the imperialist mentality and its colonialist tendencies relative to

Japan, an ideological trajectory that includes the civilizing missions of the Jesuits in the sixteenth century, Commodore Perry's forced landing in the nineteenth century, the influx of Christian missionaries in the early twentieth century, and the disciplinary rise of Japan studies in the mid-twentieth century. In each instance, Japan has been positioned as a site of instruction and an object of knowledge subject to the West's ideological gaze.[4]

I should note here that I am not unaware of the problematics in employing the monolithic term "the West," especially as it makes no distinctions between or within individual countries. Although I focus my discussion on France, England and the United States, I have opted to retain "the West" as a viable, though provisional, constitutive term since the West or "the Occident" has historically identified and represented itself hegemonically—assuming under that rubric a similarity of culture, religion, language family, mores—in relation to the East/Orient. In its dealings with "the Orient," individual western European countries have historically made little or no distinction between themselves, the West and Western civilization (Said 1978, 35). Although the terms West/Occident, East/Orient originated as geographically based distinctions, they soon came to delineate contrasting ideological poles, and the duality of West and East provided a schema that would hold any number of oppositional pairings. Further, I am in agreement with those like Chandra Talpade Mohanty who believe "it is possible to trace a coherence of effects resulting from the implicit assumption of 'the West' (in all its complexities and contradictions) as the primary referent in theory and praxis" (52). Finally, although my discussion centers primarily on the United States and Britain, I do not believe that the feminization or exoticization of Japan or the sexualization of Japanese women is a discursive or ideological practice limited to those two countries.

In his discussion of the relation between imperialism and modernism, Edward Said suggests that the bumper crop of Western modernist novels dealing with "loss and disablement" finds its compensatory complement in "not only the novel of frank exoticism and confident empire, but travel narratives, works of colonial exploration and scholarship, memoirs, experience and expertise" (Said 1993, 187). The relation Said points to is certainly manifested in one of the first outpouring of books about Japan, which took place during the period identified with European high modernism (1880–1930).[5] In these novels, and particularly in sociological, quasi-anthropological and travel writings, Japan is consistently represented as the curious and subordinate other, living either in the stasis of an indeterminate past or in a state of exotic enchantment. But the privileged, exoticizing and appropriative eye of the West is equally evident in the two other periods in which there is a concentration of writing about Japan: during the 1950s, following the Second World War and contemporaneous with the incursion of so-called war brides; and in the mid-1970s through the 1980s, those years most identified with Japan's economic rise. In all three instances, the West was experiencing a cultural crisis: the instability and fragmentation of the early twentieth century, the shock of contiguity in the 1940s (in the wartime Pacific theater) and 1950s (interracial marriages between American servicemen and Japanese or Korean women), and the economic displacement of the 1970s and 1980s. Scrambling to rearticulate the terms of its power, the West's process of self-valorization has depended largely upon the construction of Japan in terms of absolute alterity.

In a typical example, the insinuations of the following passage, written in 1903 by a sympathetic "Japan expert," find clear resonances in later and contemporary work on Japan and the Japanese:

The vast majority of the implements of our Occidental civilization have their definite place and value, either in contributing directly to the comfort and happiness of their possessor, or in increasing his health and strength and general mental and physical power. What is it that makes the Occidental longer-lived than the Japanese? Why is he healthier? Why is he more intelligent? Why is he a more developed personality? Why are his children more energetic? . . . the full significance of this point can hardly be appreciated without a perception of the great principle that underlies it. The only way in which man has become and continues to be increasingly superior to animals is in his use of mechanisms. . . . The inventiveness of different races differs vastly. But everywhere, the most advanced are the most powerful. (Gulick, 69)[6]

It is transparently clear how the use of rhetorical questions — the answers to which are assumed to be self-evident — implicitly establish the superiority and greater development of the West. Having done so, the rhetoric shifts and "development" is understood as "evolution" (the title of this book is, in fact, *The Evolution of the Japanese*). The implement-less Japanese are associated with the equally implement-less animals; thus, industrialization is implicitly understood to index the scale of human complexity, the top end of which is identified with power and dominance. This schema subtly but powerfully references nineteenth-century racial hierarchies that similarly naturalize the relation between industrial or cultural development and civilization understood as reflective of greater humanness.[7]

The relegation of the Japanese to the status of other is here configured in terms of animal and human, yet similar, if perhaps less starkly articulated, configurations are common in the literature, studies and travel narratives written by white Westerners about Japan. This type of rhetoric is not limited to the early part of this century. During World War II, for instance, a curator in physical anthropology at the Smithsonian Institution explained to a credulous President Roosevelt that Japanese skulls were "some 2,000 years less developed than ours" (Dower, 108).

According to the author of *The Evolution of the Japanese,* "Japan is . . . unquestionably the unique nation of the globe, the land of dream and enchantment, the land which could hardly differ more from our own, were it located in another planet, its people not of this world" (Gulick, 16). Some sixty years later, Pearl Buck wrote in *The People of Japan,* that even amongst Asian countries, themselves a panoply of difference, Japan was "the most different of all" (10). Such examples are not merely charming anachronisms of another and less sophisticated time. In *The Japanese Mind,* published in 1983, Robert C. Christopher argues that "as far as the rest of the world goes, Americans cope as well as can reasonably be expected. In greater or lesser degree, the thought processes of Germans, Russians, Saudis or Nigerians resemble our own sufficiently closely that when we put our minds to it we can usually deal with them. . . . Between Americans and Japanese, however, the gulf is both wider and deeper" (21). Notwithstanding the egregious and presumptuous statement that the Saudis and Nigerians are understood and can be "dealt with" by "us," the Japanese are represented here as being absolutely *different*. So different, in fact, that Russia, the Middle East and Africa, countries constructed as politically, religiously and/or racially other, are deemed comprehensible by comparison. Similarly, though without Christopher's arrogant frustration, Elisabeth Bumiller enthusiastically recalls in *The Secrets of Mariko* (1995) that "after a few months in Japan, I happily realized I was again in a wholly alien culture, more foreign even than India" (9).

Indeed, it is precisely this difference that attracts the French semiotician Roland Barthes. *Empire of Signs* (1982) presents itself as a semiotic deconstruction of Japan whose subject is less Japan than the processes of semiotics. In order that he may more accurately observe the workings of symbolic systems, Barthes chooses a country whose difference "allows [him] to 'entertain' the idea of an unheard-of symbolic system, one altogether detached from our own" (3). While he consistently foregrounds the contructedness of his own cultural symbolic, he does so in order to emphasize Japanese difference. Barthes repeatedly asserts that the excess of signifiers in Japanese culture circumscribes and circulates around ultimate emptiness, a nothingness that does not signify in "his" culture because the West's contrasting semiotic system ultimately cannot articulate this (essential, after all) trait of Japan. And of the Japanese: what is most disturbing about Barthes's book, finally, is that *nothing* is at the heart of anything and everything from tempura to lacquer boxes to the Japanese themselves. What begins as an exploration of Japanese cuisine and aesthetics eventually becomes a discussion of Japanese ontology, epistemology and morality. In the end, the difference that allows Barthes to see more clearly systems of signification and symbology is reinscribed and reified by those systems. Japan is an empire of excess signification, signifying nothing.[8]

Across different genres, and over a period of a hundred or so years, writers again and again insist on, harp on, grapple with this difference, this puzzling otherness. As Said points out in reference to orientalist discourses: "What are striking in these discourses are the rhetorical figures one keeps encountering in their descriptions of 'the mysterious East,' as well as the stereotypes about 'the African [or Indian or Irish or Jamaican or Chinese] mind' " (Said 1993, xi; brackets in original). Such utter inscrutability subverts the West's assumptions of cultural accessibility, that harbinger of the imperialist attitude, and registers as a threat, for of course if "we" cannot conquer "them," "they" may conquer "us." Because discourses of imperialism depend on the construction of the other, the inability to fully "explain" the other is ultimately the failure to establish a viable and deployable rhetoric of national identity.

The most easily identifiable reaction to this threat is to minimize or trivialize it through stereotypes. As Homi Bhabha suggests, there is perhaps more to be gained by "shift[ing] from the *identification* of images as positive or negative, to an understanding of the *processes of subjectification* made possible (and plausible) through stereotypical discourse" (71). I wish to look, then, at how the discourses of infantilization and feminization allow the West to subjectify, objectify and gain access to "the Japanese mind."

Infantilizing Threat

According to one particularly unsubtle observer in 1860, Japan "is a very paradise of babies" (quoted in Chamberlain, 255). The mix of exoticism and paternal condescension here suggests how exoticization and infantilization reciprocally lay the ideological groundwork for each other. For example, in the writings of Lafcadio Hearn (1850–1904), one of the most widely read of the early Japanophiles, it is impossible to ascertain whether his perception of the childlike benignity of the Japanese is the cause or the result of his romantic exoticization:

Elfish everything seems; for everything as well as everybody is small, and queer, and mysterious: the little houses under their blue roofs, the little ship-fronts hung with blue, and the smiling little people in their blue costumes. The illusion is only broken by the occasional passing of a tall foreigner, and by divers shop-signs bearing announcements in absurd attempts at English. Nonetheless such discords only serve to emphasize reality; they never materially lessen the fascination of the funny little streets. (Hearn [1894] 1976, 2–3)

It is difficult to see in this description, written a century ago, the Japan that was beginning the first Sino-Japanese War, a display of Japanese militarism that inaugurated, according to some scholars, the West's "taking Japan seriously" (Lammers, 195).[9] Hearn's discursive pat on the head is repeated in his more widely read *Japan: An Attempt at Interpretation*, written a decade later. The attempt of the Japanese to speak English is implicitly and comically compared to the garbling of toddlers, though nowhere does Hearn record reactions to his attempts at Japanese—if attempts there were. In this example, Japan's difference is located in its physically childlike dimensions, and Hearn's whole tone allays fears that Japan might actively resist Western access (as it did in 1853, leaving Commodore Perry's "black ships" temporarily floating uselessly in Yedo Bay). Instead, the flavor of this passage suggests that Japan and the Japanese are charmingly inaccessible much as the "fairy-land" and "fairy-folk" to which Hearn compares them ([1894] 1976, 7). The threat of difference is doubly defused: first, through the general discourse of romantic exoticization, second, through the lexicon of infantilization. Thus, no threat but "a queer thrill impossible to describe,—a feeling of weirdness" (1904, 10).

Here, as elsewhere, Hearn dehistoricizes Japan: it is the timeless land of harmless, cute little people ("Everybody looks at you curiously; but there is never anything disagreeable, much less hostile in the gaze: most commonly it is accompanied by a smile or half smile. And the ultimate consequence of all these kindly curious looks and smiles is that the stranger finds himself thinking of fairy-land" [(1894) 1976, 7]). But what is most significant here is that exoticization, dehistoricization and infantilization occur at the site of the (small) Japanese body, which, as we shall see, is variously though consistently constructed as the site of irreducible difference.

Where Hearn infantilizes the Japanese with a kind of paternal fondness, Ian Buruma in *Behind the Mask* (1984), published almost a century later, does so with a paternal contempt that masquerades under the guise of quasi-psychological analysis. This shift reflects Japan's perceived transformation from a charming little country of backward people to a military threat and economic superpower. Accordingly, the infantilization of Japan intensifies—becoming more aggressive, more contemptuous and more absurd—during the period surrounding World War II and again in the 1970s and 1980s. In these instances, unlike those around the turn of the century, the relationship between Japanese subjects and the Japanese nation is a profoundly dangerous one. As explanation for and disavowal of the significance of Japanese national identity, the relationship between subjects and nation is figured as one between infantile Japanese individuals and the Japanese mother. Thus, the threat following from a nationalistic attachment to "the motherland" is defused through the image of a country whose maternal practices produce ineptitude and/or regressive perversion. During the Second World War, for instance, John Dower notes that the Japanese were widely believed to be poor pilots because of inner-ear defects. Not satisfied with simple genetic inferiority theories, one explanation had it that the "practice of strapping babies to their mother's backs . . . caused their heads to bounce about and permanently impaired their sense of balance" (105). In a rhetorical move that illustrates the adaptive persistence of infantilist tropes, Buruma attributes what he sees as the perverse infantilism of the Japanese to the mother.[10]

Noting that Japanese mothers tend to nurse their children well past the point when Western women wean, Buruma cites a passage by the modern Japanese writer Junichiro Tanizaki in which Tanizaki's protagonist recalls the comfort of nursing and "that sweet, dimply white dreamworld" he associates with it. Buruma then generalizes this regressive fantasy to the culture as a whole, being particularly careful to include Zen, that religion most Westerners find frustratingly confusing (but which state of enlightenment they are quick to claim): "The longing described by Tanizaki is not for death so much as for that dimply white dreamworld, that supremely sensual state of unconsciousness. Many Zen-ish meditation techniques are geared to achieve exactly that: to dull, even deny the conscious mind, to sink into a state of ego-less sensuality like a warm, collective Japanese bath" (22–23). The bodily acts of nursing and bathing are compared to the supposed goal of Zen—here defined as an activity of the mind designed to deny it: all lead to an unconsciousness that is directly tied to sensuality and the body. In fact, apparently not satisfied with his infancy imagery, Buruma goes back even further. The "ever-forgiving mother" is, he writes, "what that 'sweet, dimply white dream world' of the mother's bosom is ultimately all about. Everyone is the same. All are equally sweet. Individual differences are wiped out, just as they are, ideally, in the mind of womb-like group life the majority of Japanese feel most comfortable leading. And if they don't actually lead it, they dream about it" (25). That is to say, the Japanese, most of whom Buruma feels authorized to speak for, are not just regressive, they are embryonic; they actively desire not only a preverbal and preconscious state but a gestational one. Foreclosing on the possibility that one might question his confusion of (undocumented) opinion for incontrovertible evidence, Buruma locates the authority of his claim in the fantasies and dreams of a vaguely defined group, the "majority of the Japanese."

   Behind the Mask proposes to expose the seamy, dark underside of the Japanese. It ranges from discussions of student suicide and the apparent Japanese fascination with death to illustrations from Japanese porn films and adult comic books. Its subtitle, *On Sexual Demons, Sacred Mothers, Transvestites, Gangsters, and Other Japanese Cultural Heroes*, constitutes the obscene face behind the mask.[11] Buruma, like Hearn, exoticizes the Japanese through the language of infantilization. But unlike Hearn, Buruma constructs the perceived difference of the Japanese in terms that are associated with the perverse, lawless and sexually transgressive. What cannot be appropriated is processed through the rhetoric of undesirability, of a regressive perversion inscribed as originating in an essentially infantile relation to the physical. What Hearn constructs as exotically benign, Buruma constructs as unconsciously perverse. Threat is displaced by disgusted, voyeuristic condescension.

   When the trope of infantilization is extended, however, its duality becomes apparent: children, assumed to be closer to the unconscious than adults, can be dangerously uncontrollable in their relation to pure feeling. Because of their "suppression of rational thought," the Japanese, claims Buruma, are "more than usually self-centered . . . [and] on the whole, are ruled by their emotions" (142). He argues that while the Westerner relies on "a common sense of logic," the Japanese, "only just able to keep his anger in check behind a rapidly collapsing wall of etiquette, will say: 'But don't you see what I feel?' " (143).

The projection of the physical, the emotional and the unconscious onto a feminized positionality is the fairly typical stuff of Western paternalistic racism. With the Japanese, however, emotional outbursts can be dangerous and cannot be indulged. *The Japanese Mind* (1983) analyzes Japanese emotionalism in terms of U.S. national interest. Because Christopher's analysis touches on "the Pearl Harbor mentality"—the belief that the West must be ever-vigilant to the possibilities of a fatal surprise attack—it is worth quoting extensively:

Contrary to the impression that most Westerners have of them—and contrary to the impression that they seek to give the world the Japanese are not a stolid, unemotional people. They are, in fact, exactly the opposite. "You always have to remember," a Japanese editor once told me in an attempt to explain why he opposed strong military forces for Japan, "that we Japanese are hysterics."

That, of course, was overstatement in the heat of argument. But there is undeniably a traditional highly emotional Japanese response to a continuing pattern of slights and injuries. That response is to bear one's grievances quietly, even courteously, for a prolonged period of time—and then to explode in a frenzy of destructive rage with no heed for consequences.

Obviously, what I have been drawing here is a worst-case scenario. The Japanese are not yet at the explosive stage in their relations with the United States. . . . But for too long now, the drift of Japanese-American relations has been in the wrong direction. . . . Even the most pro-American Japanese, in short, now have a mental list of grievances . . . which continue to fester away somewhere in the national consciousness.

In America's own interest, this drift must be reversed. (31–32)

The tautological rhetoric here is completely focused on the paranoid logic of a perceived threat: that is to say, the proof that the Japanese may at any point boil over lies in the fact that they have not yet done so.[12] Christopher asserts that the only way the U.S. may avoid the surprise attack of such an emotional explosion, which will happen on a national as well as interpersonal level, is "to recognize just how the Japanese differ from us" (32).[13] Japanese difference, and the infantile rage associated with it, is clearly threatening (though it also retains a comical element: thus, the Japanese editor's statement is invoked to prove Christopher's implicit point, and then dismissed as being an "overstatement in the heat of argument." The editor is presented as both agreeing with and embodying Christopher's opinion). That Christopher identifies this threat in national, not cultural, terms — despite the fact that what he describes is a sociocultural difference — suggests something about the close relation between the two. Christopher himself seems to sense something of the nationalist strains in his argument: "Invoking the national interest as a justification for any particular course of action is always a chancy business; what one person sees as a patriotic obligation may strike another as rampant imperialism" (32). One of the aims of imperialism, of course, is to suppress dangerous difference, even as it obsessively constructs difference, and appropriate the residuum through a relation of power in which the subordinated culture is, in fact, idealized or "saved" by the dominating force. In this way, the construction of the Japanese in terms of infantile emotionalism signifies both as that which poses a threat to "us" and must be suppressed, and as that which poses a threat to itself and requires a paternalistic guiding hand, much in the way of a toddler throwing a tantrum.

At stake, of course, is a dominance that is otherwise threatened by the unreadable surface of Japaneseness: whether constructed as inscrutability or ornamentality, the surface, or mask, of Japan conceals an astonishing central lack that sits uneasily beside a potentially malevolent hysteria.

In its dealing with Japanese difference, the West's alternating strategy of repression and idealization is what Bhabha characterizes as the fetishistic impulses of colonialism:

I argue for the reading of the stereotype in terms of fetishism. The myth of historical origination — racial purity, cultural priority — production in relation to the colonial stereotype functions to "normalize" the multiple beliefs and split subjects that constitute colonial discourse as a consequence of its process of disavowal. . . . The fetish or stereotype gives access to an "identity" which is predicated as much on mastery and pleasure as it is on anxiety and defense, for it is a form of multiple and contradictory belief in its recognition of difference and disavowal of it. . . . The stereotype, then, [is] the primary point of subjectification in colonial discourse, for both colonizer and colonized, is the scene of a similar fantasy and defense — the desire for an originality which is again threatened by the differences of race, color and culture. (79–80)

Bhabha locates the contradictory impulses of colonial discourse in the desire for "access" to the other, but it is an impulse that is inherently self-threatening. Thus, the stereotype of defense, the hysterical/bestial/ infantile Japanese, provides an avenue of access through the assumption of superiority while simultaneously confirming the fear that the West's dominance is imperiled to the extent that access implies a dangerous contiguity. In compensatory fashion, the stereotype of fantasy holds the promise of retaining and reasserting the West's dominance while also securing its innocence: the emotionally disabled, animals and children need a caretaker.

The fetishistic underpinnings of stereotype, which Bhabha contends point to the underlying desire for "historical origination," might be specified further as the desire for an uncontradictory and uncontingent wholeness; in other words, stereotypes index the West's desire for its own coherence. But this very desire is always thwarted by an implicit economy of alterity. If it is true that the logic of binarism dictates that the West must define itself by refraction, in obverse relation to an other, it is also true that the attendant and implicit logic of bifurcation contin- ually undermines the wholeness seemingly promised by the processes of projection and disavowal upon which orientalist fetishism depends.

We seem to face an unresolvable paradox here. That which promises to secure wholeness also subverts its possibility. However, locating dif- ference at the site of the Japanese body recuperates the possibility of wholeness and privileges the status of the stereotype as based in fantasy. Bhabha suggests that "the construction of the colonial subject in dis- course, and the exercise of colonial power through discourse demands an articulation of forms of difference—racial and sexual. Such an artic- ulation becomes crucial if it is held that the body is always simultane- ously inscribed in both the economy of pleasure and the economy of discourse, domination and power" (72). Pleasure and defense, fantasy and fear, desire and alterity mutually sustain and reciprocally construct each other. The "split subject" to which Bhabha refers is literalized by the polarization of the Japanese woman and Japanese man, and this binary schema, rooted in gender difference, becomes the framework for the seemingly contradictory, but in fact related, impulses of the West relative to Japan. Since the threat of difference must be defused but not eliminated in order for idealized or exoticized difference to function, the Japanese male, the threatening other, is discursively erased. In his place, the Japanese woman—and more crucially, the Japanese woman's body— is inscribed as the pleasurable site of racial and sexual difference that can be appropriated and mastered. She herself becomes the site of accessibility and domination, a site personifying the Japanese feminine that affirms and reaffirms its opposite: white Western masculinity.

Japanese Women and Metonymic Embodiment

As David Henry Hwang points out in the epigraph that opens this chapter, the feminization of Japan functions in relation to the masculinized West in the same way that the stereotype of the Japanese woman functions in relation to the white Western male. Both relations are inscribed by overdetermined patterns of submission and domination in which race and gender difference mark the boundaries of the orientalized other in a manner that both "invites" access and allows erasure of the threatening Japanese other gendered as male.[14] Fetishized as a super-feminized exotic object in whom the soul of the geisha resides, the Japanese woman is configured as ontologically mysterious, sexually available and hungry for contact with the West—via the white western male.

The construction of the sexualized Japanese woman is complicit with the manner in which the West and Japan are gendered through a paradigm of heterosexual complementarity that disguises an unequal power relation and reconfigures it as a willing partnership between two consenting parties. Thus, Kipling's famous dictum, "East is East and West is West, and never the twain shall meet," becomes the romanticized (girl-finally-meets-boy) prelude to the popular notion that "Japan and the United States have become perhaps the world's oddest couple" (Christopher, 33).[15]

But the extent to which the paradigm of heterosexual reciprocity depends, in fact, upon unstated structures of heterosexual mastery reveals itself if we look at what are frequent descriptions of the present economic need to "penetrate the Japanese market." Such statements are aural cousins to descriptions of Commodore Perry as "the man who opened Japan to the world" or, variously, as having penetrated Japan's isolationism (Chamberlain, 363). The twinning of sexualization and force, and their expression through tropes of phallic aggression, are even clearer in accounts of the WW II surrender ceremonies staged by General MacArthur: with the American flag flown on Perry's ship on conspicuous display, MacArthur ordered that the prow of the USS *Missouri* be pointed toward the center of Tokyo. Caroline Chung Simpson calls this "the second opening of Japan," in recognition of the similarly intrusive tactics employed by Commodore Perry in 1853–54, and notes that the imagery of forced penetration echoes the military, political and media language of rape in the postwar period.[16] H. D. Harootunian picks up on the overt positioning of the United States as a benign marital partner in his contention that the Occupation may be read "as a bourgeois wedding between the United States and Japan, the actual intent of the coupling [being] to transform the bride by bringing her into the groom's household; through marriage the bride would be resocialized into the groom's world of middle-class values and the standards of civilized life, now read as the 'free world' " (199–200).

Gendering Japan as female is central to the ease with which Western discourse, informed by both nationalism and misogyny, shifts between the romantic and the brutal, between structures of reciprocity and structures of mastery. This gendering is also the primary mechanism through which the body of the Japanese woman is conflated with and becomes a metonymic representation of Japan itself. The assignation of the feminine to Japan is thus literalized through the body of the Japanese woman, which is then metaphorized as a cultural/national landscape. The shifting interplay among metaphoric and literal registers—feminized nation/female body, geographic landscape/orientalized woman—rhetorically constructs a site that may alternately or simultaneously be inhabited by country and woman.

The figure of the Japanese woman has been variously deployed over the past hundred years. Yoshi Kuzume argues that between 1860 and 1990, American images of the Japanese woman have undergone four distinct phases: the sensual geisha girl and, simultaneously, the devoted woman (1860–1900); the heathen woman, oppressed by Japanese men and Japanese culture, who must be saved by enlightened Christianity (1910–45); the emancipated Japanese woman, freed by postwar Occupation-style democracy (1945–60); and the empowered Japanese woman, recuperated through a combination of new social history and cultural feminism (1970–90). As Kuzume rightly points out, all these incarnations of the Japanese woman are more reflective "of the changes in American attitudes concerning gender in general, and attitudes to Japanese society, than . . . of historical developments in Japan" (7). Though a distinct image of Japanese womanhood was ascendant in each period, "the Japanese woman" as an ideological construction of the West in general, and of the United States in particular, has consistently depended on variations, but not displacement, of the geisha stereotype. Contemporary versions derive much of their power from the conflation of the geisha image with the postwar construction of the Japanese woman as the direct beneficiary of the Occupation. The image of Japanese woman as up-and-coming feminist has had little impact on the stereotype of the Japanese woman as she-who-must-be-saved. (If anything, such recent images construct Japanese feminists as apprentices at the knee of Western feminist empowerment movements.) Indeed, according to one scholar (who otherwise seems to accept Kuzume's periodization of Japanese women's stereotyping), recent popular films depicting Japanese women suggest that these "beautiful heroines are so suppressed and deprived by [Japanese] society that they must be saved from their own destinies by powerful, gallant Western lovers. This insinuation repeats the age-old rhetoric that Asian women are a deprived underclass that can only be rescued by the power of the Western world — a condescending view of the East held by many white males" (Ma, 23). What this passage suggests is not so much the changes but the astonishing longevity and constancy of Western constructions of "the Japanese woman." Variations or shifts, then, reflect changes in the representational and rhetorical strategies of such constructions, rather than the images or stereotypes they convey.

As the particular inflections of her deployment vary, what remains unchanged is the Japanese woman's ideological alignment with the West in contrast to and often against the negative aspects of Japanese culture and the threat of the Japanese nation-state. Despite fluctuating levels of benignity and hostility between Japan and the West in the twentieth century, the construction of the Japanese woman as the site and sign of access has remained relatively constant.

One way in which cultural access has been figured is through the Japanese woman as the sign of an oppressive culture whose domination of the female is both cause and consequence of its archaic backwardness. More important, as Cynthia Enloe explains in relation to British colonialization, the subordinate position of woman in her own culture becomes the justification for imperialist domination by the West:

British colonial officers blamed the existing ideologies of masculinity in the colonized societies for women's degradation; if men's sense of manliness was such that it didn't include reverence toward women, then they couldn't expect to be allowed to govern their own societies. Thus, for instance, in India British commentators created the idea of the "effeminate" Bengali male, only to berate him because he wasn't manly enough to recognize his obligation to protect and revere women. (48–49)

Thus, imperialism is constructed as a large-scale domestic intervention program designed to save yellow women from yellow men.[17] Further, such imperialist moves, coded in the gestures of benign paternalism, ideologically and actively separate the colonized woman from her culture, retaining only those abstracted cultural traits that the dominating force finds appealing. Thus, according to Basil Hall Chamberlain, in 1905, the subordinate position of Japanese women is directly attributable to the oppressiveness of Japanese men and a culture archaically based on Confucianism. Significantly, more desirable, female-gendered Japanese qualities identify the Japanese woman as sympathetic, as one whose sorry lot is apparent only to the enlightened West:

Japanese women are most womanly, — kind, gentle, faithful, pretty. But the way in which they are treated by the men has hitherto been such as might cause a pang to any generous European heart. No wonder that some of them are at last endeavoring to emancipate themselves. A woman's lot is summed up in what are termed "the three obediences"—obedience, while yet unmarried, to a father; obedience, when married, to a husband and that husband's parents; obedience, when widowed, to a son. (500)

The "generous European heart" is aligned on the side of Japanese women against Japanese men, but also against their culture, as represented by the allusion to the Confucian principles of female obedience.[18] In a similar passage from *The New Japanese Womanhood*, published in 1926, the advancement of women is associated with modernization, and Japanese women are seen as the cultural bridge between East and West: "The present . . . seems to be an opportune time for the people of the West to become more intimately acquainted with Japan's 'better half.' It may very well be that, in spite of Kipling's dictum, the twain—East and West—may after all meet through the modest charm of Japan's daughters, who are fast becoming positive factors in the development of a new world for themselves" (Faust, 15).

Significantly, this type of rhetoric is particularly pervasive in the period from roughly the turn of the century through the 1920s (it takes on a somewhat different, though related, form later), a period during which the first wave of English and American feminism was demanding recognition of the oppressions of Western patriarchy. Ignoring, or in willful ignorance of, the oppression of women in the West, these writers use the rhetoric of pseudofeminism to suggest that cultural and political oppression of women happens elsewhere, in the less developed part of the world. Tellingly, this type of rhetoric is conflated with the missionary concerns of Western Christianity: "It will be noticed that the first four women on this list [of "forward thinking" women] have done their reform work as active Christians. When the history of the woman's movement in Japan will be written, the honest historian will give a large place to the Christian women for the faithful and incessant upward pull which they have contributed. They have all been conservatively progressive, not one of them destructively radical" (Faust, 158). This last is perhaps a veiled criticism of the tactics of English suffragists, a circuitous acknowledgment of the conditions of women there. What is abundantly clear is that the improved status of Japanese women is credited to enlightened, progressive Western Christianity, an implicit criticism of a predominantly non-Christian culture. The writer then connects criticism of Christianity with resistance to its "feminist" tendencies and other offered freedoms: "Greater freedom of this nature [social and educational] was formerly a fruitful source of adverse criticism of the Christians on the part of those who were opposed to this religion" (131).[19]

The imperialist impulses here are perhaps more clearly seen when we consider that in this same period, insistence on the ultrafemininity of Japanese woman runs parallel to claims for wishing to "improve" her status. One writer extols the praises of Japanese womanhood in direct contrast to the perceived aggressiveness of Western women:

How sweet . . . Japanese woman is! All the possibilities of the race for goodness seem to be concentrated in her. It shakes one's faith in some Occidental doctrines [feminism?]. If this be the result of suppression and oppression, then these are not altogether bad. . . . In the eternal order of things, which is the higher being,—the childish, confiding, sweet Japanese girl, or the superb, calculating, penetrating, Occidental Circe of our more artificial society, with her enormous power for evil and her limited capacity for good? (quoted in Chamberlain, 501)

That the American woman instead of being penetrated is herself "penetrating" suggests the anxiety underlying the leitmotiv of Japanese women's femininity and again illustrates the ways in which heterosexuality provides the structure for East/West relations. All possible virtues of Japanese culture are concentrated in the figure of the nonthreatening, girlish Japanese woman. Constructed as a benign embodiment of sexual and racial difference, her alterity becomes complementarity. Oddly enough, the paradigmatically "foreign" Japanese woman becomes the paradigmatic figure of femininity and womanliness.[20]

Similar discursive and social positionings of the Japanese woman emerge even more strongly in the years following World War II, primarily serving the purpose of remasculinizing the postwar soldier who returned home to find that "his little woman" was no longer just balancing on her high heels: now she was balancing the family checkbook, as well as the difficulties of work both outside and inside the home.[21] As Gina Marchetti notes, the abundance of films from the mid-1950s to the early 1960s that dealt with Japanese-white American relationships all "used the myth of the subservient Japanese woman to shore up a threatened masculinity in light of American women's growing independence during World War II" (158).[22] The conflated fantasies of sexual and racial domination are evident not only in numerous films, but in popular novels whose story lines focus on interracial relationships between white American men and Japanese women, a coupling made somewhat acceptable—or at least safely titillating—in the wake of Japan's defeat in WW II.

The extent to which imperialist aspirations fuel popular representations of sexual relationships between white men and Japanese women in the postwar period is apparent when those representations are understood as literalizations of the discursive feminization of Japan. It also becomes evident if we consider the ways in which popular cultural forms, such as novels and films, "participate in, are part of, contribute to an extremely slow, infinitesimal politics that clarifies, reinforces, perhaps even occasionally advances perceptions and attitudes" (Said 1993, 75). This suggests that popular cultural forms dealing with Japan in the postwar period served the purposes of representing, justifying and, to some extent, creating the reconfiguration of the United States' relationship with Japan.

Yellowfaced Nationalism in *Teahouse of the August Moon*

One of the more important aspects of the postwar reconfiguration of the relationship between the U.S. and Japan was to represent the United States not as the aggressive military body that had won the war, but as a paternally helpful country whose innate cultural and moral superiority merely revealed itself in the course of things. Popular representations of American soldiers in postwar Japan tend to depict them as anything from sensitively humane, to strongly, silently Good, to good-naturedly daffy and slightly boyish. This shift to the benevolent, tolerant and downright helpful American soldier contrasts with images of the kamikaze and the crazed, cruel Japanese soldier-patriot, still fresh in the public mind. In the novels and films of the postwar period, Japanese men, if not absented outright, are represented as either subservient and emasculated or bestial and irrational. Predictably enough, it is also in this period that the construction of the completely sexualized Japanese woman is popularized in the novel and in film. From pulp romances to Hollywood movies, Japanese women are the graceful receptacles of Western men and Western culture, represented by the figure of the American GI.

Among the earliest and most popular Hollywood films dealing with the Occupation is *Teahouse of the August Moon* (1956), a comedy starring Glenn Ford, Machiko Kyo and Marlon Brando. Set in Okinawa in 1946, the story line revolves around the bumbling but ultimately successful attempt of Captain Fisby (Ford) to bring American-style democracy to the small Okinawan village of Topiki, and the almost-romance between Fisby and the geisha, Lotus Blossom (Kyo), who falls in love with him. As in other films and the numerous pulp novels written in the 1950s and 1960s, the conflated fantasies of sexual and racial domination are evident in the trope of interracial romance between the white American man and the Japanese woman. Unlike other popular narratives, however, *Teahouse* offers a particularly transparent view of how nationalist discourses attempt to contain the incommensurability of racialized and gendered identities through narratives of coherence that ultimately rely on a phantasmal and unstable construction of the Other. Central to this dynamic is an otherwise marginal character whose purpose seems primarily to provide comic buffoonery. However, that this character, an interpreter named "Sakini," is played by Marlon Brando reveals the ways in which hegemonic racial discourse plays with and relies on the strategic deployment of essentialized alterity, even as its desire to perform alterity threatens to collapse the space between originary and scripted subjectivities.

Teahouse opens with Brando in full Asian drag, or "yellowface." Mispronouncing his *r*'s and dropping articles left and right, Brando/Sakini squats on the ground and offers, without sarcasm or irony, the following interpretation of Okinawa's troubled history:

History of Okinawa reveal distinguished record of conquerors. We have honor to be subjugated in 14th century by Chinee pirate, in 16th century by

English missionary, in 18th century by Japanese warlords, and in 20th century by American Marine. Okinawa very fortunate. Culture brought to us. Not have to leave home for it. . . . Okinawa most eager to be educated by conquerors. Not easy to learn. Sometimes very painful. But pain make man think. Thought make man wise. And wisdom make life endurable.

"So," he concludes, "Now we going to tell you little story to demonstrate splendid example of benevolent assimilation of democracy by Okinawa." The self-serving bent here is blatantly clear: who better than an Okinawan himself to wax enthusiastic about what was not, after all, a history of brutal colonialism but a traveling cultural caravan? Reconstituted as a painful but necessary life's lesson, the American military occupation is the catalyst and carrier of a wisdom that "make life endurable," though what is being endured is never made explicit.

Charged with bringing democracy to the small village of Topiki, Captain Fisby finds himself surrounded by a crude agrarian society whose members cluster en masse to hear his public addresses. He announces that a school will be built (in the shape of the Pentagon) and that all children shall be required to go to it in order to become democratized. The film makes comic use of the villager's resistance and the absurdity of a Pentagon-shaped schoolhouse, yet what it ridicules is the form, not the substance of the Occupation. The schoolhouse never gets built; instead, the village decides it wants a teahouse, a traditional symbol of leisure, refinement and culture.

What complicates this symbol is that it comes to be associated with the geisha "given" to Fisby by a Japanese dignitary of another village. Unlike the representations of the village women — up to this point physically indistinguishable from their male counterparts — Lotus Blossom is the epitome of Western fantasy. Eyes cast demurely to the floor, clad in formal kimono and coifed in high style, she is presented to Fisby by a smirkily insinuating Sakini. So insistent is she upon fulfilling her role as server and helpmate that she literally tears the clothes off a reluctant and morally outraged Fisby. It is not made clear until much later in the film that "geisha" is not synonymous with "prostitute," with the result that this opening scene blurs the line between Lotus Blossom's desire to serve and the desire to service.

Lotus Blossom quickly becomes a figure of envy in the village. The female residents of Topiki demand not only that the teahouse be built, but that Lotus Blossom teach them the art of the geisha. Fisby, for his part, is expected to provide funds, via the U.S. government, for lipstick, powder, kimonos and parasols — which he does. Finally, through a series of plot twists, the villagers, women and men alike, are transformed from the raggedly clad inhabitants of a rude and dirty village to the kimono-ed and hakama-ed ladies and gentlemen who partake of the cultural delights of classical Japanese dance, song and tea ceremony.

Thus, the "benevolent assimilation of democracy" is a civilizing encounter that individualizes and sanitizes the uninitiated masses. Of greater significance is that Occupation-style democracy is represented as that which allows the Okinawans to become more themselves: the villagers are "more Japanese" as a result of the democratic process. (The film's conflation of Okinawan and Japanese national and cultural identities both evidences American ignorance and allows the film to override the problematics of the colonial encounter.) Through Fisby, the representative of the United States, the female residents of Topiki are instructed in the art of the geisha, thereby becoming recognizably Japanese and recognizably women. The category of Japanese woman, then, signifies both the success of democratization and its basic benignity: democracy does not brutally impose Western ways onto the populace but instead ushers that populace along the road that leads back to the teahouse and the cultured sensibility it represents.

That the teahouse is built with U.S. government lumber intended for the schoolhouse, however, inadvertently reveals the similarity of their purposes. The schoolhouse and its intended function are held up to ridicule in the film, yet the teahouse with its U.S. sponsored geishas achieves what is perhaps more important than the rote learning of democratic principles: the Japanese of Topiki are instructed in how to be Japanese in ways approved of by the U.S. and, by extension, the film's American audience. The teahouse is thus the site of instruction that inducts its students into nostalgized, pre-militaristic, cherry blossomed Japaneseness. This relegation of the Japanese to American-scripted roles for the Japanese is emblematized by the film's opening sequence: Brando, eyes taped to a recognizably "oriental" slant, shuffles and squats, mumbles and grunts in nauseating imitation of a Japanese man.

In her discussion of gender performativity and the subversive possibilities of drag, Judith Butler observes: "By imitating gender, drag implicitly reveals the imitative structure of gender itself—as well as its contingency" (138). In its parodic mimicry of gender, drag foregrounds the constructed nature of gender because it relies on characteristics readily recognizable as (usually) "woman." Recontextualized and thus denaturalized, the category "woman" signifies, among other things, its own status as a category, as itself "an imitation without an origin" (138) that self-consciously and self-reflexively calls into question the dissonance within narratives of coherence.

What I am interested in here is what happens to the subversive and performative possibilities of drag when applied to instances of racial drag. In one sense, racial drag implies the possibility of interrogating originary racial difference, but only to the extent that racial parody circulates in a social or discursive arena separate from a polarized racial economy in which difference is the necessary component of self-definition. In other words, Brando's performance may be understood to unintentionally imply the subversive elements of drag only within the confines of a group that understands his parody to refer to constructed, not essential, difference. Given such conditions, Brando/Sakini could be read as foreshadowing and commenting on the performativity of Japaneseness manifested by the geishas and the teahouse, thereby revealing recognizable, scripted racial categories "as imitations which effectively displace the meaning of the original, [which] imitate the myth of originality itself" (Butler, 138). Read in this way, *Teahouse of the August Moon* becomes not only a critical commentary on the Occupation and its aims but a self-reflexive critique of its own representations.

Such hypothetical conditions, however, give this film much more credit than is reasonable. The subversion, "resignification and recontextualization" of drag do not, in fact, tend to manifest themselves when transferred from gender to race largely because the success of racial drag performances, like yellowface, relies on its ability to simultaneously transgress and reify categories of racial difference through mirroring, reconfirming race as an originary site of essential alterity. Emphatic caricature focuses on abstracted and exaggerated elements of what are perceived to be inborn racial qualities; recontextualization in this case is better defined as a kind of performative bas-relief where stereotypical characteristics are foregrounded from the clutter and complexity of individualization. Although Butler points out that the gender equivalent of racial caricature is "clearly part of hegemonic, misogynist culture," she argues that "gender meanings . . . are nevertheless denaturalized and mobilized through their parodic recontextualization" (138). However, the manner in which racially marked bodies register socially and politically in the U.S. elides the disjunctions between raced bodies, racial identity and racial performance that, in Butler's syntax of gender, create spaces for performative subversion.

At this point, it is germane to focus on Brando's performance, which is predicated on the assumption that there is, in fact, a way to recognizably imitate an Asian male. The audience, even the audience of 1956, is always highly aware of Brando himself. There is thus a crucial distinction to be made between the spectacle of "Brando acting" and "Brando acting like a Japanese." While the film capitalizes on the audience's curiosity about Brando's ability to produce a seamless image of "an Asian man," the affective upshot is simply a question of whether he successfully impersonates one or not. The issue of similitude — is Brando indeed acting "like" a Japanese — suggests the copulative function of simile: performance becomes the link between categories understood to be distinct: white and yellow. Implicit is the assumption of an originary, mirrored subject. What this suggests for the rest of the film is that there exists an essential Japanese quality that can be on one hand imitated by whites through yellowface (Brando as Sakini) and on the other properly enacted (the Japanization of the Topiki villagers).

And yet the film must contain the lingering suggestion that race is performative, not essential. Clearly, this is problematic: in the film's attempt to uphold its internal logic, the limitations and contradictions of its orientalist discourse reveal themselves as destabilizing elements that must continually be recontained. As Eric Lott states in relation to blackface minstrelsy, much of the language of "cultural exchange . . . was aimed at a racial structure whose ideological and psychological instability required its boundaries continually to be staged, and which regularly exceeded the dominant culture's capacity to fix such boundaries" (27). In *Teahouse* the issue is whether, having adopted Japanese dress and a quasi-Japanese demeanor, Captain Fisby himself is "Japanese." Is he not as instructable in becoming Japanese as the Japanese themselves? Having aligned white American men with the (re)establishment of "true" Japaneseness, the film must differentiate between who is Japanese and who is not, and must do so by reinforcing the essentialist strain that runs throughout. Since originary formulations of race rely on the assumption of atemporality and the absence of historicity (this last accounting for Sakini's opening monologue, which is less an account of history than a description of a natural process of cultural evolution), Lotus Blossom, as the feminine embodiment of idealized, dehistoricized Japanese culture, becomes the sign and marker of absolute difference. Thus, the closing scenes of the film focus on her love for Fisby, who renounces her love. "Tell her," he says to the bowing and grinning Sakini, "I'll never forget her. I'll never forget this village. On the other side of the world in the autumn of my life, when an August moon rises in the East, I'll remember what was beautiful and what I was wise enough to leave beautiful."

Similar to the manner in which the Topiki villagers have been scripted into nonthreatening and nostalgic Japaneseness, Fisby defuses the threat of the present situation by narratively projecting it into the future, thus refiguring it as already a moment in the nostalgic past. More important, given that the film backhandedly suggests the possibility that race is performative and constructed, it must somehow reassert essential racial and cultural difference. Therefore, Japanese national identity—aestheticized as culture, not patriotic militarism—is emblematized through the figure of Lotus Blossom, who falls in love with Captain Fisby, who, in turn, must renounce both her love and what she represents. In the closing scenes of the film, the captain refuses Lotus Blossom and explains his reasoning to Sakini in what is a fascinating combination of the narrative of renounced love and the rhetoric of the conqueror who is himself conquered, all cozily tucked into the platitudinous homily that one should appreciate one's lot in life: "I used to worry a lot about not being a big success. I think I felt an awful lot like you people felt, always being conquered. You know, now I'm not sure who's the conquered and who's the conqueror. I've learned in Topiki the wisdom of gracious acceptance. See, I don't want to be a world leader. I've made my peace with myself somewhere between my ambitions and my limitations."

What Fisby ostensibly recognizes are the limitations to ambition wrought by his inability, made much of throughout the film, to be more than a benign bumbler. In other words, he is constitutionally unable to realize his ambitions but has learned to reconcile himself to his limitations. Of more significance is that Fisby's realization, clothed in the friendly advice of the conqueror to the conquered—notwithstanding Fisby's professed confusion about who is who—allusively speaks to the limitations to which Lotus Blossom must consign herself. Fisby's absurd comparison between his individual situation and the history of Okinawa implies through refraction the metonymic identification of Lotus Blossom with Okinawa. The triangular relationship between Fisby, Okinawa and Lotus Blossom seems to align all three parties equally. But it is clear that while Fisby's advice to himself remains solely in the realm of the private, his statement, in relation to Lotus Blossom and Okinawa, reinforces antimiscegenist ideology and refutes the possibility of international parity. To the extent that Lotus Blossom must renounce her "ambitions" to a love relationship with Fisby, Okinawa must and should ignore its ambitions for political autonomy and reconcile itself to its limitations. Through the rhetoric of romantic renunciation, the discourse of imperialist subjugation is unmistakably clear. The implicit conflation of woman with country operates to keep both the country and the woman in their places. The power differential here—who is put into place and who has the power of assignation—is obscured by the film's comic premises and the diegetic demands of renunciation narratives.

Teahouse further refigures the confrontation with the racial/cultural other as an enabling moment of becoming that reinforces fantasies of foreign domestication and Western superiority. But that moment of becoming—in which the other becomes the Other—is always fraught with the anxiety that its ambiguity may well destabilize the boundaries that define "who's the conquered and who's the conqueror." The Japanese woman, the embodiment of racial and gender alterity, is placed alluringly in the nostalgic Japanized past, securing the West's identity and innocence at a vantage point, "on the other side of the world," from which it can spatially and temporally look back and "remember what was beautiful and what [it] was wise enough to leave beautiful."

What emerges in this film is characteristic of what is perhaps the primary rhetorical move of several films, popular novels and travel narratives dealing with Japan: reciprocity through metonymic substitution. Through the construction of the Japanese woman as the individual representative of her country, the power relation between nations is privatized and annulled by the discourse of romantic love. On the simplest level, the U.S. is exonerated from charges of nationalism and racism through the figure of the American soldier who falls in love with a Japanese woman. Understood in more complex ways, the assumed reciprocity of romance is a tropic representation of reciprocity between countries; what falls out in this equation is the mechanism of power and domination.

The Erotics of Capitulation in *Sayonara*

This romantic trope is central to the popular American film *Sayonara* (1957), based on James Michener's best-selling novel of the same name.[23] The plot revolves around a love affair between Lloyd Gruver (Marlon Brando), a U.S. airman stationed in postwar Japan, and Hana-ogi (Miko Taka), star actress of the famous all-female Matsubayashi Review (modeled after the Takarazuka Review). Sent to dissuade a junior officer (Red Buttons) from marrying a Japanese woman (Miyoshi Umeki), Gruver eventually condones the marriage and, in the film, marries Hana-ogi. The narrative of the film is in many ways the movement of Gruver from proud American antimiscegenist to compassionate, nonracist humanist for whom love conquers all. In fact, the film suggests that it is Hana-ogi, not "Royd Gluber," who must overcome her personal hatreds and hesitations.

The opening sequence of the film concentrates on Gruver's attempts to dissuade junior officer Kelly from marrying Katsumi-san, a Japanese "native," and thus functions to establish the difference of the Japanese. "There's a little difference that we need to talk about, Kelly," says Gruver, pulling out his wallet photo of his white American fiancée. Both men duly admire the physical attributes of Eileen, Kelly conceding that she "sure does something wicked to a bathing suit." But when Kelly reciprocates with a picture of Katsumi, Gruver looks at it in complete puzzlement. In Michener's novel, Gruver notes that "this Katsumi was certainly no Madame Butterfly. She had a big round face, prominent cheeks and what looked like oil-black hair. If you'd never been in Japan you'd probably have taken her for an Indian or an Eskimo maybe." In effect, Katsumi's physical attributes—or their deficiencies—relegate her to the status of Indians and Eskimos, here clearly signifying undifferentiated primitivism. Casting about for something to say, Gruver adds that "she sure looks intelligent" (10).

This scene is complemented, in Michener's text, by a later one in which Gruver and Hana-ogi go to a museum in order to look at some prints of Hana-ogi's namesake, a famous courtesan known for her great beauty. In anticipation, Gruver guesses that she will be "extraordinarily beautiful, yet with a distinctive oriental cast" (161). The oppositional "yet" indicates that the categories "beautiful" and "oriental" are, if not mutually exclusive, not ordinarily contiguous. As the curator and the present Hana-ogi proudly display the first print, Gruver recoils: "It was disgusting. The girl's face was pasty and flat. Her hair was a mass of yellow combs. She was swathed in seven kimonos that gaped at the neck. But worst of all, her eyes were caricatures, mere slants, and her teeth were a horrid black. In this portrait of dead beauty I could not find one shred of loveliness. . . . 'Why she's ugly!' I cried" (162). As each print is shown, Gruver's reaction remains the same. Finally, by explaining the conventions of Japanese representational art—and by extension Japanese standards of female beauty—the curator is able to nudge Gruver to a hedging recognition of the ancient Hana-ogi's beauty: "I think I understand," he says finally (164).

Taken together, these two scenes—one before he meets Hana-ogi, the other after they have been lovers for some time—suggest Gruver's continuing ambivalence toward the Japanese and Japanese woman. As the embodiment of both racial and sexual other, Japanese woman initially elicits disgusted aversion; in this light, Hana-ogi must be understood as an exception. If the mass of Japanese women represents disgusting otherness, Hana-ogi reveals the contradictory nature of such otherness: it is both revolting and alluring. The double figures of the past and present Hana-ogi emblematize both this contradiction and Gruver's ambivalence. That Gruver must be instructed in how to read the signs of Japanese female beauty suggest that such beauty is not immediately apparent and therefore constitutes a sign of difference not easily translatable from one cultural setting to another. Gruver suddenly thinks of the present Hana-ogi in this context: "And I could see myself back in America, about to introduce my Hana-ogi to strangers who had never known her and I could feel them cringing away from my Japanese girl—unlovely to them—as I now cringed away from the long-dead Hana-ogi" (164).

This establishment and affirmation of difference is, I believe, crucial to understanding the inscription of the Japanese woman's body in, as Bhabha says, "both the economy of pleasure and the economy of discourse, domination and power" (72). It is for this reason that Hana-ogi's difference is maintained throughout both the book and the film, particularly and most significantly at moments of romantic or sexual intimacy. And, as in *Teahouse of the August Moon,* where both womanliness and Japaneseness are allowed only in forms recognizable to and approved by the occupying force, Hana-ogi's involvement with Gruver signifies the capitulation of Japan to orientalist discourse.

From the beginning, Hana-ogi is presented as neither friendly toward the American presence in her country nor particularly feminine. As the star of the all-female Matsubayashi Review, Hana-ogi plays exclusively male roles and dresses accordingly. In the film, her first appearances are meant to contrast her with the surrounding girls who are all clad in traditional, flowing kimonos. Hana-ogi, in contrast, strides confidently in Western-style dress: pants, turtleneck and fedora. She looks directly at Gruver, showing no signs of the giggling Japanese maidenliness displayed around her. Michener emphasizes this aspect of Hana-ogi in an interesting, if superficial, role reversal that reveals her anti-American streak. When Gruver goes to see her perform, she is playing the role of Pinkerton in a stage revue version of *Madame Butterfly:*

The girl in slacks who had reprimanded us in the restaurant played this part and her Lieutenant Pinkerton was blatantly ridiculous. He was arrogant, ignorant and ill-mannered. Yet at the same time the actress herself seemed more essentially feminine than any of the other girls on stage and it was this that made her version of Pinkerton so devastating. She was all Japanese women making fun of all American men.

One act of such petty nonsense was enough for me. . . . I couldn't tolerate people making cheap fun of men in uniform, and when the people doing the burlesque were Japanese I drew the line. (80–81)

Annoyed that Hana-ogi, here representative of all Japanese, should have the effrontery to make fun of U.S. military men, Gruver is suddenly attracted to her when he sees her next number: a traditional Japanese dance in which she wears traditional Japanese dress. Though it seems possible to read Hana-ogi's Japanese femaleness as a scripted role she performs, much in the same way she performs the role of the American military male, this possibility is undercut by the implicit rhetoric of heterosexual romantic love: the Pinkerton role is simply a cheap burlesque enactment, and Hana-ogi's second role is constructed as a revelation of her "true" Japanese nature. Thus, what Gruver falls in love with is not the actress and her roles but an essential (Japanese, female) self, one unencumbered by performances that are neither true to her "essentially feminine" nature nor properly supplicant.

What is at issue is not simply Hana-ogi's snubbing of Gruver, but through her the Japanese resistance to the American presence. She is a threat insofar as she represents national/cultural resistance. It is important to remember the postwar context and the fact that the U.S. was at pains to destabilize indigenous power structures by continually asserting its superior might, while maintaining a benign presence.[24] This dynamic may also help explain why *Sayonara* was and continues to be so popular.[25]

In a filmic scene designed to both explain the reasons for Hana-ogi's dislike of Americans and showcase her capitulation to Gruver/the U.S., she is for the first time, outside a performance, clad in traditional Japanese dress (as far as one can tell, in novel and film alike, Hana-ogi never again wears her pants and fedora). Eyes cast down, she breathily, tearfully explains in charmingly accented but clear-spoken English: "My father was killed by American bomb dropped on my country. You have been my enemy. I have hated Americans. I have thought they were savages. There has been nothing but vengeance in my heart." By virtue of having fallen for her, Gruver is presented as he-who-can-overcome-petty-differences in a good old-fashioned wave of American big-heartedness. It is Hana-ogi and, by extension, the Japanese people, who harbor resentment and see the Americans in an unreasonable light, the

Japanese who generalize and stereotype. In an amazing reversal that reinforces the benignity of the Americans, Hana-ogi then goes on to admit the wrongness of her ways and beg forgiveness: "I have been watching you too. And you have not looked like a savage. And when Katsumi-san told me how gently you kissed her the day she became a bride, how tenderly you kissed my sweet little friend, I realized the hate was of my own making. That is why I came—to ask you to forgive me for what I have been feeling. Gruver-san, will you forgive me?"

Hana-ogi declares her love for Gruver, consigning herself to the difficulties they will face. Understood as the sign of both racial, national and sexual other, Hana-ogi's renunciation of her "hatred and steel" and declaration of love ("I will never fall in love again. But I will love you, Ace-san, if that is your desire") constitute the subordination of Japan and the Japanese, as well as of Hana-ogi herself. That Gruver is the son of a celebrated four-star general and is himself well known for his military prowess indicates that he has not only "won" the love of Hana-ogi, but that the U.S. and its "men in uniform" (91) have won as well. Again, what obscures a relationship marked by submission and domination is the rhetoric of romantic love.

Having consigned dangerous difference to the subordinated position through the metonym of Japanese woman, all desirable difference, configured in her sexualized body, circulates in an economy of pleasure. Once the threat of difference has been diffused, it is the site of desire. The inextricability of difference and desire is evident in Gruver's first physical contact with Hana-ogi: "[I] took Hana-ogi's hand and brought its yellow knuckles right up to my lips and kissed it. . . . I grabbed her by the shoulder and swung her around and kissed her on the lips. We kept our eyes open and I remember that in this crazy moment I could not tell whether her eyes were slanted or not, but they were very black, like the sky at night" (92).

Here, desire is clearly predicated on racial difference, and the space temporarily unmarked by a clear indication of that difference—Gruver's inability to tell whether Hana-ogi's eyes are slanted or not—is one of confusion, a "crazy moment." As I will later show, this moment is often one whose indeterminacy occasions uneasiness on the part of the white male subject because it collapses distinctions between self and other. Here, in the postwar context, that uneasiness is mitigated by the fact of Japan's defeat and the way in which it clearly demarcates the self/other boundary; given that context, the "crazy moment" signifies the boundary's temporary disruption, during which, divested of the sign of her racial difference, Hana-ogi signifies only herself. That is, however temporarily, she does not represent the nation whose submission is otherwise understood to be simultaneous to her own. (This is, perhaps, a more complex working out of Fisby's lament that he isn't "sure who's the conquered and who's the conqueror.")

Moments such as this one, however, make no further appearances. Hana-ogi's sexualization goes always hand in hand with her Japanization. Descriptions of sexual intimacy inevitably include phrases about her "sweet slanted eyes" (110) or "slim yellow body" (126). Because such moments both mark the boundary and transgress it, they are initially fraught with fear:

I was faced with the second vast occurrence of the day, for when in the fading light I at last saw Hana-ogi's exquisite body I realized with shock— even though I was prepared to accept it—that I was with a girl of Asia. I was with a girl whose complete body was golden and not white and there was a terrible moment of fear and I think Hana-ogi shared this fear, for she caught my white arm and held it across her golden breasts and studied it and looked away and then as quickly caught me to her whole heart and accepted the white man from America. (101)

Gruver's final dissociation with his formerly held antimiscegenist views is, significantly, marked by his characterization of Hana-ogi in racial/ national terms: "I was with a girl of Asia." Gruver's "terrible moment of fear" is quickly projected onto Hana-ogi. This projection creates a context in which the fear is mutual and based on the recognition of race-difference. But I would argue that Gruver's fear is consequent upon an act that destabilizes the power relationship articulated by nationalist antimiscegenation: having fallen in love and literally sleeping with the enemy radically restructures the national/racial hierarchies Gruver had previously held to: "it had never occurred to me that anyone would actually want to kiss a yellow-skinned Japanese girl. You fought the Japs on Guadalcanal. You organized their country for them in Kobe. You defended them in Korea. But it had never crossed my mind that you kissed them. . . . It was repugnant" (47).

To neutralize the threat of national and racial difference that Gruver's militarist and imperialist ideology no longer holds at bay, difference must be reconfigured within the category of exoticized and subordinated gender, which itself functions in an arena defined by American sexual politics and misogyny. Gruver's fiancée, a white American woman, and the surrounding military wives are set up to contrast with Japanese women. They are depicted as hard, determined, and ambitious—all at the cost of their femininity. For all that she is initially described in terms of conventional Anglo-American beauty, Eileen is a woman who speaks her mind in unbecoming ways. Gruver imagines married life with her:

It occurred to me that if I married Eileen we would always be a little bit afraid of each other, a little bit on edge always to be ahead of the other person. Mrs. Webster [Eileen's mother], frankly, had scared the devil out of me and now I could see the same marital tendencies in her daughter. I could see her organizing my life for me solely on the grounds that she loved me, but the definition of what was love would always be her definition; and I thought of Joe Kelly and the girl he had found . . . they were at peace. (53)

In both novel and film of *Sayonara,* white American women are categorically constructed as practical, but unromantic, asexual marriage partners who "talk about Junior's braces and country-club dances" (13). So pervasive is this "knowledge" that white American women themselves are aware of their deficiency. As one court clerk complains to Gruver, "Damn them all! They all have the same secret. . . . They make their men feel important. I try to build my husband up—as a wife should But with me it's a game. With these ugly little round-faced girls it isn't a game. It's life" (45). Gruver himself seems to share some of this anguish while looking at a white American woman: "She was beautiful and fresh and perfect and I almost cried aloud with pain to think that something had happened in American life to drive men like Mike Bailey and me away from such delectable girls" (120).

Relegating women to one of two mutually exclusive categories— willful American women and supplicant Japanese women—not only divides women along lines defined by their relation to white American men but suggests that those men have been somehow forced out of the natural current of things by the unnatural behavior of white American women. They are the innocents who have been abandoned in the name of social progress. Into this situation steps the Japanese woman, "the patient accepter, the tender companion, the rich lover" (127). Her difference, in such a context, is no longer a threat; instead, it is a restorative to white American male hegemony and an implicit criticism of white American womanhood. Japanese women do not criticize or expect anything, "they loved somebody—just simply loved him. . . . They just got hold of a man and they loved him" (51). The preference for such women keeps white women in their places or rather, through the prerogative of rejection, puts them in a different, if still inferior, place and replaces them with women who are more acceptably "women": "I concluded that no man could comprehend women until he had known the women of Japan with their unbelievable combination of unremitting work, endless suffering and boundless warmth—just as I could never have known even the outlines of love had I not lived in a little house where I sometimes drew back the covers of my bed upon the floor to see there the slim golden body of the perpetual woman" (128).

Although I have been speaking here of the construction of Japanese women in terms of gender, I want to stress that it is never separate, particularly in the postwar period, from their construction in racial and national terms. Japanese women are in one sense privileged over white American women, and yet their status as subjects (or objects, as the case may be) defined by the intersection of gender, race and nationality precludes the possibility that their gender-subordination in the context of romance is separable from the metaphorical feminization, exoticization and subordination of the Japanese race/nation. Having established the subordination of woman/country, Gruver's romance with Hana-ogi may now be read as mutually beneficial and reciprocal. Although the divergent endings of Michener's novel and the Hollywood film are significant, both support the ideal of (romantic) reciprocity.

Between its serialization in *McCall's* magazine in 1953 and the release of *Sayonara*'s filmed version in 1957, the 1952 McCarran-Walter Act had taken effect and Japanese wives of U.S. servicemen were allowed into the U.S., and this fact necessitated and made acceptable a film ending that diverged from the novel.[26] Michener's novel closes with the double suicide of Kelly and his wife, and the end of the relationship between Gruver and Hana-ogi. Hana-ogi declares that their love has helped her become a better Japanese, and Gruver a better American, though it is unclear what she means. Gruver picks up on this theme as he watches Hana-ogi dance for the last time: "her Japanese classical dance was stronger for having known [an] American not as a subject for study but as a lover—as one who cried eagerly to marry her. I understood what she had said the night before. She was now a better Japanese" (204). Again, it is unclear what constitutes Hana-ogi's being "a better Japanese" unless we recall that she and other Japanese have all along been cast as the bearers of unreasonable prejudice (there is no mention of Gruver's own improvement, or what that might constitute). Michener's narrative suggests that the romantic liaison between the white American male and the Japanese woman is not an occasion for opportunistic sexual couplings with the exotic other but an opportunity for personal growth.

Nevertheless, the rhetoric here can also be read as suggesting that because Hana-ogi and Gruver are more properly Japanese and American, a relationship between them is not possible. The novel, in this sense, ends by reinscribing the ideology of antimiscegenation. Hana-ogi refuses to marry Gruver for reasons attributed to her Japanese fatalism, appreciation for morbidity, and blind adherence to honor and duty. Gruver is cast as the impossible romantic, the one who will not renounce his love even when in the teeth of impossible circumstances. It is he who gamely recognizes the unfairness and wrongness of it all: "I was forced to acknowledge that I lived in an age when the only honorable profession was soldiering, when the only acceptable attitude toward strange lands and people of another color must be not love but fear" (214).

The film *Sayonara* machinates a similar effect, but with a very different ending. By the time the film was being shot, representations of sexual relationships between Japanese women and American men had become a frequent theme in popular entertainment, although interracial marriage was still disapproved of as a social practice. The film manages to quell this disapproval by appealing to the American taste for individualism and forbidden-love-against-all-odds story lines (the success of this strategy is evident, I believe, in the film's great popularity and several Oscar nominations).

As in the novel, Hana-ogi refuses to marry Gruver, saying that they must do the right thing, that there are duties and obligations. Gruver replies that it is a waste to do the right thing for Japanese tradition and (derisively) "the great white race," that their obligations are to themselves. Hana-ogi insists that they "come from different worlds. Come from different races" and worries about any children they might have:

Hana-ogi: But what would happen to our children? What would they be?
   Gruver: What would they be? They'd be half Japanese and half American. They'd be half yellow and half white. They'd be half you and they'd be half me. That's all it's gonna be.

Apparently convinced by Gruver's eloquence, Hana-ogi publicly announces their coming marriage:

It is very difficult for a Japanese woman to speak in public. I have never done so. But perhaps now it is the time. Major Gruver has asked me to be his wife. He knows there are many people in his country who will be disturbed by this. I know my people will be shocked too. I hope they will learn to understand and someday approve. We are not afraid because we know this is right.

Allowing the American public of the 1950s to reimagine itself, the character of Lloyd Gruver overrides the "problematic" of interracial marriage by invoking the American ideology of individual and popular narratives of true love against all odds. If military and nationalist aggression had helped win the war, it is equally true that racist wartime propaganda and fear fueled militaristic and nationalist fervor. And, however justified the internment of Japanese Americans might seem to white Americans, the underpinnings of racism were not completely invisible. What *Sayonara* allows is a vision that could accommodate the U.S.'s sense of itself as both strong enough to decimate the Japanese empire and its crazed kamikaze soldiery, and fair and big-hearted enough to take to itself the frail, exotic Japanese woman. In a penultimate scene from both book and film, Gruver faces an angry crowd of Japanese men (or "hoodlums") who are enraged by both the Occupation and the increasing incidence of American men taking on Japanese girlfriends and wives:

At the head of our alley appeared a large gang of toughs screaming, "Americans go home! America go to hell! Go home!" . . . in the lurid light of their flickering torches these fanatical faces looked exactly like the cartoons of the Japanese barbarians we had kept posted in our ready rooms during the war years. I remember one horrible face rushing at me. It was distorted, evil, brutal and inhuman. . . . The last thing I saw was a Japanese face—not one of the evil masks, but Hana-ogi's oval and yellow beauty. (188–89)

While Hana-ogi, as the sign of Japanese womanhood, may be treated with sexual tenderness, Japanese manhood, in all its inhuman barbarity, must be diligently fought. Gruver's ambivalence and the desire of the U.S. to see itself as both conquered (by love) and conquering (by military force) is figured along gender lines, in much the same manner that representations of Japanese women and men just after the turn of the century tend to polarize "good" and "bad" Japanese qualities along gender lines.

The military threat posed by Japan during the Second World War marks a decided shift in U.S. rhetoric and representations. Although the polarization of Japanese men and women is evident from before the war, it intensifies after it and continues into the present. This shift is attributable, I believe, to the military and economic threat posed by Japan, factors that must be understood to work in conjunction with the well-established sense of absolute and impenetrable difference of the Japanese. Presently, filmic representations of Japanese men and women continue to duplicate the postwar strategies I have discussed here.[27] In fact, one might argue that such representations, in various media, have both intensified and become more subtle in direct proportion to Japan's economic dominance and the corresponding economic vulnerability of Western Europe and the United States. Whereas the two films I have discussed above issue from an era in which, riding the wave of the Allied victory over Japan, the United States could confidently assert its moral and cultural dominance, the significantly stronger economic and political position of present-day Japan suggests the necessity for other discursive strategies through which it may be constructed as the feminized counterpart to the masculinized West.

Significantly, although films continue to provide a mechanism for orientalist representations, there has also been a curious return to the popularized travel narrative, a cultural product most readily associated with the late nineteenth and early twentieth centuries. Because the seemingly innocuous I-was-there narrative has long provided a discursive means for national cultures to shore up the sense of their disintegrating hegemony, and because it continues to be the expression and disseminator of imperialist, racist constructs, I want to focus on it here as offering a particularly useful way in which to understand the "processes of subjectification" (Bhabha, 71) employed by the West relative to Japan.

The Logic of Sexualized Metonymy in *Pictures from the Water Trade* and *The Lady and the Monk*

"Japanese women relate to sex somewhat differently than western women," opines the author of the *Japan Handbook,* a frequently used travel guide to Japan.[28] "Japanese women enjoy sex and unlike westerners who didn't seem to discover the clitoris until the mid 1970s, they knew that it existed at least a thousand yrs. [*sic*] ago. They are orgasmic, warm and affectionate" (35). Taken alone, this passage might be read simply as articulating the sexualized geisha stereotype so nauseatingly familiar to most Asian and Asian American women. However, as the passage continues with the bald directness of guidebook authority, the manner in which such stereotypes serve larger purposes of subjectification becomes increasingly clear. It is particularly revealing when we read what follows as encoding the West's political and cultural practices in relation to Japan:

Japanese women have also heard stories about the sexual prowess of western men and they, too, are curious. . . . A Japanese woman expects you to be the aggressor, and in the old-fashioned sense to "make" her. Obviously, this by no means includes force, but it does include directness. You lead and she responds. Ther's [sic] a bit of Scarlett O'hara [sic] in the Japanese woman. She wants Rhett Butler to sweep her off her feet and manfully carry her to the bedroom. This in a way exonerates her from responsibility because, after all, she couldn't refuse. (35)

The near endorsement of rape here is itself highly problematic, but particularly so because it is placed within the context of cultural reciprocity—that is, overt sexual aggression is not just the correct way to "make" a Japanese, and therefore clitorally aware woman, but it confirms the sexual prowess about which she is "curious." Rape is recast as the consensual satisfaction of cultural curiosity wherein both parties are "exonerated from responsibility." Thus the rhetoric of cultural and sexual reciprocity obscures the underlying imperialist/rapist mentality.[29]

There exists a significant body of writing wherein the white, Western male protagonist seeks and presumes to understand Japan through a sexual relationship with a Japanese woman. It articulates the entrenched perception that consort with the Japanese (female) other somehow transmits experiential and therefore "authentic" cultural knowledge.[30] The salient characteristic of this writing is not only that the Japanese woman is placed in metonymic relation to Japan, but that she is the site of both difference and desire, the space where cultural alterity is both constructed and collapsed. As a raced subject, she is the sign of absolute racial/cultural alterity. As a gendered subject, she is constructed as sexually accessible. The West's obsessive articulation of racial and sexual alterity places the Japanese woman's body in a fetishistic economy of difference, in which it is discursively and literally the site of the East's receptivity to the West, a vestibulary conduit to Japanese culture. In other words, sexual penetration equals cultural entrance.

Such narrative strategies characterize the contemporary phenomenon of overtly autobiographical travel narratives, which have proliferated in concert with quasi-sociological studies and books on the business culture of Japan: all, I argue, rework and sanitize gestures of cultural imperialism as the desire for access and "understanding."

Travel narratives have a particularly long tradition in France and England, and, as Lisa Lowe notes, both countries have shown great interest in "the Orient." Lowe, like many others (Edward Said and Mary Louise Pratt among them), points out that the ideology of the travel narrative implicitly comments on the status of the home country. In reference to eighteenth-century orientalist travel narratives, Lowe writes that "travel as a representation of territorial ambition became a predominant discursive means for managing a national culture's concern with internal social differences and change . . . [and] addressed national anxieties about maintaining a hegemony in an age of rapidly changing boundaries and territories" (1991, 31).

In the past decade, travel guides and travel narratives about Japan have enjoyed a great deal of popularity as more and more Westerners have gone there to exploit Japan's economic prosperity. As this might suggest, the economic conditions in the West, and particularly in Britain—the country of origin for the two writers I discuss here—have not been comparably fortunate during the late 1970s and 1980s. Lowe's analysis of eighteenth-century Britain certainly has parallels in this period, in which economic, social and political anxieties have made serious inroads into the ideal of the British empire of the earlier part of this century. In addition, the analyses of British feminism have cast further doubt upon the primacy of British nationalist patriarchy.

The two texts at issue, John David Morley's *Pictures from the Water Trade: Adventures of a Westerner in Japan* (1985) and Pico Iyer's *The Lady and the Monk: Four Seasons in Kyoto* (1991), suggest that the narrative strategies in the present historical moment differ significantly from those of, for instance, the postwar period. Earlier representations of the Japanese woman tend to emphasize submissiveness, servile femininity and the possibilities of interracial marriage; difference is the site of cultural appropriation coded through the rhetoric of heterosexual romance and the institution of marriage. In contrast, Morley's and Iyer's narratives position difference as the site of titillating desire, which cannot be domesticated matrimonially but can be mastered sexually. The failure of the romantic relationships that structure these narratives reaffirms racial and national alterity, the threat of which is defused through the constructs of infantilization and feminization. In this context, these narratives may be read as attending to two separate, but related, agendas: a nationalist one in which the primacy and superiority of Britain and/or the West is (re)established, and a personal one that confuses sexual and gender dominance with a relationship of mutuality and reciprocity.

This dynamic of consensus or reciprocity is central to many travel narratives about Japan. Morley's and Iyer's books both replicate the sexual-conquest/cultural-difference narrative set up in the *Japan Handbook*, though each in a different way. Distributed by major publishing houses and fairly popular for their genre, both rely on what Mary Louise Pratt, in her study of transculturation and travel writing, identifies as the sentimental mode of the "anti-conquest" travel narrative (Pratt, 39).[31] In contrast to overt "conquest" narratives in which the omniscience of an unidentified narrator implies cultural mastery, the anticonquest travel narrative constructs the protagonist "as a non-interventionist European [or Western] presence. Things happen to him and he endures and survives. As a textual construct, his innocence lies less in self-effacement than in submissiveness and vulnerability, or the *display* of self-effacement" (Pratt, 78). Moreover, the sentimental anticonquest narrative relies heavily on transgressive plot lines featuring taboo interracial relationships. In Morley and Iyer's texts, both narrators are the central figures in what are topically books about Japan. More particularly, their narratives revolve around what Pratt identifies as the "mystique of reciprocity" (78), in which the protagonist is, at least in his mind, as much a figure of curiosity and conduit as the Other, and therefore innocent of establishing an asymmetrical relationship of which he is the beneficiary. And yet, the discourse of self/other clearly manifests itself in the metaphors of seeing that run through both narratives. Rey Chow argues in her theory of "ethnic spectatorship" that, relative to China, such metaphors are crucial to the "demarcation of ontological boundaries between 'self' and 'other' " (3).

Morley's *Pictures from the Water Trade* establishes this rhetoric of sight immediately. As the title unintentionally suggests, Morley's "pictures" are static representations articulated from a fixed, Western point of view. Interestingly, Morley's narrative is told in the third-person, with the effect that his point of view is obscured as such, resulting in a wholly fictive voice that presents itself as neutral. In the opening pages, this totalizing perspective undermines what at first seems to be a moment of reciprocal observation. A Japanese woman sits next to Boon, Morley's semifictional alter ego, then she "turned to look at him, as if noticing him for the first time." He responds with a description that both objectifies the woman and privileges his own status as subject:

She had the most beautiful head, superbly coiffeured, and a very striking face. The slant to her large, oval eyes was barely perceptible, with the curious effect that one was kept guessing, in Boon's particular case as to whether he was looking at a Japanese or a European face, but also more generally, as to quite what one should make of her: the chief characteristic of the face was its ambiguity, which was why Boon found it increasingly difficult to keep his eyes off her. (4)

What I find significant here is not that Morley/Boon obviously seems to expect the exaggeratedly slanted eyes of Western stereotype, but that the absence of such a slant should launch him into a sort of racial existentialism. Unable to differentiate between self and other in racialized terms, Morley's language immediately shifts modifiers: he speaks no longer of *her* face but of "the face," not of *her* ambiguity, nor even *an* ambiguity but "its ambiguity." The discursive result is that agency is granted to his eyes, not hers.[32]

The ambiguity of which Morley speaks is more accurately understood as his sense of himself as an ambiguous subject. Throughout his narrative, Morley repeatedly states that Boon's reasons for coming to Japan were unclear to him, but it soon becomes evident that Japan serves as the cultural backdrop that animates the primacy of his search for himself. In the above passage, *sight* both calls into question and reestablishes the territories of self and other, but that reestablishment of boundaries takes place only after Morley/Boon has visually transgressed them. His intrusive gaze recalls the intrusive sexualization with which Morley characterizes Japanese culture. The eroticization that permeates his perceptions clearly illustrates the ways in which he both feminizes and sexualizes Japanese culture, a move predicated by highly aggressive rape metaphors that recall the above *Japan Handbook* passage. As Chow notes, the rhetoric of sight involves much more than marking "positivistic taxonomic juxtapositions of self-contained identities" (3). At stake is the articulation of a power relationship in which the narrating eye/I implicitly grants itself subject status vis-à-vis its chosen object of scrutiny.

Shortly after his encounter with the "superbly coiffeured" woman, Boon watches a dancer perform to the traditional music of the *shamisen*. It is notable that Morley describes the eros of dance in terms of dominance and submission:

The last note shuddered into silence, the dancer was obediently still. The *shamisen* attacked at a high pitch; her body jerked with a spasm, as if she had been stung, and with sharp, stiff movements of her hands and arms, warding off the jangle of chromatic sounds, the dancer began to retreat . . . her body in profile to the audience displaying the classic *kimono* figure . . . both suppliant and erotic. (13)

Clearly, what interests Boon is the agonistic interplay between music and dancer. As he continues, his fascination centers on the gradual submission of the dancer:

The rhythm of the *shamisen* became faster and more aggressive, breaking the dancer's controlled sequence of movements and forcing her into confusion; the straight neck suddenly buckled and slumped. . . . She stopped, flounced, pitching her head back and her buttocks out, straightened, shuffled . . . as if searching for an escape and fluttered submissively to her knees. The strident, masterful music of the *shamisen* beat her still further down, she drew her arms into her sleeves and gently sank, nothing but white and gold, back into exhausted repose. . . . Boon was entranced; it was the most ravishing, sensual dance he had ever seen. (13)

The Cio-Cio-San, or Madame Butterfly, imagery here is unmistakable, and Morley uses its clichéd familiarity as the informing lens through which to view an otherwise unfamiliar cultural performance. In a mode similar to that in which he describes the woman's face in the passage quoted earlier, his narration here relies on the parsing of individual features: the focus on her foot, neck, back and buttocks suggests that Morley's attention fixes on only one feature at any given moment. What is thereby confirmed is his own status as a coherent subject, conferred by the implicit primacy of his gaze as the locus at which these various details come together. (Tellingly, at a later point in the narrative, Boon replies to the question of whether he is half—meaning half Japanese—with the statement, "I'm whole. I'm English" [207].) While the need for descriptive detail and specificity demands distance and focus, Morley decontextualizes isolated details in order to arrive at generalizations that confirm his construction of Japan in sexualized terms. Thus, just as in this passage he orders isolated details into an aesthetic narrative of sexual domination and submission, so does Morley construct Japan generally from the isolated details he gleans in the water district's various bars and Pink Cabarets.

The metaphorical rape that Morley/Boon reads into this dance is indicative of the way in which he both sexualizes Japanese culture and identifies himself with the role of aggressor. In this, it is significant that Morley's generalizations are almost always realized through Japanese women, in relation to whom he constructs himself as dominant and dominating. In one of his most absurd and striking passages, Morley equates the art of Japanese calligraphy, or *shodo,* with "dark, illicit sexuality" (86): "it was largely the sensual friction of contrasts, black and white, wet-dry, hard-soft" (86). He notes that this realization comes simultaneously with his awakening "to the attractiveness of Japanese women" (86). As Boon improves his *shodo* stroke, Morley's account takes on greater sexual overtones, borrowing the image of the pen/paintbrush *cum* penis: "Suzuki-san was mildly surprised [by his marked improvement], calling her mother in from the kitchen to watch Boon wreak black mischief with his dripping lance. *'Ara!'* crowed the old lady, guarding her lap with folded hands. Unfolded, knees parted, her daughter quivered" (88).[33]

Ultimately, and hardly surprisingly, Boon's attempt to assert a self in the world centers on Mariko, a woman who works in a bar. For all the metaphors of sight and seeing, Mariko is never described in detail; she is effaced both within and by the narrative. Of Boon's aggressive pursuit, Morley notes that "his approaches were so reckless and imperious that they obliterated their object. It was less a courtship than an assault" (136). He continues:

Yet when Mariko remarked in one of her letters that she felt herself spiritually raped she was not registering a complaint; it was in the nature of Mariko's consent, as it was of her entire self, to appear as something taken rather than given. . . . This was not what she thought but what was thought in her, a conclusion that followed naturally from an irreducible fatalism lodged at the core of her soul. . . . He was the agency of an effect in her, with her response they were complete. (137)

Boon's search for completion, finally, powers both Morley's narrative and Boon's relationship to Mariko and Japan. His complaints about the essential and baffling difference of Japanese culture become indistinguishable from his frustration that "Mariko was an enigma. The ambiguity about Mariko, the ambiguity that Mariko herself was, began to torment him" (146). Boon's attempt to understand Japan ultimately rests on his ability to understand Mariko. His "spiritual rape" of her, then, must be understood in the context of his desire for access to a culture that confounds him. In terms of Pratt's notion of the anticonquest narrative, Morley/Boon is subjected to the confounding difference of Japan/Mariko; though he is an active subject, he retains his "innocence" by repeatedly emphasizing his status as a stranger in a strange land.

More significantly, Boon confirms this innocence through his sexual relationship with Mariko. Morley includes several graphically described sexual trysts in which Boon's ability to please Mariko both justifies his self-described role as "predator" and reasserts her essential difference. Each time he "takes her like an animal," Boon simultaneously feels her "aloofness," that she is as "remote from him as her prickling flesh was close" (161). Moments of physical intimacy mark most clearly the gulf between Mariko and Boon, and he soon realizes that "she was simply opaque. He had not understood her at all" (174). Boon blames the failure of the relationship on "cultural premises very different from his own" (176), which he can neither understand nor appropriate through Mariko, but he ignores the possibility that his own aggressive "spiritual rape" is in any way responsible for her resistance. Ultimately, however, it doesn't matter. For what the failed relationship with Mariko accomplishes is the quelling of Boon's own racial/cultural ambivalence: "his capacity to assimilate the new culture would depend on his willingness to sever, or at least temporarily suspend, the attachment to his own in a much deeper sense. The relationship with Mariko made plain to Boon that this was a sacrifice he was not prepared to make" (176). Ultimately, *Pictures* is not about Japan: it is about Morley/Boon's reaffirmation of his own Westernness.

The construction of Japanese woman as the figure of desire and difference is similarly present in Pico Iyer's *The Lady and the Monk*. Iyer, like Morley, seeks to understand and gain entry into the culture through the sexualized site of Japanese woman. And, like Morley, Iyer uses the rhetoric of complementarity to characterize "the pairing of Western men and Eastern women" (79). However, where Morley/Boon discovers or reaffirms his "Englishness" through overt gestures of sexual domination, Iyer ossifies the categories of "Japanese" and "Western" through the mechanism of a cultural nostalgia that is variously configured as sexual and/or cultural innocence.

Iyer reinscribes the figure of Japanese woman as the exotic embodiment of Japan, even as he wryly and feebly tries to resist that conflation. As with most travel narratives about Japan, the protagonist foregrounds his status as male and as a Westerner; however, unlike most of those protagonists, Iyer—born in England and currently residing in the United States—is ethnically South Asian. With the exception of one section in which he briefly takes stock of the characteristics of his identity (and then only to illustrate the ways in which his Japanese romantic interest cannot seem to see him except through the limited categories of "mysterious Indian, history-steeped Brit, fun-loving Californian, romantic loner, wandering writer, sometimes monk" [192]), Iyer's own positioning in relation to British and American culture is rendered invisible, particularly to the extent that he can identify himself as the arbiter of Western cultural values and the bestower of its various freedoms. Thus, one of the unstated agendas of his narrative is to assert a seamless relation between himself and the Western cultural tradition he can lay claim to in distinction to those who are not part of it. Throughout Iyer's narrative, Sachiko Morishita, as an emblem for Japanese culture, is consistently portrayed as one who parrots a set repertoire of imported images from Mozart to Michael Jackson. "When it came to names at least," writes Iyer, "and surface responses, there seemed no limit to her range. Trying to find some weakness in her repertoire, I chided her about her indifference to baseball" (172). Sachiko's ability to elide national boundaries through commodified popular culture presents a moment of anxiety for Iyer, who attempts to reestablish the upper hand by invoking the quintessential American sport of baseball. As one who himself crosses and moves between national borders—suggested both by his personal background and his status as a travel essayist for *Condé Nast Traveler* and *Time* magazine—Iyer might reasonably be expected to identify with Sachiko.

In fact, he does just the opposite. To the extent that he can identify Sachiko—and Japan—as parochial innocents, Iyer's investment in the privilege of his mobility suggests a concept of transnationality to which only a select few have access. In order to shore up the terms of that privilege, Iyer must continually redraw national boundaries even as he himself transgresses them. But Iyer has an arguably more insidious purpose: his residence in Japan and his relationship with Sachiko are the conduits for his nostalgic longing for "a better time and self" (251). He repeatedly states his desire for "innocence," projecting this quality onto Japan generally and Sachiko in particular. It is this quest for a kind of prelapsarian—or perhaps more accurately, atemporal—innocence that ultimately reinscribes the discourse that Iyer professes to reject. A crucial part of that project involves conflating the discourse of nationalism with the discourse of romance, both powered by the logic of oppositions.

Iyer's book takes its title from a fairy tale of his own invention that furnishes the narrative's primary metaphor. The story, about a "beautiful lady" (120) and a Buddhist monk, concerns the ways in which the lady's presence distracts the monk from his meditations. Finally, he invites her across the threshold of the temple and, though "that night was the coldest of the year . . . neither the monk nor the lady knew it." On the morning after, the monk asks that the lady come no more. "I want to keep my image of you as clear as running water," he says. "And know that, though we should not meet again, it is you I always think of" (121). This act of renunciation serves a dual purpose: the encounter between the monk and the lady is transformed into a talisman for the monk's meditations, and her absence proves the primacy of the spiritual over the physical. In other words, she is the corporeal transition point to a spirituality defined by her absence. Once she serves her purpose, the purpose itself requires her absence. As Hortense Spillers writes in reference to black women: "She became . . . the principal point of passage between the human and the non-human world. Her issues became the focus of a cunning difference — visually, psychologically, ontologically — as the route by which the dominant male decided the distinction between humanity and 'other.' At this level of radical discontinuity in the 'great chain of being,' black is vestibular to culture" (76).

Of key importance in Spillers's formulation is her notion that the black woman is constructed not only as the site of difference but as the "vestibule" that connects one state of being to another, one site to another. In Iyer's fantasy narrative, woman is the vestibule to a spirituality encoded as culturally and racially Japanese. It is everywhere clear that Iyer finds this story not only touchingly instructive but prescriptive, and his whole book becomes a narrative attempt to keep his image of both Japan and the Japanese woman with whom he becomes involved "as clear as running water." It is the woman's image, infinitely manipulable by virtue of its stasis, not the woman herself that powers his narrative. Clearly, Iyer makes use of an age-old trope: spirit is gendered as male, sensuality, and the distractions thereof, as female. In his own, tediously typical, search for Zen enlightenment, Iyer presumptuously places himself in the role of monk, and Sachiko in the role of lady.

What seems to complicate this pedestrian setup is that Iyer regards with a certain amount of skepticism the tradition of "Western men seeking Asian wives, as well as Asian wisdom, and not always troubling to distinguish between the two" (59). He even makes a passing and somewhat disapproving mention of the *Japan Handbook*. However, though he notes that "Japanese girls had long been the subject of romantic fantasies of our own in the West" (79), Iyer excuses such fantasizing as a natural consequence of "the attraction of opposites" (78). "Besides," he continues, "the pairing of Western men and Eastern women was as natural as the partnership of sun and moon. Everyone falls in love with what he cannot begin to understand" (79). Iyer naturalizes a perceived absolute difference and constructs Sachiko's difference as the site of both eternal innocence and inherent Japanese sexuality, conveniently blurring the line between "wives and wisdom."

Opening his account of his year in Japan, Iyer retrospectively rhapsodizes about Japan as a timeless zone of "romance" and "charm" (Iyer's favorite adjective describing things Japanese). His glimpses of Japan reveal a "gallery of still lifes" (3), a *tableau vivant* (7) in which "everything looked exactly the way it was supposed to look" (3). These visual metaphors, and the various ways in which they are sustained throughout his account, suggest that sight, the act of seeing, provides an important means by which Iyer will organize his experience. But "seeing" here assumes a transparent relation between object, perception and apperception, and therefore it is precisely the question of "who is 'seeing' whom" (Chow, 3) that Iyer never interrogates. Japan and the Japanese are constructed as containers of inherent difference. The Japanese, who, Iyer "assum[es], as always . . . were not like other people" (41), live in a country that occupies "a different kind of universe, which rarely made contact with our own" (159).

Given that absolute difference is synonymous with Japan, it is easy to understand why Iyer is unable to deal with the factual existence of the out-Westing-the-West Japan of the 1980s, a Japan that increasingly exemplifies the transnational possibilities of global capitalism. Instead, he consistently refers to Japan in atemporal terms, in static metaphors of sight. Though Iyer often evokes Heian Japan (A.D. 794–1190), it is because he sees this period as paradigmatically Japanese; his nostalgia for a pre-Westernized Japan dehistoricizes twelfth-, and obscures twentieth-, century Japan.

Heian Japan, whose images give most Westerners their stock of samurai and cherry blossom stereotypes, is the basis for Iyer's sweeping characterizations as well. This period, identified by many as the greatest of Japanese literature was, significantly, the era of the great women writers and poets. Completely ignoring their tensile undercurrents and sharp political sense, Iyer characterizes the writing of Sei Shonagon and Lady Murasaki by "its charm, [which] lay in its girlishness, its womanly refinement, its sensitivity to nature, and to the lights and shades of relationships" (54). Iyer then extends his inaccurate and gendered view of these two writers to Japanese literature in general, and this characterization ultimately is the ground for his gendering of Japan as female:

I was struck again and again by how much Japanese writing was touched with a decidedly feminine lilt and fragrance, a kind of delicacy and a lyricism that I associated, however unfairly, with the feminine principle. This softness was apparent not just in the watercolor wistfulness of Japanese poems, but also in the very themes and moods that enveloped them—loneliness, abandonment, romance. . . . Clearly, too, in a society whose public life was close to formal pageant, it was only in private, behind closed doors, that people began to seem interesting to themselves. Yet, whatever the reasons—or the qualifications—poetry and femininity seemed almost interchangeable in Japan, as they would never be in the literature of Chaucer, Milton, and Johnson. (53–54)

In addition to the masculinist construction of English literature in distinction to feminized Japanese literature, the themes Iyer identifies in the latter, "loneliness, abandonment, romance," closely parallel the themes of his lady and monk story. What is more crucial here is the move he makes to privatize Japan and Japanese relations. In this passage as elsewhere, he dismisses Japanese public life as empty ritual and pageantry; thus, it is in the realm of the private that the "real" Japan reveals itself (or, rather, herself), and this is the rationale for learning (or "doing") Japan through his relationship with a Japanese woman.

Sachiko, like Shonagon and Murasaki, is consistently described in terms of her girlish charm: "a small and pretty figure bounced up to me . . . a tiny figure of casual chic . . . hands shyly crossed behind her back, and bouncing on the soles of her feet" (47, 61). Though Sachiko is, in fact, a thirty-year-old woman with two children, Iyer is unable to describe her in language that represents her as anything other than a "girlishly dressed" (87), "bouncing girl" (135). By reducing her to a twelve-year-old, Iyer is able to associate her with the principle so dear to his heart, the reclamation of his own innocence: "Often, with Sachiko, I felt as if I were . . . auditioning to play the part of a freewheeling foreigner in the long-running romantic picture she'd been screening in her mind. . . . Sachiko, like many Japanese perhaps, was an uppercase Romantic, with an innocence that idealized experience and turned it into a reflection of itself. . . . Her innocence seemed almost proof against the world, making the world seem innocent" (131, 300).

This insistence on her childlike innocence obscures her to such an extent that Iyer does not consider that Sachiko's stilted English (the transcription of which reads like Japlish gone awry) frustrates the ways in which she can represent herself with complexity; instead, the limited communication between himself and Sachiko makes them "gentler, more courteous, and more vulnerable . . . returning us to a state of innocence" (131). Innocence, like Iyer's Japan, can be located only in the past. Introducing Sachiko into the matrix of his images of Japan in order that she may represent them, she must be not the woman she is in the present but the girl she was in the past.

In addition, such language defuses the sexuality represented by Sachiko, who, as a Japanese "girl" possesses an "innocence . . . touched by a hint of guiltless sensuality" (78). In Iyer's narrative, difference and desire reciprocally construct each other, each is implied by the other. Iyer's attraction to both Japan and Sachiko is inextricably tied to their alterity. Just as "romance" signifies both sexuality (romantic love) and idealization (the romance of Japan), so, too, does "desire" signify sex (desire for Sachiko) and spirit (desire for Zen enlightenment). Instead of parsing sexual and spiritual desire, Iyer locates both outside himself, projecting those qualities onto Japan: "I had not even set foot in Kyoto on my way back to Japan before enlightenment and seduction—and the intertwining of the two—were all about me once again" (162).

By articulating desire through his construction of Japan and (Japanese) woman, Iyer places himself in the position of one who must merely differentiate between modes of desire understood as existing in the world, not in the self. In addition to being a much less threatening process, it allows Iyer to retain his construction of the Japanese woman as the titillating site of the sex/spirit dyad. Sachiko, then, is its unknowing and, more crucially, unconscious carrier (since consciousness, like enlightenment, is territory Iyer claims): "Her emotions seemed as exquisitely worn as her seasonal bracelets or earrings, and the words she used had a kind of other-worldly, romantic Zen flavor—or, at least, a sense of clarity and calm that seemed to cut to the heart of Zen" (131).

Sachiko's inborn Zen-like qualities manifest themselves unconsciously, naturally, unconnected to her will or intent. What agency Iyer does allow her—wearing her emotions like jewelry—suggests the intention of allure and attractiveness. Indeed, this is borne out in Iyer's description of Sachiko's attentiveness to his "preferences," which "she stored away . . . as diligently as a courtesan" (261). This attentiveness, apparently, has nothing to do with gender expectations inflected through cultural forms of politeness, and everything to do with her latent, courtesan sexuality, which is itself understood to be identified with her racial difference.

It is for this reason that moments of intimacy and desire immediately give rise to physical descriptions that signify Sachiko's essential difference:

There was . . . a curious kind of intimacy that Sachiko-san established—she seemed to draw a net around one as if to shut out the rest of the world. And as she explained the symbols of Zen to me in the giddy autumn sunshine, I caught snatches of her perfume, saw silver bracelets jangling on her tiny wrists, realized that her eyes—finely folded and alight—were the first Japanese eyes I had ever really seen. (62)

Again, the conflation of desires is evident here: Sachiko is explaining Zen to Iyer, but he is taken up with other, more worldly concerns. Far from locating distracting sexuality in his own perceptions (the sunshine, not Iyer, is "giddy"), this passage confirms the trope in his lady and

monk story: Sachiko cannot be the carrier of spirit, but merely the per-
fumed, braceleted handmaiden of Iyer's spiritual quest. She can be the
vestibule to spirituality but not its embodiment. Significantly, the intimacy she creates, which Iyer frames in sexual terms, focuses his attention
on her eyes. As though glimpsing a mythic species, Iyer directs his (and
our) attention to what is for him the ultimate and most characteristic
marker of Japanese difference. Much later, when he has arguably had
time to get used to Sachiko's "finely folded" eyes, he again focuses on
them in a moment of intimacy: "I could feel her perfume all around me,
and as we watched the clouds catching the last of the light on the city
below, she sighed, and a chill came into the air. I had never seen eyes
shaped like hers before, with ocher eye shadow and folded lids, and
when she looked up at me, I felt a shudder" (119). Iyer's "shudder" here
is telling, as it is unclear whether he is shuddering with anticipatory
desire, distaste or a sense of the delicious strangeness of it all. I would
argue that all three possibilities are, in fact, one and the same.

Iyer, as the culturally determined I/eye of the West, is fascinated with
Sachiko's eyes, and his fascination reinforces the primacy of his gaze. By
isolating and objectifying her eyes, he precludes the possibility of a subject whose gaze meets his own. Iyer controls the discursive field in which
Sachiko is constructed and is therefore able to delineate the boundaries
of self and other, as well as accept, reject, exoticize or appropriate difference according to how he wishes to manipulate it. He is able to identify as a Western "us" in noting Japanese difference, but he can also
claim to be one of "them" (after ten weeks in the country, Iyer professes
to be "quasi-Japanese" [156] and "Japanese enough" to think and act like
one [157]). Difference is both fixed relative to the Western norm and
floating in terms of its deployment by the West.

In a similar way, Iyer can read or "see" Sachiko's difference as simultaneously signifying her mystically atemporal innocence and her essential, exotic sexuality. Since the structure of his desire rests on the
fulcrum of Sachiko's racial and sexual difference, it is crucial that he
maintain her alterity. Through images that closely parallel the lady and
the monk story, Iyer describes what we are to assume is the long awaited
union of opposites:

I held her, shivering, against the windless night, and together we looked up
at the hazy moon of monks. "I dream of sea," she said, "and many star."
Above us, the moon was balanced on the branches.
    Then I felt her hot whisper in my ear, and saw her lying down, her curved
eyes flashing in the dark.
    The moon, the mild, warm air; the silent, sleeping dogs. (305–6)

Sachiko, like the lady at the temple, interrupts Iyer's lunar meditations with a sexual heat that warms up the night in which they had
previously shivered. And here, as in earlier passages, the site of sexuality
is marked by the ludicrous description of Sachiko's eyes — a description
that subtly echoes the inanity, circulated and widely believed during
World War II, that Japanese women's vaginas, like their eyes, were horizontal slits.

Iyer recuperates, through the rhetoric of woman as vestibule, what
might otherwise be seen as a lapse in his spiritual quest:

As winter deepened, and I continued reading, the theme of the lady and the
monk continued to pursue me, and everywhere I turned, I found new variations on the theme. . . . What was more surprising, though, was that
sometimes the woman's virtue could be stronger than the monk's, that, in
a sense, the woman could become an agent of belief and a gateway to a
heaven not only seen in earthly terms. (179)

The vaginal imagery here is telling, for it reveals the convenient conflation of that which signifies difference and that which enables passage
from woman to spirit, thereby justifying sexuality as the (regrettable,
but not too regrettable) means to the end. "Sometimes," Iyer concedes,
a woman "could" be identified with virtue or the spiritual, but that
concession does not confirm female spirituality; rather, it (re)asserts the
primacy of male spirituality. Having walked through the gate and onto
the other side, the gateway can now be left behind, its purpose fulfilled,
much as the lady in Iyer's story is renounced only after she has provided
the monk his meditative image. Sachiko's sexuality is thus constructed
in terms of its *a*ffect. Shortly after Iyer's coyly vague account of Sachiko
and her curved eyes, he realizes "I drew closest to the discipline [Zen]
only when I did not know that I was doing so — in the utter absorption
of writing about Sachiko, say, or talking with her sometimes" (309).
Or, say, when sleeping with her. Sachiko's "innocence" leavens her sexuality, and, in conjunction with it, is transformed into a kind of sexual
koan of Iyer's spiritual (con)quest. The metaphor of "seeing" that surfaces throughout the text ultimately functions to constrain Sachiko's
complexity within the static confines of the eternal paradox: the sexualized woman as the gateway to male spirituality.

Earlier in his account, Iyer declares that "Kyoto had installed itself
inside me. . . . No other place I knew took me back so far or deep, to
what seemed like a better time and self." Significantly, he comes to this
epiphanic realization only after Kyoto has become for him an ossified
"album of photographs" (251). What is particularly interesting here is

the way in which Iyer occupies the feminized position of receptivity. This reversal ironically underscores the extent to which the innocence he seeks and eventually claims conflates the spiritual and cultural *via* the sexual. As the spiritual/cultural innocent who is himself, so to speak, penetrated, Iyer further distances himself from the tradition of "Western men seeking Asian wives, and Asian wisdom, and not always troubling to distinguish between the two" (59).

At the close of his narrative, Iyer similarly ossifies his experience through the metaphor of (hind)sight, which allows him an atemporal, feminized but asexually innocent, snapshot of Japan: "It was only later, after I left Japan, that I realized that everything had been there that night: the lanterned dark, the moon above the mountains, the dreamlike maiden in kimono [Sachiko]. There was the Heian vision I had sought since childhood. And yet, by now, it was so much a part of my life that I had not even seen it till it was gone" (338).

One could more simply say that Iyer has seen nothing at all, since forcing correlations to projected fantasies is less an act of seeing than of selective looking. What Iyer, like Morley, is ultimately looking for, of course, is himself. In the end, the line of Shinsho's poetry that Iyer quotes says much more about the project of Japan travel narratives than Iyer most likely intended: "No matter what road I'm traveling, I'm going home" (251).

Though the idea that in writing the other one ultimately says more about oneself has been stated in any number of disciplines, including anthropology, sociology and history, Morley's and Iyer's narratives suggest much more than a distasteful personal and national self-absorption. Ultimately, *Pictures from the Water Trade* and *The Lady and the Monk* participate in and justify a discourse that desires to see Japan as sentimentally innocent and engagingly obtuse so as to ameliorate an increasing fear that Japan's present economic status presents a serious challenge to Western hegemony. In an age when global capitalism and a growing transnational culture render discreet national and cultural borders increasingly unstable, the practice of defining national identity within an oppositional model itself becomes untenable. In this context, Iyer's description of Japanese difference—its very outlandishness suggesting the extent of his investment—reads like a last-ditch effort to reestablish that model:

The analogy [of Japan's difference] here was not so much with Gulliver as with Alice; in Japan, one felt as if the world had been turned upside down and inside out, all its values and assumptions turned on their heads—as if, one might say, the force of gravity had been so radically altered that one had ended up on another planet. It sometimes seemed—and Japan liked to make it seem—as if Japan had a different epicenter from the rest of the world, as if, indeed, all the rest of the world inhabited a Copernican, and Japan a Ptolemaic, universe. (159)

Iyer's analogy recalls the old cliché that digging to the antipodes leads to a literally backwards China, an Asian Wonderland of inversion. Needless to say, the normalizing point of reference, the point from which one starts digging, is Western. Iyer's association of Japan with a Ptolemaic universe suggests, beyond a laughable backwardness, a failure to progress from what everyone else knows to be an archaic, obsolete mentality. Iyer justifies his perspective, so to speak, by claiming that the Japanese themselves wish to be seen as inhabiting another planet—indeed, another universe. Clearly, such a notion of Japan's self-concept does much to quell xenophobic anxieties that prefer an old world order of separate and impermeable national spheres. Like Morley, whose protagonist concludes that his Japanese lover, and through her Japan itself, "was simply opaque" and best left so, Iyer retreats to a nostalgic view of a premodern Japan that charms, rather than threatens, with a supposedly self-promoted image of its own alterity. However, the inherent instability of these constructions—encoded through the contingencies of mastery and nostalgia—suggests that the East-West dichotomy invoked in Morley's and Iyer's narratives can function at best only as a provisional and bracketed fiction.

Although the geisha stereotype is very familiar and its use ubiquitous, there has been little inquiry into how it has functioned as more than simply an erotic projection of male sexual fantasy. As we have seen here, the Japanese woman has consistently been troped, through the geisha figure, as a nonthreatening site of appropriable difference. And let me point out what may be in the realm of the obvious: Japanese woman has been constructed not as a subject with subjectivity but as a subject of serviceability. She has been granted agency only insofar as it has served the interests of those other than herself. Through the logic of metonymy, essentialized Japanese womanhood has been used to both feminize and dominate Japan in ways that obscure the imperializing impulses of the West. Employed as the central figure in narratives molded through the rhetoric of sexual romance, she serves as both the sign of willing Japanese capitulation to aggressive acts of military paternalism and the vestibular site through which white Western manhood reassures itself of its coherence and primacy. Thus, the "geisha-ized" Japanese woman as both racial and sexual other is not merely a distasteful expression of Western stereotyping but the necessary mechanism of a paradigm in which Japan, femininely infantile and sexually exotic, may be mastered.

CHAPTER 2

In/Visible Difference

Japanese American Female Subjectivity

I really love Japanese films, almost as much as I love Asian girls!
I'm going to Taiwan next month to meet this woman I've been
corresponding with. I really prefer Oriental women to American
because (he whispers) there are so many "feminists" in this town.
You're Asian aren't you? Don't tell me, let me guess. Japanese?
Chinese? Hawaiian? Eurasian?

Elena Tajima Creef, "Notes from a Fragmented Daughter"

Let's face it. I am a marked woman, but not everybody knows my
name. . . . I describe a locus of confounded identities, a meeting
ground of investments and privations in the national treasury of
rhetorical wealth. My country needs me, and if I were not here, I
would have to be invented.

Hortense J. Spillers, "Mama's Baby,
Papa's Maybe: An American Grammar Book"

The racial economy of the United States, as many have
noted, is structured by several related binaries that powerfully position
racially marked others along axes of difference that both assert and maintain white dominant ideology. The most significant structural binary,
one that has shaped and continues to shape the national consciousness,
is based on a black-white paradigm in which blackness is coded as difference and is determined in relation to normative whiteness. The implicit reliance on alienated difference—in which what one *is* and *is not*
simultaneously define each other—subtends the logic of binary oppo-

sitions, and the belief in the objective veracity of sight naturalizes the metaphor of color as a fact of the body. While a number of corollary dichotomies structure identities within the black-white dyad, the color scale—with its obsessive gradations of "blood" and attendant assignations of social, moral and ontological value—provides the master schematic for racialized identity in American culture.

As Robyn Wiegman argues, this "economy of visibility" (6), with its heavily invested assignations of ontological difference plotted along a seemingly self-evident trajectory of increasing epidermal darkness, has overtly structured racial categorization since at least the nineteenth century. If racial marking, however, is artificial, contingent and socially constructed, its legitimation and naturalization derive from confusing the line between perception and apperception, between what people "see" and what they are looking for. That is, the logic of racial marking grounds itself in bodies that, in the closed circle of a tautology, are then perceived to be "really" black or white. "Of course," writes Wiegman, "bodies are neither black nor white, and the range of possibilities accruing to either designation contradicts the assurance of these categories to represent, mimetically, the observable body. Our cultural trust in the objectivity of observation and the seemingly positive ascription we grant representation are part of the history of race's discursive production" (9).

"Is Yellow Black or White?"

The slippage between ideological structures and what is assumed to be observable difference is perhaps nowhere clearer than in the positioning of Asian Americans within the racial structure of the United States.[1] In a configuration in which what signifies is primarily black and white, Asian Americans, Native Americans and Latinos have been assigned the intermediary spaces. Although these spaces are internally configured along other organizational binaries (West/East, North/South, domestic/foreign, citizen/native) that place whiteness at the far (or top) end of a line whose opposite point defines everyone else, the overarching symbolic of black-white configurations reduces these ideological spaces to sites ranging from relative undervisibility to structural invisibility.

For Asian Americans, this hierarchy of pigmentation has resulted in an invisibility whose potency is in direct relationship to their placement near the "white" end of the color scale, a positioning Angelo Ancheta names "white by analogy" (4). The powerful ideology of this pigmentocracy has been naturalized as the perception that since Asian Americans supposedly are not "dark," they are therefore closer to whites than other groups whose bodies read as "brown" or "black." But of course such readings of epidermal shading are highly questionable and always contingent. That such assignations and positionings are in fact not natural or given is evidenced by the historical shiftings of Asian Americans in the American racial landscape. As Gary Okihiro notes, "Asian Americans have served the master class, whether as 'near-blacks' in the past or as 'near-whites' in the present or as 'marginal men' in both the past and the present" (34).

Asian Americans are further ideologically invisibilized as "model minorities" or "honorary whites." The conflation of color (or the supposed relative absence of it) and character (or the supposed relative presence of it) reveals not only the socially constructed and historically contingent nature of the "racial formation" in the U.S., but the ways in which the arbitrary nature of that formation allows for both difference and nondifference to circulate at the same site.[2] As the inhabitants of this site, Asian Americans are vulnerable to the ways in which, as Okihiro illustrates, relationally defined difference or nondifference is deployed by the dominant order for its own purposes.

The contradiction inherent in the positioning of Asian Americans results directly from the signifying paradigm of black and white. With its conflation of ontological/moral status and seemingly observable color difference, the black-white dyad renders Asian Americans invisible as subjects. And yet the logic of visuality, coupled with the ideology of East-West difference (noted in chapter one), results in the status of Asian Americans as highly visible racially marked objects. This contradictory status registers at a site that foregrounds the extent to which the material and ideological form and inform one another: the body—and more specifically, as I explain in the latter part of this chapter, the Asian face.

Whereas this study as a whole addresses the subjectivity of Japanese American women, one of this chapter's significant sections discusses Asian American women as a group. I broaden the focus for two primary reasons: the ways in which Japanese American women specifically and Asian American women generally have been rendered invisible as subjects in this country are structurally similar, if not tactically identical. And the racial history of the United States, as it pertains to Asian Americans, has continually failed to differentiate between Asian ethnic groups, as it has failed to distinguish between Asian Americans and Asian nationals.

Given that history, I must make a somewhat contradictory move in simultaneously arguing for the ethnic specificity of this study and concentrating on Japanese American women at crucial points in this chapter. The persistent conflation of Asian and Asian American women, and of Asian ethnic groups, has resulted in all too real violence against Asian American women, especially when they do not conform to pervasive stereotypes and expectations of passivity and sexual servitude.[3] Because their invisibility as subjects has been the social and discursive condition of Asian American women, to critically or theoretically replicate the persistent absence of ethnic differentiation is to take part in the further erasure of Asian American female subjectivity.

Owing to their invisibility, and to the erasure of ethnic specificity in American racial discourse, I have chosen to err on the side of insisting on a particularity that allows me to draw connections between the figure of the Japanese woman and Japanese American women.[4] There is thus an unavoidable awkwardness in my attempt to account for both the specific ways in which Japanese American women construct themselves as subjects and their simultaneous construction as objects in an orientalist discourse wherein the failure to mark ethnic specificity subtends the erasure of individual subjectivity.

Gendering Asian American Invisibility

I begin with the ways in which the Asian American female body is encoded in an economy of racial and gender difference. One involves the conflation of Asian nationals with Asian Americans, which keeps them forever foreign in this country. A second is the way in which Asian American women often find themselves cast in an undifferentiated pool of Asian women whose (assumed or enforced) foreignness and physical exoticism promise a range of delights: Lotus Blossom, China Doll, Madame Butterfly, Geisha Girl, Suzy Wong, Dragon Lady.[5] Whether delicately or dangerously sexual, such images are all inflections of the same trope and reveal the extent to which the Asian American woman's body is invested in an orientalist economy of sexual power and fantasy.

The construction of Asian American women in highly sexualized terms has a long tradition of American cultural production, from novels and plays to legitimate films intended for mass-market audiences to porn films and skin magazines.[6] The commodification of Asian women's sexuality in such venues, however, is just one expression of the manner in which Asian and Asian American women are, and have been, fetishized in American culture and in the American imaginary. As James S. Moy observes:

The nineteenth-century construction of the sexually available Asian female has recently been transformed into the "super Jap" or "sleazy Asian girl" (SAG). In general, Asian women in America have come to be perceived as possessing special mastery of sexual practices. Indeed, in California this belief has given rise to what could be called the cult of the SAGophile, Anglo men whose pursuit of SAGs can be read on the personal ad pages of the *San Francisco Bay Guardian*. (136)

Far from representing an attitude on the extreme fringes of the socially inept or the sexually ignorant and desperate, the perception of Asian American women as domestic English-speaking versions of Madame Butterfly and Miss Saigon is evident in less easily dismissable places. In Pulitzer Prize–winning author Richard Rhodes's critically acclaimed *Making Love: An Erotic Odyssey* (1992), for instance, one finds the following passage of sexual self-examination: "For as long as I can remember I've been compulsively attracted to women with Asian features. Living most of my life in the Middle West, I met very few; I've never dated or slept with an Asian or an Asian-American" (74). He writes that his immediate attraction to his second wife, a white woman, was largely based on the fact that "her features were slightly Mongolian . . . her eyes had nearly epicanthic folds" (75). These days, he goes on, his fantasies about Asian women have become quite specific, involving being the owner of a whorehouse filled with Asian "girls," attractive because "the bodies of Asian women are small by Western standards and relatively hairless, relatively childlike" (77).

Attending such images of sexual exoticism is the widespread belief that Asian American women have somehow been untouched by decades of social and political feminism. The distressing popularity of the Asian Bride catalog business attests both to the continuing perception of Asian women as "cute (as in doll-like), quiet rather than militant, and unassuming rather than assertive" (except sexually), as well as more "feminine, loyal, [and] loving" (Lai, 168). While this image of Asian women ultimately says more about the self-styling of white masculinity than anything else, the widespread perception of Asian women as inherently, exotically sexual is too often taken as fact.

Yet for all their visibility as sexually exotic objects, Asian American women remain invisible as subjects, within both dominant discourse and much feminist discourse. As a recent study on Japanese American women observes, "They have been largely invisible throughout the one hundred years of their lives in this country" (Nakano, xiii). And, as Mitsuye Yamada reminds us, "invisibility is an unnatural disaster."[7] The experiences of Asian American women have either been defined as identical to that of Asian American men or subsumed within the experience of white women; both moves attest to the failure of representing Asian American women as sites of the complex intersections of race, gender and national identity.

As I argue in the previous chapter, constructions of the orientalized other—and specifically of the infantile and hyperfeminine Japanese woman—function primarily to reassert the coherence and primacy of the Western subject. It is at this juncture that the relation between sites of visibility and invisibility must be carefully drawn out. If the contradictory nature of the economy of racial visibility in this country results in the Asian American as an invisible subject who is nevertheless highly visible as a racially marked object, then—given the inherent binarism of visuality—there is plenty to suggest that the differing levels of Asian American in/visibility will have as their complement the subjective visibility/racial invisibility of the dominant white subject. As the work of scholars examining the construction of whiteness asserts, the structural visibility of white subjects relies on the ideological invisibility of their race.[8] "One can name only a part of one's racialization," writes Ruth Frankenberg, "by making a spectacle of an Other" (1996, 5). In order to secure itself, whiteness is visible only by the default resulting from the specularity of the other. Thus, the racially marked body—and in this case, the Asian American body—is forced to function in a context not of its own making, one in which the spectacle of the orientalized body secures the terms of difference.

In order to anchor my inquiry into the nature of the Asian American female subject's problematic relationship to her hypervisible, sexualized and overdetermined body, I take up the narrative structure of Alan Parker's 1990 film, *Come See the Paradise,* as providing a particularly clear example of how the Asian female body is visually deployed to recast the reality of white racism and reassert the centrality of white masculinity.

Parading beneath a present-day ethos of liberal multiculturalism that flouts the reality of 1940s antimiscegenist sentiment and the rarity of Asian-Caucasian marriages, the film nevertheless capitalizes on the spectacle of interracial sex and a lingering sense of its illicit allure.

Come See . . . What?

Come See the Paradise hinges its superficial exploration of the internment of Japanese Americans on a romantic narrative that ultimately renders the Asian American subject invisible while refiguring white racism as an anomalous character flaw, instead of as a pervasive ethos. Central to this process is the specularity of the visibly Asian, female body constructed as a site of both difference and desire that undermines the film's putatively liberal protest against race-based injustice.

In the film's closing scenes, Lily (Tamlyn Tomita), the Japanese American wife of a white American, and her daughter wait to meet the train that carries husband/father Jack (Dennis Quaid) back home. Punished for going AWOL during WW II because he left duty to visit his wife and child in the internment camp where they had been forcibly sent, Jack has spent the last few years in a military prison. He alights from the train into the waiting arms of wife and child, in a scene that recalls films whose culminating moment depicts the game soldier at last returning home from the private hells he has endured. Lily and Jack's reunion is the closing scene in what is supposed to be a film about the injustice of the internment of Japanese Americans during the war. But as the music swells and eyes glisten with meaningful sentiment, the discourse of true (romantic and familial) love effectively erases the depictions of hardship (sanitized as they are) that Lily, her daughter and 120,000 other persons of Japanese descent incarcerated by the United States government suffered for years. The film's ending suggests that all has come aright and that Jack, not Lily, has been victimized by a rigid military code and his own admirable refusal to forsake his Japanese American wife. Compared to Lily's internment, a situation she had no choice but to experience, Jack's suffering is chosen, and therefore heroic. What Lily has experienced is rendered invisible; what she has endured, the film implies, is offset by the fact that Jack has sacrificed himself for her. The imprimatur of a white man's love compensates for the branding suffered because of white racism.

This moment of reunion provides the dramatic frame of the film, which opens with Lily and her daughter walking to the train station. Their stroll down dusty lanes through fields of mustard flowers is the occasion for Lily to tell her daughter the story of how Lily and Jack met, fell in love and married, as well as to recount the war years and the internment: stories to pass the time. If the closing scene, as I have suggested, reduces the impact of the internment by privileging Jack's experiences, the film compounds that reduction by structurally subordinating Lily's experience to the framing narrative of the family's imminent reunion. This diegetic obfuscation has two functions: it downplays the impact of white American racism on Lily and the Japanese American community and simultaneously foregrounds Jack's lack of racism. This second purpose, however, relies on emphasizing Lily's racial difference. That is, the extent to which Jack is recognized as a noble antiracist is in direct proportion to how Lily is recognizable as representative of racial otherness. The result is that the film structurally downplays Lily's social and political difference (and the effects thereof) while it visually emphasizes her physical, sexual difference.

As many feminist film theorists have pointed out, the history of Hollywood film has depended on the sexualization of woman through the male gaze. As the object of desire within the film, woman must also be constructed as an object of desire for the audience. In *Come See the Paradise* (a title unexplainable except by reference to Lily herself *as* Paradise), Japanese American womanhood is constructed not only as sexually desirable but as sexually desiring. Within the introductory sequences of Lily's retrospective narrative, a Japanese man makes a fumbling pass at an impatiently dismissive Lily, who is shortly thereafter introduced by her father to a new acquaintance as having "every man in Little Tokyo chasing her. But can she find a husband?" Embarrassed, Lily is pulled away by a giggling girlfriend. They join a group of young women peering through a doorway at a man and woman kissing passionately in an empty room. The woman, however, is married, and the man she so fervently embraces is not her husband, as Lily's friends explain in the happily hushed tones of scandalous titillation. Later that evening, the community learns that Mr. Oka, the woman's husband, has committed suicide because his wife's publicly witnessed infidelity has caused him to lose face.

Jack's first glimpse of Lily, then, is preceded by representations of Japanese American female sexuality as transgressive and dangerous. Looking at her through the window of the tailor's shop where Lily is seated at a sewing machine, Jack is immediately attracted to her. Lily's brother, who works with Jack in the family's Japanese movie house, tries to dissuade Jack from inviting Lily to lunch with them, warning that "it's no good. You should find a nice American girl, Jack." Later, left temporarily and fortuitously alone at the restaurant, Jack and Lily engage in a few minutes of stilted conversation. Suddenly, Jack says, "You're really beautiful, Lily . . . Can I kiss you?" Lily seems taken slightly aback at first, but her expression suggests that the idea of kissing a near-total stranger appeals to her sense of daring. From this point on, virtually all sexual contact between Jack and Lily is initiated by Lily. By that night Lily is in the projection booth that doubles as Jack's room, apparently well versed in the ways of sexual seduction. It is Jack who puts a stop to the action by insisting, in tones perfectly straddled between increasing desire and gentlemanly restraint, that he take the disappointed Lily home. The following night, and a few scenes later, Lily again comes to Jack's room. As they embrace, they inadvertently turn the film projector on and make love in its flickering light. Significantly, Lily, in the stereotypical position of the sexually aggressive woman, lies naked on top of Jack; as the film continues to roll, a Japanese woman's voice can be heard singing on the film track. Thus, Lily's sexuality is constructed as latent, not virginal, and is specifically identified, through the voice of the singer, as Japanese.

The emphasis on visuality and spectacle in *Come See the Paradise* reveals, though inadvertently, the role sight plays in the construction of raced sexuality. That the projection booth doubles as Jack's living quarters suggests that his desire for Lily literally inhabits the realm of spectacle. The lovemaking scene, dominated by the tick and flicker of the projector, visually echoes the earlier scene of Mrs. Oka's witnessed infidelity. Although Lily herself was a spectator of another (Japanese American) woman's sexual transgression, seeming to align her with the cinematic gaze referenced by the running projector, she is in fact positioned as the object of that gaze. Literally framed within the tailor shop's window when Jack first sees her, as well as visually beheld by the projector lens that mimics *Come See*'s audience, Lily's body is the focal point that collapses Jack's and the audience's gaze.

It would be perhaps too easy to suggest that this collapse alone functions to make Lily invisible as a subject, and indeed it is here that the narrative structure of the film figures significantly. That the story of Jack and Lily's meeting and subsequent relationship is framed by Lily's retrospective narrative would seem to necessitate the dominance of her point of view. In fact, however, as the scene discussed above illustrates, the film implicitly foregrounds Jack's point of view. Thus, through a structural sleight of hand, what Lily narrates is her own desirability in terms that contain any implied sexual agency within the realm of male desire. The prevalence of visuality and sight, in addition to the filmic structure, renders Lily's sexuality, and her view of her own sexuality, as mediated through the gaze identified, through Jack, with white masculinity. In short, Lily, like the woman she watched kissing her lover, is a spectacle.

While the film at various points suggests Lily's cultural difference from Jack (and white America), it is her sexualized racial difference that is most persistently visible. The inseparability of the discourses of romantic love and gendered, racial essentialism is suggested by a scene that weds the epiphanic and the conjugal. Lying in bed together, Jack explains to Lily what he has come to realize about her.

You have a happiness inside that makes you so beautiful. It's as if someone gave you a little bag of magic. Is that what you can dip into? And I see that way that you look at Mini [their daughter] and then your eyes are something so perfect no one can touch it. No one can cheat you or steal it away from you because it's something no one else can have. I love you so much, Lily. You're braver than anyone I ever knew. You have everything that I never had. And I was still so blind and stupid that I didn't see that . . . you were just giving me a little handful of that magic. And no one and nothing is ever going to take that away from us. No one. Never.

Given that Lily and the Japanese American community she represents are, in fact, cheated and stolen from, Jack's monologue might be taken as ironic if not for the way in which it both naturalizes Lily's difference and suggests that this difference, this "magic," and its retention are of ultimate importance. Material losses need not be personally devastating if one has that "little bag" (of womanly forbearance, Japanese stoicism?) to "dip into." But Lily's magic and untouchable perfection cannot be dissociated from the spectacle of her prone, postcoital nakedness. Lauren Berlant suggest that "when the body of the woman is employed symbolically to regulate or represent the field of national fantasy, her positive 'agency' lies solely in her availability to be narrativized—controlled . . . by her circulation within a story" (1991a, 28). Jack not only reconstitutes the figure of the essentialized Japanese woman as possessing some secret that is expressed, among other ways, sexually, but narrates Lily's place in their story in terms that metonymically inflect to the national realm. Though Jack's epiphany is occasioned by Lily having taken their child and left him because of an argument, all seems well once they are near enough each other to let physical, sexual attraction work its magic. Lily's concerns, serious enough to have initiated a separation, seemingly evaporate in a sexual heat, after which she lies silent and placid in Jack's arms.

Indeed, this tendency on Lily's part is suggested in the first few minutes of the film. As mother and daughter walk toward the train station, Mini complains that her feet hurt. Interestingly, Lily's response accompanies her first (of many) soft-focus, face-front shots: "Try not to think about it. You want to look pretty now, don't you?" Through this innocuous piece of dialogue, Lily is cleverly represented as one who does not dwell on hardship (of either sore feet or of the internment), concerning herself instead with matters of prettiness. Her focus is on her physical affect, not her personal experience. As the family walks off into the distance, one can only surmise that Lily and Jack's reunion will be, once again, punctuated by Lily giving him "a little handful of that magic."

Fragmenting the Subject: Negotiating Difference and Identity

Filmic representations of Asian American women have been a particularly potent source of their construction as embodiments of racialized sexual difference. The relation between visibility and invisibility played out in *Come See the Paradise* is paradigmatic of the construction of Japanese American women specifically, and Asian American women generally. Such constructions are crucial not only to the maintenance of structures of domination but to the formation of national identity understood to be synonymous with white racial identity. Lauren Berlant, among others, argues that national identity is formulated through the ways in which historical or "everyday" persons are abstracted and "reconstituted as a *collective* subject, or citizen" (1991a, 24). That is, the individual person "acquires a new body by participation in the political public sphere. The American subject is privileged to suppress the fact of his historical situation in the abstract 'person': but then, in return, the nation provides a kind of prophylaxis for the person, as it promises to protect his privileges," one effect of which "is to appear to be disembodied or abstract while retaining cultural authority" (1991b, 113). Yet this process of privileged abstraction implicitly assumes a subject whose particularities of race, gender, class and sexuality are coded as normative and therefore invisible. The male, white, heterosexual and propertied subject is structurally visible in direct proportion to that subject's invisibility as a site of marked embodiment.

But what obtains for those whose "humiliating particularity" remains, in a sense, uncollectible, unabstractable, who are marked "as precisely not abstract, but as imprisoned in the surplus embodiment of a culture that values abstraction" (1991b, 113)? Women, people of color, the poor, the queer are subject to an enforced embodiment wherein the particularity of their hypervisible bodies defines their status as the obverse of American ideality, or more accurately as the obverse on which the idea of American national identity depends.

The relation between hypercorporeality as spectacle and the marking of Asian/Americans as the vanishing subjects of the American imaginary is central to Janice Mirikitani's poem, "Looking for America," which references a catalog of standard movie-house male Orientals. The stanza comprising Asian female stereotypes, however, ambiguously references (to the extent that they are separable) both filmic and social images:

> I found myself
> in a bar, dancing for a tip,
> cheong sam slit to my hip,
> or in a brothel, compliant and uncomplicated,
> high-heeled in bed, wiping some imperialist's lips
> with hot scented towels.
>
> (*We, the Dangerous*, 4)

What the speaker finds in the search for an Asian American subject, Mirikitani concludes, is a "foreigner / who is invisible / . . . / on America's pages." The shift from visual, filmic representations where the Asian body is visible only to be dominated sexually or in combat by white masculinity ("shot by John Wayne / conquered by Stallone / out-karated by Norris, Van Damme, Carradine and Seagal") to the discursive realm, in which the Asian American subject is not to be found, signals the constantly shifting social registers that fetishize and undermine racially marked subjectivity. While Asian American men have been routinely portrayed as asexual (either as bestially crazed warmongers or spectacled geeks), the female Asian body seemingly cannot be racially marked without hypersexual encoding. That is, engendering of the Asian body is always inscribed through the sexual, either in terms of lack or excess. Given this fact, one might ask, in terms borrowed from Hortense

J. Spillers in her essay, "Mama's Baby, Papa's Maybe: An American Grammar Book," how to "speak a truer word." How "to come clean" under the weight of one's own appropriated (Asian, female) body? How can identity be claimed when it is tied to a racial construction so sexually encoded and overdetermined? Because the body itself serves as both the locus for projected otherness and as the referent of specularity, it is a profoundly problematic site at which to deal with questions of subjectivity and agency.

It is perhaps for this reason that direct, explicit mention of sexuality and the body has been until recently largely absent from the writings of Asian American women. Where the body does appear, it is often represented as the catalyst for humiliation or represented in order to be disowned. In the poem "Corrosion" by Gisele Fong, for instance, the speaker first dissociates from all those who remind her of her own shamed racial identity: "Immigrant, sweatshop woman, / kung fu man, laundry worker, / Chinese waiter, computer nerd. / You are not a part of me." Strikingly absent from this litany are images of the sexualized Asian American woman. Yet the closing lines of the poem signal that their absence involves more than simply authorial preference or oversight. With an abruptness that itself serves as a transition, the poem ends: "Eyes, tongue, / leg, breast, / heart / You are not a part of me" (117). Because the Asian woman's body is so heavily encoded as sexual, the speaker here recognizes no possibility for its reappropriation and disavows it altogether. But with the rejection of the body is an attendant splitting from the ethnic community and from ethnicized identity. The fragmentation of the self and the dissociation from the body are experienced not only as an abstract ontological state but as a physical sensation of the absolute alterity of one's own self.

Writing by Asian American women suggests that feelings of invisibility compete with feelings of being all too visible, resulting in images of fragmentation, splitting and corrosion. Whereas many poststructuralist accounts of subjectivity privilege indeterminacy, fragmentation and the infinite deferral of a "self" and valorize "difference" as the site of multiplicity and provisionality, subjects who are racially marked and marginalized cannot approach such theories uncritically.[9] As Gayatri Spivak observes, much current theory tends to reassert the sovereignty of the (white, male, propertied) Western subject, even as it claims to undermine coherent subjectivity by defining it in terms of "pluralized 'subject-effects'" (271–72). What Spivak's analysis points to, I think, is that moves toward privileging indeterminate fragmentation must and should involve recognizing the ways in which dominant culture subjects rely on a granted, assumed coherency that may then be both bracketed and deconstructed. For subjects marked by race, or by gender and race, fragmentation is very often the condition in which they already find themselves by simple virtue of being situated in a culture that does not grant them subjecthood, or grants them only contingent subjectivity.

Poststructuralist articulations of subjectivity are rife with the language of contingency, relativism and spatial marginalization, and concepts of a fragmented, deconstructed subject are central to its grammar.[10] Humanist notions that assume a unified ground of being are dismissed as totalizing constructions based on illusions of an originary self. As many theorists have noted, ideas about the unified self ignore the extent to which history and language construct the subject and thus open the door to essentialism. Similarly, political inflections of poststructuralism recognize that discourses of unity and coherence are often the discourses of hegemony, and thus oppressive. Yet for the raced subject, an ontology and epistemology based on fragmentation not only pose serious political problems but also tend to subvert the attempt to integrate the several and disparate aspects of being and bring them to bear on a sense of self. The language of rupture and physical rending characteristic of poststructuralism depends on a coherent subject that is then "taken apart," and it is in this sense that Spivak accuses such discourses of valorizing the Western or dominant culture subject, even as those discourses seem to refuse that subject's commensurability. In other words, while dominant culture subjects may experience subjectivity as constantly shifting, indeterminate and fragmentary in an ontological, internal sense, subjects marked by race and gender not only experience such contingency ontologically, but socially as well. Collapsing the important differences of positioning between these two groups obscures the extent to which discourses of fragmentation refuse the raced subject any stance other than that of the disempowered.

I want to turn briefly to Frantz Fanon who, in his groundbreaking book *Black Skin, White Masks,* describes the dynamic between visually marked, ideologically loaded, difference and the negation of subjectivity, the moment when the racially marked subject realizes that s/he is regarded as "an object in the midst of other objects":

Sealed into that crushing objecthood, I turned beseechingly to others. Their attention was a liberation, running over my body suddenly abraded with nonbeing, endowing me once more with an agility that I had thought lost, and by taking me out of the world, restoring me to it. But just as I reached the other side, I stumbled, and the movements, the attitudes, the glances of the other fixed me there. . . . I was indignant; I demanded an explanation.

Nothing happened. I burst apart. Now the fragments have been put together by another self. (109)

Crucial to the understanding of this passage is Fanon's equation of fragmentation with nonbeing. Subjugated to "the movements, the attitudes, the glances of the other," the shattered and disparate aspects of one's being undermine the very possibility of being. The "glance" or gaze that fixes and fragments the other allows for no "ontological resistance" (110), resulting in a state in which one is ontologically nonexistent to, because completely alienated from, oneself. Clearly, valorizing the fragmentation of multiple subject-positions alone as a positive alternative to the unified and coherent self is an exercise in absurdity when applied to a raced subject whose experiences tell him/her that to celebrate the fragmented is to celebrate his/her own dismemberment. Difference understood as an abstraction separable from the context of specific material and social conditions of racism will always modulate into the absurdity of privileging precisely those things that have denied subject-status and agency to the marginalized and oppressed.

Yet to evacuate the possibilities of a more fluid subjectivity would suggest that such a sense of the self as subject could somehow avoid the reification that has typically been the cornerstone of racist ideology. Fanon's articulation of the ways in which subjectivity must somehow be "put together" again by "another self" whose own existence is understood to be provisional—always already threatened with dispersal—suggests the process through which the raced subject must continually attempt to reconstruct him/herself from his/her own burst fragments.

The difficulty of so doing, however, involves the extent to which the internalization of oppression precludes what Fanon calls "disalienation" (231). Though the poststructuralist understanding of difference is one in which " 'difference,' unlike 'otherness,' has no exact opposite against which to define itself" (Hutcheon, 6), "difference" for the raced subject must always first be extricable from *different from*, since that suggests an always contingent self.

But what many poststructuralist theorists of subjectivity have failed to adequately account for is the status of the racially marked body whose visibility precludes the free play of discursive signifiers. Though I by no means argue that the body is a site of irreducibility, nor that an assumed facticity of the body in and of itself sets the limits on discursive play, I reemphasize that the racialized body is one for which distinctions between denotative and connotative are particularly difficult to establish.

In the following passage from *Black Skin, White Masks,* Fanon illustrates the manner in which the connotative possibilities of the body are not in the control of the raced subject. What he describes throws into question whether or not issues of identity and reality can be so easily dismissed as "reactionary" (Lyotard, 75):

In the train it was no longer a question of being aware of my body in the third person but in triple person. In the train I was given not one but two, three places. . . . It was not that I was finding febrile coordinates in the world. I existed triply. . . . I subjected myself to an objective examination, I discovered my blackness, my ethnic characteristics; and I was battered down by tom-toms, cannibalism, intellectual deficiency, fetishism, racial defects, slave-ships, and above all else, above all: "Sho' good eatin.' "

On that day, completely dislocated, unable to be abroad with the other, the white man, who unmercifully imprisoned me, I took myself far off from my own presence, far indeed, and made myself an object. What else could it be for me but an amputation, an excision, a hemorrhage that spattered my whole body with black blood? But I did not want this revision, this thematization. (112)

Fanon's use of physical images to describe feelings of fragmentation is not a mere metaphor. For raced subjects, perceived as being physically marked by difference, the body itself is a contested site of subjectivity.

The imagery of the passage above recalls a similar language of fragmentation and disavowal in Gisele Fong's "Corrosion." Both vacate the body as an irredeemable site of fetishization. Yet such moves leave one at a problematic site of psychic disembodiment. Asian American women face a difficult task in attempting to create themselves as subjects: on the one hand, they must refuse totalizing, essentialist discourses that would construct them as the forever foreign Other and timeless handmaiden of male sexual fantasy; on the other hand, they must somehow reconcile the notion of shifting identities and provisional coherence with the fact that people of color need to move from already feeling fragmented to an embodied sense of coherence and agency. In addition, the discourse of racial and gender essentialism means that the Asian female subject must negotiate issues of difference, essentialism, identity and subjectivity in an environment that assumes a direct, synonymous relation between them. Without contesting the discursive structure that allows little differentiation between the four terms, difference—and the body as the bearer and manifestation of difference—becomes that which must be refused wholesale in order to controvert an essential and forever foreign "Japaneseness," thus resulting in a dualistically constructed identity that isomorphically stands in for subjectivity. That is, subjectivity is based on what one is not and therefore straddles a racial lacuna. Alternatively, difference embraced as identity itself results in an essentialized subjectivity, as though one is constructed by and through difference alone. Trinh Minh-ha formulates the problem this way: "The difference (within) between *difference* and *identity* has so often been ignored and the use of the two terms so readily confused, that claiming a female/ ethnic identity/difference is commonly tantamount to reviving a kind of naïve 'male-tinted' romanticism" (1989, 96). If one is to extricate oneself from difference defined as "different from," a stance that clearly remains tied to normative (white, male) constructions of subjectivity, the assumption of an essential self that underpins the ideology of dualized difference must be dismantled; thus, "difference should neither be defined by the dominant sex nor by the dominant culture" (Trinh 1990, 372).

But defining difference outside the constructs of dominant ideology is no easy task. Paradoxically, the racially marked and marginalized must refer to dominant culture constructions of themselves in order to claim the agency of self-naming.[11] As the Fanon passage quoted above attests, stereotypical subject positions simultaneously construct the raced object and destruct the raced subject. Such subjects must therefore both dismantle and (re)construct themselves as subjects. While "both" implies that these processes are separable, they are not. The complexity of negotiation for raced subjects involves "insist[ing] first what they are *not* and then affirm[ing] what they are, who they are, and their place in this historical space" (Ortega and Sternbach, 14). Clearly, the danger lies in mistaking what one is not for what one is; and yet the raced subject cannot construct a positive, nonreactive self completely without reference to imposed constructions because they make up a significant part of one's experience of subjectivity in the first place.

One way in which raced subjects attempt to circumvent defining subjectivity and identity through any reference to dominant culture constructs is to resort to what I might call a self-defined racial essentialist position. It claims racial identity as full-blown, an essential self that must simply unburden itself of social racism in order to thrive. In an environment that denies viable subjectivity to people of color, the temptations of essentialist-based constructions of the self are understandable, if problematic. Cultural nationalist movements posit a stable, determinate identity that seems to answer to the need for the self as a *functional* totality. In fact, such identities posit an *absolute* totality that reinscribes the conflation of identity and difference. The inherent danger of this confusion is that it inevitably leads to the circumscription of racial difference within exploitative notions of racial "authenticity." To accede to an authentic ethnicity is to accede to racial stereotypes promoted with a patronizing and ultimately self-serving concern for "diversity" or "variety" by the dominant culture, as though race and ethnicity are exotic commodities whose value is in direct proportion to how tolerant dominant culture wishes (for the moment) to be. Trinh identifies this move as "planned authenticity":

As a product of hegemony and a remarkable counterpart of universal standardization, it constitutes an efficacious means of silencing the cry of racial oppression. We no longer wish to erase your difference. We demand, on the contrary, that you remember and assert it. At least, to a certain extent. Every path I/i take is edged with thorns. . . . i play into the Savior's hands by concentrating on authenticity, for my attention is numbed by it and diverted from other, important issues. (1989, 89)

Delimited within the confines of an assumed and largely invisible normativity, difference uncritically understood as an authentic identity remains within the discursive field defined hegemonically, and thus subject to capricious appropriation, marginalization or erasure.[12] Joanne Harumi Sechi illustrates how, in fact, such hegemonic definitions of difference are unconsciously internalized so that the Japanese American subject becomes bounded by his/her own self-commodification:

I felt that I had to be expert on things Japanese. I had to know the proper Japanese names for objects, the correct origins of ceremonies. I always tried to present "my" culture to others on a silver platter before they could attack it. When the little awareness I did have about Japanese culture led to questions I couldn't answer, I felt ashamed and guilty. I had internalized the greater society's expectations to be culturally aware of a country I'd never lived in, let alone wanted to be responsible for. I was made to feel that cultural pride would justify and make good my difference in skin color while it was a constant reminder that I was different. (446)

Sechi describes the inevitable failure of the "authenticity" route as a means to claiming identity and agency through difference defined in relation to white American normative models.

Difference, then, must be redefined as that which both "undermines the very idea of identity" (1989, 96) and as that which "does not annul identity. It is beyond and alongside identity" (1989, 104). The seeming contradiction between these two definitions of difference suggests how difference is continually negotiated and constantly shifting. Understood this way, difference is accorded no absolute value and is removed from the ideology of "different from." Thus, there can be no easy equation of difference with identity since both are neither static nor discrete. The continual negotiation between difference and identity is thus itself constitutive of subjectivity.

In other words, the subject must self-consciously position herself in relation to difference, as well as understand how she is positioned by and within it. Subjectivity will always labor under the threat of subjection when its own status remains bounded by nonpermeable models of self/other, subject/object, that is, when it continues to be unaware of its own agency in constantly negotiating meaning and its basis in an ongoing process of constitution. For Trinh, this awareness involves a critical distance from the self:

The difficulties [of constructing the self as subject] appear perhaps less insurmountable only as I\i succeed in making a distinction between difference reduced to identity-authenticity and difference understood also as critical distance from myself. The first induces an attitude of temporary tolerance— as exemplified by the policy of "separate development"—which serves to reassure the conscience of the liberal establishment and gives a touch of subversiveness to the discourse delivered. (1989, 89)

In such a scheme, Trinh argues, the "I" can be realized as that which is constituted by "infinite layers" and allows the "free reign of indeterminacy" (1989, 94). However, if this conceptualization resists the ideological traps of a unified, essentialized subjectivity, it does not fully address the problematics of indeterminacy and fragmentation it seems to valorize. For if "differences that cause separation and suspicion . . . do not threaten [because] they can always be dealt with as fragments" (Trinh 1989, 90), difference defined as a series of continually negotiated stances circulating within a discursive field of indeterminate signifiers threatens to fragment from within a subjectivity that is already fragmented from without. The infinite play of signifiers becomes the endless deferral of one's own viability as a subject. Difference must be theorized in ways that are not indiscriminate and totalizing, that do not obscure the realities and consequences of embodying identifiable difference. Difference understood as an abstraction separable from the context of the specific conditions of racism and sexism will always modulate into the absurdity of privileging precisely that which has been used to deny subject-status and agency to the marginalized and oppressed. Put another way, if the constant shiftings of identity, difference and subjectivity are necessary as a strategic deployment of resistance to hegemonic codes of representation that themselves continually change in order to adopt new modes of appropriative power, marginalized subjectivity must somehow be grounded if it is to include both the possibilities of multiplicity and a sense of coherent functionality.

The sexual saturation of the Asian American female body inaugurates a disavowal of the body and the fragmenting of subjectivity, resulting in an invisibility that is both determined by the culturally dominant discursive field and enacted by the Asian American female subject in an attempt to reclaim subjectivity. Yet if we are to accept, however skeptically, the claim of identity politics that political viability and community are grounded in lived experience defined by the ways in which subjects are visibly marked, then the rejection of the sexually raced body also implies a separation between the subject, ethnic identity and community. In the terms I have delineated so far, there would seem to be no avenue by which the Asian American female subject can claim visibility without on the one hand finding her subjectivity under erasure within a matrix that identifies Asian American female embodiment with hypersexualization, or on the other hand disclaiming the sexualized body at the expense of ethnic subjectivity.

At this point, I turn to two autobiographical texts that, in very different ways, interrogate the relationship of the Japanese American female subject to the body as a site of visible identity. I argue that the sense of fragmentation that inaugurates these textual narratives is recuperated, through reclamation of the body, as a disjuncture that is nevertheless experienced as itself the ground of a viable subjectivity. Further, I suggest that this process of reclamation is enabled by the subject's temporary positioning outside the geographic boundaries of the United States.

Originary Essentialism Revisited: Going "Back to" Japan

Until recently, Japanese American autobiography consisted solely of narratives written by Nisei (second-generation Japanese Americans). Beginning with Dorinne Kondo's *Crafting Selves: Power, Gender, and Discourses of Identity in a Japanese Workplace,* published in

1990, two additional autobiographical narratives by Sansei (third-generation Japanese Americans) appeared in quick succession: David Mura's *Turning Japanese: Memoirs of a Sansei* (1991) and Lydia Minatoya's *Talking to High Monks in the Snow: An Asian American Odyssey* (1992). (Because this study concentrates on Japanese American women, I will limit my following discussion to Minatoya's and Kondo's texts.) All three texts share important characteristics: they have been published fairly recently, they deal with questions of identity and subjectivity and, most striking, they all focus on journeys to Japan. This last suggests that the struggle to define and construct Japanese American subjectivity is intimately connected to the process of coming to terms with "Japaneseness." "Going back to Japan"—a phrase I use ironically, in distinction to white Americans who often fling it derisively—is not, however, a sentimental journey to recover "roots" or an authentic Japanese self. It is a necessary journey in the process of disentangling Japanese American identity and subjectivity from racist configurations that elide the differences between Japanese Americans and Japanese. What such journeys provide is a space for claiming a connection to "Japaneseness," a connection that is usually threatening in an America only too ready to point to any connection to Japan as justification for keeping Japanese Americans forever foreign. As Trinh Minh-ha observes, "i do feel the necessity to return to my so-called roots, since they are the fount of my strength, the guiding arrow to which i constantly refer before heading for a new direction" (1989, 89). Such journeys counteract the fragmentation Asian Americans constantly face when confronted with the disjunction between how they see themselves and how others see them. Paradoxically, this process is enabled by recognition of how "Japanese" one is/not.

Elena Tajima Creef's essay "Notes from a Fragmented Daughter" (in *Making Face, Making Soul*) provides one account of how the Japanese American subject resists an unproblematic connection to Japaneseness while also claiming Japaneseness understood in more complex ways. Creef opens with several short, numbered vignettes, each depicting how white Americans conflate an ill-defined Asian identity with an Asian American identity: a white man assumes she has made the Asian foods at an art gallery opening; a friend's aunt wonders where she has learned English so well and notes how much she admires "your people"; a Mexican American schoolmate inaccurately calls her "a flat-faced chinaman." Creef's response to this fragmenting by others is to attempt to define herself with a dizzying list by which she identifies herself:

Nine months out of the year, I pose as a doctoral student—a historian of consciousness; the rest of the time, I am your basic half-Japanese postmodernist gemini feminist, existentialist would-be writer of bad one-act comedy revues, avid cat trainer, and closet reader of mademoiselle, cosmo, signs, diacritics, elle, tv guide, cultural critique, representations, people magazine, critical inquiry, national enquirer, feminist issues, house beautiful, architectural digest, country living, cat fancy, bird talk, mother jones, covert action, vogue, glamour, the new yorker, l.a. times, l.a. weekly, and sometimes penthouse forum. (83)

But if such self-proclaimed declensions offer to complicate the images of herself offered by others, they also further fragment an already fragmented consciousness. Significantly, Creef ends the essay with a discussion of her mother in a section entitled, "Deconstructing My Mother as the Other."

> I am the daughter of a World War II Japanese war bride.
> ....
> My name is Elena June.
> I am the youngest daughter of Chiyohi,
> who is the only surviving daughter of Iso,
> who was the daughter of the Mayor Of Yokoze
> and was the Village Beauty
> born in the last century to a Japanese woman
> whose name is now forgotten,
> but who lived in the Meiji era
> and loved to tell ghost stories. (84)

Creef's recitation of her lineage does much more than simply claim connection to the women in her family. As a so-called war bride, Creef's mother represents Japan and Japanese identity. Connecting to a matrilineal line is thus inseparable from the connection to a racial and ethnic identity. The fragmentation that characterizes (and titles) the piece narratively grounds itself in Japan, both geographically (Yokoze) and temporally (the Meiji era). Far from resorting to an easy nostalgia for a one-dimensional Japanese identity, however, Creef's positioning at the close of her essay is complicated by the earlier litany of self-naming. Thus, she discursively redefines the context in and through which she identifies herself with difference.

Similar moves of resistance and claiming characterize Lydia Minatoya's 1992 memoir, *Talking to High Monks in the Snow: An Asian American Odyssey*. Minatoya begins with a long section in which she describes her childhood in the 1950s. Growing up on the East Coast, Minatoya knew no Asian Americans outside her immediate family (elsewhere, she says she was twenty before meeting a Japanese American who was not related to her) and keenly felt her racial difference. By the time she is in elementary school, difference has already insinuated itself as the wedge leading to fragmentation. Minatoya becomes fascinated with the mother of one of her white girlfriends: smoking cigarettes and unconcerned with the niceties of maternal order, Ellen Lindstrom is a figure of romance to the young Minatoya. But more than that, Minatoya sees her as a role model who represents the potential freedom of being different:

Ellen Lindstrom knew no need to belong. She fit nowhere and believed she fit everywhere. She always felt at home. I thought I could learn from her. I thought I could absorb her easy confidence and shed my anxious ways. *My* differences dislocated me, made me simpering or sullen. In those days, I was vigilant for role models. I was always searching for clues. (40)

The reluctance to identify herself directly as a subject of racial difference is implied by Minatoya's generalization of difference such that the social iconoclasm of a white woman becomes a potential "clue" for how Minatoya might deal with her own difference. Such a strategy can only fail. The sense of dislocation Minatoya describes intensifies during her adolescence and young adulthood, and by the time she is in her early thirties, dislocation has become dissociation. Minatoya describes her whispered and hesitant acceptance to attend a Day of Remembrance Ceremony to commemorate the Japanese Relocation Act, noting "I am surprised at how frightened I feel" (57). As she sits in the audience, Minatoya observes a Japanese American wife with her white husband. What is striking about this passage is that Minatoya's description takes the point of view of the white husband:

His wife leans forward, like an alert student enrapt in a lecture. Her expression is composed. Her shoulders slightly shake. Tears roll steadily down her cheeks, and her husband does not know what to do. Should he put his arm around her? Rigidly, his arm grips the back of her chair. Would that be intrusive? Should he leave her alone with her thoughts? He leans away, trying to achieve enough distance so that he can keep her entire face in focus. Would that be abandoning? He has never seen her like this before. Never knew that this was important. What will this mean in their marriage? His wife is oblivious. She crosses her arms. Enfolded in her own embrace, she shifts forward and away. (57)

Minatoya does not include her own reactions to the ceremonies. But her fright and hesitancy over the initial invitation suggest her reservations about including herself in an occasion during which she must identify as Japanese American surrounded by sixty other Japanese Americans, an unusual event on the East Coast at that time. Indeed, her impulse to dissociate from her Japanese American identity finds its expression in this passage where she again, as with Ellen Lindstrom, identifies with a white subject. I do not want to imply self-hatred on Minatoya's part, but rather a sense of estrangement from the Japanese American self, a distance that manifests itself in a narrative that adopts the white husband's point of view. Further, it is possible to see the couple Minatoya describes as a metaphor for her own reactions to the situation. Apparently equally puzzled about how to react as the husband she observes, Minatoya narratively displaces her own emotional reactions onto the figure of the Japanese American wife who sits attentive and crying.

Shortly after the Day of Remembrance ceremony, Minatoya attends the first gathering of East Coast Asian American women at Boston University. Two hundred women attend: "Gathering together is a new experience," Minatoya writes, "and the conference hums with the confessional excitement of a consciousness-raising session" (58). The women there share stories, school each other on correct terminology, talk about hating to be confused with F.O.B.s. Minatoya writes that she felt many of the women were judgmental and recalls how she differentiated herself from the rest of the women at the conference: "I'm glad I'm not judgmental, like these *other* women, I think with relief" (59). Already disinclined to identify as Japanese American and surrounded by women who represent a greater threat of identification because they embody similarities of both race and gender, Minatoya casts them into the role of Other, disavowing her connection to them.

Finally, Minatoya's sense of dissociation, exacerbated by the performance demands of graduate school and the end of a romantic relationship, comes to a crisis during which she becomes physically alienated from herself:

That summer, I begin to suffer from periods of "otherness." I go out to move my car and find myself, for a second, standing in the street not knowing the city or decade I am in. Or I am swimming my laps—churning with determination and without purpose through my day—when suddenly I imagine that my departed boyfriend is in the next lane, like a twin, separated yet connected through a warm and fetal fluid. Finally, before the fall semester starts, I go to a doctor. I have walking pneumonia. I have been running a fever for months. (62)

Significantly, Minatoya's alienation from herself is accompanied by distancing from her own body and a complete unawareness of her illness. In longer narrative form, Minatoya's crisis here shares much in common with the dissociation described in Gisele Fong's poem—a refusal to identify with the Asian other and the refusal or dismissal of the body that manifests that otherness: her own.

Whereas the first third of Minatoya's book clearly foregrounds her profound feelings of alienation as a Japanese American woman, the remaining two-thirds are curiously lacking in self-reflection and tend more toward a straightforward narrative. However, I would argue that far from indicating a lack of awareness, Minatoya's narrative strategy to some extent reenacts the deintensification of her self-consciousness, for the latter part of her book deals with her travels through Asia and, ultimately, Japan. As in Creef's essay, Minatoya responds to her crisis of dislocation and self-alienation by claiming what she has previously ignored: she goes "back to" Japan. And, like Creef, Minatoya begins her journey of healing by locating herself geographically and temporally in Japan. Tracing her ancestral line back to 1185, Minatoya begins: "I am the product of eight hundred years of inbreeding. . . . My mother's ancestral home is in the prefecture of Wakayama" (87, 88). In many ways, Minatoya's journey is the journey back through her mother's history to find the family stories of which she has only previously heard scraps. Cutting between the past and present, Minatoya's travels through Japan, China and Nepal are the frame through which she recalls pieces of memory, shards of remembrance. In some ways, one could argue that Minatoya experiences more, not less, fragmentation as she attempts to move between her present identity as a Japanese American woman and her inheritance of a Japanese past. Yet the effect is not one of dislocation and otherness. "In Asia I had found acceptance" (265), Minatoya writes near the close of her narrative. In fact, this sense of belonging leads Minatoya to a sense of home: the last section of the book is ambiguously entitled "The Journey Home" and refers both to her return to Japan from Nepal (the majority of the section) and her return to the United States.

The ambiguity and potential doubleness of "home" is paralleled by a closing passage that relies on a familial image in striking contrast to the way in which Minatoya had earlier "othered" both herself and the Japanese American women represented earlier in the book:

While I had been living in Asia, Asia had begun living in me. She pulsed through my heart. She traveled through my bloodstream. She changed my perceptions, my thoughts, and my dreams. Like a mother who kisses her bruised daughter and shoos her back to play, Asia had transformed the ache of my lapsed career. But, O America—my stern, beloved fatherland—would I be worthy in your eyes? (264)

Minatoya's use of physical imagery reverses her earlier dissociation from her body; perhaps more important, configuring Asia in maternal terms not only signifies acceptance of the Japanese self represented by Minatoya's mother but indicates a conceptualization of identity that can include both the "mother" (Japaneseness) and the "father" (Americanness). But Minatoya's imagery also calls up complex issues of essentialism. Is this passage, in fact, a reinscription of racial biologism? Does it reinforce ideas about the incompatibility of reductively defined Japanese and American identities? Admittedly, Minatoya's somewhat romanticizing stance seems to suggest a nostalgic return home to a place she has never been. But I believe this impulse is tempered by Minatoya's identity as a Japanese American, an identity that does not allow for easy claims to Japaneseness as a home site.

Minatoya writes that she began to wonder, "Was I now Asian? Was I still American? Would I have to choose between the two?" (264). While such questions might at first seem to reflect a dual identity concept, in which one must choose between two identities defined as mutually exclusive, Minatoya's questioning destabilizes the viability of the terms "Asian" and "American." The impossibility, and indeed irrelevance, of choosing between the two is suggested by an earlier passage in which Minatoya finds herself scrutinized by two Japanese men and a boy who cannot quite conceptualize the idea of a Japanese American:

"But you are Japanese. You are speaking Japanese. You have a Japanese face!" They peered at me closely.
"My ancestors were Japanese. I was born in America. I am an American."
The trio exchanged looks of disbelief and plunged into lively discussion. They seemed to forget about our presence as they argued as to whether such a thing, an American with a Japanese face, really could exist. (90)

After finally figuring out Minatoya's family line and parsing out the possibilities of immigration and return, what might have happened and when, the two men exclaim, " 'So it is! An American with a Japanese face.' The two men and the boy nodded solemnly and started at me with satisfaction. I was a puzzle to which they had found a most successful solution" (91).

Minatoya's strangeness to the Japanese is one that many Japanese Americans in Japan have experienced. Mirroring the ways in which white Americans can often not conceive of Americans with nonwhite faces, many Japanese find the figure of the Japanese American a curious one. Faced with such puzzlement, Minatoya insists on her own possibility: one can in fact be a Japanese American. Her very existence proves the point. But Minatoya's insistence on her identity in Japan is, for all its seeming similarity, markedly different from the ways in which Japanese Americans must insist on their identity in the United States. The differences in contexts, assumptions and power relations form a matrix within which questions of identity take on differing valences. Thus, insisting on one's viability as an American in the United States is always in answer to unspoken assumptions that one, in fact, does not belong, cannot be a "real" American with a Japanese face. However, asserting one's identity as a Japanese American in Japan is often in response not to *ex*clusion but to *in*clusion and the assumption, at first, that one is Japanese. In both cases, the Japanese American subject contests entrenched notions about the confluence of national, ethnic and cultural identities, especially as each is initially determined by physical appearance. But I would argue that a Japanese context allows the Japanese American subject to see more clearly the complex structures of identity because one's Japanese face does not, as in the U.S., signify a difference that both inaugurates and reinforces the processes of alienation that construct one's own body as other. Rather, what has been the sign of difference is read as the sign of identificatory sameness, which is then destabilized by the perceived disjunction between how "Japanese" one looks and how "not Japanese" one acts. These readings of the body in relation to how one acts, or performs, foreground both how one is and is not "Japanese."

But this process of negotiation is neither simple nor unproblematic. If "going back to Japan" remaps the possibilities of identity, it does not do so without first destabilizing the idea of Japanese American identity itself, much in the way that the men Minatoya met questioned its possibility. Dorinne Kondo's study of Japanese work sites provides valuable insight into how questions of identity are never separable from the context in which those questions arise. Although not an autobiography in the traditional sense, I include it here because Kondo's approach is based on the belief that her own positioning as a Japanese American woman was crucial to the ways in which she theorized, acted on and was acted upon by the Japanese with whom she worked and lived; the result is something of an autobiographical anthropological narrative. Thus, Kondo writes, "In this text, the deployment of the first-person is strategic, intended to show the ways my experiences as a Sansei woman were different from those of a white ethnographer and to argue that those differences were not inert—either for the Japanese people I encountered or in the crafting of this text" (302–3). What is most fascinating in Kondo's text is the way in which identity—or identities—emerge as constantly shifting entities that can nevertheless be provisionally fixed or labeled, as well as the potential of and the limits to the performative nature of "identity."

Kondo notes that "for most third-generation returnees to the 'mother land,' the temptations of romanticism or apologism are great" (303). Yet in many ways such impulses are compromised by the difficulty for Japanese in conceptualizing Japanese American identity. In a passage that echoes Lydia Minatoya's first encounter with the Japanese, Kondo writes that

as a Japanese American, I created a conceptual dilemma for the Japanese I encountered. For them, I was a living oxymoron, someone who was both Japanese and not Japanese. . . . For me, and apparently for the people around me, this was a stressful time, when expectations were flouted, when we had to strain to make sense of one another. There seemed to be few advantages in my retaining an American persona, for the distress caused by these reactions was difficult to bear. In the face of dissonance and distress, I found that the desire for comprehensible order in the form of "fitting in," even if it meant suppression of and violence against a self I had known in another context, was preferable to meaninglessness. (11–12)

Of key importance in this passage is the relation Kondo draws between "fitting in" and "meaningfulness," suggesting that any easy confluence between being ethnically Japanese and culturally Japanese is mistakenly illusory. More significantly, Kondo's formulation points toward the idea that "Japaneseness" is performative to the extent that it can be identified with fitting into certain prescribed roles whose ability to order perceptions produces meaning. To ease the jarring effect she had on the people around her, Kondo writes that "my first nine months of fieldwork were characterized by an attempt to reduce the distance between expectation and inadequate reality, as my informants and I conspired to rewrite my identity as Japanese" (12).

Although Minatoya and Kondo both recount their attempts to act properly "Japanese" and recognizing in the process just how "American" they are, their experiences as Japanese Americans in Japan differ in one significant way: for the benefit of her anthropological fieldwork, Kondo, unlike Minatoya, consciously attempts to present as seamless a relationship as possible between *looking* Japanese and *acting* Japanese. In addition, because Kondo is specifically concerned with "craftings" of the self in a way that Minatoya is not, Kondo interrogates the constructed nature of subjectivity and puts pressure on categories of identity. The recasting of Kondo's identity in Japanese terms reveals the slippage between persona, identity and subjectivity and suggests intriguing questions about the performative aspects of identity in relation to the body.

While Kondo begins by self-consciously adopting a Japanese persona that is often at odds with her American persona, the line between self-conscious performance ("fitting in," as Kondo puts it) and performance-as-identity blurs in direct proportion to Kondo's ability to decrease the awareness of her Japanese informants of her Americanness. Finally, the Japanese read Kondo's "acting Japanese" not as performative at all but as a natural outcome of her essential Japaneseness. "Frequently," Kondo recalls, "correct behavior was simply accepted as a matter of course. *Naturally* I would understand, *naturally* I would behave correctly, for they presumed me to be, *au fond,* Japanese" (16). Comments like these, coupled with conditions that necessitated isolation from other Americans in Japan, Kondo writes, "increased my susceptibility to identifying with my Japanese role" (16). And, as Kondo makes clear, the elision between self-conscious performance of a role and identity collapses the sense of subject-agency: "Identity can imply unity or fusion, but for me what occurred was a fragmentation of the self. This fragmentation was encouraged by my own participation in Japanese life and by the actions of my friends and acquaintances. At its most extreme point, I became 'the Other' in my own mind, where the identity I had known in another context simply collapsed" (16).

For Kondo this collapse extended beyond a simple disjunction between what could be "labeled Japanese and American pieces" (14), for that collapse destabilized those identities as discrete categories. In addition to reinforcing the point that the privileging of fragmentation can result in self-alienation and disorientation, Kondo's account of her experience suggests that, for a Japanese American, the body is a crucial factor because of the ways in which its markedness limits the agency implied in performance. In a sense, the success of Kondo's ability to "act Japanese" is predicated on the fact of her physical appearance—that which confuses the Japanese sense of racial/cultural identity—and thus points to the ultimate instability of performance as the line of differentiation between "role" and a more essentially defined "being." That is, the agency implied in performance conflicts with the limits to one's propriety over one's own body and how it signifies to others.

Significantly, the disorientation Kondo experiences is occasioned by seeing her own reflection. As she is shopping for the evening meal, she is suddenly confronted with what she is and is not:

> As I glanced into the shiny metal surface of the butcher's display case, I noticed someone who looked terribly familiar: a typical young housewife, clad in slip-on sandals and the loose, cotton shift called 'home wear' (*homu wea*), a woman walking with a characteristically Japanese bend to the knees and a sliding of the feet. Suddenly, I clutched the handle of the stroller to steady myself as a wave of dizziness washed over me, for I realized I had caught a glimpse of nothing less than my own reflection.
>
> Ultimately, this collapse of identity was a distancing moment. It led me to emphasize the *differences* between cultures and among various aspects of identity: researcher, student, daughter, wife, Japanese, American, Japanese American. In order to reconstitute myself as an American researcher, I felt I had to extricate myself from the conspiracy to rewrite my identity as Japanese. (17)

What Kondo narrates is a moment when she becomes her own double, and it foregrounds the ways in which the body is visually conscripted into structures of difference, even in an environment where physical difference, as defined in another context, would not be expected to signify as difference. What Kondo pulls away from, I should make clear, is not Japaneseness per se, nor does it indicate a refusal of the identificatory role of "Japanese." What she pulls away from is the loss of agency over identity as a consciously deployable category. The loss of agency here is intimately tied to the lack of control over how the racially marked body signifies, particularly in a context (Japan) where physical similarity is assumed to imply cultural and identificatory similarity.

Identity, then, may be performative, but its ability to function *as* performance is itself unstable and contingent on the extent to which one can/not delimit how the racially marked and gendered body signifies to those other than oneself. Near the close of her book, Kondo writes: "Rather than bounded, essential entities, replete with a unitary substance and consciousness, identities become nodal points repositioned in different contexts. Selves, in this view, can be seen as rhetorical figures and performative assertions enacted within specific situations within fields of power, history and culture" (304). And yet the question of visible difference (or in the Japanese context, visible indifference) remains. For what Kondo experiences in the reflection of the display case is both

seeing herself through the other's eyes and seeing herself as other. Physically removing herself from the conditions that had so successfully recast her identity in fully Japanese terms allows Kondo the necessary
distance to reclaim propriety over her own body.

"Going back" to Japan in these narratives is the occasion for the
moment of contradiction when the Japanese American subject both does
and does not fit in. The recognition that "everyone looks like me" and,
conversely, that "I look like everyone else" is a significant recontextualization of the physical difference of Japanese Americans in the United
States. But, as these narratives attest, that recognition does not lead to
embracing an authentic Japanese self. Instead, Japan offers an opportunity to assert a Japanese American identity in an environment of assumed "belonging," a situation markedly different from the assumption
of not belonging with which Japanese Americans are confronted in the
U.S. But if these narratives suggest the ways in which Japan is a site to
which one can "constantly refer before heading for a new direction"
(Trinh 1989, 89), it nevertheless problematizes the role of the body and
its relationship to subjectivity.

Faced with Difference

*"Face" is the surface of the body that is the most noticeably
inscribed by social structures. . . . The world knows us by our
faces, the most naked, most vulnerable, exposed and significant
topography of the body. When our* caras *do not live up to the
"image" that the family or community wants us to wear and
when we rebel against the engraving of our bodies, we
experience ostracism, alienation, isolation and shame. Since
white AngloAmericans' racist ideology cannot take in our faces,
it, too, covers them up, "blanks" them out of its reality. To
become less vulnerable to all these oppressors, we have had to
"change" faces. . . . Some of us . . . have been forced to adopt a
face that would pass.*

Gloria Anzaldúa, *Making Face, Making Soul*

The Asian body has long both repelled and fascinated white Westerners.
The Asian face, in particular, seems to attract all manner of commentary.
As I discuss in greater detail in the following chapter, writing by Asian
Americans, and particularly by Japanese Americans, frequently attests to
the ways in which non-Asians read the Asian face as a mask that they

cannot or will not see beyond. The title of Daniel Okimoto's autobiographical narrative, *American in Disguise* (1971), suggests the ways in which the visibility of the Asian face fundamentally precludes recognition of the (for Okimoto, American) subject beneath or within: "Our physical characteristics made a kind of mask that prevented the 'others' . . . from seeing us as we truly were" (5). While Okimoto's implicit assumption of an essential, true subject is somewhat problematic in this age of postmodern sensibility, it is important to remember that his statement is in response to a dominant order whose working assumption, until fairly recently, was that Asian Americans—like other racially marginalized groups—were somehow other than human.[13] The sense that there exists a disjunction between how one sees oneself and how one is seen by others is, of course, experienced by nearly everyone in varying degrees. But the significant difference for those who are racially marked and marginalized is signaled by Okimoto's invocation of collectivity ("our physical characteristics," "as we truly were"). Inasmuch as the structure of racism depends on differentiating between normative and collective whiteness—within which dominant subjects are accorded the distinctions of individuality—and deviant and imposed group identity, the difference between self-perception and one's apperception by the cultural dominant always involves the power and agency of assignation: *who* gets to make distinctions and *whose* distinctions circulate crucially determine the relationship between the other's body and the signs that fix and determine that body as other.

Asian Americans, subject to an imposed group identification that takes as one of its organizing principles facial appearance, are literally faced with difference. "Sometimes when I was growing up," writes Kesaye E. Noda, "my identity seemed to hurtle toward me and paste itself right to my face" (243). Although other people of color are also subjected to derision and group identification ("they all look alike") on the basis of physical appearance, Asian Americans are consistently identified as other on the basis of their facial features: their "flat" face, "low" nasal bridge and "slanted" eyes. While the sense of estrangement many whites feel in relation to Asian Americans no doubt admits cultural and often religious or linguistic differences, I maintain that the inaugural moment of alienation is one marked by the perception of physical difference.[14]

In *Empire of Signs*, for instance, Roland Barthes indulges in several passages about the Japanese face. While reveling in what he calls the scriptural as opposed to sculptural qualities of the Japanese face, Barthes ultimately serves up a more sophisticated version of a cultural stereotype: "Reduced to the elementary signifiers of writing (the blank of the page and the indentations of its script), the face dismisses any signified, i.e., any expressivity: this writing writes nothing (or writes: *nothing*); . . . it does not 'lend' itself . . . to any meaning" (89). "The Japanese face," concludes Barthes, "is without moral hierarchy; it is entirely alive, even vivid (contrary to the legend of Oriental hieratism), because its morphology cannot be read 'in depth,' i.e., according to the axis of an inwardness" (102). While calling attention to the metaphorical convention that reads the (non-"flat") Caucasian face as the surface and sign of a deeper, inward self, Barthes in fact reinscribes that convention by implicitly relying on it. His reading of the Japanese face/script is inseparable from cultural conventions that construct the Japanese other as lacking "moral hierarchy."

Although Barthes privileges the nonsignifying properties of the Japanese face, he inadvertently points to what is so problematic for Asians and Asian Americans whose faces must circulate in a field of meaning where whiteness and white features have normative value: the conventions do not "read" the Japanese face and therefore (as Anzaldúa notes) blank it to accommodate the script/ing of racist projections. The pure signification that Barthes celebrates ("it writes: *nothing*") is possible only within constructions that assume the "readability" of Western morphology.

Of all Asian features, the "Oriental eye" is the most likely to be identified as what differentiates Asians from everyone else. Barthes devotes a section of his book to "The Eyelid," describing it in terms that reduce the Japanese to no more than the carriers of a fascinating anomaly:

The eye is flat (that is its miracle); neither exorbital nor shrunken, without padding, without pouch, and so to speak without skin, it is the smooth slit in a smooth surface. The pupil, intense, fragile, mobile, intelligent (for this eye barred, interrupted by the upper edge of the slit, seems to harbor thereby a reserved pensivity, a dose of intelligence kept in reserve, not *behind* the gaze but *above*) — the pupil is not dramatized by the orbit, as in Western morphology; the eye is free in its slit . . . 'life' is not in the light of the eyes, it is in the non-secret relation of a surface and its slits: in that gap, that difference, that syncope which are, it is said, the open form of pleasure. (102)

In this passage, as in the previous passage about the Japanese face, Barthes relies on a common stereotype — here, one that equates the Japanese eye with "reserved pensivity" (known in plainer terms as sneakiness) — that is recontextualized in a purely semiotic field.[15] Most significant, however, is the identification of the "slitted" eye with difference ("in that gap, that difference") and with pleasure. Thus, the Japanese eye is the site of pleasure in both morphological and semiotic terms. Barthes's description of the Japanese eye, for all his intention to speak of it in terms of its signifying properties, echoes cruder popular myths. Without the accouterments of semiology, others, too, have equated "slanted" eyes with difference. As I show in the travel narratives of John David Morley and Pico Iyer (see chapter one), the eyes of the Asian woman are fetishized as the ultimate indicator of her racial/sexual otherness, which is then encoded into the economy of sexual pleasure.

Japanese American women are denied agency the moment their physical difference registers within this economy. As Minatoya's and Kondo's narratives about their experiences in Japan suggest, *looking* Japanese can easily undermine the performative agency of *acting* Japanese. In order to problematize strategies of resistance within the context of the United States, I turn now to what many Asian Americans consider a disturbing phenomenon: the popularity of cosmetic eye surgery among Asian American women.

Making (a) Face:
The Politics of Cosmetic Surgery

When my cousins saw my newborn son for the first time, they crowded around and peered intently into his tiny face. Expecting the usual parsing of features (his nose is like yours, the mouth is like his), I was somewhat taken aback when the first comment was a jubilant, "He's got the fold! He's got The Fold!" Since I, too, have "the fold," I was congratulated roundly for having passed it on. One of my cousins, in particular, was especially pleased. For over twenty years now, since she was eight, she has taped her eyelids every night before she goes to bed. Born with the epicanthic lid that characterizes many Asian Americans' eyes, she has often expressed envy for those born with the double lid.[16] When I asked recently whether this process wasn't too bothersome to be worth the trouble, she replied that she was so used to doing it that it was as automatic as brushing her teeth. "The only thing is," she said, "I just have to make sure I don't cry. If I cry, my eyes puff up and then I lose the fold."

Eyes occupy a contested space for Asian Americans: from grade school on, few have not been subjected to taunting by white classmates, fingers pulling out the corners of their own eyes to what must be a painful slant. Asian American women, exposed to the visual rhetoric of American beauty magazines, learn quickly that large, deep-set, heavy-lidded eyes are the standard toward which they ought to wield their arsenal of cosmetics. Asian American women's eyes are the site of images that run the proverbial gamut: slant-eyed Jap and sloe-eyed beauty, the mysteriously lidded eye that conceals nefarious intelligence and the weird slit that promises a weirder and titillating slit below. Above all, the eyes are the physical marker that has been fetishized as the determinate sign of Asian difference.

In the 1980s and 1990s, my cousin's nightly eye-taping has been superseded by a surgical procedure called upper blepharoplasty, an operation highly popular in Hawaii, Japan and various countries throughout Asia. According to the American Society of Plastic and Reconstructive Surgeons, over 39,000 Asian Americans sought some form of cosmetic plastic surgery in 1990; the overwhelming majority of those cases involved reconstructive eyelid procedures.[17] Magazines targeted for Asian American women often include articles on eyelid surgery.[18]

Cosmetic eye surgery has been highly criticized by many in the Asian American community, and Asian Americans who have undergone the procedure have been accused of "trying to look white" or, at the very least, accused of trying to look "less Asian." I do not deny that such purposes may completely or partially motivate a number of those who surgically alter their eyes. But while it is reasonable, perhaps even necessary, to decry the violence of plastic surgery and the ways it is an accomplice to images of what women, in particular, should look like, I take issue with the assumption that such a procedure, perforce, implies racial self-hatred and the rejection of ethnic identity. Instead, I want to examine the possibility that it may involve resisting the framework of value that divests biology of personal significance and imbues it with essentialist assumptions that place social and moral value on isolated physical features. As a practice that provides another avenue for the various discussions of problematized agency throughout this book, I want to consider the phenomenon of cosmetic eye surgery not as simply "good" or "bad," as something to either endorse or reject, but rather as an act of both contestation and complicity, an act of reappropriation as well as an act of reinscription that foregrounds the impossibility of any "pure" space of resistance or affirmation. At the very least, the popularity of the procedure indexes the extent to which the body is never a neutral site and that its very availability as a readable surface means that its markings—given or made—are never simply "there."

I do not intend to imply that a radical resides in the heart of every Asian American who walks through the doors of the plastic surgeon's office, but it is also improbable that most Asian Americans who seek cosmetic surgery are completely unaware of the issues involved or of the potentially loaded nature of their act or that they look toward such procedures as a necessary step toward whiteness. Thus, while my cousins' reactions to my son's eyes may be read as an uncritical privileging of a feature associated with Caucasians, it may also be read as a kind of shorthand reference to the problematic meanings assigned to Asian features in white American culture. That is to say, I did not interpret their reaction, nor did they, I think, intend it to be read as relief that my son "looked white," and one indication of that is that I, not my son's Euro-American father, was credited for having passed on "the fold."

If I press too much on this point, I do so because it illustrates what is too often overlooked: those who assume that cosmetic surgery implies the desire to look white have themselves fallen into a framework of value that assumes "folded" eyes to be a Caucasian feature and the lack of it to be an Asian feature. Approximately half of all Asians and Asian Americans are born with the double eyelid, but it is easy enough to forget this fact in the miasma of racist representations that identify Asianness with epicanthically "small" eyes.[19] Clearly, it is impossible to talk about the popularity of cosmetic eye surgery without recognizing that the negative connotations with which many Asian Americans and white Americans regard "Asian" eyes are intimately related to a racist "ideological code in which biological attributes are invested with societal values and meanings" (Mercer, 249). While there can be no easy separation between individually constructed meanings and socially constructed meanings, it is highly problematic to assume that those negative connotations and meanings and an attendant desire to disavow Asianness are always present when an Asian American seeks cosmetic surgery. To do so implicitly asserts that the very existence of socially constructed meaning precludes any exercise of agency, however compromised, reactive or limited it might be.

It is only too easy to assume that cosmetic eye surgery implies capitulation to normative models of whiteness but, again, doing so itself uncritically reinscribes a framework of assignation wherein the terms

"Asian eyes" and "Caucasian eyes" signify along rigidly—and inaccurately—defined physical characteristics. Few Asian Americans who seek cosmetic procedures labor under the illusion that the result will be looking white (Chen), since it is clear that "looking Asian" involves more than the configuration of one's eyes. In fact, as Eugenia Kaw notes in her discussion on this point, "many Asian American cosmetic surgery patients explicitly request that their noses and eyelids not be made to look too Caucasian" (85). Changing the appearance of the eye is perhaps less an attempt to change one's Asian appearance with the goal of looking white than a way of asserting control over the uncontrolled meanings that others associate with the epicanthic lid. If white hegemony, in other words, reads the eyes as the sign of difference, one must consider that cosmetic surgery may be an attempt to control the eye/sign. Kaw, who studied the medical files of several plastic surgeons and interviewed Asian American female patients, writes that the decision to undergo reconstructive nose or eye surgery is primarily

an attempt to escape persisting racial prejudice that correlates their stereotyped genetic physical features ("small, slanty" eyes and a "flat" nose) with negative behavioral characteristics, such as passivity, dullness, and a lack of sociability. . . . For the women in my study, the decision to undergo cosmetic surgery was never purely or mainly for aesthetic purposes, but almost always for improving their social status as women who are racial minorities. (75, 78)

The very arbitrariness of social constructions that place an equal sign between Asianness and "slanted," "lidless" eyes reveals not only the way that racist ideology reinforces "meaning" with biological categories but points to the possibility of disrupting such frameworks of value by foregrounding their own arbitrary constructedness. And yet, as the criticisms by Asian Americans who see cosmetic surgery as rejection of raced identity indicates, the power of racist ideology lies in the way it both dictates the field of value and imposes it on those it seeks to control. Kobena Mercer suggests that the real power of racist construction lies in the extent to which the raced subject becomes responsible for upholding that structure of value: "Dominant ideologies such as white bias do not just dominate by 'universalizing' the values of hegemonic social/ethnic groups so that they become everywhere accepted as the 'norm.' Their hegemony and historical persistence is underwritten at a subjective level by the way ideologies construct positions from which individuals 'recognize' such values as a constituent element of their personal identity" (250). Thus, those who equate cosmetic eye surgery with capitulation may themselves participate in upholding dominant constructions by holding fast to the epicanthic fold as a (or *the*) constitutive element of racial identity. The racist essentialism that assigns negative value to physiological difference ironically finds its corollary in simplistic forms of social politics that replace negative fetishization with an affirmative valorization of isolated features as the sign of authentic ethnic identity.[20]

While the phenomenon of cosmetic eye surgery and its popularity among Asian American women is disturbing, many criticisms of the procedure are equally so. As Dorinne Kondo's experience suggests, "looking Asian" accommodates a range of meanings. However, the positionings of those who "make" meaning and the context in which that meaning circulates and acquires value are crucial elements that inform what "looking Asian" means. In Kondo's case, looking Japanese at some point undermined her agency in deploying her identity through "acting Japanese." Her response was to remove herself from the immediate context (living among and with Japanese families) in order to realign the relationship between appearance and act. In a similar way, I suggest, cosmetic eye surgery may also signal an attempt to displace (a part of) oneself from a context in which the individual cannot control or limit the social meanings attached to physiological features. Such actions are not necessarily an attempt to adopt a face that will pass for or into whiteness, especially given the fact that changing one's eyelid is highly unlikely to result in being (mis)taken for white. Cosmetic eye surgery can divest the value assigned to difference and thus refuse identification with the face—and all that it signifies—that one has been forced to adopt. If visible difference has resulted in the invisibility of Asian Americans and the denial of their agency, accusations of "wanting to look white" can also participate in the erasure of the Asian American subject through the implicit denial of agency.

Masking Selves

For many white Americans, Asian/American women remain a site of orientalist fantasy, of projections, of half-baked idealizations that do not idealize but demean and erase. Faced with that reality, one wonders about the viability of claiming one's own face in a culture that fetishistically appropriates it the moment it becomes visible. And yet, if Asian American women are compelled to wear the mask of their own faces, what is revealed and distorted within those who find the mask so compelling? And can the Asian American subject redeploy or signify upon that which is revealed to both protect the self that walks through the world and reappropriate the ground of subjectivity?

Recent theorizations of masquerade have, in Kaja Silverman's words, "stressed the dislocation between subjectivity and the role which is thereby assumed" (11). That dislocation is precisely where I want to locate the possibilities for reappropriative and resistant Japanese American female subjectivity. In speaking of and for that possibility, however, I use the less theory-accrued term "masking" for two reasons. "Masking," unlike "masquerade," retains its more direct relation to "mask" and, as I note above, the Asian face/mask is a recurring motif in Japanese American writing. The mask thus takes on a physiological dimension that is largely absent from the notion of masquerade, which often invokes the language of costuming.[21] This distinction is a crucial one because it points to the difference between the registers of simile and (literalized) metaphor: the face is *like* a mask versus the face *is* a mask. In the move between "like" and "is," the synonymity between masquerade and masking collapses.[22]

The second reason bears on an implicit assumption of agency in the concept of masquerade. That is, masquerade is enacted, within whatever social or discursive strictures, by the subject-who-masquerades. But for those whose subjectivity has been placed under erasure by an imposed mask that is inseparable from their physical appearance, from their very faces, the issue of agency cannot be understood as an enactment that exploits the disjuncture between subjectivity and (chosen) roles. Where masquerade focuses on the realm of the performative and discursive, masking directly foregrounds the racial markedness of the body/face.

Thus the first part of the book's title, "Masking Selves," gestures grammatically toward both the limitations on and possibilities of Japanese American women's agency. Its phrasal ambiguity evokes an implied subject/agent who masks the selfhood of the (Japanese American) other, as well as the Japanese American subject whose self is, in a sense, defined by its own participation in reappropriative acts of masking. In various metaphoric, textual and psychological forms, masking protects a sense of self and is itself constitutive of subjectivity. Inaugurated by the trauma of the racially marked, gendered and sexualized body's positioning in the social economy of the United States, masking is a resistant strategy by which the body and, through the body, subjectivity may be claimed. Its enactment by Japanese American woman writers is the subject of the following chapters.

CHAPTER 3

"That other, private self"

Masking in Nisei Women's Autobiography

*But always we were split in two, straddling silence, not sure where
we would begin to find ourselves or one another. From this division,
our material dislocation, came the experience of one part of ourselves
as strange, foreign and cut off from the other which we encountered
as tongue-tied paralysis about our own identity. We were never all
together in one place, were always in transit, immigrants into alien
territory. . . . The manner in which we knew ourselves was at
variance with ourselves as an historical being, woman.*

Sheila Rowbotham,
Woman's Consciousness, Man's World

*The extraordinary central-government apartheid reflex that effected
this policy [of internment], and its ghostly echoes in the popular
press, were predicated solely on the visible and the inferred biologies
of facial difference and "Oriental" blood. The constitutional
guarantees of citizenship (where applicable) were summarily
suspended; and a mass of faces was interned.*

John C. Welchman, *Modernism Relocated*

    Although the "we" in the quoted passage above denotes
"women," Sheila Rowbotham movingly describes the experience of
Asian Americans in an often hostile dominant white culture, as well as
the situation of the Japanese American woman writer as she attempts
to write herself as an autobiographical subject. Already aware of the
disjunction between how she sees herself and how she is seen, the Japanese American autobiographer must also come to terms with the nec-

essary disjunction between the "I" who writes and the "I" who is written about. These two selves continually negotiate between themselves across the generic limitations of the autobiographical form, a form traditionally neither defined by marginalized subjects nor defined with them in mind. As Sidonie Smith writes, the female autobiographer reveals in the writing act "the degree of her self-consciousness about her position as a woman writing in an androcentric genre. Always, then, she is absorbed in a dialogue with her reader, that 'other' through whom she is working to identify herself and to justify her decision to write about herself in a genre that is man's" (50). Positioned as both gendered and raced subjects, Japanese American women autobiographers address themselves to a doubled other. They must write themselves in a form that is both andro- and Anglo-centric.

Within this context, I want to begin my discussion with an observation and a question: Nisei women's autobiographies are frustratingly *un*autobiographical, not given to personal disclosure or passages of intimate self-reflection. They are not, to use a pejorative term often applied to those who speak about themselves, self-indulgent. Tonally, they are the equivalent of pleasant acquaintance. My question is similar to one posed by Doris Sommer in her essay on Latin American women's *testimonios* and the "Janus-faced nature of autobiography": "Is [autobiography] the model for imperializing the consciousness of colonized peoples, replacing their collective potential for resistance with a cult of individuality and even loneliness? Or is it a medium of resistance and counterdiscourse, the legitimate space for producing that excess which throws doubt on the coherence and power of an exclusive historiography?" (111).

To link my observation to my question, is the congenial flatness—or *seeming* congenial flatness—of Nisei women's autobiographies a necessary consequence of taking on a discursive form whose field is hegemonically constructed? On a more basic level, do the material circumstances of production—the machinery and criteria of publication—assure a complicit voice? Or is the very act of articulation, taking on the assumption of the right to speak the self, a gesture of resistance sufficient to refuse the pressures of hegemonic autobiographical representation?

What is at stake here is not simply the question of whether the autobiographical form, as though it had a life of its own, empowers or disempowers its practitioners. At issue are crucial acts of discursive agency and the (re)appropriation of representational power, both of which are directly related to whether one reads these autobiographies as simply benign remembrances of things past or as self-conscious narratives that construct and assert subjecthood and agency.

Until very recently the entire, if small, body of Japanese American autobiographies was produced by Nisei. Although a discussion including both Nisei and Sansei autobiographies would undoubtedly reveal intriguing parallels and distinctions, I focus on Nisei women's autobiographies in this chapter in order to argue that these narratives constitute an identifiable tradition that distinguishes them from Sansei autobiographical writing. The historical specificity of the internment provides the impulse for Nisei autobiography and directly informs textual self-presentation in a way that is not the case for Sansei autobiography. Further, because of the race-based justification for the internment during a war pervaded with racial overtones, issues of ethnic identity take on a particular and immediate urgency that is not characteristic of later Sansei autobiography. This urgency, which I explore later in this chapter, derives from the contradictions between legal, cultural and ideological forms of citizenship, and between national and community identities. While such contradictions still obtain in the present, the years surrounding World War II bring them into particularly sharp relief.

Within the genre of Nisei autobiographical writing, the most widely read are those by women: Monica Sone's *Nisei Daughter* (1953), Jeanne Wakatsuki Houston's *Farewell to Manzanar* (1973) and Yoshiko Uchida's *Desert Exile: The Uprooting of a Japanese-American Family* (1982).[1] Yet these texts have been primarily recognized as sociological and/or historical documents and taken at face value. Recognition of their status as autobiographies has been cursory at best, as evidenced by the dearth of critical work concentrating on Asian American, and particularly Japanese American, autobiographies.[2] While it is crucial to recognize the documentary elements of these texts, it is equally important to recognize that shifting from a social/historical focus to an autobiographical one shifts critical attention from these narratives as straightforward reconstructions of events to constructions of the self within the context of historical, social and material realities. As Domna C. Stanton points out, "autobiography" negatively understood as "femininely" spontaneous and natural has been consistently used "to affirm that women could not transcend, but only record, the concerns of the private self" (1984, 6–7). For Japanese American women autobiographers, marginalized by both gender and race, the issue of representation is particularly acute: failure to extend the critical range results in the exclusion of their texts from the canon of American autobiography and the refusal of their claims to discursive agency.

At least some of the critical inattentiveness I am speaking of is a consequence of what Shirley Geok-lin Lim identifies as "the paradox ruling much Japanese American autobiographical writing": "Although the autobiographical impulse seeks to express a unique life, almost in contradiction, these life stories repeat a common plot of race difference and conflict with white American hegemony. They therefore come to represent something other, both more communal and more abstract than the particular life" (1990, 292). Lim's analysis notes the characteristic of nondisclosure in Japanese American autobiography, as well as the possible reason for it. The reality of conflict is present in virtually all Nisei autobiographies because all deal with the watershed event of the internment, a defining and deeply dispiriting moment in the history of Japanese Americans. In one sense, speaking as hostilely marginalized subjects whose individuality was denied, much of the impulse driving Japanese American autobiographers involves witnessing a group wrong in order to prevent a recurrence of a historical event, the national memory of which is threatened by the occlusions of time and apathy. In this, these autobiographies share something of the moral purpose of the African American slave narrative.[3] Yoshiko Uchida, for example, ends her autobiography by noting that she wrote it so that other Japanese Americans could find a "sense of continuity with their past." She continues: "But I wrote it as well for all Americans, with the hope that through knowledge of the past, they will never allow another group of people in America to be sent into a desert exile ever again" (154). This didactic end may help explain why these autobiographies at first seem somewhat two-dimensional. The avoidance of overt conflict with those readers whom these authors desire to educate necessitates the nonthreatening presentation of the individual as paradigmatic rather than particular.

However, we should also recognize that Japanese American autobiography exists between two impulses: historical motive and cultural reticence. On the one hand, Nisei autobiographies are the written record of a community betrayed by the dark side of democracy—majority rule or, in this case, majority racist hysteria. On the other hand, the autobiographical form is fundamentally at odds with the Nisei tendency to downplay the individual self, a behavioral adaptation largely shaped by the desire to "fit in" and thus avoid racist discrimination.[4] The result is an autobiographical tradition grounded in the desire to witness, not in the introspective impulses of self-contemplation. And yet, as Jeanne Wakatsuki Houston writes in the foreword to *Farewell to Manzanar:*

It became [clear] that any book [I] wrote would have to include a good deal more than day-to-day life inside the compound. To tell what I knew and felt about it would mean telling something about our family before the war, and the years that followed the war, and about my father's past, as well as my own way of seeing things now. Writing it has been a way of coming to terms with the impact those years have had on my entire life. (ix–x)

While these narratives function as records of "day-to-day" life in the camps, they are also the statement of a subject whose constitution is intimately tied to the fact of the internment. To write about the intern-ment is to write about an event whose very basis was the denial of subjectivity, and it is thus an act of writing the self—and by extension the community of interned Japanese Americans—as subject. Because much of their narrative is addressed to a potentially defensive and hostile white American audience, Nisei autobiographers are selective in their use of personal detail and guarded in their criticisms of white America. If, as Sidonie Smith writes, the female autobiographer "can speak with authority only insofar as she tells a story that her audience will read" (52), Nisei women who assume autobiographical authority must be even more careful to present their stories in "acceptable" terms. However strongly they might feel about their experience of the camps, there is also a reluctance to speak about those experiences and feelings, a guard-edness about the act of revelation. Already marginalized and delegiti-mized by race, gender and, often, class as they critiqued, however subtly, an audience whom they were largely addressing, these writers had every-thing to lose and little to gain by revealing the private self.

Selwyn Cudjoe notes that African American autobiography indicates "a much more *im-personal* condition, the autobiographical subject emerging as an almost random member of the group, selected to tell his/her tale. . . . [It is] a *public* rather than a *private* gesture, *me-ism* gives way to *our-ism* and superficial concerns about *individual subject* give way to the *collective subjection* of the group" (9). Certainly, the same can be said of Nisei women autobiographers who, like many contemporaneous African American women autobiographers, "eschew . . . the confes-sional mode—the examinations of personal motives, the searchings of the soul—that white women authors so frequently adopt. Black women's autobiographies seem torn between exhibitionism and secrecy, between self-display and self-concealment" (Fox-Genovese, 71).

Yet revelation would seem to be inevitable in any autobiographical gesture, and while Nisei women autobiographers might be reticent, that reserve needs to be recognized not as a reductive symptom of an essentially Japanese female sensibility but rather as an encoded means through which to express and construct the self and community—a means I refer to as masking, and which I will later discuss in detail. Foregoing the revelatory confessional mode does not mean that Nisei women's autobiographies are simply a recounting of events. If indirectly, these autobiographies reveal the circumstances of their production and the personal investments of their authors. In the process of reclaiming agency through the trope of masking, Nisei women's autobiographies contradict many standard critical definitions of autobiographical texts. As we position this body of work within the tradition of autobiography generally and American autobiography in particular, it is crucial that we simultaneously recognize how these narratives reshape our understanding of those traditions.

The Subject(s) of Autobiography

In his discussion of American autobiography, Robert Sayre argues that "there is no great American autobiographer . . . [because of] the very identification of autobiography *in* America *with* America. An American seems to have needed to be an American first and then an autobiographer, and this places some limits on his or her achievement" (147). Whether or not we agree with this assessment of absent greatness in American autobiography, most scholars of the genre agree that it differs from the European tradition through its consistent inquiry into the nature of what it is to be an American, into what constitutes Americanness. James Holte agrees with this point in his study of ethnic American autobiography, adding that "ethnic and immigrant autobiographers used the autobiography as a means to impose order on an experience that was both disruptive and confusing" (28). He goes on to trace out what he sees as its connecting line to the European tradition: "The conversion narrative has provided writers with a structure to evaluate the life of the individual within the culture, or ask, again and again, what is an American. . . . the imagery of the journey and conversion become the standard features in nearly all American autobiography" (30–31). Ethnic autobiography, Holte argues, takes on the conventions

of the conversion narrative either to describe the journey of assimilation—"the transformation of outsider to insider" (34)—or to point out
the failures of a society that has barred some from entering, and thus to
show the transformation of one who has failed to or "chosen" not to
become part of mainstream culture into a spokesperson for other cultural "outsiders" (35).

Much of the critical work on American autobiography follows on the
assumption of individuality that underpins these arguments: the failure
or force of American autobiography lies in how it articulates or reflects
the *autos* (self) of autobiography. Either the American autobiographer
fails because s/he does not identify her/himself as an individual autobiographical stylist or, as in Holte's argument, the force of the autobiographical text is in its assessment of the individual's relation to the culture as a whole. This emphasis on the individual characterizes not only
American autobiographical theory but general theorization of the genre
as well. In James Olney's work, widely recognized as standard, the individual is more than simply a single, particular being: the individual is
an autonomous consciousness unbounded by circumstance or time:

We can understand . . . the life around which autobiography forms itself . . .
as the vital impulse—the impulse of a life—that is transformed by being
lived through the unique medium of the individual and the individual's
special, peculiar psychic configuration; we can understand it as consciousness, pure and simple, consciousness referring to no objects outside itself,
to no events, and to no other lives; we can understand it as participation in
an absolute existence far transcending the shifting, changing unrealities of
mundane life; we can understand it as the moral tenor of the individual's
being. Life in all these latter senses does not stretch back across time but
extends down to the roots of individual being; it is atemporal, committed
to a vertical thrust from consciousness down into the unconscious rather
than to a horizontal thrust from the present into the past. (239)

Olney's definition omits and precludes what is perhaps the most salient
feature of autobiographical writing by women, people of color, and
other marginalized groups: group consciousness, a sense that the individual is not an extirpated self gamely trudging along with a timeless
consciousness "pure and simple." As many feminist theorists of autobiography point out, the inappropriateness of individualistic models becomes clear once one considers "the importance of a culturally imposed
group identity for women and minorities. . . . [and] the differences in
socialization in the construction of male and female gender identity.
From both an ideological and psychological perspective, in other words,

individualistic paradigms of the self ignore the role of collective and relational identities in the individual process of women and minorities" (Friedman, 35). Mary Mason agrees with this point in her assessment that women autobiographers tend to construct themselves relationally, not individually (82). Further, Asian/American models of identity tend to emphasize intersubjectivity and the individual's relationships to family and ever-widening circles of community.[5]

For Japanese Americans, particularly of the Nisei generation, the fact of the internment is the crucial and inescapable ground for the construction of self, all the more so because the internment was an event based on and forged by the denial of individual subjectivity, resulting in a negativized group identity. Writers of this generation take up and reverse the collective identity it imposed, insisting on a resistant subjectivity that does not assume identity to be synonymous with individuality. For them, the assertion of Americanness is not simply "I am an American," but rather "We are Americans." The collectivity of that claim is thus grounded in the particular author's life, but that life is to be understood as representative. While the deployment of a collective or representative voice might seem to be implied in American autobiography generally, one should note that while the term "American" is a nationally collective, though abstracted, identity, it is also one predicated upon the American ideology of individuality.

In addition, because "collective subjection" for Japanese Americans is directly related to white America's doubts about their "Americanness," the conversion model of American autobiography, as exemplified by Holte, is especially problematic. The force of the question "Who is an American?" is particularly strong for Japanese Americans whose mass internment was the result of the narrow perimeters within which what constituted Americanness was understood. Clearly, to read these autobiographies as conversion narratives whose transformative moment is the internment or to read them as statements of cultural "outsiders" is to undermine one of their primary purposes, which is to claim the status of "American" and to assert the legitimacy of that claim prior to World War II. That is, though the internment experience is both an historical and personal watershed, it does not mark, as the conversion narrative would have us do, the transition from a Japanese-based identity to an American-based one. Furthermore, individual conversion models impose a model of identity and subjectivity that is not entirely appropriate when speaking of racially marginalized communities.[6]

Ann Rayson's "Behind the Mask: Autobiographies of Japanese-

American Women," the only article written to date on the subject, suggests that the autobiographical act marks the leaving behind of a "muted culture in order to become a part of the larger culture" (44) and that "now a part of the larger culture through conversion, they [Japanese American autobiographers] are permitted to remember the indignities of the past" (45).[7] There are several problems with this thesis: it reinscribes a cultural split and a hierarchy of cultures, and it assumes that belonging to a so-called subculture precludes full participation in so-called dominant culture without ever interrogating the terms of belonging and participation. It also works against what is perhaps the only trait that Japanese American autobiography *does* share with the conversion narrative—the narrator who has become spokesperson and defender for the community. The standard structure in these autobiographies includes descriptions of life before the camps, where the "Americanness" of the Nisei and the humanity of their Issei parents is emphasized. The narratives are an implicit argument against dehumanization and speak from within and for the community of Japanese Americans.

Most problematically, Rayson's model—or any such conversion model—undermines the assertion of belonging that runs through all Japanese American autobiography. Again, conversion narratives imply a movement from outside to inside, and that movement is propelled primarily by "an emerging sense of self-discovery" (Holte, 29). But the terms "outside" and "inside" are always culturally loaded, defined by a dominant culture deeply invested in its assumed centrality and power to determine who is "inside" and who is not. In other words, to read these autobiographies as narratives about "becoming an American" suggests that the writers themselves have accepted the terms and their own implied status as (former or present) outsiders. Instead, we need to recognize that these autobiographies self-consciously redefine the idea of home/land and their own relationship to it, mediated as it is by external and internalized racism.

Yoshiko Uchida's *Desert Exile,* for instance, opens with a scene in which the contestation of "home" is literalized. She describes her parents' purchase of a new house in an all-white neighborhood, which until that point had remained white because of a "tacit agreement" that non-whites could not rent or buy in that area. Predictably, the neighborhood "Improvement Association" pays a call, claiming to represent the whole area. "They came," writes Uchida, "not to welcome my parents, but to tell them to get out" (4). In the ensuing altercation, Uchida's father asks that those members who object to his family's presence present themselves: "If they can bring proof that we are undesirable elements in the neighborhood, we will leave immediately. Otherwise, I feel their request is unreasonable" (4). Uchida concludes: "Those members never came and their three representatives never returned. My father had won, and my parents remained in the house, but it was only a small victory, for those were days of such intense anti-Asian sentiment, there were billboards bearing signs that read, 'Japs, don't let the sun shine on you here. Keep moving.' " (4)

In many ways, the daughter speaking in her autobiography and the father she writes about are in parallel positions. But with a difference. While the father's claim to "home" is self-admittedly contingent ("If they can bring proof that we are undesirable . . . we will leave immediately"), Uchida's contextualization of this incident within the climate of anti-Asian sentiment foregrounds her own implicit assertion that the U.S. as "home" for Japanese Americans is only debatable in a society that condones racism. The house, or home, as a site of contestation and instability is one defined by racist group identification. Uchida reclaims home, much as her father originally claimed it, but retrospectively denies agency to the racist nativism of the "Improvement Association."

Uchida's telling here is more than simply the account of what happened to one particular family; still less is it an account of what happened to *her* family. There is no indication of what her father's personal feelings were, what the family might have said about it, and little, even in retrospect, that details Uchida's own sense of the impact of this event on her personal sense of self. The fact that she places this account at the opening of her narrative directs our attention to its symbolic function as a narrative of the attempt and difficulty of, as well as the resistances and barriers to, claiming "home," thus lending force to the notion of exile that entitles Uchida's text. Significantly, both Sone and Houston record similar incidents in their autobiographies; as such, Uchida's account must be read as representative of a group experience.

Perhaps more important, Uchida's retelling/rewriting of the incident empowers her father: instead of presenting him as one whose purchase of an American house marks his entry into the American "homeland," and thus marking his conversion from immigrant to resident, she represents him as laying claim to what is already rightfully his. Reading Uchida's text as either following a conversion model or as simply a revelation of a personal nature is to privatize this event, and thus trivialize it to the dimensions of an unpleasant moment in the life of a single family on their journey to Americanization.[8]

If moments like the one Uchida describes do not mark the transition from one culture to another, however, they do mark the moment of realization that the status of "American" could not be assumed. The post–World War II emergence of Japanese American autobiography is a direct consequence of the ways in which the phantasmal category of "American" was used against Japanese Americans to justify the internment and the denial of personal agency. Thus, the motivation and ground for Nisei autobiographers is this loss of agency, both on a personal and group level.

Until the advent of feminist and poststructuralist autobiography theory, autobiographical writing was identified with a culturally reinforced sense of agency and power. Following on George Gusdorf's groundbreaking essay, "Conditions and Limits of Autobiography" (1956), autobiography theory argued that the autobiographical act predicates the sense of an empowered self or, as Susan Stanford Friedman puts it, assumed that "autobiography is the literary consequence of the rise of individualism as an ideology" (35). In the following passage by Gusdorf, for instance, self-recognition as an individual is commensurate with the assumption of power:

At the moment it enters into history, humanity, which previously aligned its development to the great cosmic cycles, finds itself engaged in an autonomous adventure; its own reckoning, organizing them, by means of technical expertise, according to its own desires. Henceforth, man knows himself a responsible agent: gatherer of men, of lands, of power, maker of kingdoms or of empires, inventor of laws or of wisdom, he alone adds consciousness to nature, leaving there the sign of his presence. The historic personage now appears, and biography, taking its place alongside monuments, inscriptions, statues, is one *manifestation* of his desire to endure in men's memory. (31)

As Friedman notes, autobiography, as defined by Gusdorf, "represents the expression of individual authority in the realm of language. The 'sign' to which Gusdorf refers is, literally and literarily, the 'mark' or 'imprint' of man's power: his linguistic, psychological, and institutional presence in the world of letters, people, and things" (35). I have been emphasizing the extent to which Nisei women's autobiographies do not participate in individualistic models wherein agency is the ground for articulation. I should point out, however, that I do not intend to suggest that Japanese American women do not consider themselves individuals capable of self-determined action. After all, Japanese American women, like Japanese women, have been plagued with images of themselves as selfless, dependent vessels of service to others. Rather, I want to convey the idea that the Japanese American woman as autobiographer neither speaks as an autonomously defined self writing about the particulars of her life nor as a subject for whom agency has been granted, assumed or allowed by the dominant culture. Though denied, Japanese American women's sense of their own agency is not contingent on whether someone else decides to confer it on them; however, to the extent that a disjunction remains between internal and external constructions of Japanese American women, their motivations as autographs are significantly different from those of white, heterosexual male subjects. Agency for the self written about is not an a priori condition; rather, the "I" self-reflexively confers that agency through the autobiographical act.

Insofar as Gusdorf's model describes an empowered male subject, it also assumes a determinate coherence within the subject and thus cannot articulate the complexities of multiple subject-positions without resorting to the problematic and overdetermined language of fragmentation. As Rowbotham eloquently notes in the quotation that begins this chapter, women are split at the moment of realization that how they know themselves is not how they are "known" by others. Sidonie Smith further develops this point in her study of women's autobiographies: "The autobiographer who is a woman must suspend herself between paternal and maternal narratives, those fictions of male and female selfhood that permeate her historical moment" (19). For Japanese American women, who must "suspend" themselves not only between paternal and maternal narratives, but between white dominant culture and their own cultural narratives, linear representative coherence necessarily involves discarding those parts of themselves that do not fit the dominant culture model. In other words, the necessary fiction that is the discursive "I" of autobiography can become a narrowly synecdotal fragment that must, impossibly, represent the complexities of the entire subject.

Although most autobiographers must submit to a sense of the different selves that write and are written about—usually expressing it as a temporal difference accentuated by the variations of hindsight—Nisei women enter the discursive field of autobiography already conscious of themselves as split subjects. For the Nisei in particular, the generation that until very recently produced all Japanese American autobiography, World War II and the internment made abundantly clear that birth and the legal status supposedly following therefrom did not qualify them for more than cursory citizenship. What before the war had been an awareness of participating in two cultures became during and after the war a split self. "I felt," writes Monica Sone, "like a despised, pathetic two-headed freak, a Japanese and an American. . . . I found myself shrinking inwardly from my Japanese blood, the blood of an enemy" (158, 145). The bifurcation of self is a theme that runs throughout all Nisei autobiographies. That is to say, both women and men experience this same sense of being split. Daniel Okimoto, for instance, the best known of the male autobiographers, refers to a sense of his "racial freak-ishness" (69). He goes on to describe the feeling of fragmentation and self-loathing that many Nisei felt during and after the war: "Since they had done no wrong, the only way they could possibly interpret intern-ment was to assume that they were being punished for being Japanese. . . . The result of this assumption was that they grew to despise the Japanese part of themselves" (29).[9]

I do not wish to suggest, however, that Nisei autobiographers write solely out of self-loathing or that they use the forum of autobiography as a public stage for self-healing. Such motivations would necessitate an overt agenda of self-revelation that is not to be found in these texts. What is true, however, is that the feeling of being divided runs through-out all these texts and cannot be dismissed as merely manifesting the internalized racism of a pre–civil rights era. Analyses that ignore this division unwittingly may reinscribe single-subject narratives that under-mine the complexity of autobiographical presentation and, in fact, erase the ways in which these writers claim agency. In *A Poetics of Women's Autobiography*, Sidonie Smith writes that "because the autobiographer can never recapture the fullness of her subjectivity or understand the entire range of her experience, the narrative 'I' becomes a fictive persona" (46). Here and elsewhere, Smith locates the birth of the "fictive persona" in the space between what is remembered and what happened. In other words, the subjective nature of memory suggests that the textual self created through the processes of selection and the (re)construction of the past is a necessary fiction:

Involved in a kind of masquerade, the autobiographer creates an iconic rep-resentation of continuous identity that stands for, or rather before, her sub-jectivity as she tells of this "I" rather than of that "I." She may even create several, sometimes competing, stories about or versions of herself as her subjectivity is displaced by one or multiple textual representations. (47)

Smith's use of the word "masquerade" here suggests the manner in which the autobiographical text costumes or disguises the writing/writ-ten subject. But unlike Smith, who argues that the autobiographical form itself functions as "a kind of masquerade," I emphasize the agency of the autobiographer and the choices she makes in relation to the trope of masking and, in turn, how those choices function in relation to the construction and protection of the self as subject, as well as to the processes of projection and the disavowal of the Japanese self.

Masking "that other, private self"

"I made up my mind," writes Monica Sone in *Nisei Daughter,* "to make myself scarce and invisible, but I discovered that an Oriental face, being somewhat of a rarity in the Midwest, made people stop in their tracks, stare, follow and question me" (219–20). Sone's account of the way people reacted to her Japanese face (in this case, after her release from the Minidoka internment camp) is painful to read for the way in which it tries to work through what Asian Americans and other people of color are constantly confronted with in white-dominated America: their (nonwhite) faces. Sone writes that she was mistaken for a local fan-dancer and for Anna May Wong ("I felt the vicarious thrill of a celebrity" [220]). Nevertheless, Sone concludes that "sometimes there were decided advantages to having an Oriental face . . . clerk[s] would spot me instantly and rush up to wait on me, burning with curiosity. The clerks were inevitably pleasant and sociable and they complimented me on my English" (221). Sone transforms being objectified, stared at in unabashed curiosity and patronizingly complimented into the shallow advantage of getting faster customer service. But what lurks beneath is the self-conscious awareness of racial difference signified by one's unchangeable, always different, socially marked, Asian face, a site of signification that, as I argued in the preceding chapter, is largely uncontrolled by the Japanese American subject.

Yoshiko Uchida also recounts instances when her face seemed to be all that signified to white Americans. When a white woman comments on Uchida's ability to speak English, Uchida realizes that "she had looked at my Japanese face and addressed only my outer person" (20). And in *Farewell to Manzanar,* Houston writes that "part of me yearned to be invisible. In a way, nothing would have been nicer than for no one to see me. . . . I felt that if attention were drawn to me, people . . . wouldn't see me, they would see the slant-eyed face, the Oriental" (1973, 114). For Houston, this feeling quickly translates into the conviction that "easy enough as it was to adopt white American values, I still had

. . . a Japanese face to thwart my social goals" (1973, 122). Asian features, once circulated in a white American context, become the wedge in a reaction of disavowal of the Japanese self.

It is significant that these writers choose the imagery of the mask since it results from the recognition that "slanted eyes and high cheekbones" (Houston 1973, 29) become not simply Japanese physical characteristics but floating signifiers of difference, which, as Eugenia Kaw notes, are correlated "with negative behavioral characteristics" (75). In one of the most interesting examples of the attempt to claim the power of naming the mask through which others see her, Houston recounts a postwar high school beauty contest. Recognizing that she "couldn't beat the other contestants at their own game, that is, look like a bobbysoxer," yet also knowing that dressing up in kimono would be "too Japanese-y," Houston decides to turn the mask of Asian femininity to her advantage: "I decided to go exotic, with a flower-print sarong, black hair loose and a hibiscus flower behind my ear. When I walked barefoot out onto the varnished gymnasium floor, between the filled bleachers, the howls and whistles from the boys were double what had greeted any other girls" (1973, 124). Houston wins but is troubled, though she doesn't understand quite why at the time. With hindsight, she recognizes that while she can use the mask dominant culture places over her face, that is, use her knowledge of "how an Oriental female can fascinate Caucasian men . . . that even this is usually just another form of invisibility" (1973, 117). What Houston finally realizes is that her deployment of the mask, originally intended as a subversive gesture, is quickly reappropriated within the intersection of raced and gendered stereotypes.

The feeling of one's Japanese face as an obstructing mask that white Americans refuse to or cannot see beyond is not limited to Japanese American women by any means. The title of Daniel Okimoto's book, *American in Disguise,* alludes to his feeling that "our physical characteristics made a kind of mask that prevented the 'others' . . . from seeing us as we truly were" (5). But for women, as Houston's account reveals, the mask is defined in terms of raced gender constructs and is thus experienced as doubly impenetrable. The mask and masking, then, involve a literal dimension that is absent for other groups to whom the trope of masking might be applicable. That all the writers quoted above choose the imagery of the mask suggests their overriding sense that their faces, in a social context defined by white dominant culture, are what is most visible about them, and that this visibility renders them invisible.

Implicit is the sense of a "true self" trapped beneath the mask of a

Japanese face that continually undermines the subject's attempts to breach the disjunction between self consciousness (consciousness of one's self) and self-consciousness (consciousness of the self through the consciousness of an-other). And while masking can be used against the self, used by others to deny singularity and subjectivity, its function as concealment points to its potential doubleness. That is, if the mask of Japanese physical features conceals the unwilling Japanese American subject, it can also be used to actively conceal, and thus protect, that same subject. I do not wish to imply that racist perceptions projected onto Japanese Americans are in any simple way also that which they use to their advantage. Nor do I wish to suggest a facile argument for making the cheerful best of a bad situation. Beginning with the understanding that masking involves metaphorical dimensions that follow from the literal level, I want to propose masking as a double-sided trope that addresses the often difficult and painful strategies Nisei subjects have adopted to preserve a sense of dignity and selfhood. Masking foregrounds the complex nature of agency and the careful ways in which modes of agency should be understood.

Although Okimoto is a particularly problematic source for discussing Japanese American subjectivity because of his uncritical acceptance of dominant culture constructions, he inadvertently identifies a critical trope in the autobiographies of Japanese American women.[10] In the following passage, Okimoto discusses the importance of masks in Japanese culture and explicates a cultural practice that significantly affected the Nisei generation:

The Japanese are masters at hiding their true feelings behind expressionless masks. Masks, significantly, are used in several art forms, such as Noh, and are common literary themes. Stoic expressions may be the reason Westerners complain of Oriental inscrutability; seeing only a frozen face it is difficult for one to know what is passing through a Japanese person's mind. . . . However, behind their masks the Japanese are highly emotional. While nodding and maintaining an impassive front, they may be seething with anger inside. (108)

While this passage ultimately functions to reiterate and justify stereotypes about the impassive, mask-like and, hence, sneaky Japanese face, it nevertheless points up the necessary distinctions that need to be made between cultural practices and the ways in which those practices are misread and appropriated by dominant white culture. But Okimoto also describes a cultural trait that the Issei and Nisei adapted for a survival strategy in the internment camps. Powerless to change the situation, the internees could only accept it with a stoicism that was often misread as indicative of covert intentions or, most often, as happy and willing acquiescence. But there was often a great disparity between what one showed outwardly and the "emotional substance" beneath (Okimoto, 29).

Houston, describing her mother in camp, recounts how the concealment of intensely negative feelings also marked out a space of personal, psychological privacy:

She would quickly subordinate her desires to those of the family or the community, because she knew cooperation was the only way to survive. At the same time she placed a high premium on personal privacy. . . . Almost everyone at Manzanar had inherited this pair of traits. . . . But the entire situation there . . . the packed sleeping quarters, the communal mess halls, the open toilets—all this was an open insult to that other, private self, a slap in the face you were powerless to challenge. (1973, 23–24)

Houston's account suggests how the concealment of internal reactions to hardship and turmoil functioned not only to get one through difficulty but also to maintain the appearance of normalcy and some sense of personal dignity. Sone, Uchida and Houston all attest to the ways in which masking the humiliation and boredom of internment through activity provided a containing surface for the emotional lives of the evacuees. "Sunday was the day we came to an abrupt halt," writes Sone, "free from the busy round of activities in which we submerged our feelings" (185). And as Houston observes, more than a simple diversion, masking through activity was a survival strategy:

The present, the little bit of busywork you had right in front of you, became the most urgent thing. In such a narrowed world, in order to survive, you learn to contain your rage and your despair, and you try to re-create, as well as you can, your normality, some sense of things continuing. (1973, 72)[11]

In addition to providing at least the appearance of normalcy, masking also, I argue, allowed the only bit of privacy available in a place where four or more might be crowded into a stall eighteen by twenty feet, as well as a way of protecting the private self whom one was otherwise powerless to protect. Deployed by its wearer, the surface provided by masking was a barrier behind which singularity and dignity might have some kind of free reign.

The strategy of masking feelings as a way of protecting "that other, private self" takes on further valences when we turn to not just *what* these writers represent, but *how* they employ representative strategies. Critics such as Shirley Geok-lin Lim, Ann Rayson and Sau-ling Cynthia Wong have all noted what is perhaps one of the most striking characteristics of Monica Sone's *Nisei Daughter*, a characteristic that exists in varying degrees in all three autobiographies I examine here and one that brings us back to the observation of congenial flatness with which I began this discussion. Rayson writes that Sone's tone is "throughout cheerful, enthusiastic, even breezy" (51). Lim describes it as "a curiously muffled tone that deadens the expression of . . . internal violence" (1990, 296). As these critics note, it is singularly inaccurate, for numerous reasons, to take the narrative tone at face value. On the simplest level, Sone and Uchida were both in their early twenties at the time of their internment and were thus already heavily influenced by Issei cultural habits. Uchida notes, for instance, that "those early Issei . . . women must have had tremendous reserves of strength and courage to do what they did, often masked by their quiet and unassertive demeanor" (6). This "demeanor" (note the denotative connections to the face) modeled by the Issei mother is internalized and practiced by the Nisei daughter. But on a more complex level, we must recognize the congeniality of these narrative voices as a version of the masking Houston describes in relation to her mother. That is, through the use of tonal masking, these writers are able to protect "that other, private self" even as they "unmask [their] transgressive desire for cultural and literary authority . . . [through] choosing to write autobiography" (Smith, 50). Taking on that authority holds even greater risks for women who are racially marked because they are doubly likely to be dismissed by an audience defined by hegemonic standards assumed to be normative. In addition, because Sone, Uchida and Houston are addressing an audience whom they hope to enlighten, none are overtly critical or confrontational. Sone, who is particularly careful when addressing issues of prejudice and racism, published her autobiography only eight years after the internment camps were finally closed. She routinely employs "humor, anecdote, and oblique reference to engage the American public of the 1950s" (Rayson, 51). Uchida's narrative is characterized by a matter-of-factness lightened by humor; because her autobiography was written during the 1980s, Uchida is somewhat more willing to speak directly about white American racism. Nevertheless, the prevailing voice is genial, reasonable, ungrudging. Houston, much younger than the first two writers, seems more willing to reveal her internal thoughts, at least in comparison to Sone and

Uchida. Still, she also is nonconfrontational, careful not to allow her anger to speak clearly.

However, there are ruptures in Sone's and Uchida's narratives where we catch glimpses beneath the tonal mask. In the epilogue of what has been an autobiography spanning the period from her parent's marriage to the family's release from camp, Uchida writes that her parents had "helped my sister and me channel our anger and frustration. . . . Our anger was cathartic, but bitterness would have been self-destructive" (148). The intense anger and frustration to which this statement alludes, however, is never represented in the text. In a single passage, Uchida hints at, but does not fully articulate, her anger. Instead, she writes about internment life at the level of an acute irritant:

After three months of communal living, the lack of privacy began to grate on my nerves. There was no place I could go to be completely alone. . . . There was no place to cry and no place to hide. It was impossible to escape from the constant noise and human presence. I felt stifled and suffocated and sometimes wanted to scream. But in my family we didn't scream or cry or even have a major argument, because we knew the neighbors were always only inches away. (96)

Immediately, however, Uchida reverts to humorous anecdotes about the sometimes extreme measures people took to gain some privacy.

Sone, in a similar gesture that alludes to emotions unrepresented in detail, writes about her exit from camp, saying, "I had been tense and angry all my life about prejudice, real and imaginary" (186). While she acknowledges the effect of racism (referred to here as "prejudice," a much less threatening term), she quickly undercuts that acknowledgment with her closing phrase, "real and imaginary." Still, such an admission, however modified, comes as something of a surprise, because there has been, up to this point, little evidence of any anger at all, let alone an anger that Sone had lived with all her life—the life we have been reading about. Even, and especially, Sone's descriptions of camp life are vague and quickly underplayed. She tells us she felt "riotous emotion" (170), "a knot of anger" (177), "burning thoughts" and "quiet hysteria" (178), but these feelings, and their textual presence, are submerged beneath Sone's generally "breezy" tonality. These breaks in the text, or rather these cracks in the mask, suggest a whole other self but give us no access to it. Sone, like Houston, uses the language of a private self masked by endurance:

We had often felt despair and wondered if we must beat our heads against the wall of prejudice all our lives. In the privacy of our hearts, we had raged, we had cried against the injustices, but in the end, we had swallowed our pride and learned to endure. (124)

Although *Farewell to Manzanar* is, in many ways, more reflective than either Sone's or Uchida's autobiographies, Houston employs similar techniques of tonal masking to avert the reader's attention from potentially threatening emotions. Houston's narrative focuses on the effects of war and internment on her father, characterizing him as bullying, impulsive, and finally broken. But a closer reading reveals that Houston rarely differentiates between the effects of internment and the effects of the father's increasing drunken sullenness on the Wakatsuki family. Further, it is unclear whether she considers her father's drinking to be directly related to the internment. Houston's tone throughout is elegiac, sad, but not threateningly angry or accusatory. Following a blowup in . the family, caused by the father's anger and frustration, Houston writes that she "felt the miserable sense of loss that comes when the center has collapsed and everything seems to be flying apart around you" (1973, 50–51) — a description that might well convey the emotional effects of being uprooted, imprisoned and treated like so many head of cattle. This sentiment echoes an earlier passage in which Houston reflects on the change in her family after the war:

My own family, after three years of mess hall living, collapsed as an integrated unit. Whatever dignity or feeling of filial strength we may have known before December 1941 was lost, and we did not recover it until after Papa died and we began to come together, trying to fill the vacuum his passing left in all our lives.

The closing of the camps, in the fall of 1945, only aggravated what had begun inside. (1973, 27)

This passage is the most direct in its indictment of the internment and its effect on Japanese American families, a rending that occurred in many families. But what finally permeates Houston's description is the privatization of her family's loss of familial feeling. She implies, here and elsewhere, that, finally, while the internment is the context for what happened to her family, the father is the direct cause. By the time we reach the closing passages, it is difficult to read the young Jeanne's thoughts about her father without irony and as sadly misplaced. As her father drives crazily about in the car he has bought to drive his family out of the Manzanar internment camp, she thinks:

Watching Papa bounce and weave and shout in front of me, I was almost ready to laugh with him, with the first bubbly sense of liberation his defiant craziness had brought along with it. I believed in him completely just then, believed in the fierceness flashing in his wild eyes. Somehow that would get us past whatever waited inside the fearful dark cloud, get us past the heat, and the rattlers, and a great deal more. (1973, 144–45)

In the end, Houston's autobiography has turned into an examination of her father, whom she by turns admires, pities, fears, loves and resists. If Sone and Uchida mask their individual, private thoughts through the collective form of their narratives, Houston privatizes what is ostensibly a book about life in the internment camps. And yet even Houston does not employ the autobiographical form as a private arena for confession and self-examination. Personal details enter only where they relate directly to Houston's overall purpose.

Citizenship and Cultural Identity

If they use tonal masking to protect a vulnerable interiority, why do these women nevertheless choose to write autobiography? Again, we have to remember the didactic purpose that lies at the heart of these narratives. The autobiographical form, as practiced by Nisei women, provides a container for the tension between the communal act of witnessing and having to do so through the specific experiences of the individual self—that is, the tension between the collective and public, and the individual and private. In addition, autobiography creates a narrative mask that allows for the articulation of a self critical of the U.S. and its inability to live up to its ideals.

Narrative masking allows Sone, Uchida and Houston to assert their status as Americans by both interrogating and claiming the national ideologies of democracy and individualism as a way of resolving the contradictions between juridical and cultural Americanness. That is, there is an inherent tension between the denotative legality of American citizenship, conferred by birth, and the national culture's connotative ideals about what Americanness means, and to whom. Lisa Lowe suggests that it is through the

terrain of national culture that the individual subject is politically formed as the American citizen: a terrain introduced by the Statue of Liberty, discovered by the immigrant, dreamed in a common language, and defended in battle by the independent, self-made man. The heroic quest, the triumph over weakness, the promises of salvation, prosperity, and progress: this is the American feeling, the style of life, the ethos and spirit of being. It is in passing by way of this terrain of culture that the subject is immersed in the repertoire of American memories, events, and narratives and comes to articulate itself in the domain of language, social hierarchy, law, and ultimately, political representation. (1996, 2)

What Lowe points to here is the crucial connection between culture understood as a national enterprise and political/juridical citizenship. For those of the Nisei generation, the fact of their juridical citizenship signified little in the face of an American cultural imaginary unable to conceive of the Asian subject as (Asian) American. What these writers attempt is to bridge that tension through the direct invocation of the ideological. I suggest that the ideological partakes of both the denotative and connotative registers of citizenship—that is, the ideological register cites both the juridical and cultural "meanings" of citizenship—and thus provides a potential and privileged avenue of resolution for those subjects who inhabit the site of contradiction between them.

Sone and Uchida's autobiographies employ narrative masking not only to critique political and social hypocrisy but to stage the contradictions and incommensurabilities between juridical, cultural and ideological citizenship. It is for this reason that both include events that specifically highlight conflicts between Issei fathers, immigrants denied citizenship status, and white Americans for whom the category of citizen is assumed and reinforced on both legal and cultural levels. In both narratives, the fathers—and thus their Nisei offspring—emerge as articulating and embodying "Americanness." Through accounts of their childhood before the war, Sone and Uchida indirectly establish their families' belief in the American ideological code of justice and fair play. Uchida's father, she tells us, "cherished copies of the Declaration of Independence, the Bill of Rights, and the Constitution of the United States, and on national holidays he hung with great pride an enormous American flag on our front porch, even though at the time, this country declared the first generation Japanese immigrants to be 'aliens ineligible for citizenship' " (36). This passage reverberates with Uchida's account of her father's conflict with the white homeowners who had objected to a Japanese/American family in the neighborhood. Thus, Uchida asserts that "citizenship" is an ideological site that can be, and is, claimed by "aliens."

In a similar fashion Sone recounts her father's run-in with some crooked police who attempt to frame, then blackmail, him on charges of violating Prohibition laws. Writing several years after the actual event, Sone recalls her family's harassment by the local police in terms that function as a gloss on the internment:

During those impressionable years, the police became our sworn enemies, especially after two of them shoved their way into our household one night and arrested Father as a bootlegger. It happened so suddenly and it was so unexpected that we magnified the incident as catastrophic and the most harrowing experience of our lives. (34)

Notwithstanding her characteristic manner of minimizing what happened as an "incident" that the family "magnified" out of proportion, Sone's phrasing is purposefully suggestive and subtly ironic. From the family's limited vantage point in the past, the illegal use of force by local representatives of state power becomes "the most harrowing experience" they have undergone. But from the perspective of the future point in time at which Sone writes, this event could hardly compete in terms of catastrophic significance with the national abuse of state power during the war years. Rather, this passage serves as a textual harbinger, a masked "little-did-we-know" commentary that clearly parallels the unfairness of this remembered event with the injustice of what was to come. Sone's long description of her father's framing by the police *re*frames him as the legitimate representative of American ideals of good citizenship, in comparison to those whose claims are merely based on the accident of birth. (Interestingly, Sone concludes this section in a way that reveals some of the motivation behind her narrative strategies. After the matter has been straightened out, a family friend calms Sone's father by telling him, "The police have the upper hand. If you try to settle scores, there's no telling what other miseries they might think up for you" [42].)

Such passages suggest a concept of Americanness that has little to do with actual citizenship, and still less with race, and more to do with the beliefs that govern individual acts. In their accounts of the internment, Sone and Uchida both stress the reaction of the Japanese American community—a disbelief that white America could so easily turn its back on its own professed principles. In Sone's narrative, she subtly criticizes the hypocrisy of patriotism and hints at its potentially racist underpinnings:

We had heard the clamoring of superpatriots who insisted loudly, "Throw the whole kaboodle out. A Jap's a Jap, no matter how you slice him. You can't make an American out of little Jap Junior just by handing him an

American birth certificate." But we had dismissed these remarks as just hot blasts of air from an overheated patriot. We were quite sure that our rights as American citizens would not be violated, and we would not be marched out of our homes on the same basis as enemy aliens. (158)

Of course, they were treated as enemy aliens. Written from a future point in history, Sone's narrative ironically suggests how misplaced was the belief that racism—or, in Sone's terms, "superpatriotism"—would not take precedence over the American ideal of democracy. Her juxtaposition of patriotic racism and the Japanese American community's faith in democratic principles points out the potential failures of American ideology and recasts the category "American."

Uchida also uses quotation to ironic effect, embedding within her text a statement from President Roosevelt in which he claimed, "The principle on which this country was founded and by which it has always governed is that Americanism is a matter of the mind and heart. Americanism is not, and never was, a matter of race or ancestry" (135). The statement was not released in conjunction with the closing of the internment camps: its purpose was to encourage Nisei males to join the armed forces, which had been previously denied them. Sone's use of Roosevelt's 1943 recruiting statement is clearly meant to be read against similar statements made by Japanese Americans in 1941–42. Thus, Uchida suggests a selective and retarded response to American ideals, even by its representative figurehead. Here, as in her stated purpose for writing her autobiography, Uchida assumes for herself and for the Japanese American community the role of teaching white America the very principles it espouses as its own.

Using the textual mask of a simple narrative that recounts the crossed paths of national and personal history, Sone and Uchida address an audience whom they do not directly indict. But beneath that narrative surface, each is highly critical of a society that so easily, as Sone says in her 1979 foreword, "overlooked the vital American principle that consideration of guilt and punishment is to be carried out on an individual basis, and is not to be related to the wrongdoing of others" (xvi).

The didactic purpose of Japanese American autobiography implicitly points toward the shift these narratives trace from uncritical, naive notions of the American ideals of democracy and respect for the individual to a perspicacious awareness of the failures and limits of those ideals. The conversion in these texts, then, is not that of Japanese Americans moving from immigrant to citizen; if anything, the conversion element lies in their hoped-for effect, the conversion of white American aware-ness.

Even through both hindsight and the invocation of American dem-ocratic ideology, however, these writers are unable to fully resolve the contradictions of American citizenship in relation to the Nisei subject. While the critiques of American political reality and the articulation of its ideological narrative are strategies of the writing subject temporally distanced from the subject-who-is-written-about, there remains the painful memory of the internment and its illustration of how easily the guarantees of legal citizenship could be overturned and denied on the basis of cultural exclusion inflected through racial difference. Nisei subjects suddenly found themselves identified with their Issei parents and thus accorded no more civil rights as citizens than their noncitizen parents. The contradictions between legal and cultural citizenship were, in a sense, resolved by the American government's collapse of both terms, rendering all those of Nikkei heritage "aliens." But that collapse simultaneously reinforced and ossified those terms, such that the Nisei were faced with a narrowly conceived notion of Americanness that placed them in conflict both with their Issei parents and with their own identities as Americans of Japanese descent.

In the attempt to articulate their legal and political legitimacy, Nisei were forced into the juncture at which, as Lowe writes, "in being rep-resented as citizen within the political sphere . . . the subject is 'split off' from the unrepresentable histories of situated embodiment that contra-dict the abstract form of citizenship" (1996, 2). As Lauren Berlant also suggests, inclusion in the American nation and body politic always im-plies and has historically required a trade-off in which the particular, embodied person becomes an abstract citizen.[12] But for many immigrant groups and for people of color in particular, such a trade-off is by no means unproblematic or guaranteed in its results. For Nisei subjects during and immediately following the war years, the extent, though limited, to which they might be "represented within the political sphere" came at the high cost of splitting themselves off from those "unrepre-sentable histories" symbolized by their parents and by Japanese culture. But it also came at the cost, in many cases, of a split within the self, a split inaugurated by the recognition that what was unrepresentable was a fully realized Nisei subject.

The Disavowed (Japanese) Self

If reading the autobiographies of Japanese American women is, to use Nancy K. Miller's phrase, like a gloved handshake (57) or like a face-to-face meeting behind masks, the effect is deliberate, not simply a by-product of a narrative form that determines the degree of intimacy or "truth." These writers self-consciously use the disjunction between written and writing selves to mask the painful nature of memory and omission. The powerful conflict between both rejecting and retaining racial/ethnic identity and the resultant splitting of the subject force themselves through the narrative masks Sone, Uchida and Houston employ to tell their stories; however, any turmoil is quickly masked through tonal geniality or flatness.

Having considered autobiographical masking for didactic purposes in relation to white America, however, we must further articulate the trope of masking in Japanese American women's autobiographies in order to clarify that it is not a written form of passive aggression or simply a reactive response to a potentially hostile audience that would be alienated by overt accusations of racism. The most significant of these writers' uses of masking is as a psychological defense mechanism.

Implicit in many of the passages we have examined earlier is the sense of a disorienting disjunction between one's "real" or "true" self and the self defined by one's Japanese face. While I have argued here and in the preceding chapter that it is crucial to recognize the multiple positionings of the Japanese American female subject, I feel it is important to reiterate and emphasize the point that while multiplicity in the abstract sense is able to articulate complexity in a way that forcing coherent subject narratives cannot, the feeling of being painfully split in a day-to-day context is something quite different. For while dominant culture subjects are no less complex, no less articulable in terms of multiple subject positions, they nevertheless function, on a daily basis, in a world that assumes their status as subjects and allows for a functional, if provisional, sense of themselves as coherent beings. For Japanese Americans, particularly in the period of which these autobiographies speak, the refusal to recognize subjecthood for Japanese Americans meant that they labored under the constant strain of having to "prove" themselves, whether or not they felt they should have to. In this context, the following discussion recognizes the legitimate need for a coherent, viable subjectivity — a sense of self—capable of agency, without forcing a single-subject narrative to articulate the range of Japanese American female subjectivity.

The concept of a dual personality along reductively defined "American" and "Asian" categories has come under attack, most notably by the editors of *Aiiieeeee!* (1974), one of the earliest anthologies of Asian American writers. This concept, they argue, has largely been created by whites as a way to justify continued exclusion of Asian Americans from full participation in American culture. Because it suggests "that the Asian American can be broken down into his American part and his Asian part" (7), the dual personality or dual heritage theory underpins arguments that "the Asian part" is forever unassimilable, incompatible with "Americanness." The *Aiiieeeee!* editors trace what they see as a long tradition of Asian American writers buying into this concept and reinforcing it with autobiographies and novels featuring protagonists who feel they are straddling two incompatible cultures and identities (19).

While I agree that the "dual personality" concept does not provide a viable means to a functional sense of self, I take issue with the reinscription of essentialized notions of subjectivity within the context of a reductive cultural nationalism. Critics of the "dual personality" concept substitute an essentialized Asian American identity for an essentialized Asian one, as though one's multiple subject positions are always discrete and coterminous. Further, applying notions of dualized selfhood to these autobiographies can too easily lead to their dismissal. Instead of reading these narratives as exemplifying a total rejection of the Japanese self, as the dual personality model would lead us to, I read them as struggling with the impulse to retain a sense of that self in resistance to the impulses of rejection and disavowal. This contradiction, and the pain of it, necessitates tonal, narrative and psychological masking in order to diffuse what is too threatening to the self. Whereas the dual personality implies two mutually exclusive personae that lead to cultural schizophrenia, concepts of the split or bifurcated self acknowledge the agency of the subject in terms of how s/he defines and negotiates between often competing subject positions. Although the sense of a split self is by no means unproblematic, I want to stress that it does not, so far as I am formulating it, involve outright and total rejection of Japanese identity.

Because white American racism is the causal element in the sense of a split self, the terms "American" and "Japanese" become extremely loaded and imbued with issues of national loyalty and primary versus secondary identities. Yoshiko Uchida, for instance, recalls an Olympic Games event she attended as a child. While several of her Japanese American friends cheered on the Japanese nationals, Uchida felt that for "the first time I became acutely aware of the duality of my persona and the fact that a choice in loyalties might be made" (40). Although she recognizes that supporters of the Japanese team were not "any less loyal to America than I," Uchida contradicts herself by immediately associating choice of identity with American patriotism: "I was startled and puzzled by their action. As Japanese as I was in many ways, my feelings were those of an American and my loyalty was definitely to the United States" (40).

Sone and Houston both recount similar moments of realization but negativize them in ways much more overt than Uchida. Sone begins her autobiography with her "shocking discovery" that she is of Japanese heritage when her mother announces that she must begin attending Japanese school in addition to American public school:

The first five years of my life I lived in amoebic bliss, not knowing whether I was plant or animal, at the old Carrollton Hotel on the waterfront of Seattle. One day when I was a happy six-year-old, I made the shocking discovery that I had Japanese blood. I was a Japanese. (3)

Sone's account of events conflates the twin horrors of being Japanese and being forced into more schooling, suggesting that racial anxiety is being displaced into a realm much less threatening than that of identity. The intensity of the reaction hints that school is not, in fact, the issue:

Until this shattering moment, I had thought life was sweet and reasonable. But not any more. Why did Father and Mother make such a fuss just because we had Japanese blood? Why did we have to go to Japanese school? I refused to eat and sat sobbing, letting great big tears splash down into my bowl of rice and tea. (4–5)

I had always thought I was a Yankee, because after all I had been born on Occidental and Main Street. . . . I didn't see how I could be a Yankee and Japanese at the same time. It was like being born with two heads. It sounded freakish and a lot of trouble. (19)

As Shirley Geok-lin Lim points out, the announcement of racial difference results in a feeling of "division and psychological deformation" (1990, 294).[13] Sone increasingly, and unconsciously, articulates an uncritical acceptance of essentialized "American" and "Japanese" identities. However, her placement of this moment at the opening of her narrative suggests that the dramatic movement of her autobiography will focus on resolution of this painful dualism. Indeed, the final line of Sone's autobiography—"The Japanese and the American parts of me were now blended into one" (238)—compels us to recognize that within or perhaps underlying her acceptance of hegemonically defined racial traits is the desire to create a space for agency with which she can ultimately claim the resolution of cultural conflict and a sense of wholeness.

What Sone's autobiography details is the process by which she attempts to claim agency, while still not being able to dismantle her own internalized and essentialized images of "the Japanese." Thus, she depicts herself as a spunky and lively "Yankee" not to be confused with the "Japanese maiden" (92) represented by her cousin Yoshiye. In a chapter entitled "We Meet Real Japanese," a title that conveys the exotic othering most often associated with whites who find themselves face-to-face with an "Oriental," Sone writes that Yoshiye "made me feel like a tomboy with her restrained, delicate movements while I rustled and hustled around as I pleased" (92). In a fit of rage after Yoshiye laughs at her for talking "funny," Sone slaps her cousin across the face. Thus, she strikes out not only at the Japanese face from which she wants to dissociate, but also at everything she has accepted as representing the despised Japanese female self. Sone closes with a description that further negatively characterizes that self:

I was removed to another room. Although I was not sorry I had slapped my cousin, it had been an odd sensation. It was like striking a sack of flour. There had been no resistance or angry response, only a quiet crumbling away. (94).[14]

The division of the self into positivized American and negativized Japanese qualities is especially strong in passages where Sone (born Kazuko Monica Itoi) describes her experience of public American school and Japanese school. At Bailey Gatzert School, Kazuko is "a jumping, screaming, roustabout Yankee, but [at Japanese school] I suddenly became a modest, faltering, earnest little Japanese girl with a small, timid voice" (22). Later, in high school, Sone writes that she had become, because of Nihon Gakko, "a polished piece of inarticulateness" (131). While cultural standards of behavior are quite different in American public school and Japanese school, Sone ascribes the difference between herself and her white classmates to essential, racial difference:

Some people would have explained this [silent self-consciousness] as an acute case of adolescence, but I knew it was also because I was Japanese. Almost all the students of Japanese blood sat like rocks during discussion period. Something compellingly Japanese made us feel it was better to seem stupid in a quiet way rather than to make boners out loud. I began to think

MASKING IN NISEI WOMEN'S AUTOBIOGRAPHY   131

of the Japanese as the Silent People. . . . Only after a long, agonizing struggle was I able to deliver the simplest statement in class without flaming like
a red tomato. (131)

By dehistoricizing Nisei cultural adaptations and identifying "Japanese
blood" as the cause of her painful self-consciousness, Sone effectively
displaces blame from the effects of white American racism and the ways
in which it has crucially shaped the characters of both her and her fellow
Japanese American classmates. This displacement allows Sone to maintain the necessary fiction that what bars her full acceptance to and participation in American society is only the residuum of "Japaneseness"
conferred by blood, instead of a racism that she can do little to change.
While Sone's construction of the categories "American" and "Japanese"
evidence an internalization of stereotypes, it also suggests her denial of
the inevitability of her exclusion from American society. Sone fashions
a means by which she can actively gain entry—that is, by dissociating
herself from her Japanese ancestry. Though disturbingly problematic a
solution insofar as it still grants white American hegemony the power
of discriminating between what is desirable and salvageable and what is
undesirable and discardable, we should recognize the gesture toward
agency buried beneath. We should also recognize what is almost a psychological truism: that people most need denial—in this case of the
power of hegemonic racism—in direct proportion to the intolerability
of a situation to which there is no foreseeable solution.

   If Sone reinscribes the parsing of good and bad character traits along
racial lines—at one point writing that in the aftermath of the Pearl
Harbor bombing "an old wound opened up again, and I found myself
shrinking inwardly from my Japanese blood, the blood of an enemy"
(145)—Houston seems to have absorbed this sense of bifurcation to such
an extent that "Japanese" is associated with fear. After Pearl Harbor,
seven-year-old Jeanne's family moves to Terminal Island in the hope
that living among other Japanese will help them feel less isolated. Instead, Jeanne reacts with fear and revulsion to the Japanese faces she
sees around her:

It was the first time I had lived among other Japanese, or gone to school
with them, and I was terrified all the time. . . . When I had entered kinder-
garten two years earlier, I was the only Oriental in the class. They sat me
next to a Caucasian girl who happened to have very slanted eyes. I looked
at her and began to scream, certain that Papa had sold me out at last [to the
Chinese, as he had threatened]. My fear of her ran so deep I could not speak
of it, even to Mama, couldn't explain why I was screaming. For two weeks
I had nightmares about this girl, until the teachers finally moved me to the

other side of the room. And it was still with me, this fear of Oriental faces, when we moved to Terminal Island. (1973, 8–9)

The intensity of Jeanne's fear, which predates Pearl Harbor, is a direct consequence of her internalization of the fear and loathing with which Asians were regarded before, during and after the war. But her terror of the Caucasian girl reveals the extent to which Jeanne identifies her own repulsive Asianness in terms of isolated physical features in order to dissociate from them. That is, if "slanted eyes and high cheekbones" (1973, 29) are read not as Japanese physical features but as floating signifiers of difference, radical otherness can be projected onto an other. Yet this strategy fails because Houston/Jeanne has internalized essentialized notions of racial identity. Like Sone, Houston identifies consciousness of racial difference with fear, chaos and a fall from feelings of self-confidence and the sureness of one's own power to move in the world. Sone personifies projected Japanese qualities into the figure of an "enemy," a "two-headed freak"; Houston completely objectifies her Japanese identity, referring to it literally as "it." By the time she is ten, Jeanne has come to identify totally with white standards of beauty and goodness. She takes to baton-twirling, that childishly glamorous marker of quintessential American girlhood, obliterating, or trying to obliterate, her Japanese ethnicity: "Even at ten, before I really knew what waited outside, the Japanese in me could not compete. . . . It tried—in camp, and many times later, in one form or another" (1973, 79).

In her thematic analysis of Asian American literature, Sau-ling Wong refers to the figure of the double in relation to the numerous instances of the projection of disavowed racial characteristics onto another Asian or Asian American. Wong points to "the recurrent pattern of the double," in which

a highly assimilated American-born Asian is troubled by a version of himself/ herself that serves as a reminder of disowned Asian descent. The racial shadow draws out mixed feelings of revulsion and sympathy from the protagonist, usually compelling a painful reassessment of the behavioral code which has thus far appeared to augur full acceptance into American society . . . the "good" and "bad" halves of the ambivalent self are distributed not in two visibly different races but in two unequally assimilated characters of the same race. (92)

Sone slapping her cousin, as Wong notes, is a clear example of this doubling motif. Yoshiye represents everything from which Kazuko has dissociated herself. But what of Houston? The fear of "Orientals" she describes reveals its irrationality in her fetishization of isolated physical features. Explaining her reaction in terms of reversal—that is, placing the white girl in the position of the Oriental other and inhabiting the space of dominant white American—cannot account for the miasma of terror that characterizes the incident. What is unaccounted for is what Julia Kristeva calls the process of "abjection."

Kristeva describes the abject as that which "show[s] me what I permanently thrust aside in order to live. . . . Abjection [is caused by] what disturbs identity, system, order. What does not respect borders, positions, rules. The in-between, the ambiguous, the composite" (1982, 3–4). Although Kristeva locates this phenomenon at the site of the individual—who, as is common in psychoanalytic theory, is racially unmarked—the process she describes can be usefully employed to articulate the situation of the raced subject who, because of normative models of the self defined by white American hegemony, rejects his/her racial descent in the attempt to delineate identity in externally generated terms (which are then quickly internalized). Sone's revulsion and Houston's fear arise from being faced with their own racial otherness in the face of an other, a confrontation that reminds them of their own difference and of the differences within. Their reaction is, in Kristeva's terms, one of revolt:

There looms, within abjection, one of those violent, dark revolts of being, directed against a threat that seems to emanate from an exorbitant outside or inside, ejected beyond the scope of the possible, the tolerable, the thinkable. It lies there, quite close, *but it cannot be assimilated*. It beseeches, worries, and fascinates desire, which, nevertheless, does not let itself be seduced. . . . The abject has only one quality of the object—that of being opposed to "I" . . . the jettisoned object is radically excluded and draws me toward the place where meaning collapses. . . . From its place of banishment, the abject does not cease challenging its master. (1982, 1–2; first emphasis mine)

The abject is characterized by disgusting corporeality and deformation; it is associated with decay, illness, defilement. It is Sone's "old wound" (145), the "two-headed freak" (19, 158), Houston's terror and nightmare. The abjected racial self is the "it" that cannot compete with Jeanne's baton-twirling but remains to "thwart" her goal of white-defined acceptance. It is what comes to be associated with the filth of internment, where "dust, dirt, and wood shavings covered the linoleum that had been laid over manure-covered boards, the smell of horses hung in the air, and the whitened corpses of many insects still clung to the hastily white-washed walls" (Uchida, 70).

But where Kristeva's formulation leaves little room for any kind of agency, however limited and however reactive, I want to extrapolate from it and move the process of abjection into the context of systemic racism and the legitimate desire for acceptance. This foregrounds two issues: first, this contextualization resists Kristeva's emphasis on the unconscious and the characterization of abjection as largely self-generated, irrespective of social and political forces. Second, it denies the completely unconscious and therefore unwilled nature of Kristevan abjection. I am not equating abjection with total self-conscious choice, nor do I imply that abjection is simply negative agency. I do, however, want to suggest that the subject-who-abjects (who is also the subject-who-is-abjected) is not merely a passive embodiment of unconscious forces.

The most important difference, relative to my discussion here, is that for Japanese Americans abjection cannot be read as unequivocal rejection of the Japanese self. If what is abjected cannot be completely extirpated from the self since the formation of that self depends on the process of abjection, it is also true that for Japanese Americans of the Nisei generation, complete disavowal cannot happen without a similarly complete break from the Japanese American community—often the only source of social acceptance—and from their Issei parents. Even the abjection of the "Japanese" from "Japanese American" is fraught with ambivalence because "Japanese" is associated with the familial and, in terms of culture and cultural practices, with the maternal. As I note in greater detail in the following chapter, the Japanese mother is consistently identified with Japanese culture and, by extension, with the raced self from which the Japanese American subject attempts to dissociate. In all three women's narratives, the mother is constructed, as Lim notes in Sone's autobiography, as "the absolute pole of Japanese identity. She instructs her daughter on Japanese foods, customs, and literature" (1990, 295). Uchida, in fact, includes her mother's haiku between the chapters of her autobiography. This intertextuality suggests the degree to which intersubjectivity between mother and daughter, between Issei and Nisei, is a crucial element in the formation of Japanese American subjectivity. But if the association with the Japanese mother offers a sense of emotional connectedness, it also threatens identification with the raced self. The resulting ambivalence manifests itself in intense conflict both between generations and within the Japanese American subject.

Sone and Uchida illustrate their mothers' racial/cultural difference through humorous vignettes that function as humanizing comic relief. But these anecdotes, the written equivalent of the fond chuckle, mask a much more serious sense of humiliation and shame. In a passage striking for its sudden use of the collective "we" instead of the personal "I," Uchida writes briefly of the effects of white American racism on the Nisei psyche:

Society caused us to feel ashamed of something that should have made us feel proud. Instead of directing anger at the society that excluded and diminished us, such was the climate of the times and so low our self-esteem that many of us Nisei tried to reject our own Japaneseness and the Japanese ways of our parents. We were sometimes ashamed of the Issei in their shabby clothes, their rundown trucks and cars, their skin darkened from years of laboring in sun-parched fields, their inability to speak English, their habits, and the food they ate. (42)

We can clearly see here in this description of the Issei the characteristics of the abject. Immediately following this passage, however, Uchida reverts to humorous anecdotes that allow her to substitute feelings of embarrassment (or as Uchida puts it, mortifi[cation] beyond words" [42]) —for the more threatening feelings of shame, disavowal and the wish to dissociate from the mother or parents who act in such humiliatingly "non-American way[s]" (42).

Differences in cultural practices, communication styles and social rituals were, before the war, primarily benign conflicts taking place within the family. Uchida, for example, writes that her mother tried to teach her Japanese during summer vacations: "We had many stormy sessions as Mama tried to inject a little knowledge of a difficult language into two very reluctant beings. Learning Japanese to us was just one more thing that would accentuate our 'differentness,' something we tried very hard to overcome in those days" (40). Uchida's account echoes Sone's opening passages in at least two important ways: the resistance to identifying as Japanese is conflated with the resistance toward schooling, and the representative carrier of racial consciousness is the mother. With the onset of the war and the internment, however, what were once private tussles become openly confrontational arguments that parallel the increasingly public conflicts between Issei and Nisei. In a passage that actively seeks to represent the Nisei as loyal to the U.S., in contrast to their sometimes more ambivalent parents (who were legally barred from becoming U.S. citizens), Sone reveals the escalating tension between Japanese parents and their American-born children. In the following passage, a twenty-one-year-old Sone takes issue with her mother's seeming defense of Japan. In a tone of resignation, the mother

replies, "I suppose from now on, we'll hear about nothing but the humiliating defeats of Japan in the papers here" (148):

Henry and I glared indignantly at Mother, then Henry shrugged his shoulders and decided to say nothing. Discussion of politics, especially Japan
versus America, had become taboo in our family for it sent tempers sky-
rocketing. Henry and I used to criticize Japan's aggressions in China and
Manchuria while Father and Mother condemned Great Britain and America's superior attitude toward Asiatics and their interference with Japan's
economic growth. During these arguments, we had eyed each other like
strangers, parents against children. They left us with a hollow feeling at the
pit of the stomach. (148)

That "hollow feeling," symptomatic of the rejection of a vital part of the
self, reverberates throughout Sone's narrative. Her awareness of that
feeling indicates the push-pull of her desire to disavow "Japaneseness"
and her desire to remain connected with her mother and her Japanese
cultural heritage. Exacerbated by the narrow parameters within which
"Americanness" was defined by the dominant culture, as well as by
mounting anti-Japanese hysteria, the tension between Issei and Nisei
increased greatly during the years directly preceding and following the
internment. As Uchida and Houston both attest, accusations of disloyalty or of complicity with camp authorities flew between Issei and Nisei.
Violence between the two groups was common (as was strife within
each group). Many families, unable to resolve intergenerational tensions, broke apart during the war years. But Sone quickly turns away
from the turmoil and strife, watering it down with a story of comic
cultural misunderstandings between Issei and Nisei during a "most curious tea party" (190) given in honor of her brother's engagement.

Uchida mentions briefly that "the corrosive nature of life in camp
seemed to bring out the worst in many people" (132), noting that the
incidence of crime rose in direct proportion to the amount of time the
internment went on. Although Uchida's love and respect for her parents
comes through clearly, she also hints at the increasing level of friction
within the family. She writes that feelings of "helplessness, personal in-
security, and inertia . . . were overtaking me . . . and increased my desperation to get out of camp. Internal squabbling spread like a disease"
(133). I find it significant that here, as in an earlier passage, Uchida's
descriptive viewpoint suddenly shifts from the subjective and specific
("were overtaking me") to the seemingly objective but ambiguous ("internal squabbling spread" within the family? throughout the camp?),
thereby distancing herself from what may be painful personal state-

ments. But this distancing also indicates a desire to transcend the model of conflicted intergenerational relations and to align the Nisei self with the Issei parents, a desire sharpened by hindsight. "It was only in later years," Uchida writes, "that we came to realize how much they had done for us; how much they had given us to enrich and strengthen our lives" (142). What comes through quite strongly in Uchida's closing pages is the recognition that her Japanese parents, and particularly her mother, have been a source not only of shame, but of strength as well:

During the war . . . they [the Issei] all suffered enormous losses, both tangible and intangible. The evacuation was the ultimate of the incalculable hardships and indignities they had borne over the years.

And yet most of our parents had continued to be steadfast and strong in spirit. Our mothers had made homes of the bleak barrack rooms, just as my own mother, in her gentle, nurturing way, had been a loving focal point for our family and friends. (142)

This passage echoes Uchida's opening pages, where she represents her father claiming the U.S. as home. Here, it is the mother who is identified with home in its emotional and psychological connotations. Through her, the family is able to retain some sense of its emotional coherence. To abject the Japanese self through the mother, then, would be to reject connectedness and emotional agency. In this light, Houston's account of the breakdown of her family is significant: in what is ostensibly a narrative about the effects of internment, she privatizes her family's struggles and focuses on the figure of her father, nearly erasing her mother from her autobiography altogether.

In Sone's autobiography, too, love and respect for her parents cannot be doubted, but these feelings must compete with the need to differentiate from the parents who represent unassimilable foreignness. Near the end of *Nisei Daughter*, she describes her parents as looking "like wistful immigrants" (237) who are literally positioned on the other side of the gate of the internment camp from which Kazuko is being allowed to leave. The guilt that arises from this conflict—evident in the way that negative encounters with the Japanese mother, the symbol of disavowed Japanese ethnicity, are glossed over or elided—is compensated for by the fetishization of Japanese cultural objects. Because objects must carry all the positive qualities of the culture, the result is a shallow appreciation for Things Japanese: manners, food, church socials and picnics are compared to the pleasures of American holidays and represent what is "good" about Japanese/Japanese American culture.

The ambivalence suggested by this polarization does not, I think, indicate only that Sone rejects Japanese culture in all but its most trivial forms. Instead, it indicates guilt over the impulse toward rejection and disavowal. It is with this in mind that I read Sone's closing pages, which are otherwise puzzling in their gung-ho enthusiasm for a rather shallowly defined "American democracy." Upon the daughter's exit from camp, the mother makes a startling apology: "When the war came and we were all evacuated, Papa and I were heartsick. We felt terribly bad about being your Japanese parents" (236). The daughter's reply is even more startling:

I don't resent my Japanese blood anymore. I'm proud of it, in fact, because of you and the Issei who've struggled so much for us. It's really nice to be born into two cultures, like getting a real bargain in life, two for the price of one. The hardest part, I guess, is the growing up, but after that, it can be interesting and stimulating. I used to feel like a two-headed monstrosity, but now I find that two heads are better than one. (236)

Lim observes that all the turmoil Sone has experienced (which is only, as I've said, alluded to) is "collapsed in the conclusion to the single weak adjective 'nice.' The psychological, economic, and cultural price the family has had to pay for being Japanese is distorted here to 'a bargain . . . two for the price of one.' " While Lim sees this as evidencing the "utter defeat of the Japanese self" (1990, 299), Sone's recognition of the Issei suggests to me that she retains, however uneasily and problematically, a sense of connection to the Japanese self, that she cannot completely cut her ties to the "mother('s) culture." Her transformation of the two-headed freak image to the homiletic "two heads are better than one" implies that the split self with which Sone's narrative opens remains; yet it must be recognized that she does not simply cut her losses and run. To put it another way, if Sone's statement that two heads are better than one is puzzling almost to absurdity, she has nevertheless not beheaded the Japanese self.

What Sone does do is disempower it through the rhetoric of patriotic self-determination:

In spite of the war and the mental tortures we went through, I think the Nisei have attained a clearer understanding of America and its way of life, and we have learned to value her more. Her ideas and ideals of democracy are based essentially on religious principles and her very existence depends on the faith and moral responsibilities of each individual. I used to think of the government as a paternal organization. When it failed me, I felt bitter and sullen. Now I know I'm just as responsible as the men in Washington for its actions. Somehow it all makes me feel much more at home in America. (237)

It would be comforting to be able to read this passage ironically, but there is little to indicate that Sone speaks anything but genuinely. Given that Sone cannot conceive of a mode of agency that legitimizes and includes Nisei identity, her solution is to claim agency for herself through the ideology of individual self-determination. Unable to end her narrative with the terror of racial difference that begins it and the humiliating sense of an illegitimate identity that runs throughout, Sone transforms the internment into a hands-on civics lesson, the upshot of which is that all has been for the interesting, stimulating best. The pain of bifurcation is masked by Sone's better-for-having-suffered platitudes. Nevertheless, Sone's discourse suggests that, in fact, the sense of bifurcation persists.

While Uchida does not so overtly articulate Sone's enthusiastic embrace of "America and its way of life," she also gives in to the impulse to transform herself into the "ideal American" in ways that suggest not a resolution of her turmoil but an ungrudging dismissal of it:

I left Topaz determined to work hard and prove I was as loyal as any other American. I felt a tremendous sense of responsibility to make good, not just for myself, but for all Japanese Americans. I felt I was representing all Nisei, and it was sometimes an awesome burden to bear. (149)

Like Sone, Uchida implies that the internment experience has actually motivated her toward a greater acceptance and embodying of the "American values" of hard work, responsibility and respectability. Like Sone, Uchida alludes to feelings of anger and bitterness only in retrospect, when both the "I" of the narrative and the "I" writing it are temporally distanced from those feelings.

The masking of negative emotions results in narrative voices that at once invite and refuse entry into the private internal realm of these women about whose lives we are reading. Removed in time from the events she describes, the autobiographer may be overinvested in distancing herself from disturbing memories and overeager to represent any traumatic internal conflicts as past events available for description by a subject who has since come to a sense of reconciliation. Sone's incessantly upbeat narrative, Uchida's generally matter-of-fact account, and Houston's tone of elegiac closure represent a strategic deployment of discursive masking and indirectly suggest the risks and circumstances on which the autobiographical act is predicated, as well as feelings of guilt, disavowal and bifurcation.

In the attempt to speak a self into being that is perhaps finally more a wished-for self than an existent one, Sone, Uchida and Houston complicate our understandings of the discursive relation between revelation and concealment in the autobiographical act. However guardedly, however problematically, however frustratingly, in their desire to speak for the community of Japanese Americans, they also construct, protect and give voice to "that other, private self."

CHAPTER 4

Mothers, Daughters and the Trope of Maternal Absence in Japanese American Women's Fiction

Silent Mother, you do not speak or write. You do not reach through the night to enter morning, but remain in the voicelessness. From the extremity of much dying, the only sound that reaches me now is the sigh of your remembered breath, a wordless word. How shall I attend that speech, Mother, how shall I trace that wave? . . . I am thinking that for a child there is no presence without flesh. But perhaps it is because I am no longer a child I can know your presence though you are not here.

Joy Kogawa, *Obasan*

"My daughter denies she is like me," begins "Breaking Tradition" by Sansei poet Janice Mirikitani, "her secretive eyes avoid mine" (1987, 27). The poem describes the separation between the speaker and her Yonsei daughter, and the ways in which they cannot communicate. Remembering her own daughterhood, the speaker describes her sense of separateness from her Nisei mother:

I deny I am like my mother. I remember why:
    She kept her room neat with silence,
    defiance smothered in requirements to be otonashii,
    passion and loudness wrapped in an obi,
    her steps confined to ceremony,
    the weight of her sacrifice she carried like
    a foetus. Guilt passed on in our bones.
I want to break tradition—unlock this room

where women dress in the dark.
Discover the lies my mother told me.
The lies that we are small and powerless
that our possibilities must be compressed
to the size of pearls, displayed only as
passive chokers, charms around our neck.
Break Tradition.
I want to tell my daughter of this room
of myself. . . .
. . . .
My daughter denies she is like me. . . .
her pouting ruby lips, her skirts
swaying to salsa, Madonna and the Stones,
her thighs displayed in carnivals of color.
I do not know the contents of her room.
She mirrors my aging.
She is breaking tradition. (1987, 27–28)

The room is the site of what is hidden and what must be renounced: the mother's room is identified with repression and concession to cultural prescriptions, the speaker's "room of myself" is ignored by her daughter, and the daughter's room remains concealed. The room is also a metaphor for the self, discrete and contained within its own walls. Defining the self seems to have as much to do with rejection of the mother's room as with maintaining the separate space of one's own. What one is *not* defines identity and subjectivity, and the viability of one's subjectivity largely depends on the process of rejection.

Mirikitani's poem traces the search for separation from the mother and marks the differences between each generation—Nisei, Sansei, and Yonsei—suggesting that the daughter's identity is not based solely on differentiation from the mother but involves distinctly generational differences. A number of Asian American literary works deal in varying degrees with questions of generational difference and intergenerational conflict, and these thematics have been popularly accepted as characterizing Asian American literature in general, despite the fact that a significant percentage of it does not focus primarily on generational issues.[1] Two of the most well known novels by Asian American women, Maxine Hong Kingston's *The Woman Warrior* and Amy Tan's *Joy Luck Club*, have been widely read as dealing specifically with such conflict in the mother-daughter relationship. But while the Asian American literary canon lends itself to the generational model, that model also decontextualizes it, flattening much of its complexity. As Lisa Lowe observes:

Interpreting Asian American culture exclusively in terms of the master narratives of generational conflict and filial relation essentializes Asian American culture, obscuring the particularities and incommensurabilities of class, gender, and national diversities among Asians; the reduction of ethnic cultural politics to struggles between first and second generations displaces (and privatizes) inter-community differences into a familial opposition. (1991b, 26)

The filial/generational model often assumes that cultural transmission is unidirectional, beginning from an originary source and following down the generational line. Furthermore, it treats generational differences as emblematic of cultural/national differences; the result is a model that encodes generation *as* culture, and whose implicit structure is one of development or progression. In other words, those who are "earlier" are more Asian, less American and therefore a problem. The unspoken reliance on assimilation narratives — marked by a clear trajectory from a point A characterized by lack to a point B characterized by realization and fulfillment — ideologically and structurally requires an understanding of culture as a process of assent but cannot account for culture as also a process of contestation and resistance.

The generational model is especially problematic when applied to mother-daughter relationships, not only because it does not account for the specificities of gender and does not adequately acknowledge intersubjective modes of agency, but also because it focuses on intergenerational tensions and differences that must be renounced in order to define both one's self and one's generation. As a result, the filial/generational model neatly reinforces psychoanalytic models of individuation wherein, as Marianne Hirsch writes, "a continued allegiance to the mother appears as regressive and potentially lethal; it must be transcended. Maturity can be reached only through an alignment with the paternal, by means of an angry and hostile break from the mother" (168). And yet Japanese American women must both differentiate from and identify with the mother in order to construct a viable subjectivity in which gender and race are mutually constitutive. Certainly Mirikitani's poem would seem to follow the psychoanalytic pattern of daughterly individuation. But it also hints at the necessary connection between the generations: Mirikitani discursively connects each woman to the other through the act of "breaking tradition." Ironically, this act becomes itself a tradition, a connective act of disavowed connection carried through the generations. In one sense, the speaker who is both daughter and mother passes down the necessary act of breaking away from the mother's model of female subjectivity. The closing line, "She is breaking tradition," is both celebratory and sad as the speaker simultaneously identifies with the daughter and finds herself identified with her own mother. If the tonal ambiguity here represents connection in somewhat ambivalent terms, "Generations of Women," an earlier poem in the same volume, directly voices the need for connection:

> Mother, grandmother
> speak in me.
> I claim their strong fingers
> of patience, their knees
> bruised with humiliation,
> their hurt, their longing,
> the sinews of their survival.
> Generations of yellow women
> gather in me
> to crush the white wall. (1987, 15)

"Mother, grandmother / speak in me" is at once descriptive and plaintive; the speaker claims and desires a univocal connectedness. The doubleness of these lines is perhaps most significant for how they articulate the intersubjective agency between generations: as third-person description, they point to how the mother and grandmother find voice and agency through the voice of the daughter. As second-person address, these lines illustrate the daughter's recognition that her articulateness and sense of empowerment come from her connectedness to generational mother figures. The agency implicit in speaking thus depends on the agency of the mother and grandmother.

This recognition is subtly indicated in "Breaking Tradition," where the speaker grants agency to her daughter while also claiming her own agency as mother. Unlike her mother, whom she represents as "smothered" and "confined," the speaker identifies herself as an active agent who "want[s] to tell [her] daughter of this room" where she is the maker of poems and music. The doubled positioning of the speaker complicates the earlier image of her own mother by suggesting that as she has perceived her mother without subjectivity, so does her daughter perceive her.

In *The Mother/Daughter Plot,* Hirsch argues that psychoanalytic models, including feminist models, figure the mother as an absent subject and that they articulate the mother/daughter dyad "only from the point of view of the developing child" (167). The child's, and in this case daughter's, development is privileged and "the mother's own part in that process remains absent, erased from theoretical and narrative representation" (169).[2] Mirikitani's poem, then, may be read as an attempt to represent the mother's agency, though that representation is complicated by the fact that the speaker positions herself as both mother and daughter. Nevertheless, "Breaking Tradition" and "Generations of Women" suggest the importance of creating a space for maternal agency, a space for which traditional and many feminist psychoanalytic models do not provide.

The latter poem points out why agency and connection are crucial aspects of the mother-daughter relationship for Japanese American women: the necessity for identification with the mother relates to issues of survival and resistance, which contextualize mother/daughter identification within the conditions of historical racism ("the white wall").[3] In contrast to models that posit the necessity for a "third term [the father] that *must* break the asocial dyadic unit of mother and child" (Steedman, 79), the structure of racialized motherhood suggests that the mother is a crucial figure for enculturating the daughter in modes of material and psychological survival in a social realm where she will be defined by both her race and gender. The absence of race in much of the literature on mothers and daughters reveals a highly problematic, because incomplete, model that implicitly assumes similar processes of socialization among different ethnic groups.[4] Patricia Hill Collins notes that

For Native American, African-American, Hispanic, and Asian-American women, motherhood cannot be analyzed in isolation from its context. Motherhood occurs in specific historical situations framed by interlocking structures of race, class, and gender. . . . Despite the significance of race and class, feminist theorizing routinely minimizes their importance. In this sense, feminist theorizing about motherhood has not been immune to the decontextualization of Western social thought overall. (45)

Constructed within the interlocking structures of racism and patriarchy, relationships between Japanese/American mothers and daughters cannot adequately be understood in the context of gender alone. To do so ignores issues that question the universality of mother-daughter conflict as the primary characteristic of their relationships and its primacy as a way of understanding the subjectivity of these women.

Reading Motherwork in *Beyond Manzanar*

To ground these concerns, I take up two personal essays by Jeanne Wakatsuki Houston, which provide a clear example of the potential failures of models in which "maternal subjectivity must be erased for daughterly subjectivity to develop" (Hirsch, 171), as well as those that assume the primacy of gender. Several years after completing *Farewell to Manzanar,* Houston wrote "Beyond Manzanar" (1978) and "The Geisha, the Good Wife, and Me" (1983).[5] If the mother is largely absent from *Manzanar,* represented primarily as a background figure who reacts to her husband's actions, these essays focus exclusively on and attempt to define the mother as an active subject. Their motivating force is clearly grounded in Houston's attempt to define herself, and, significantly, she finds she cannot do so without coming to terms with her mother. As a young woman, trying "desperately to be as American as Doris Day" ([1978] 1985, 8), Houston finds her mother's tendency to serve and defer to her father "embarrassing" and says, "I would not declare my love for her" (10). Houston divides identity between the seemingly mutually exclusive categories of "the good Japanese wife" and "assertive American" and attempts to construct herself in the image of her white friends: "I wanted to be like my Caucasian friends. Not only did I want to look like them, I wanted to act like them. I tried hard to be outgoing and socially aggressive, and to act confidently, like my girl friends. At home . . . I still tried to be as Japanese as I could" (17). Yet formulations of subjectivity that rely on the logic of opposition inevitably backfire and fix both the other and self into untenable and essentialized positions. Judith Butler's analysis of the roles of repudiation and abjection points to the inevitable "cruelties that sustain coherent identity, cruelties that include self-cruelty as well" (Butler, 115):

To the extent that subject-positions are produced in and through a logic of repudiation and abjection, the specificity of identity is purchased through the loss and degradation of connection, and the map of power which produces and divides identities differentially can no longer be read. The multiplication of subject-positions along a pluralist axis would entail the multiplication of exclusionary and degrading moves that could only produce a greater factionalization, a proliferation of differences without any means of negotiating among them. (114)

The importance of Butler's analysis is that it recognizes the self-defeating moves of a wholly oppositionally defined subject. Ironically, Houston comes to something of a similar realization when she takes a psychology course in college and is exposed for the first time to Freud's theories of the mother. It is unlikely that psychoanalytic theory was introduced in any complex or perhaps even very detailed way, but Houston's reaction to it reveals the felt inappropriateness of such models:

During my freshman year at San Jose State College I took the required General Psychology course and was exposed for the first time to Freud and Jung, as were most of my classmates. I was stunned to hear them discuss their mothers so impersonally and often with great hostility. It seemed everyone had something negative to say about a "domineering, materialistic, guilt-evoking, aggressive" mother. I did not understand then that this was merely a way of asserting independence, of striking out at the one authority in their lives that emotionally held them to the "nest." ([1978] 1985, 10)

While Houston senses that what Freud describes does not describe her own experience, it is striking that she neither overtly challenges a model that equates rejection of the mother with the need to assert one's own identity nor recognizes her own actions as similar to those of her class-mates. Although it could be argued that Houston sentimentalizes her mother, perhaps from residual guilt over her earlier attitude, her reaction is not simply a compensatory one: what she recognizes is that her mother is not represented in Freudian and Jungian discourse.

Houston continues to divide actions along "Japanese" and "Ameri-can" axes, at times to the point of essentializing each.[6] Paradoxically, it is her tendency to essentialize that brings her to the realization that in refusing to identify with her mother, she rejects a vital part of her own identity, an act of self-cruelty in Butler's terms. Having grown up in a culturally Japanese household, Houston's sense of herself as a woman is intimately tied to the figure of the mother. When Houston marries a white American, she finds that her identity as a woman is inseparable from her identity as a Japanese American; more important, she recog-nizes that her identity as a Japanese American woman is inseparable from that of her mother. "My natural inclination," Houston writes, was "to do as she did" ([1978] 1985, 24). Clearly, to reject the mother is to reject one's own gendered and racial identity; to be "as American as Doris Day" implicitly is also to be as American as her mother is not, to disavow the subjectivity represented by the mother.

But the task here is not simply to reconcile with the mother in a facile celebration of reclamation and identification. Much as the daughter/mother in Mirikitani's "Breaking Tradition" finds herself identified with her mother, so is Houston identified by others as inhabiting the space of "the good Japanese wife" associated with her mother. She writes that she does not feel free to act "Japanese" in front of white friends who misinterpret her actions as "psychological subservience" ([1978] 1985, 22) and tells the story of a Chinese American acquaintance who "remarked to a Caucasian friend that she polished her husband's shoes. Her friend turned to her in mock fury and said, 'Don't you dare let my husband know you do that!' My friend," Houston continues, "said she felt ashamed, humiliated, that she had somehow betrayed this woman by seeming subordinate to her husband" (21). The shame and humiliation, with which Houston clearly empathizes, result from the assumption that female agency is defined in accordance with normative (white) standards, any deviation from which is interpreted as servile passivity.

Having internalized these values, Houston must move toward redefining Japanese female subjectivity in terms that will allow her to recuperate her mother's agency and, by extension, her own. These essays are, in large part, her attempt to locate agency at a site with which she had formerly avoided identifying. Central to this project is recontextualizing her mother and the Japanese womanhood she represents within the intersection of Japanese cultural practices and white American racism. Thus, Houston writes that a crucial difference between white American and Japanese culture is the attitude toward service: "In my family, to serve another could be uplifting, a gracious gesture that elevated oneself. For many white Americans it seems that serving another is degrading, an indication of dependency or weakness in character, or a low place in the social ladder. To be ardently considerate is to be 'self-effacing' or apologetic" ([1978] 1985, 20). "At times," she notes, "my willingness to give was misconstrued as a need to be liked or an act of manipulation to get something" (21). While the Japanese concept of serving another is often, though by no means always, gender-marked, Houston draws attention to the ways in which the server's agency is implied in the act of serving. Houston identifies service with attentiveness, not with servility — "to serve meant to love" (13) — and by so doing creates a space for Japanese female agency denied by dominant cultural standards.[7]

Moreover, Japanese/American cultural practices cannot be read apart from the historical and social circumstances of racism. Houston also explains her mother's tolerance for her father's often rudely imperial behavior at home by pointing out his powerlessness in the world outside:

He had to earn a living for his family in an environment both alien and hostile to him. My mother, already inherently prepared to subordinate herself in their relationship, knew this and zealously sought for ways to elevate his position in the family. He had to absorb the humiliations "out there": she would absorb them at home. After all, was he not doing this for his family, protecting her, acting as the buffer between herself and that alien *hakujin* [white] world? ([1978] 1985, 12)

Problematic as this passage may be in its relegation of the female to the domestic sphere and the male to the social and economic domain, it reveals the extent of the mother's awareness of the difficulty for the husband in dealing with white society. Sylvia Junko Yanagisako observes in her study of Japanese American tradition and kinship patterns that although many of the Issei women she interviewed expressed awareness and some resentment of the power differential in their marital relationships, they nevertheless preferred to work in realms that kept them circumscribed within the home and away from contact with outsiders, "nonkin and strangers" (99).[8] Although Yanagisako ascribes this attitude to cultural traditions, presumably implying that Issei women's resistance to working outside the bounds of their traditionally defined sphere would also be true in an exclusively Japanese environment, I hold that the need for such boundaries is perceived in markedly different ways in the context of U.S. racism, functioning in a more overtly protective capacity. Thus, the power imbalance between the mother and father relates to the father's lack of power in the world at large. It is also crucial to recall that the time about which Houston is writing is after the internment, an event that shattered the hierarchical order, stability and often the very existence of many Japanese American families. The willingness of Houston's mother to "absorb humiliation" at home, then, should not be interpreted as merely acquiescence to traditional Japanese female roles but rather as a strategy, albeit a culturally sanctioned and problematic one, meant to stabilize both her husband and the family itself. As Houston writes of her parent's marriage in comparison to her own: "what . . . emerge[s] as a basic difference is directly related to the Japanese concept of cooperation for group survival and the American value of competition for the survival of the individual. My Japanese family cooperated to survive economically and spiritually" ([1978] 1985, 23). In this view, the mother's role benefits the whole family, not just the husband. Collins writes that this element of ensuring survival is crucial in understanding the role of what she calls "motherwork" in communities of color:

Racial ethnic women's motherwork for individual and community survival has been essential. Without women's motherwork, communities would not survive, and by definition, women of color themselves would not survive. On the other hand, this work often extracts a high cost for large numbers of women. There is loss of individual autonomy and there is submersion of individual growth for the benefit of the group. While this dimension of motherwork remains essential, the question of women doing more than their fair share of such work for individual and community development merits open debate. (Collins, 50)

Evelyn Nakano Glenn similarly observes that for communities of color, the family is simultaneously the site of female subordination and resistant female agency: "Japanese American women['s] . . . reproductive labor maintained the family as a bastion of resistance to race and class oppression, while at the same time it was the vehicle for their oppression within the family" (1986, 193). Thus, while the family may delineate the boundaries of maternal influence, it may also be seen as a "culture of resistance" in which women play a vital role (192).

It is not my intention to portray traditional Japanese marital relationships as egalitarian, nor do I wish to imply that male privilege is inoperative or unperceived by Issei women themselves. The difficulty here is to define modes of female agency that do not ignore the fact of power imbalances between men and women or translate that differential into terms that reduce Japanese American women (particularly Issei women) to passive subjects. This is, of course, precisely Houston's dilemma: having been "influenced . . . by the women's movement" of the 1970s ([1983] 1985, 27), she resists replicating her mother's model of Japanese womanhood; at the same time, to reject her mother's model completely would be to cut herself off from the very strength that kept Houston and her family together. This conflict, or doubleness, in the mother's role is precisely what Houston must come to terms with. Complicating the whole issue of identification are significant differences between the Issei and Nisei. To this extent, intergenerational models of Japanese American culture are useful in delineating shifts between generations. But such an interpretive lens alone privileges the agency of the daughter in deciding what to accept or, most often, what to reject. And, again, it largely obscures the mother's agency. The importance of constructing maternal agency not only recuperates the mother as subject but is an integral part of the daughter's own subjectivity.

For Houston, coming to an understanding of her mother involves understanding how she was able to retain a sense of self within and alongside the role Japanese women were culturally expected to play. Only by doing so can Houston accept her own identity as a Japanese American woman. Although she employs the language of "the inner self" in the following passage, what Houston comes to recognize is a mode of Japanese female subjectivity defined at once by acquiescence and by resistance:

She never confused her tasks with who she was. This concept of the inner self, which I have begun only recently to understand as a result of my attempts to rediscover my Japanese "roots," allowed her to form her own image, distinct from the one in the exterior world. This ability to create a psychological privacy, inherited from a people who for centuries have had to create their own internal "space" in an overpopulated island, gave her the freedom, of which she was so deprived in her role as Japanese wife and mother. This was her way to survive . . . and to succeed. ([1978] 1985, 9; ellipsis in original)

It is precisely this double nature of the Japanese woman's role that makes the daughter's recognition of her mother's agency so difficult, particularly since the most highly visible aspects of that role easily disappear within racist configurations of the passive and servile Japanese woman. But beyond this, as Houston's passage suggests, the daughter must recognize the difference between a role and the sense of self, much as her mother "never confused her tasks with who she was" ([1978] 1985, 9)

The way in which the mother "create[s] a psychological privacy," finding inner freedom in the restricted space of Japanese womanhood, echoes the strategies of camp internees finding a space of freedom in the restrictions of barrack life. What Houston's mother teaches her are necessary tools for survival, strategies of masking, in a community and dominant society that constructs restricted spaces for Japanese/American women. After her father's death, Houston realizes that for all his dominance within the family, "she had been the strong one. The structure had been created for him; but it was her essence that had sustained it" ([1978] 1985, 14). It would be easy to read this recognition as nostalgically compensatory, as one that romanticizes women and mothers as the "real" power in the house, when everywhere outside it they are denied freedom and restricted in their access to social forms of power. But such a reading gives short shrift to the dignity with which Houston's mother negotiated the meanings of agency and powerlessness, containment and freedom. Houston herself comes to understand her mother in more complex terms and, in doing so, provides a space for maternal agency and representation.

Fiction written by Japanese American women is striking in its steady use of the trope of the absent mother. While some novels represent the mother as literally absent, others depict the mother as emotionally absent. Still others textually absent the mother. I want to call attention to the absent/ed mother as a trope rather than as a condition because it highlights what at first seems to be a puzzling contradiction at the heart of these fictional narratives: despite her perceived absence, the mother remains a central figure. According to traditional models of female development, maternal absence is at some critical point a necessary element of differentiated identity; that is, maternal absence is itself constitutive of daughterly subjectivity. But these models cannot explain the centrality of the mother except in negative terms, as a dominating presence. As such, the erasure of maternal subjectivity would be the necessary condition and expression of the daughter's agency.

If we move away from models that implicitly privilege the daughter's development, and hence her point of view, and toward one that attends to maternal subjectivity in conjunction with the daughter's own, then it is necessary to look at how the daughter must depend on, not simply individuate from, the mother, as well as how the need to recuperate, not reject, maternal agency and subjectivity is crucial to Japanese American mother-daughter narratives.

Thus, the trope of maternal absence must be understood as the problematic that powers these narratives, one of whose central concerns, then, is how to connect and identify with, as well as how to differentiate from, the mother.[9] The critical challenge is to theorize the mother with purposes that parallel those of the daughter without uncritically replicating the daughter's point of view. Thus, we must "look at the mother *as subject* constituted in a particular relation to social reality, to sexuality, to work and historical experience, to subjectivity" (Hirsch, 165–66).

Because these fictional narratives are almost entirely written from the daughters' point of view, it is all too easy to forget that representations of mothers and maternality are mediated by their narrative authority. That is, the mothers in these works are not, for the most part, literally absent; rather, they are experienced as absent, often because the daughters fail to "read" their mothers or are unable to "see" them as subjects. In the following discussion, I examine the roles of ideal motherhood, maternal sexuality and maternal silence in terms of how each complicates the issues of presence and absence, the difficulties of generational and cultural differences, the seemingly competing discourses of speech and silence, and the ways in which the mother negotiates the simultaneity of raced and gendered identities.

Ideal Motherhood and the Nisei Mother in *The Floating World* and *The Loom*

In *Mothers and Daughters: The Distortion of a Relationship*, Vivien E. Nice writes that the "massive cultural expectations" (226) of mothering and mothers are largely responsible for the perception of failure in many mother-daughter relationships. "The idealisation of mothering," writes Nice, "sets the scene for the demonisation of the mother" (135).[10] But in an environment where racism marginalizes the Japanese American family, as Houston illustrates in *Beyond Manzanar*, a dynamic that leads to outright rending within the family is one likely to be avoided. If mothers are not demonized in Japanese American women's fiction, the figure of the idealized mother nevertheless remains a spectral presence that shapes the mother, the daughter, and the relationship between them. Nice writes that the "search for the ideal mother is also a search for oneself" (152). But where Nice refers here to the daughter's projections onto the mother as an integral part of the search for herself, I want to examine this idea in relation to the mother. That is, the way in which the mother interacts with the construct of the ideal mother provides one angle from which to examine maternal agency and the trope of absence. In the work of the following two authors, resistance to or compliance with this ideal is crucial to the daughter's experience of maternal absence.

I begin my discussion with a novel that seems textually to absent the mother. Cynthia Kadohata's 1989 novel, *The Floating World*, tells the story of a Japanese American family in the 1950s. Narrated from the Sansei daughter's point of view, the novel chronicles the family's constant migrations through the United States and the coming-of-age of Olivia (the daughter). Sau-ling Wong observes that Kadohata's novel participates in the tradition of mobility and dislocation narratives in Asian American literature (120). What is perhaps most interesting about Kadohata's novel is that, as a work that most actively employs the trope of mobility and/or dislocation, it is also one that depicts a mother who clearly and actively resists her traditionally defined role. I do not, however, intend to imply that the family's dislocation and uprootedness are a consequence of the mother's refusal to define herself solely in terms of her maternity. However, I think it is possible to read the family's constant search for a home site as a symbolic parallel to the mother's active search for an identity outside the bounds of the socially defined ideal mother. Significantly, the mother's name is barely mentioned in the entire text and is only introduced as parenthetical information by the daughter: "Eventually, my grandparents . . . moved to Hawaii. (That's where my mother, formerly Mariko, became Laura)" (32).

The family, as Olivia tells us, constantly travels because the father must find work and also because her parents "were dissatisfied with their marriage, and, somehow, moving seemed to give vent to that dissatisfaction" (4). Although the constant packing and unpacking that moving requires is hard on her mother, Olivia notes that the family's life on the road seems to offset their accumulation of material goods and the structured life they imply:

I think she felt both affection and resentment toward our possessions. No matter how hard she tried to stanch the growth of the number of things we owned, we seemed to be accumulating more and more. At times she seemed to feel that soon her life would be ruled and defined by our pink kitchen chairs, the embroidered bedspreads she'd made, the stained kitchen towels. (69)

It soon becomes clear that the dissatisfaction to which Olivia refers is primarily the mother's unhappiness at having been forced to marry Charlie O.—the man Olivia calls father, but who is not her biological father—because she was pregnant. Pushed into the marriage by her mother, Olivia's grandmother, who lives and travels with the family, Mariko nevertheless resists capitulating fully to the role expected of and assigned to her:

My mother read a lot in a community where men rarely—and women never—read books. A couple of times at parties, I watched the women scurry back and forth cleaning up as the men dropped nutshells on the carpet and ashes on the coffee table. When the women went into the kitchen to clean, my mother remained in the living room to talk, and I felt faintly ashamed, and unsure whether I ought to stay in the living room or go into the kitchen. Usually I stayed in the living room, but I didn't really talk to anyone. So I never had to help clean up. (73)

The mother models for Olivia an alternative to the strict gender roles in the Japanese American community. Olivia associates her mother with the discursive—she reads and talks, instead of cooking and cleaning— but her reaction is primarily one of embarrassed ambivalence that her mother does not act like the other women. Olivia's feeling of being "faintly ashamed" merges with one of not knowing what her own role should be. She is too young to understand fully that her mother's gift is to not constrain Olivia in those socially dictated roles. As she admits elsewhere, "Often my mother gave me advice I couldn't yet fathom" (43).

Olivia's narrative generally refrains from identifying her mother with any "traditional" wifely or motherly roles at all. Instead, and in direct contrast to Olivia's grandmother, an almost obnoxiously present personality who talks so incessantly that her grandchildren and daughter tune her out whenever possible, the mother evokes distance and silence. "We always got extra quiet when my mother spoke," says Olivia,

My mother rarely initiated small talk, and usually when she spoke she had something she especially wanted to say. She had an elegant, lush face, and always had about her a slight air of being disoriented, as if she could not quite remember how she came to be wherever she was. I think sometimes people interpreted that disoriented air as aloofness. (7)

In some ways, it is possible to read the mother's disorientation as the desire to retain a sense of self amidst the details of her life that restrict her freedom. The mother, in effect, psychologically absents herself from the family that would otherwise define her. This absence is paralleled in Olivia's narrative, which generally avoids focusing on the mother directly. Instead, Olivia is often associated with her grandmother, at one point commenting that "my life intertwined with my grandmother's" (8). While this might seem to suggest that Olivia identifies with her grandmother because she is more palpably present, even after her death, I argue that the largeness of the grandmother's presence is easier for Olivia to deal with than the distance and dissatisfaction associated with her mother. And if grandmother's and granddaughter's lives intertwine, surely they do so through Olivia's mother.

Indeed, there is much to indicate that Olivia identifies and is identified with Mariko. Both, for instance, have lost their fathers: the mother's through death, Olivia's through her mother's forced marriage to Charlie O. At one point Olivia notes that "my allegiances were shifting to my mother. She was moody, but also graceful and pensive and intellectual, things I wanted to be when I grew up but already knew I would never be" (44–45). This difference between their personalities, however, is an important indicator of the bond between them. The mother's pensive moodiness is a result of her unhappiness; Olivia understands early on that it is this unhappiness her mother wishes her to escape: "Once, my mother started crying suddenly, and I knew it was over something from a long time ago. Nobody said anything, but everyone looked pointedly at me. The looks meant it was my obligation to leave Arkansas someday and have a happier life than my parents had" (114).

What happened "a long time ago," of course, is Mariko's marriage to a man she did not love. At one point, Olivia recalls her mother gesturing toward some opened morning glories and saying, " 'That's the way you'll feel inside the first time a boy you love touches you.' Later we passed the same flowers, closed into tight little twists. 'And that,' she said, 'is how you'll feel inside the first time a boy you don't love touches you' " (43). Sexuality is thus closely associated with the mother's sense of freedom and restriction. Olivia, the child of a man other than her mother's husband, is simultaneously the sign of the mother's emotional freedom and the sign of the end of that freedom. Olivia's very existence is connected to the mother's sexuality and emotional agency.

One night, Olivia hears her mother and Charlie O. making love in one of the hotel rooms where they have stopped. It is not the intimacy of their lovemaking that captures her attention, however, but its despair: "Something about their lovemaking that night, about the sound of it, seemed somehow hopeless. . . . It was not the sex I thought I ought not to have heard but the hopelessness. . . . Walker [Olivia's brother] had probably heard our parents making love. I wished he hadn't. It seemed to me a burden to have heard, and I didn't want him to have that burden" (52–53). The burden is Olivia's understanding that her mother "didn't want anything [Charlie O.] could give her" (57), and from that understanding she takes on the responsibility of somehow redeeming her mother's life. Paradoxically, she can do so only by separating from that life.

The need to separate, however redemptive, would seem to imply that Olivia must separate from her mother in order to come to her own adulthood and, indeed, her narrative appears to pull farther from the mother as it progresses. How then might maternal agency operate here? It is implicit in silence, in absence. That is, Mariko's absence and silence directly contrast with the grandmother's volubility and interfering presence. Instead of replicating the ways in which her own mother, Olivia's grandmother, has shaped her life, a life with which she is dissatisfied and unhappy, Mariko pulls away, leaving Olivia room to define her own life. It is this pulling away that allows Olivia to identify with her mother without reliving her mother's life.

As an adult, Olivia takes over her dead father's vending-machine service route. Olivia's search for the ghost of her biological father, however, is less a search for him than an attempt to rescue her mother's agency and sexuality from the hopelessness and loss with which they are identified. Although the narrative ends after Olivia's encounter with her father's ghost, she comes to terms not with the father, but with Mariko. She recalls that her mother once told her she loved Charlie O., the man Olivia calls her father:

Though she once told me she loved my father, I wasn't really sure. A few months earlier, when my parents had visited Andy and me, she kept staring at us in a funny way. Later, when I asked what made her stare, she said we'd both had the same look on our faces, as if we'd been washed over with the same water. I used to try to picture her with Jack [Olivia's biological father], both of them washed over with the same water. (185)

Beyond simply wanting to place her mother in a happier time, Olivia's need to imagine her mother feeling "washed over with the same water" as her lover, Olivia's biological father, is the need to create a space in which her mother's subjectivity can be identified with her own. Thus, Olivia's encounter with her father's ghost is the moment in which her mother's agency is clearest:

I noticed for the first time that Jack was quite young. . . . I think he met my mother around that time. But perhaps this was still in the future for him, a few months or years away. I hadn't been born yet as he sat there. When my mother fell in love with Jack, she must have realized how young they were and that things wouldn't turn out well. But she didn't care. I liked to think of her then, not caring. (195)

Interestingly, Olivia's search ends not with finding her father or even herself—she actually absents herself at this moment—but with finding her mother. The textual absenting of the mother (an absenting that I believe involves more than the simple exigencies of the plot) is reversed at the end of the novel: the mother's presence emerges at the point where Olivia can imagine her as an active and emotionally free agent.

The Floating World addresses a number of crucial issues: the connection between maternal and filial agency and the ways in which the daughter's identity is intimately related to the mother's sexuality and resistance to social norms. Idealized motherhood functions as a construct that the mother resists and from which she absents herself. In contrast, she is present to her internal and emotional life, and it is this, finally, that allows Olivia the freedom of mobility and departure.

In contrast, two short stories in R. A. Sasaki's *The Loom* (1991) focus on mothers who seem to define themselves completely in terms of the ideal mother, and whose agency goes largely unrecognized by their daughters. The depiction of mothers in these stories reveals how idealizations of mothering affect mothers, as well as how constructions of the mother are imbricated with raced subjectivity.

In "Seattle," a Sansei daughter and her Nisei mother try to relate across generational and cultural differences. The mother, an avid watcher of Japanese family dramas, is "especially fond of the mother-daughter stories" (107) and assails her daughter with each minute detail of the various plots. The daughter, however, tells us she neither enjoys nor understands "the pathos and self-sacrifice" that are the hallmark of the Japanese story line. Differences between mother and daughter are represented by the dissimilarities between Japanese family dramas and American movies, and the contrasting expectations that inform each:

But I am not Japanese. . . . Perhaps I've just seen too many American movies. In American movies getting everything you want constitutes a happy ending. A satisfying Japanese ending, in contrast, has to have an element of sadness. There must be suffering and sacrifice—for these are proof of love. I've always hated stories where everybody sacrifices themselves and nobody ends up happy. It is a compulsion that strikes me as a form of mental illness, and I don't want to hear about it, much less do it. (108)

"Seattle" revolves around one of the daughter's regular visits with her mother, recently widowed. She wants to tell her mother that she is going to Japan to marry a Japanese man who already has children and has not yet divorced his wife. She debates how to break the news, deciding finally on an indirect method, "something gradual but ominous." But before she can get to the purpose of her visit, her mother, perhaps also beginning with something gradual but ominous, asks, "Guess who I ran into the other day?" (109). The mother goes on to say that a couple the family knows, Rhonda and Kenji, are separating. As it turns out, the circumstances are disturbingly similar to those of the daughter and her lover. "Apparently," says the mother, "he has a girlfriend in Seattle, someone he met and used to visit on his business trips. Rhonda found out about it and kicked him out of the house. The kids won't speak to him. . . . The Japanese programs are always like that." The daughter, taken aback, wonders whether her mother is "psychic. Is she being incredibly subtle, indirect, and Japanese—or am I being paranoid? I search her face for a clue." The conversation, or the conversation that doesn't happen, descends into silence: "she is silent; and I can think of nothing to say" (110).

On first impulse, we might read this interaction as evidence of the gulf between mother and daughter, their failure of communication. Yet, in many ways, the story illustrates the ways in which the two communicate in a manner that implies a deep similarity between them. Like the mother, the daughter decides to break her news in a "subtle, indirect, and Japanese" manner. In response, the mother's story about Rhonda and Kenji seems to speak directly to the daughter's situation. The story might hold a pointed purposefulness on the mother's part or the daughter may be reading into the story from a Japanese cultural point of view. Either way, the daughter herself is implicated in the "Japaneseness" of the interaction, suggesting that mother and daughter understand each other far better than the daughter might suppose. The mother's avoidance of speaking directly about her daughter's life and her eventual silence create a space that the daughter is unsure of: within an American context, it could mean nothing. But within a Japanese context, what is unsaid is quite clear to the daughter. Ultimately, it is through the mother's verbal indirection and silence that her daughter feels her influence.

But the daughter/narrator downplays the mother's purposefulness, or initiative agency, by suggesting that she acts within the unreal framework of Japanese dramatics:

Maybe I will tell her my story the next time I come. Or perhaps she will have one to tell me, another mother-daughter tale from the Japanese program. It is always the same story. There are minor variations. Sometimes the mother is very old-fashioned, sometimes modern, even outrageous. But underneath it all she always has the same Japanese heart. Sometimes the daughter marries and leaves, sometimes it's the mother who marries, unexpectedly, or fabricates a fictitious marriage proposal so that the daughter will not feel obligated to stick around. What is always the same is the invisible wires that bind them, the bond of obligation, of suffering, of love—and this is why my mother likes these dramas; because this is the way she would like real life to be. (112)

According to these story lines, the daughter would be expected to renounce her lover and live with her mother. As she says, "From the Japanese standpoint, it was the expected thing to do. A divorced daughter, over thirty—a mother, over sixty, left alone. I wavered" (108). But to the extent that she can dismiss these cultural expectations as dramatic story lines whose values she finds "a compulsion that strikes me as a form of mental illness," she can both ameliorate her own guilt and lessen the impact of her mother's implied wishes by attributing them to the fact that her mother simply watches too much TV, even "in the middle of the afternoon" (107). But the daughter's own American movie-influenced values are equally in play here, though their workings are obscured by her first-person narration. Just as the mother wishes "real life" were more like what is depicted in her Japanese family dramas, so does the daughter implicitly wish real life to follow American movie endings: everyone gets what they want and everyone is happy.

However, the potential conflict between Japanese and American values must be read in the context of the daughter's relationship to a man who is a Japanese national. This relationship contradicts any easy notions that the daughter wishes to reject her mother and the Japanese cultural values she represents. Instead, the daughter's ambivalence about her lover is displaced onto the mother. The fact that her affair seems to conform to the plot lines of the Japanese programs her mother watches brings up the uneasy possibility that she herself is unconsciously or unwillingly playing a role in a cultural script that suits her lover. Because that potential is threatening, the daughter defuses both the mother's agency (expressed here as real concern about her daughter's relationship with a married man) and dismisses the Japanese programs she watches.

Thus, much of this story hinges on the mother's resistance to capitulating to her daughter's happy American endings (which surely involve their own forms of compulsion). In one sense, this is a story about competing "ideal mother" narratives, each informed by differing cultural values and expectations. The daughter implies she would like her mother to be happy about her coming marriage, that she would like to talk about it. "I had wanted to tell my mother" the narrator says twice, seemingly unable to mark their connection in other than verbal terms. But if the mother is unable to participate in a revelatory mother-daughter chat, the daughter is equally unable to fully read her mother's silences. The mother's own image of the ideal mother may be represented in the dramas she watches, in whose structure of value she would be expected to sacrifice her own desire for her daughter to live with her in favor of the daughter marrying and going to Japan. After all, the "moral" of her story about Rhonda and Kenji involves marital fidelity, not filial duty, as the daughter seems to recognize when she responds, "You were lucky, Mom. Daddy wasn't like that." Nowhere does she indirectly hint that her daughter should rightly come to live with her. But the daughter in some sense misinterprets what might be called the mother's silence of renunciation as the silence of unspoken expectations. She assumes that "it is always the same story" (112), that within the script of Japanese culture a mother would expect her daughter to renounce personal happiness for the mother's sake. The daughter, in effect, assumes that the action of renunciation is hers, the passivity of unspoken expectation her mother's. In fact, the mother enacts an unrecognized reversal of the daughter's expectations through her own conception of ideal motherhood.

The pressures of such an ideal and the daughter's attempt to locate maternal subjectivity are most explicit in the title story of Sasaki's collection. "The Loom" is, again, narrated from the daughter's point of view, though in the third person, allowing greater distance between narrator and daughter. The story opens with the accidental death of a sister and the surviving sisters' puzzlement at their mother's reaction:

It was when Cathy died that the other Terasaki sisters began to think that something was wrong with their mother. . . . Sharon had to raise her voice so her mother could hear the awful words, choked out like bits of shattered glass, while Jo watched what seemed like anger pull her mother's face into a solemn frown. (16)

What disturbs the sisters so much is that the mother's initial reaction is one of anger that Cathy hadn't listened when told not to go mountain climbing. "It was as though she didn't feel anything at all," one sister says, "It was as though all she could think about was that Cathy had broken the rules." Their mother, the sisters note, does not cry over her daughter's death until their father, devastated by the news, stands "sobbing his dead daughter's name" (16). Only then does the mother cry, "but it seemed almost vicarious, as if she had needed their father to process the raw stuff of life into personal emotion. Not once since the death had she talked about her own feelings. Not ever, her daughters now realized." The mother's emotional repression, the sense that she is somehow absent from her own life, becomes the focus of the story. The daughters' delayed recognition that their mother had never expressed her own feelings leads them to wonder "just who was this little person, this person who was their mother?" (17). For the first time, the daughters realize that they have no sense of who their mother is outside her role as their mother. They decide that she needs to get away from the house and the wifely/maternal role it represents, but they soon realize that the changes such trips bring are only temporary: "When Jo visited two months later, her mother was once again effaced, a part of the house almost, in her faded blouse and shapeless skirt, joylessly adding too much seasoned salt to the dinner salad" (30).

The use of the word "effaced" here is significant, for "The Loom" is in many ways about the strategies, as well as the potentially high costs, of masking—one of which is that Mrs. Terasaki's daughters have no idea just "who was their mother" (17). The story also represents an attempt to focus on maternal agency from outside the restricted realm of the daughter's subjectivity, and Sasaki's use of a third-person narrator, by turns intimate and distant, allows for a doubled perspective that suggests that the mother's self-effacement and emotional absence is both deliberate and unintentional in its effects.

The narrative diverges from the event of Cathy's death to the mother's childhood and young adulthood, during which she goes from being someone who "met life headlong and with the confidence of a child" (18) to someone who "always acted with caution in new surroundings, blending in like a chameleon for survival" (20). What marks this radical shift is her entry into the "outside world—the *hakujin* world" (21) when she starts school, where she soon learns that her visible racial difference makes her vulnerable. Her solution is to make herself invisible:

She did her best to blend in. Though separated from the others by her features and her native tongue, she tried to be as inconspicuous as possible. . . . If she couldn't be outstanding she at least wanted to be invisible. She succeeded. She muted her colors and blended in. . . . [But] she was not really herself. (20)

It is here that the mother's process of "effacement" begins: she masks her difference, as much as possible, by muting its visible and verbal features. Unable to literally hide the Japanese face that is the target of other children's vicious taunts, she mutes it by "rigorously edit[ing] out Japanese words and mannerisms" (21) in order to blend into white America, and grows up "wearing the two faces of second-generation children born of immigrant parents. The two faces never met; there was no common thread running through both worlds" (17).

However, there are also indications that the mother's retreat to silence and invisibility are not only passive adaptations but also strategies of defense and resistance. She decides "there were two things she would never do again: one was to forget the girl's name who had called her a Jap, and the other was to cry" (20). Vulnerable as a person of color in a racist society, she decides early on to make herself as invulnerable as possible, an action markedly different from simply making oneself unnoticeable.

In the outside world—the *hakujin* world—there was a watchdog at work who rigorously edited out Japanese words and mannerisms when she spoke.

Her words became formal, carefully chosen and somewhat artificial. She never thought they conveyed what she really felt, what she really was, because what she really was was unacceptable. In the realm of behavior, the watchdog was a tyrant. Respectability, as defined by popular novels and Hollywood heroines, must be upheld at all costs. . . . She could admit to no weakness, no peculiarity. (21)

Though the mother's strategy of masking is in many ways similar to those I discuss in relation to Nisei women's autobiographies, there is a marked difference. In her effort to blend in, the mother in this story strictly relegates Japanese identity to the realm of the private and abject: it is a weakness, a peculiarity. Whereas the split self evident in the autobiographies indicates the simultaneous and contradictory pulls of racial disavowal and connection, the mother's split self—the two faces—evidences an almost complete break from all that which does not fit into the normative white model.

This code of behavior is also imposed on her daughters and "as a mother, she was without fault" (28). Here, notions of the ideal American and the ideal mother intersect, suggesting the ways in which discourses of motherhood are always defined along categories of race. The mother's decision to conform to these models is a complex one. On the one hand, it shows her capitulation to normative and ideal standards; on the other, her decision represents the desire to protect both herself and her daughters from reproach or humiliation for failing to behave in accordance with those models. If the search for the ideal mother is also a search for oneself, as Nice asserts, the mother in this story can be seen as trying to find a sense of self within the image of the ideal mother implicitly coded as white, an attempt that necessitates the exclusion of "what she really was." This strategy results in fragmentation, the sense that events become "just another loose thread in the fabric of her life" (30) and that "there was no common thread" (17) binding things together. As a result, she is alienated from her own emotional life and from the emotional lives of her daughters.

For her daughters, the mother's initial inability to cry at the news of Cathy's death and her silence surrounding her feelings about it are unfathomable. But to cry or speak would threaten the interiority she has protected under the carapace of formality and respectability, as well as threaten that which, in her mind, has protected her children. Her resistance to her daughters' efforts "to bring her out" (32) is, in one sense, a refusal to remake herself in their visually and verbally oriented terms. What she cannot express verbally, she ultimately expresses silently through the loom given to her by Sharon, the daughter identified as "not hav[ing] much to say" (30). Weaving becomes both a metaphor for and expression of the mother's life; it allows her a way to bring together "the diverse threads of life into one miraculous, mystical fabric" (35), and the fabric she weaves becomes the means through which she can reveal her self:

One could pick up threads from the warp selectively, so there could be a color on the warp that never appeared in the fabric if it were not picked up and woven into the fabric. With this technique she could show a flash of color, repeat flashes of the color, or never show it at all. The color would still be there, startling the eye when the piece was turned over. The back side would reveal long lengths of a color that simply hadn't been picked up from the warp and didn't appear at all in the right side of the fabric. (33)

Her daughter Jo notices that in the scarf her mother has woven "there's actually red in there . . . and even bits of green. You'd never know it unless you looked real close." To which Sharon replies, "Most people don't" (34–35). These closing passages open the possibility of the daughters seeing beyond the mother's effacement and recognizing "just who . . . this little person, this person who was their mother" (17) might be.

The organizing textile metaphor that runs throughout the story culminates in the scarves and fabrics the mother weaves, presumably suggesting that her former negative self-image as an unacceptably colored thread in "the larger fabric of society" (24) is positively transformed through the creativity, and thus agency, of her loom. The tactile/textile image of weaving links the mother's subjectivity to a nonverbal mode of expression whose possibilities of registering her as a subject mirror the visibility of the flashes and bright swaths beneath the "subdued, muted colors." Metaphorically, the cloth offers an alternative to the daughters' former reading of their mother's emotional absence: beneath the surface, the headlong and confident girl remains, transformed into modes of silence and invisibility that signify her presence. At the close of the story, as one daughter departs for home, her mother stands in the airport crying. Afterwards, the mother sits at her loom, "weaving the diverse threads of life into one miraculous, mystical fabric with timeless care" (35).

In such a reading, the subjectivity of silence and the strategies of protective masking are a subtle critique of the daughters' seemingly American-influenced inability to translate their mother's subjectivity. And yet, the resolution of the story simultaneously subverts, or at least complicates, its own possibilities. The gendered connotations of the loom compound the traditional association of silence with passivity, resulting in a reading in which the mother is relegated to an arena of speechlessness gendered as female—all of which can easily be appropriated within the construction of Japanese American women as passively silent. Further, while her daughters, looking carefully, see the mother's "hidden colors . . . [come] alive in the sunlight," those colors nevertheless remain deeply buried beneath the dull "brown fabric" (34).

These two readings of the mother's cloth are not so much contradictory as they are indicative of the doubleness of the mother's masking strategies. While masking and muting her interiority and the Japanese identity with which it is associated are protective strategies of survival, those very strategies have come at the high cost of emotional absence and repression. In identifying with white America and its constructions of ideal motherhood, the mother is almost completely unknown by the daughters whom she mothered "without fault" (28).

Enculturation and Resistance in Yamamoto's "Yoneko's Earthquake" and "Seventeen Syllables"

The daughter's inability to perceive maternal subjectivity and her resulting perception of the mother's absence are explored in relation to language and sexuality in two stories by Hisaye Yamamoto, "Yoneko's Earthquake" (1951) and "Seventeen Syllables" (1949). In these stories, the importance of the mother as a model of enculturation and resistance to the structures of patriarchy is central to her own agency, as well as fundamental to the necessity of the daughter's identification with her. While the mothers in these stories are not literally absent or experienced as absent, they are symbolically absented by their daughters' inability to fully understand the lessons of their mothers' lives.

This inability undermines the extent to which Japanese American daughters must both differentiate from and identify with their mothers. In an environment structured by racism and sexism, one of the most crucial aspects of "motherwork" is the enculturation of children in modes of survival and resistance. However, that process of modeling and enculturation is not always overt. One of the stories' most interesting formal aspects is that Yamamoto positions the reader from the point of view of the daughters, whose narratives are unreliable and whose perceptions are limited by youth and inexperience. The subtle revelations of the mothers' lives foregrounds the disparity between what the reader comes to understand and what the daughters do not—that the daughters' emotional and psychic survival depend on identifying with the mother and recognizing her as an active and resistant agent within the realm of domesticated sexuality and the culture of patriarchy.

"Yoneko's Earthquake" (1951) relies heavily on the parallel situations of the ten-year-old daughter, Yoneko, and her mother, Mrs. Hosoume. Yamamoto employs Yoneko's limited point of view to tell the mother's story through suggestion, highlighting the disjunction between Yoneko's perception and her mother's reality, and revealing, through Yoneko's unknowing disclosures, the mother's resistance to the ways in which her life is circumscribed.

Yoneko's crush on Marpo, a Filipino farmhand hired by the Hosoumes, hints at the mother's involvement with him. Marpo, as Yoneko describes him, has a "face like brown leather, the thin mustache like Edmund Lowe's, and the rare, breathtaking smile like white gold" (47). Unlike her father, whose struggles for the family's economic survival leave him no energy or interests outside the exigencies of farming and necessity, Marpo is variously ascribed the talents of athlete, artist, singer, musician and radio technician. However, "Marpo's versatility was not revealed . . . in a lump. Yoneko uncovered it fragment by fragment every day, by dint of unabashed questions, explorations among his possessions, and even silent observation, although this last was rare" (49). Yoneko's eventual conversion to Christianity has much less to do with her belief in God than her infatuation with Marpo. Yoneko's growing admiration for Marpo suggests her mother's own attraction to him as she, too, works around him day after day in the field. Mrs. Hosoume spends even more time with Marpo, alone, after an earthquake that disables Mr. Hosoume and reverses the traditional roles of wife and husband:

After the earth subsided . . . , life returned to normal, except that Mr. Hosoume stayed at home most of the time. Sometimes if he had a relatively painless day, he would have supper on the stove when Mrs. Hosoume came in from the fields. Mrs. Hosoume and Marpo did all the field labor now. . . . Marpo did most of the driving, too, and it was now he and Mrs. Hosoume who went into town on the weekly trip for groceries. In fact Marpo became indispensable and both Mr. and Mrs. Hosoume often told each other how grateful they were for Marpo. (51)

The earthquake so terrifies Yoneko that it is thereafter referred to as "Yoneko's earthquake." It completely destabilizes the family's traditional hierarchy. Incapacitated, Mr. Hosoume is identified with the feminized and domestic, Mrs. Hosoume experiences greater autonomy from her husband, and Marpo's increasing importance to and within the family subverts Mr. Hosoume's role as husband. Symbolically, while aftershocks continue to roll the ground, the house is determined to be unstable, and the Hosoumes and Marpo live outside "between the house and the rhubarb patch" (51).

This rupturing of the domestic space, the site of traditionally defined gender roles, familial hierarchy and sexual monogamy, results in Mr. Hosoume's further dislocation from the structure of patriarchal power, which is symbolically indicated by Yoneko's perfunctory rejection of Christianity after her frantic prayers fail to stop the earthquake: "God was either powerless, callous, downright cruel, or nonexistent." Following his injury during the quake, Mr. Hosoume's constant presence in the home is a pathetic parallel to his former dominance within the family as its head and primary provider. Yoneko finds him annoying and complains that he "cramped her style" (51). Yoneko's minor infractions of her father's authority suggest Mrs. Hosoume's own feelings. Not long after the earthquake, she asks Yoneko to keep a secret for her:

Her mother came home breathless from the fields one day and pushed a ring at her, a gold-colored ring with a tiny glasslike stone in it, saying, "Look, Yoneko, I'm going to give you this ring. If your father asks where you got it, say you found it on the street." Yoneko was perplexed but delighted both by the unexpected gift and the chance to have some secret revenge on her father, and she said, certainly, she was willing to comply with her mother's request. Her mother went back to the fields then and Yoneko put the pretty ring on her middle finger, taking up the loose space with a bit of newspaper. (52)

As Stan Yogi observes in his discussion of this story, "These actions not only link mother and daughter in their attraction for the hired hand but signal serious changes in the family. Mrs. Hosoume's adultery is a direct violation of patriarchal dominance, and Yoneko's unknowing compliance and silence about the ring's origin suggest generational rebellion against the patriarchy" (140). The several implicit parallels between Yoneko and her mother culminate in the passing of the ring between them. While the ring, on the most obvious level, symbolizes the relationship between Mrs. Hosoume and Marpo, the matrimonial connotations of the ring and the promise of secrecy more significantly represent the connection between mother and daughter. Yamamoto's use of the metaphor of marriage between Mrs. Hosoume and Yoneko not only implies their bonding against the father's authority but also signifies

Yoneko's initiation into an adult world ordered by marital, religious and social institutions. However, the circumstances under which this initiation takes place—the mother's affair with Marpo—undercut those institutions, represented by her father.

The mother's continuing challenge to the father's authority becomes overt in an argument between them; significantly, the disagreement begins with issues of sexuality and race. Mrs. Hosoume directly contradicts her husband's opinion that Yoneko is too young to wear nail polish and that it makes her "look like a Filipino" (54). Mr. Hosoume's racist comment is clearly a veiled insult to Marpo, and its underlying assumptions of flagrant sexuality—the narration dryly noting that "it was another irrefutable fact among Japanese in general that Filipinos in general were a gaudy lot" (52)—register Mr. Hosoume's feeling of sexual threat. Mrs. Hosoume continues to press her point but remains calm until her husband, angered at being contradicted, calls her "nama-iki, which is a shade more revolting that being merely insolent." When she angrily objects, Mr. Hosoume, in an attempt to reassert his power in front of the children and Marpo, slaps her across the face: "It was the first time he had ever laid hands on her. Mrs. Hosoume was immobile for an instant, but she resumed her ironing as though nothing had happened, although she glanced over at Marpo. . . . 'Hit me again,' said Mrs. Hosoume quietly, as she ironed. 'Hit me all you wish.' " The silent glance between Mrs. Hosoume and Marpo reinforces her open act of defiance, and her enjoinder to her husband indicates a willingness to challenge his place by having Marpo come to her aid (which he does). All the while, Yoneko and her five-year-old brother, Seigo, "stared at their parents, thunderstruck" (53). Although the children are shocked at their father's violence, which is new to them, they are equally taken aback by their mother's defiance.

Shortly following this incident, Marpo suddenly leaves and the family drives into the city "on a weekday afternoon, which was most unusual" (54). Yamamoto reveals the purpose of the trip, to obtain an abortion, through a framing metaphor. Driving to the Japanese hospital, Mr. Hosoume hits a dog but drives on. "Yoneko, wanting suddenly to vomit, looked back and saw the collie lying very still at the side of the road" (54). On their return drive from the hospital, while Mr. Hosoume tells the children to tell "absolutely no one" (54) they had gone into the city during the workweek, "Yoneko looked up and down the stretch of road but the dog was nowhere to be seen" (54).

The sudden death of Seigo moves Mrs. Hosoume to convert formally

to Christianity, paralleling Yoneko's earlier, though much more superficial, conversion. Both daughter and mother's conversions are connected to their relationship to Marpo. The mother believes Seigo's death
is a result of having had an abortion. She tells her daughter, "Never kill
a person, Yoneko, because if you do, God will take from you someone
you love" (56). Yoneko responds by rattling off her reasons for having
rejected God: " 'Oh that . . . I don't believe in that, I don't believe in
God.' And her words tumbling pell-mell over one another, she went on
eagerly to explain a few of her reasons why" (56). Yogi notes that the
mother and Yoneko speak at "cross purposes" (142), illustrating just
"how far apart mother is from daughter" (141). Further, the story ends
with Yoneko's loss of the ring her mother entrusted to her.

While the failure of communication between mother and daughter
seems to indicate a gulf between them, an indication reinforced by the
loss of the ring "somewhere in the flumes along the cantaloupe patch"
(56), there is also much to suggest that the bond represented by the ring,
lost because it was too large for Yoneko's finger, may be reestablished
in the future when she is older. Her continued rejection of God and his
authority suggests that her identification with the mother may help her
to resist acquiescing to patriarchal dominance and its disciplining of
female sexuality.

The parallels that have been drawn throughout the story continue
through the mother's acceptance and Yoneko's rejection of Christianity,
opposed as they might at first seem. Just as Yoneko defines Christianity
in her own terms—God exists depending on whether or not her prayers
for the earthquake to stop are answered—so the mother accepts it in
terms that indicate a residuum of skepticism. The mother's statement to
Yoneko to "never kill a person" indicates her guilt over the abortion but
expresses no regret over her sexual infidelity. The mother's resistance to
the patriarchal authority represented by her husband is thus carried
through in the aftermath of her affair and the abortion of Marpo's child,
significantly modifying any reading that would interpret the mother's
conversion as concessive and wholly conformist. Further, as King-Kok
Cheung observes, Mrs. Hosoume's statement is an "oblique indictment"
of her husband and, while avoiding explicit reference to her husband, it
expresses her view that "her presumably involuntary abortion [is] an act
of killing by her husband" (45).

The persistent, if temporarily weakened, connection between mother
and daughter is significant for two reasons. The mother's rejection of
patriarchal authority provides a model for her daughter who, as a female,

will also be subject to the strict gender hierarchy in Japanese families.[11] Mrs. Hosoume also models survival as a person of Japanese descent in white America. Yamamoto subtly indicates the ways in which race is operative in this story. The family is isolated by their rural livelihood, as evidenced by the drive into the city (which is something of an event in itself, notwithstanding the circumstances of Mrs. Hosoume's pregnancy). But they are also isolated from the larger white society because of racial difference. Yamamoto suggests a segregated existence by specifying that the family's trip is to the Japanese hospital, for instance. When Mr. Hosoume is incapacitated, the family depends on Filipino and Mexican, but not white, labor. As Houston describes in the passage quoted earlier, the racial climate for Japanese Americans was a hostile one and families had to pull together in order to survive. For a Japanese woman in an anti-Asian society, leaving a marriage that represents familial, social and economic stability was rarely an option. Mrs. Hosoume, then, must remain circumscribed within the gendered and racially marked sphere to which she has been relegated; nevertheless, she exercises, if only briefly, both agency and resistance within that sphere. Yoneko's identification with her mother is thus highly crucial to her own survival. The ring that Yoneko loses may be read as both indicating a connection between mother and daughter that has not been destroyed and opening the possibility that Yoneko's life will not replicate her mother's experience.

The mother as the central figure of the daughter's enculturation is also present in an earlier story by Yamamoto. "Seventeen Syllables" (1949) similarly explores maternal subjectivity but specifically connects it to issues of language, silence, and sexuality. Like "Yoneko's Earthquake," "Seventeen Syllables" is narrated through the point of view of the daughter, this time a teenager, Rosie Hayashi. Again, the doubled plots of mother and daughter underscore the parallels between them. Rosie, on the brink of adulthood, undergoes the process of sexual awakening; her mother, throughout the story, becomes more and more focused on writing her haiku. Sexuality and art are closely associated, connected through their relation to language and silence.

From the beginning, Mrs. Hayashi is identified with culture and language, but the opening of the story points to the double function of language as that which allows for expression but is also a barrier to communication:

The first Rosie knew that her mother had taken to writing poems was one evening when she finished one and read it aloud for her daughter's approval.

It was about cats, and Rosie pretended to understand it thoroughly and appreciate it no end, partly because she hesitated to disillusion her mother about the quantity and quality of Japanese she had learned. . . . Even so, her mother must have been skeptical about the depth of Rosie's understanding, because she explained afterwards about the kind of poem she was trying to write. . . . "Yes, yes, I understand. How utterly lovely," Rosie said, and her mother, either satisfied or seeing through the deception and resigned, went back to composing. (8)

The linguistic difference between the Issei mother and Nisei daughter illustrates the cultural and generational differences between them, but Rosie's reaction indicates a fundamental lack of understanding about her mother that goes beyond her dismal proficiency in Japanese. Mrs. Hayashi's writing is not merely a hobby that her daughter cannot appreciate; rather, it is connected to a crucial element of her subjectivity that Rosie perceives as alien to herself. In accordance with the conventions of haiku, Mrs. Hayashi takes a pen name, Ume Hanazono; however, within the context of the story, this pen name represents a separate self undefined by the roles of wife and mother:[12]

So Rosie and her father lived for awhile with two women, her mother and Ume Hanazono. Her mother (Tome Hayashi by name) kept house, cooked, washed, and, along with her husband and the Carrascos, the Mexican family hired for the harvest, did her ample share of picking tomatoes. . . . Ume Hanazono, who came to life after the dinner dishes were done, was an earnest, muttering stranger who often neglected speaking when spoken to and stayed busy at the parlor table as late as midnight scribbling with pencil on scratch paper or carefully copying characters on good paper with her fat, pale green Parker. (9)

Yamamoto's description illustrates the difficulty Issei women faced in their attempt to pursue any identity beyond the constricting boundaries of daily necessity.[13] This passage also, through the character of Mrs. Hayashi/Ume Hanazono, collapses easy distinctions between speech and silence as indicative of agency or its absence, representing both as associated with subjective agency. For instance, while her writing sets the boundaries of a separate self, her silence—the refusal to speak when spoken to—similarly marks those boundaries.

Yamamoto follows this characterization of silence, however, with two images that suggest its darker side. The Hayashis visit some friends, where Mrs. Hayashi happily converses with Mr. Hayano, who shares her enthusiasm for haiku. In contrast, Mrs. Hayano rocks silently in her chair, "motionless and unobtrusive" (10). Rosie notes that "something had been wrong with Mrs. Hayano ever since the birth of her first child.

Rosie would sometimes watch Mrs. Hayano, reputed to have been the belle of her native village, making her way about a room, stooped, slowly shuffling, violently trembling" (9–10). Where Mrs. Hayashi's haiku-writing silence indicates an animate self, Mrs. Hayano's silence suggests that the strictures and demands of domesticity have almost completely effaced her. In fact, the only time Mrs. Hayano speaks, it is in her role as hostess, and she "quaveringly" (10) calls to her oldest daughter to prepare snacks for their guests. Most ominous is the subtle indication that the four lively Hayano girls—Haru (spring), Natsu (summer), Aki (autumn) and Fuyu (winter)—will, like their mother, have their season and fade into silence and depression.

A second image of silence identifies its potential to erupt suddenly out of frustration, foreshadowing later events. Isolated at the end of the couch, Rosie's father leafs through a copy of *Life,* which he periodically holds out to Mrs. Hayano, who rocks silently nearby. His verbal ineptitude, symbolized by the picture magazine he looks through as his wife and Mr. Hayano discuss haiku, is reinforced by his apparent belief that he must shout to Mrs. Hayano, as though she were deaf. An earlier evening at home where he was reduced to playing solitaire while his wife "scribbled" into the night compounds his isolation at the Hayanos. He abruptly and angrily announces that there is work to be done the next morning and forces his wife's departure.

Against this background, Rosie becomes interested in the son of one of the Mexican laborers her family has hired. One day, telling her he has a secret, they meet in the family's packing shed. When he kisses her,

she could find no words to protest; her vocabulary had become distressingly constricted and she thought desperately that all that remained intact now was yes and no and oh, and even these few sounds would not easily out. Thus, kissed by Jesus, Rosie fell for the first time entirely victim to a helplessness delectable beyond speech. But the terrible, beautiful sensation lasted no more than a second, and the reality of Jesus' lips and tongue and teeth and hands made her pull away with such strength that she nearly tumbled. (14)

The connection Yamamoto draws between sexuality and silence carries both positive and negative connotations. The pleasure implicit in Rosie's gasping fragments of speech is in direct contrast to the glibness she displays with her mother and the failure of communication between them. Her physical and emotional connection with Jesus, however, is problematized by the attendant initiation into male/female sexual politics. The ambiguity of Rosie's silence links her both to her mother, or rather to Ume Hanazono, for whom silence signifies subjectivity and to Mrs. Hayano, whose silence indicates the erasure of subjectivity.

Yamamoto capitalizes on this ambiguity in the closing scenes of the story. Mrs. Hayashi submits her poetry to a haiku contest in the Japanese newspaper. At the peak of the tomato harvest, when the tomatoes must be quickly packed before they spoil, a representative of the paper comes to the family's farm to tell Mrs. Hayashi she has won first prize. Speaking "in a more elegant Japanese than [Rosie] was used to," Mr. Kuroda gives Mrs. Hayashi her prize, a beautiful Hiroshige print. Rosie notices that her mother responds in similarly formal Japanese, "falling easily into his style" (16). As in the opening of the story, Yamamoto again employs language to indicate the mother's singularity. Rosie's reaction to the editor's "elegant Japanese" indicates she has heard it infrequently, presumably because her father speaks a common form that marks his lower-class status.

Mrs. Hayashi invites Mr. Kuroda for a cup of tea, leaving the tomatoes. Mr. Hayashi and Rosie continue packing, working "in silence." Suddenly, "her father uttered an incredible noise, exactly like the cork of a bottle popping, and the next Rosie knew, he was stalking angrily toward the house, almost running in fact" (17). Mr. Hayashi chases Mr. Kuroda out of the house, grabs the Hiroshige print, and violently smashes it with an ax and burns it in the bathhouse woodpile. "Having made sure that his act of cremation was irrevocable," he stalks back to continue the tomato packing. Rosie runs into the house, and mother and daughter stand silently watching the fire: "They watched together until there remained only a feeble smoke under the blazing sun. Her mother was very calm" (18). Only months after the "birth" of Ume Hanazono, Mr. Hayashi's "cremation" signals her silencing and death. The mother's reactive retreat to calm and quiet is in marked contrast to the scribbling silence of her poetry writing and indicates her profound despair.

But it is also here that Yamamoto illustrates the darker aspect of language. Without turning away from the window, the mother asks, "Do you know why I married your father?"

It was the most frightening question [Rosie] had ever been called upon to answer. Don't tell me now, she wanted to say, tell me tomorrow, tell me next week, don't tell me today. But she knew she would be told now, that the telling would combine with the other violence of the hot afternoon to level her life, her world to the very ground. (18)

The foreboding hinted at in her father's silences is now present in her mother's words. In contrast to her resigned acceptance that Rosie understands neither her haiku nor the discursive freedom it represents, Mrs. Hayashi proceeds to tell the story of her past in blunt terms: "Her mother, at nineteen, had come to America and married [Rosie's] father as an alternative to suicide" (18). After giving birth to her lover's stillborn child in Japan, a child who would now be seventeen years old, a marriage was hastily arranged with a young man "of simple mind . . . but of kindly heart" (19), who was never told the circumstances under which his future wife had fled Japan. The mother's telling of her sexual past reaches back to and recasts the moment of Rosie's speechlessness when Jesus kisses her. Rosie's experience of sexuality is paralleled with her mother's affair, but Rosie's silence of pleasure is overlaid with the silencing that culminates her mother's experience of sexual agency.

In an attempt to save Rosie from a similar fate, Mrs. Hayashi suddenly kneels on the floor, grasps Rosie's wrists and entreats her never to marry. "Promise, her mother whispered fiercely, promise" (19). Yamamoto's omission of quotation marks conflates the mother's voice with Rosie's narrative, suggesting the simultaneous identification with and erasure of the mother. Cheung observes that at the moment Mrs. Hayashi begs her daughter to avoid the entrapment of marriage, her actions "oddly and ironically correspond to the posture, gesture, and entreaty of an ardent suitor proposing marriage" (41). This scene, in fact, parallels the matrimonial imagery of the ring Mrs. Hosoume passes on to her daughter in "Yoneko's Earthquake." Similarly, both stories depict mothers trying to protect their daughters from the disappointments of their own lives. But Rosie's sexual awakening resists and is already implicated in the narrative of the mother's thwarted desires. Her mother's desperate clutching recalls "the memory of Jesus' hand, how it had touched her and where" and Rosie "silently" calls out his name. Her silent call to Jesus is, in one sense, a desperate call that reminds her of her singularity and the specificity of her own experience. Yet her sexual initiation simultaneously threatens that sense of singularity and points to the potential collapse of distinctions between her life and that of her mother. "Yes, yes, I promise" (19) she finally says, but the promise is as shallow as her espoused understanding of her mother's poetry. Mrs. Hayashi's response foregrounds the failure of language and substitutes a nonverbal gesture that conveys to Rosie what words cannot:

Her mother, hearing the familiar glib agreement, released her. Oh, you, you, you, her eyes and twisted mouth said, you fool. Rosie, covering her face, began at last to cry, and the embrace and consoling hand came much later than she expected. (19)

Cheung and Yogi read the mother's reaction of delayed maternal comforting as her "unspoken reprimand" that Rosie "is now expected to face life's muddles (Cheung, 42), thus initiating her "into the excitement, pain and disillusionment of adult life" (Yogi, 146). However, it also the moment at which Rosie, paradoxically, is most identified with Ume Hanazono. The silence that formerly indicated the mother's subjectivity and autonomy from the family now characterizes Rosie's resistance to her mother. Like her mother's poetic silences, which are signifying, not absent, silences, Rosie's silence here is completely readable: this is the one point in the story where mother and daughter seem to understand each other clearly.

Rosie is also linked to her mother's poetic subjectivity in another, more disturbing, way. Both Cheung and Zenobia Baxter Mistri note that "in Japanese, the name *Ume* stands for an exquisite flowering tree which blossoms early in spring and bears fruit by the end of spring — that is, in three months" (Mistri, 198; quoted in Cheung, 36). The life of the poet spans three months, as the narrative itself tells us (9), suggesting a brief seasonal flowering. This links Ume Hanazono to the four Hayano daughters, whose names portend the brevity of their vitality before growing into the restricted space occupied by their mother. Rosie's own floral-inspired name carries connotations of cultivation and domesticity and suggests the potential fragility of the sexual agency she is only just discovering — an agency linked in an ambiguous relationship to female silence.

Further, Rosie's moment of confusion when she calls out to Jesus, "not certain whether she was invoking the help of the son of the Carrascos or of God" (19), contrasts starkly with Yoneko's rejection of God and, by association, her father's patriarchal authority. Thus, the mother's response is one of bitter and frustrated disappointment, the words that issue from her "twisted mouth" a terrible parody of the poetry she speaks aloud at the beginning of the story. Paralleling her earlier dismissal of her mother's haiku, Rosie, unable to bear the weight of her mother's experience, absents her mother, an action that finds its corollary in the delayed act of maternal consolation.

"I want more": Disappointment and Anger in Wakako Yamauchi's *Songs My Mother Taught Me*

If the two mothers in Yamamoto's stories are examples of what Sau-ling Wong would identify as "extravagance," the mothers in Wakako Yamauchi's stories and plays are largely defined by "necessity." The daughter's desire for a life different from that of her mother often parallels the mother's desire for a life of dreams, art, sexuality and creative freedom. However, because the mother either identifies with wanting something more and lives in disappointment or represses that desire and lives in the realm of the practical, their daughters experience them as absent to their needs for a figure of the imagination.

In the title story of Yamauchi's collection, *Songs My Mother Taught Me: Stories, Plays, and Memoir* (1994), the song the daughter, Sachiko, learns is one of isolated longing. Cut off from the emotional imagination, the sentiments of the song turn out to have devastating consequences for both mother and daughter. Hatsue Kato, the mother of three children, is initially presented as a woman for whom the imagination and art provide an escape from the rigors of the family's farm life. "Often," the daughter/narrator observes, "I found her sitting at the kitchen table writing, nibbling at the stub of a pencil, and looking past the window. It was also true that she played the Victrola, usually the same record over and over" (34). The daughter also notes that these occupations mark an emotional shift in the household: the mother seems depressed and joins the family's trips less and less often. When a handsome Japanese man is hired on as temporary labor, the change in the mother's spirits is evident: "He was the affirmation of my mother's Japan—the haunting flutes, the cherry blossoms, the poetry, the fatalism. My mother changed when he was around. Her smile was softer, her voice more gentle" (35). The man moves on after harvest, and the mother, already the mother of three, finds herself pregnant. Depressed throughout her pregnancy, after the baby's birth "she grew despondent from this perpetual drain on her body and her emotions, and slipped farther and farther from us, often staring vacantly into space." Nevertheless, Sachiko loves the baby who so pains her mother, giving him the maternal love that the mother herself cannot. She also attempts to compensate for the mother's depression with prayers to the Buddha, through an imaginative ritual that is an uninformed blend of "eastern deity" and "western methods" (37).

The mother slips farther into her depression, at one point laying the blade of a hatchet on the baby's forehead while the daughter watches, horrified. The mother pulls her daughter to her, sobbing, "I didn't want this baby—I didn't want this baby . . ." (38; ellipsis in original). The baby's later death, by drowning in a tub of water in which he was playing, is determined to be accidental; however, the narrative leaves open the strong possibility that it was not a moment's inattention but a deliberate act by the mother that caused the death. What Sachiko learns, then, is the high price of imaginative longing and an emotional life. The saddest aspect of the story, finally, is the daughter's concluding thought "that if my tears would stop, I would never cry again. And it was a long time before I could believe in God again" (40). While the retrospective aspect of the narration implies that Sachiko's faith eventually does return, it is clear that she is marked by the experience: she closes down emotionally and turns from the faith that represents the spiritual and imaginative life.

The conflict between the practical and the imaginative is also present in what is Yamauchi's best-known piece, *And the Soul Shall Dance* (1976), a play developed from a short story of the same title.[14] Because the play represents a fuller realization of mother-daughter thematics implied in the story, the following discussion focuses on the former. The play concerns the Murata family, whose eleven-year-old daughter, Masako, eventually befriends the second wife of a family friend, Mr. Oka. The unfolding events are largely the culmination of past history, brought into play by the arrival from Japan of Oka's daughter, fifteen-year-old Kiyoko, from his first marriage to the present Mrs. Oka's sister. Technically the girl's aunt but expected to act as her mother, Emiko Oka longs for her life of art and culture in Japan, bitterly resenting her life in the United States and the man she was forced to marry. For the purposes of this discussion, I want to focus on the two daughters, Masako and Kiyoko, who represent contrasting needs in relation to their mothers.

From the beginning, Masako is fascinated by the figure of Emiko Oka, who refuses to conform to the expectations of proper Japanese womanhood, much to the disapproval of Masako's mother, Hana. Mrs. Oka not only neglects social niceties but is clearly more interested in music, dance and the life of the soul, all of which she identifies with Japan. She is drawn to Masako and explains that the song "And the soul shall dance" is about longing and retaining dreams. Later, in a violent argument with her husband, Emiko says, "I must keep the dream alive. The dream is all I live for. I am only in exile now. If I give in, all I've lived before will mean nothing . . . will be for nothing. Nothing. If I let you make me believe this is all there is to my life, the dream would die. I would die" (180). This most clearly contrasts her with Masako's mother, who tells her daughter, "Sometimes the dreaming makes the living harder. Better to keep your head out of the clouds," to which Masako replies, "That's not much fun" (182).

Masako, identified early on as one who has a passion for reading, is clearly drawn to Mrs. Oka's intense emotional presence. In one scene, Masako and Mrs. Oka are talking about romance while Hana intermittently calls for her daughter. "You'll fall in love one day," Mrs. Oka says,

Someone will make the inside of you light up and you'll know you're in love. Your life will change . . . grow beautiful. It's good, Masa-chan. And this feeling you'll remember the rest of your life . . . will come back to you . . . haunt you . . . keep you alive . . . five, ten years . . . no matter what happens. Keep you alive. (187; ellipses in original)

This scene perfectly encapsulates the choice that lies before the young girl. Masako sits with Mrs. Oka outdoors in the evening, when day and night are inseparable, captivated by this example of extravagant longing and artistic sensibility. Meanwhile, from within that paradigm of domestic spaces, the kitchen, the mother calls for her daughter to come inside and be properly sociable.

Perhaps the greatest strength of this play is that it does not relegate Masako's mother to a dry realism so unattractive that there is no real conflict for the daughter. For while Mrs. Oka represents an emotional life that is almost palpably present, Hana is not without her own emotional life. She, too, misses Japan and her life there. But unlike Mrs. Oka, whose constant longing for Japan makes it both present and all the more absent for her, Hana carefully manages her emotions—not to ignore them, but to preserve them. When Masako asks about Japan, her mother answers, "I didn't want to hear that sound too often . . . get too used to it. Sometimes you hear something too often, after a while you don't hear it anymore. I didn't want that to happen. The same thing happens to feelings too, I guess. After a while, you don't feel anymore. You're too young to understand that yet." This passage is significant because it suggests a different kind of emotional economy from the one that attracts young Masako. Though she replies, "I understand, Mama"

(203), Hana is right in her perception that she cannot fully understand what her mother is telling her.

For the fifteen-year-old Kiyoko, however, the experience of her aunt's emotional life is one of violence and neglect. Her vague childhood recollections of Mrs. Oka in Japan are characterized by her primary memory that "she was gone most of the time" (186). Now, several years later in the United States, Mrs. Oka's disappointment in her life has contributed to domestic havoc: Kiyoko flees the house in an attempt to escape the escalating violence between husband and wife and runs to Hana for comfort. In comparison to the emotional chaos of Kiyoko's home, Hana's matter-of-factness and practical mothering are precisely what the girl needs. Though Hana admits that "sometimes the longing for home . . . fills me with despair," she counsels, "you can make the best of it here, Kiyoko-san. And take care of yourself. You owe that to yourself. Eat. Keep well. It'll be better, you'll see. And sometimes it'll seem worse. But you'll survive. We do, you know" (193).

Just what survives is the central question in this play. Unable to find a way to return home, deeply unhappy with her husband and the drudgeries of rural life, Mrs. Oka dances into the waste of the surrounding desert as the play ends. It is night, and as she dances off singing fragments of "And the soul shall dance," Masako watches her. In the final scene, Masako picks up the branch of sage dropped by Mrs. Oka. Rich with ambiguity, the ending may be read as either a scene of renunciation—Masako does nothing to stop Mrs. Oka out of some knowledge that she must release her—or one of inheritance, as the sage branch passes from Mrs. Oka to Masako.

The play refrains from making any final evaluations of either woman, instead presenting two very different possibilities of female resistance: resistance as physical and emotional survival or resistance as the refusal to compromise the life of the imagination. Masako emerges as the primary figure: she must negotiate between the possibilities of a relatively absent imaginative life, represented by her mother, and a life that leads eventually to one's total erasure, represented by Mrs. Oka.

These choices are even more sharply drawn in a later play, *The Music Lessons* (1980), also developed from a short story.[15] Many of the thematics of *And the Soul Shall Dance* may also be found in this play, with one significant difference: here the figure of the imagination is male, not female. The mother, Chizuko Sakata, and her fifteen-year-old daughter, Aki, are both attracted to him; thus, the differences between them—the mother once again identified with the exigencies of practical life, the daughter with the desire for a different kind of life—are inflected through issues of sexuality.

Chizuko, at thirty-eight years of age, is a widow with three teenage children, two of them boys. She is described as "gaunt and capable looking, hair bunned back, wearing her dead husband's shirt, pants, heavy shoes, and hat" (54). She has been, in a sense, de-gendered by a life of hard labor, poverty and worry, a fact of which she is not unaware. At one point, she tells Kaoru, the man she hires as temporary help, that she "never thought my life would be so hard. I don't know what it is to be a . . . woman anymore . . . to laugh . . . to be soft . . . to talk nice" (74; ellipses in original). However, she realizes, with some regret, that such forms of womanliness must compete with the reality of raising her children to survive: "I hear myself: 'Don't do this; don't do that. Wear your sweater; study hard. . . . ' I try to say other things: 'How smart you are; how pretty you look . . . ' but my mouth won't let me. I keep thinking, life is hard. I shouldn't let them think it would be easy." Kaoru replies by noting that "The important thing is, you're here. It's no good without a mother" (74).

From the family's reaction to the artistic Kaoru, it is clear that in her struggle to make a living Chizuko's mothering has lacked the soul-nurturing elements of art and the imagination. Kaoru is identified with music—he plays the violin—and poetry, but also with sexual vitality, suggested by his trips into town when he gets paid. Returning from one such trip, he buys some magazines and candy for the boys, and a book of Elizabeth Barrett Browning's sonnets for the daughter, Aki. Soon after, he offers to teach Aki to play the violin. But it is his gift of a pretty scarf to Chizuko that most clearly evokes the sexuality that will eventually become a source of tension between the mother and daughter. The scarf, originally bought for another woman, presumably a past lover, symbolizes the kind of impractical, decorative prettiness that Chizuko's life has denied her. Her offer, not long after, for Kaoru to stay as a partner in the farm is something akin to an awkward proposal characterized more by the practical than by the romantic.

The conflict Chizuko feels, pulled between the struggle for survival that de-genders her and the desire for engenderment and beauty, is externalized in her culminating conflict with Aki. At fifteen, Aki is just entering young womanhood, and she is very sure that her mother is no model for what womanhood might or should mean. "You're going to drive Kaoru-san away from here—bossing him around like that," she tells her mother, "Nobody likes that. Especially a man like him" (85).

As Aki's violin lessons continue, it becomes clear that she doesn't so much want to learn to play well as "to hear it and feel the romance and mystery of that other world out there. I want to be part of it" (82). Because of the close association between "the romance and mystery" and Kaoru himself, Aki, predictably, falls in love with him. Chizuko's growing concern that her daughter is spending too much time alone with a man so much older results both from her concern for Aki and from her own unacknowledged feelings for Kaoru. Aki reads her mother's concern as a characteristic resistance to imagination and emotion, accusing her of having no emotions and living in a fear that leaves her emotionally dead: "I'm not going to live like you. I'm not going to live all tied up in knots like you: afraid of what people say, afraid of spending money, afraid of laughing. . . . Afraid you're going to love someone" (86). Chizuko defends herself by pointing out that she has had to live a life of worry in order to support her family. Significantly, it is after pointing this out that she voices her own feelings of maternal concern most clearly and revealingly:

Chizuko: I don't want you to get hurt, Aki.
  Aki: It's *my* life!
Chizuko: Your life is my life. We're one.
  Aki: No! We're not! We're not the same!
Chizuko: I mean when you hurt, I hurt.
  Aki: That's not true. I hurt when I see how you live: dead! Nothing to look forward to. You think that's good. You want me to live like that. Well, I won't. I want more.
Chizuko: You will have more. Things are not like they were for me. You're young. You have lots to look forward to. (87)

Chizuko's slip, "Your life is my life. We're one," is telling, not because it suggests that she wants to lock Aki into the life she has led, but because it reveals the extent of the similarity between them: Chizuko, like Aki, desires "that other world out there" (82). She too wants more, both for herself and for her daughter. Aki, however, dismisses her mother's concern, accusing her of jealousy.

Terrified that her life will replicate her mother's, Aki is unable to recognize the extent to which her own and her mother's emotional desires overlap, instead literalizing that overlap as competitiveness over Kaoru. One evening, after Aki has put the violin away, she embraces him: "Aki will not let him go. His vision blurs; he sees Aki's innocent longing and responds to her embrace. They kiss and hold for a long moment before Kaoru puts her down on the cot. The embrace grows sensual" (90: stage directions). Chizuko, suspicious at the long silence, enters Kaoru's cabin and sees him with Aki. She kicks him out, furious that he has betrayed her trust. Although an argument could be made that Chizuko reacts out of her own thwarted desire for Kaoru, her response problematically tends to reinforce the notion that a break from the mother is necessary in order for Aki to move forward into womanhood. Moreover, Chizuko's anger is directed at Kaoru for taking advantage of her trust, not at Aki for competing sexually with her.

In fact, such a reading does not fit Aki's own actions. Misunderstanding her mother's motivations and shouting angrily that "I don't want to stick around to be the kind of woman you are" (92), Aki prepares to leave with Kaoru, who is clearly uncomfortable with such a prospect. In the end, he tells her he can't take her with him and, as gently as possible, disabuses her of the notion that what has passed between them is love. The play ends as Kaoru hitches a ride to "another town, another job" (96), and quite possibly another woman. Aki retreats to the bedroom of her mother's house.

The failure here is not the failure of the imaginative life, nor is it a failure of the mother's love. Rather, the play suggests the extent to which the daughter fails to see the mother's subjectivity as anything but stunted, and thus to recognize what her mother knows: that Aki's inexperience and longing for a different kind of life would in fact have led her into precisely the kind of life her mother has led.

Like *The Music Lessons,* "So What; Who Cares?" focuses on the daughter's mistaken assumption that her mother lacks interiority. Strikingly, the story is narrated from the mother's point of view as an internal monologue that is in ironic counterpoint to her complete outward silence. The absence of speech causes the daughter to assume her mother is just barely a sentient being, as though she isn't present in any significant way. "She thinks," narrates the mother, who has been slightly disabled by a stroke, "because I don't talk, I can't hear," but in fact "not much gets past me." What doesn't get past her is that her grown daughter's impatient visits to leave dinners for the week or administer a bath are perfunctory and resentful, punctuated with alternating "coos" and "harsh words" (231).

Much of the story is taken up with the mother's retrospective musings, which obliquely suggest why the daughter seems to do things more out of duty than love. Through the course of the narration, we learn that the mother married fairly young, had her daughter, was sent into internment and was widowed shortly after her husband volunteered for the armed services. After her husband's death, her mother dies in camp, her beloved younger sister and father die, her in-laws repatriate to Japan "and it was just the baby and me." Her next statement is revealing: "Sometimes in my dreams it all comes back with a suffocating longing. Then I wake up and see it's just another day" (233). Again, hardship and heartbreak cause a mother to tamp down her grief in order to survive and raise her daughter. The difficulties of making a living render impossible the kind of ideal mothering both mother and daughter might have wished for. The daughter grows up into a kind of independence that suggests she has learned from her mother how to survive with few others on whom to depend: "She grew up fast, learning to start dinner, learning to mend and sew her own clothes. She was proud of her competence." Now that competence provides the primary avenue of relationship between the daughter and mother. The emotional repression necessary to survive those years is now evident in the daughter, whom the mother regards with regret: "It seems so sad to me now. I want to grab her and say, 'I couldn't help it, Baby, forgive me.' But she wouldn't like that. She hates tears. She won't let herself cry, and she won't forgive anyone who does" (234). The extent to which the daughter has distanced her mother is emblematized by the separate rooms from which she shouts during much of the visit, as well as by her rigorous maintenance of separate spaces: the mother lives alone and the daughter "never invites" her to visit the grandchildren (231).

Paralleling the strained relationship between the mother and daughter is a memory that is slowly revealed through a series of fragmented memories whose narrative associates the mother's interiority with sexuality. During the internment, the mother had or almost had or might have had, a sexual relationship with the one man who saw her as other than "a widow with a baby" (232), whose eyes "looked through you, past your fluttering heart, and all the way down to you-know-where." The rapid reversals and revisions that mark the emergence of this memory make what actually happened difficult to ascertain, even for the mother herself: "I've told myself so many variations of the story, I can't separate fact from fiction anymore." The fact that she has "clung to this memory through four decades" indicates that its importance lies less in what actually did or did not happen than in its function as a site of imagination and subjectivity. It is an element of her interior life and sexual embodiment to which she returns, "embellishing it, stripping it to its bone, and putting on the flesh again" (233).

Significantly, this memory emerges again when the mother, under her daughter's direction, is in the bathtub, denied even the agency of deciding the temperature of the water ("Not too hot," the daughter calls from the kitchen, "I don't want you to faint in there"), or whether to forgo the usual capfuls of Mr. Bubbles (which "prevent a ring" that the daughter must clean) (235). She returns to the moment of decision that has reverberated throughout her life:

I should have done it the night he came over. The baby cried and he held her and began to sing. He drew me close (what a leaping in my heart), and we put her to bed. He said, "Let's go to bed too."
   "I can't," I said.
   "Why?" he asked.
   "I don't know."
   "Don't you want me to?" He ended the sentence with a preposition.
   "No," I lied.
   "Well, then, we won't." He put his hands up. "Good-bye," he said and left.
   No, he didn't. He stayed and kissed me and we made love and it was the most wonderful. . . . "Wonderful, wonderful," is that the only word I know? He said good-bye and left. (235)

The mother's attention to grammar, her critique of her own narration, and the vague adjective "wonderful" are the clearest indications that nothing happened after all. However, these details also suggest a narrative agency that provides a contrasting parallel to her earlier exercise of negative narrative agency—lying about her own desire at a moment when either honesty or silence might have led to an outcome that might, the mother feels, "have changed my life" (236). Language has fraught associations, running the gamut from creativity to deception. This sense of language is reflected in what she misses most about not seeing her young grandchildren, whose "silly chatter" is unburdened by facticity because "they live in a storybook world now. . . . [But] soon their words will grow too clever, their eyes will change" as they move into the adult realm "of reality" (232).

Storytelling and narrative are thus associated with a discursive freedom that contrasts sharply with the mother's present situation in the bathtub. A significant detail, however, indicates that this memory is not only a recalled moment of sexual being. The memory is linked to the internment years, about which the mother says very little except that they were "awful . . . the price of being a Japanese in America" (232). Her focus on the almost-affair instead of on the humiliations and restricted agency of camp life evidences not so much denial as a way of

recasting those years into a single moment when choice, though ultimately exercised to the mother's regret, was possible. That memory signals a moment of agency in a place otherwise intended to deny agency;
similarly, that moment's continual narrativization and renarrativization—
the story the mother tells herself about it—signals an inner freedom
unrestricted by the narrow facts of what "really" happened and the subjectivity ignored by her daughter. Silence becomes a way to protect that
interiority.

Indeed, that the mother's silence is chosen and not simply the result
of her stroke is soon evident. The daughter comes into the bathroom,
complaining at her mother's silence and the difficulty of communicating
with her. Meanwhile, the mother, held in the intensity of regret, berates
herself, "I should have done it. . . . I should have. I should have." Finally, she resolves that the whole thing is "something to remember." It
is at this moment of acceding to the facticity of what did, or did not,
take place that the mother inadvertently speaks out loud, "At least it's
something to . . . ," but trails off before finishing with "remember." The
daughter is completely stunned, " 'You can talk!' she screams." "So
what?" her mother replies, "What's the use of talking? There's nothing
to say anymore" (236).

The piece ends on an ambiguous note: the daughter who does not
cry dashes around, heaving "great humps of dry tears" and preparing to
bring her mother to her house. Her sudden willingness to bring her
mother into her life, however, does not necessarily signal a future of
mother-daughter intimacy, for the daughter's actions are precipitated by
the mother's burst of speech and it seems likely that the mother will
again lapse into silence because "there's nothing anyone wants to hear
anymore" (236). The daughter "wipes her eyes with the sleeve" of the
shirt she has gotten for her mother, which both symbolizes the tenuous
connection between them and gestures forward to the daughter's continued insistence on directing the details of her mother's life on her own
terms.

The daughter's focus on the particulars of her life and situation, notwithstanding what may be a genuine concern for her mother's well-
being, neatly metaphorizes the pervasive critical and psychoanalytic approach to the maternal in relation to daughterhood. The daughter
mistakes practical independence for emotional growth (hence, her reaction to the mother's slight disablement is to treat her like a child),
associates maternal silence with absence ("she thinks because I don't talk,
I can't hear"), does not recognize or is impatient with the mother's

modes of agency (although the mother can feed herself, "I'm slow and she . . . sometimes tak[es] the fork from me") and, finally, gestures toward reconciliation when the mother acts in accordance with the daughter's desires.

Paradigmatic acts of maternal erasure by the daughter, here and throughout this chapter, are enacted in the mistaken belief that separation from the mother is the necessary condition for the daughter's subjectivity to individuate. But such assumptions preclude the recognition of the mother as a model for actively negotiating structures of race and gender that are neither inert nor neutral for the female children of women of color. The extent to which the mother is a key figure in her daughter's survival and development is most fully realized in Joy Kogawa's novel *Obasan,* which structurally revolves around the trope of the absent mother. This novel, perhaps more than any other in the body of Asian American literature, suggests the failures of any critical or theoretical method that implicitly or otherwise assumes the daughter's point of view.

Obasan: Reconstructing Maternal Semiotics and Absence

Kogawa's poetic novel focuses on the character of Naomi Nakane, a thirty-six-year-old woman profoundly wounded by the absence of her mother, whose disappearance is associated with the Japanese Canadian relocation and Naomi's childhood sexual molestation by a neighbor. At the time the novel opens, Naomi is emotionally repressed, disconnected from her own body and unable to move forward in her life. When her uncle dies, Naomi returns to her aunt, Obasan, who raised her after her mother's departure to Japan, a trip from which she never returned. Obasan, holding fast to the promise of silence she made to Naomi's mother, has never told Naomi the story of the mother's disfigurement from the atomic blast at Nagasaki and her subsequent death. Naomi knows nothing of her mother's fate, only that its withholding has always been shrouded in the phrase *kodomo no tame ni,* "for the sake of the children." Kogawa parallels Naomi's process of healing with her developing understanding of the silences that have shaped her life and with the recovery of her mother's presence.

Since its publication in 1981, *Obasan* has been the focus of considerable commentary, much of it directed to the thematics of speech and silence that clearly run throughout it.[16] Ironically, in response to a narrative that seeks to critique and reconstruct the configural opposition of speech and silence, many reviewers and critics have read the novel in terms that reinscribe that opposition and uncritically privilege speech as the vehicle and indicator of subjectivity. King-Kok Cheung persuasively argues against such interpretive frameworks, noting that they ignore Eurocentric assumptions about the role of language and fail to recognize the full force of Kogawa's narrative and the ways in which it subverts any easy distinctions between speech and silence.[17] Cheung astutely observes that *Obasan* "shows a mixed attitude toward both language and silence and reevaluates both in ways that undermine logocentrism" (128). Gayle K. Fujita, in an early and often-cited reading of the novel, writes that its "essence . . . is Naomi's nonverbal mode of apprehension summarized by the term 'attendance.' This sensibility, rooted in Naomi's *nikkei* inheritance and her before-the-war Vancouver home, is therefore not simply the novel's stylistic achievement but a form of Japanese Canadian and American culture" (34).

Kogawa's use of silence as a mode of signification has been well argued by Cheung and Fujita. I want to extend their analyses to look more specifically at the trope of maternal absence in relation to the way in which locating subjectivity from the mother's point of view is crucial for both Naomi and the reader. The connection between silence and absence in the novel suggests that not only must silence be understood as a mode of agency, but that absence also must be recuperated as a site of subjectivity. The failure to do either relegates the maternal to passivity and erasure. In her essay, "Not You/Like You," Trinh Minh-ha reveals the psychoanalytic underpinnings of such associations:

Silence can only be subversive when it frees itself from the male-defined context of absence, lack and fear as feminine territories. On the one hand, we face the danger of inscribing femininity as absence, as lack and as blank in rejecting the importance of the act of enunciation. On the other hand, we understand the necessity to place women on the side of negativity and to work in undertones, for example, in our attempts at undermining patriarchal systems of values. Silence is so commonly set in opposition with speech. Silence as a will not to say or a will to unsay and as a language of its own has barely been explored. (1990, 372–73)

The problematic Trinh lays out is particularly evident in relation to Kogawa's novel, in which silence, absence and the maternal are inextricably linked. The mistake is not in the alignment of these elements, but rather in ways they are read in accordance with the uncritical privileging of speech and/as presence.

Such privilege is the implicit underpinning of psychoanalytic, psycholinguistic readings of *Obasan,* which tend to argue that Naomi's journey enacts the crisis of maternal separation that marks entry into language. A. Lynne Magnusson, for instance, writes that "the crisis of separation from the mother's body coincides with entry into the symbolic order of language [that] presupposes the absence of the object it signifies. Hence to enter into a world of relationships mediated by language is to enter into a world of endless yearning" (61). This reading seems to predicate any entry into signification on separation from the maternal, however regrettable; it closely resembles arguments that the daughter's development depends on individuating from the mother. Indeed, Eleanor Ty goes so far as to demonize the mothers in *Obasan* and Jamaica Kincaid's *Lucy,* citing Adrienne Rich's observance of the daughter's "wish to be purged 'of our mothers' bondage,'" the result of which is "guilt, self-hatred, and sexual anxiety." These "paradoxically are the very bases of [the daughters'] selves and identity" (120).

The separation from the mother that informs these arguments correlates with a second critical stance whose primary assertion is that Naomi "progresses" to speech. Donald C. Goellnicht argues that Naomi eventually learns to negotiate between the preoedipal language of the "mother tongue/culture" and the "figurative language of the new 'father land'" (124):

Once the daughter has negotiated a successful balance within this play of differences, her liability becomes an asset, that of being able to juggle the positions of a multiple, shifting identity, and to utilize a multiplicity of discourses so as to critique the Law of patriarchy and the totalizing voice of dominant history. Paradoxically, but significantly, Naomi discovers this empowered voice for the breaking of silence in the very "amniotic deep" of prefigurative, literal mother-child communication. (128)

In what is otherwise a subtle and insightful reading, this final critical dependence on an apparent paradox suggests a critical structure that retains the binarisms of mother/father, silence/speech, absence/presence from which such paradoxes arise. Similarly, Shirley Geok-lin Lim reads Naomi's emotional journey as evidencing the "eruption of the semiotic into the symbolic, in Kristeva's terms" and her passage "through the stages of muteness or aphasia (Obasan's character), logocentric documentation ([Naomi's Aunt] Emily's character), and a speaking voice (the narrator's poetic voice)" (1990, 307, 309).

The Kristevan notion of the semiotic poses a particularly acute problem here because on the one hand, by reversing the order of value that traditionally denigrates the maternal, it opens the possibility for a reevaluation of the maternal. On the other hand, however, that reverse occurs through valorizing and privileging the relation of the maternal to biology, nature and (nonsignifying) silence.[18] Reversal alone as Jacqueline Rose comments, does not disrupt or subvert the identification of the maternal as the "primitive semiotic" and "the hidden underside of culture" (154). Further, Rose asks, "What does it mean . . . to place the mother at the source and fading-point of all subjectivity and language — a point which, as Kristeva herself has argued, threatens the subject with collapse?" (155–56).[19] A simple reversal that privileges silence without fundamentally redefining it or realigning the terms with which it is associated would necessarily lead to the critical absurdity of claiming that maternal absence is to be read positively as itself evidence of a nonphallic linguistic economy. However, *Obasan* clearly illustrates the deep wounding Naomi has suffered because of the loss of her mother, so any reading that would seek to valorize absence defined as lack is highly problematic and counterintuitive.

Psychoanalytic and Kristevan articulations of the maternal may initially help explicate the thematics of silence in Kogawa's novel, but because they posit the mother as "a continuous separation, a division of the very flesh . . . [a]nd consequently a division of language" (Kristeva [1976] 1987, 254), they read Naomi's recovery of her mother as indicating either a regressive return to the preverbal or as evidencing the "eruption" of the maternal semiotic into the symbolic, thus giving rise to a maternal language that cannot fundamentally challenge existing structures of representation and precluding the possibility that the reestablishment of connection to the maternal includes discursive agency.[20] For Hirsch, this framework depends on the mother as speechless other:

Since the phallus (as lack) is the tool of representation, and since the mother does not have it (in Lacan's terms, women lack lack), any other articulation of her own becomes an impossibility. The child, coming to language, becomes subject to the name-of-the-father, accepting the exigencies of symbolizing desire in language and thereby transcending the mother's silence. The mother herself remains absent even to herself. The place she inhabits is vacant. Although she produces and upholds the subject, she herself remains the matrix, the other, the origin. (168)

For Eleanor Ty, "this sense of 'otherness,' being so closely related to the maternal, often manifests itself as a mythic conflict and struggle with

[the] real or bodily" mother (126), which reinscribes the mother's total difference from the daughter's subjectivity and implicitly suggests a hostility that identifies such a reading with generational-conflict schemas.

Finally, the psychoanalytic narrative of phallic lack relegates the mother to a position of complete and unrecoverable absence. If we are to read Naomi's recovery of her mother as neither a retreat to the oedipal prelinguistic or Kristevan semiotic, nor as a triumphant realization of "transcending the mother's silence" (Hirsch, 168), but as the recovery of "the speech that frees [and] comes forth from the amniotic deep" (Kogawa), we need to look carefully at the powers of signification Kogawa attributes to silence and the ways in which the mother's absence prompts the fragmentation of Naomi's subjectivity and the polarization of speech and silence. Kogawa challenges the necessity and inevitability of this split in her conception of a maternal language that encompasses the range of both the silence that speaks and the words made flesh, locating them at the site of the recuperated maternal body.

Obasan begins and ends in silence, which is the clearest indication that this is not a novel about the attainment of speech after its long repression. It is a novel that traces Naomi Nakane's growing understanding of the many different modalities of silence in her life. Indeed, two different kinds of silence are indicated in the opening invocation:

There is a silence that cannot speak.
   There is a silence that will not speak.
   Beneath the grass the speaking dreams and beneath the dreams is a sensate sea. The speech that frees comes forth from the amniotic deep. To attend its voice, I can hear it say, is to embrace its absence. But I fail the task. The word is stone.

What is immediately clear is that the narrator distinguishes between oppressed silence and willed silence, each denoting a differing position of the subject to silence. In the first, the subject is denied agency and is silenced. In the second, agency exists within a self-defined silence, a refusal to speak. But the thematic of absence is also present in these lines. The necessity of reconstructing absence as more than lack is suggested by the physicality of the word "embrace." That is, Naomi must both accept and read her mother's absence as an embraceable presence. Without that tactile relation to the "sensate sea," both words and silence are hailstones that pock the earth and lack the fluidity of a living language, and absence can only be read as emptiness.[21]

Naomi's disembodiment and erasure of self, homophonically suggested by her nickname Nomi, "no me," is frequently associated with images of disappearance. At one point, for instance, she likens herself to dust: "Sometimes when I stand in a prairie night the emptiness draws me irresistibly, like a dust speck into a vacuum cleaner, and I can imagine myself disappearing off into space like a rocket with my questions trailing behind me" (222). Such imagery suggests that the thematic of absence in this text is no facile reversal of absence as presence: just as there are different modes of silence, so are there different kinds of absence. Absence as disappearance and emptiness is connected to death and nonsignifying silence. Naomi's sense of absence from her own life is paralleled by the general situation of Japanese Canadians, for whom "the message to disappear worked its way deep into the Nisei heart and into the bone marrow" (219), as well as by the specific situation of her own family: "Some families . . . disappear from the earth without a whimper" (25).

The literalization of silence as the opposite of speech and absence as the opposite of presence both figure lack as the privileged category of determination. Naomi's later identification with the nightmare figure of the Grand Inquisitor associates her sureness of the absoluteness of her mother's absence with his insistence that silence does not speak. Despite her memory of reading the Japanese ideographs for "love" and "passionate love," Naomi follows this recollection with an account of her dream that suggests her inability to similarly "read" her mother's dance: "Why, I wonder as she danced her love, should I find myself unable to breathe?" Unable to believe in her mother's embodiment, even within the unconscious of the dreamworld, Naomi does not breathe, an act of "judgement and a refusal to hear" (273) that link her to the Grand Inquisitor as "accuser and murderer" (273–74): "How the Grand Inquisitor gnaws at my bones. At the age of questioning my mother disappeared. Why, I have asked ever since, did she not write? Why, I ask now, must I know? Did I doubt her love? Am I her accuser?" (274). This passage makes clear that it is not so much Naomi deeply missing her mother that identifies her with the Inquisitor but her insistence, into adulthood, on a child's reasoning: if her mother loved her, she would be there or write letters. That no letters ever came signals both the absence of the mother and of love. Naomi's literalism, which sometimes manifests itself in an awkward pedantry, may be both understandable and forgivable, but it is also partly responsible for the great pain and emotional immobility of her present life.

This kind of literalization tellingly figures in Kogawa's use of photographs throughout the novel, which for both Obasan and Naomi are the only link to the family's existence prior to being fragmented by death and relocation. However, the pictures' stasis serves primarily to remind their viewers that what was once present has disappeared. Obasan gazes at the photos and sighs, "Such a time there was once" (23) or "This is the best time. These are the best memories" (56), which contrasts with Naomi's young students who "know that you can't 'capture life's precious moments,' as they say in the camera ads" (24). Thus, these representations of presence in the past seem mostly to exacerbate the sense of absence in the present. Indeed, photographs always evoke a sense of loss, as when the snapshot of Naomi's father and Uncle leads directly into the memory of their hand-built boat being impounded by the police and the subsequent arrest of Uncle (25–26). Prompted into memory by the photograph of her mother and herself as a child, Naomi can now read the picture only as evidence of what no longer is. The past is cut off from the present, the resultant fragmentation mirrored in the narrative syntax: "The woman in the picture is frail and shy and the child is equally shy, unable to lift her head. Only fragments relate me to them now, to this young woman, my mother, and me, her infant daughter. Fragments of fragments. Parts of a house. Segments of stories" (64).

Photographic literalization of presence and its location of presence in the past are most painfully evident in the picture of the mother and Naomi as a young child. Holding it, Obasan murmurs, "Mukashi mukashi o-o mukashi. . . . In ancient times, in ancient times, in very very ancient times" (65), underscoring the distant unrecuperability of such a time. The photograph evokes painful memories for Naomi that do not "bear remembering" (60): the mother's presence in the picture is associated with the family's home in Vancouver. This memory is significant because it contains two elements that will later help Naomi to heal emotionally. While many have noted the mother's association with silence, few have recognized that Naomi's memories of her childhood home associate the mother with "laughter, music and meal times, games and storytelling" (69). Here is a key contrast to the mother's silent stasis "in a black-and-white photograph, smiling your yasashi smile" (291). This memory, in which the mother is connected to nonsilent modes of communication (laughter, music and stories), suggests a capacity for signification that contradicts readings of the mother as a figure of an irredeemable silence characterized by lack.

The second element is one that has been identified by Gayle K. Fujita in her reading of Naomi's bicultural sensibility, which is Naomi's inheritance of "a vital *nikkei* culture including the positive use of silence exemplified by Naomi's attendance" (40). Naomi's Vancouver memories are associated not only with maternal connectedness and happy embodiment, symbolized by the creature comforts of a warm bath and fresh *nemaki,* but by a mode of presence that parallels the different uses of silence. She recalls the family's evenings, when her father and brother Stephen would play instruments and her mother would sing. Fujita notes that "only Naomi neither sings nor plays instruments, but her listening and simple presence are accepted as participation" (38). That is, Naomi's nonactive physical presence signifies a level of emotional presence. The reconfiguration of presence is even more clear in a following memory where the absolute presence of attentiveness, what Naomi calls "alert and accurate knowing," is linked with silence: "When I am hungry, and before I can ask, there is food. . . . A sweater covers me before there is any chill and if there is pain there is care simultaneously" (68). What Naomi's mother and grandmother react to is the understood presence of unstated needs: to attend is to anticipate another's needs, to experience the world from another's point of view and thus act on what need not be literalized and made obvious.

This mode of attending to that which is not literally present is most evident in Naomi's memory, at five, of witnessing a hen pecking her chicks to death. Frightened, Naomi calls out, "Mama—":

Without a word and without alarm, she follows me quickly to the backyard. . . . With swift deft fingers, Mother removes the live chicks first, placing them in her apron. All the while that she acts, there is calm efficiency in her face and she does not speak. Her eyes are steady and matter of fact—the eyes of Japanese motherhood. They do not invade and betray. They are eyes that protect, shielding what is hidden most deeply in the heart of the child. . . . Physically, the sensation is not in the region of the heart, but in the belly. This that is in the belly is honoured when it is allowed to be, without fanfare, without reproach, without words. What is there is there. (71)

Central to this passage is the mother's concentration not on calming her daughter's fear itself so much as on preserving a sense of self "hidden most deeply in the heart of the child" (71) and threatened by fear. What is not seen is nevertheless honored and "allowed to be" in a way that is profoundly aware of what we might call the child's subjectivity. It is simply accepted: "What is there is there." This response closely ties attendance and its nonverbal modes of acknowledging nonvisible presence to the maternal and nurturing. Far from being characterized by lack,

this realm of maternal attendance is defined by the protective, the accepting, and also by a kind of apprehension that is associated with the
intuitive and poetic.

It is this poetic of attendance, the realm of multiply signifying silences, words, presences and absences, that is ruptured and bifurcated
into contradictory opposites by Naomi's molestation at the hands of
Old Man Gower. Significantly, the structure of this episode links it to
the memory of the mother and the chickens. Unlike the mother who
takes care not to "invade and betray" (71), Gower both psychically and
physically splits Naomi. And unlike the mother's story of Momotaro,
when Gower asks, "Would you like me to tell you a story?" (75), his
narrative—his molestation of Naomi—pushes Naomi into a realm
where language is duplicitous, silence is the withholding of truth, presence is what renders one most vulnerable, and absence signifies both the
erasure of self and the loss of the mother. By lying about a cut on Naomi's knee, Gower duplicitously uses language to name what isn't there:
"He lifts me up saying that my knee has a scratch on it and he will fix
it for me. I know this is a lie. The scratch is hardly visible and does not
hurt. Is it the lie that first introduces me to the darkness? . . . 'Don't tell
your mother,' he whispers. . . . Where in the darkness has my mother
gone?" (75, 77). Here, Gower's tending to what is not literally present—a
cut—enacts a terrible parody of maternal attendance, and his deception
symbolically inaugurates the mother's meaningless absence into darkness.

Gower's symbolic function as a figure of literalism, death and nonsignifying silence/absence is reinforced by his identification with the
Grand Inquisitor. While Naomi's own identification with the Grand
Inquisitor is associational, based on her insistent questions, Gower's
identification with the same figure is direct. Both are identified with the
abuse of masculine, hegemonic power (particularly in terms of Gower's
symbolic representation of white Canadians in relation to Japanese Canadians). Both are described in terms of encroaching darkness and by
their bare scalps, which are compared to "a shiny skin cap" (72, 273).

But Naomi's associational identification with the inquisitor leads her
to a recognition that disidentifies her with that figure, and this recognition involves her recovery of attendance. "To hear my mother," she
realizes, "to attend her speech, to attend the sound of stone, he must
first become silent. Only when he enters her abandonment will he be
released from his own" (274). For Naomi, who has perceived her
mother's absence as abandonment, this realization suggests that she
must enter her mother's absence, inhabit that space, much in the way

that acts of attendance imply a profound and active identification with another's consciousness. In doing so, Naomi, like the Grand Inquisitor, must abandon the kind of literalization that has brought the mother to voiceless silence and endless absence.

It is after this point that Naomi finally learns what happened to her mother, as well as why her silence was not an act of abandonment but of love. It is not, however, learning the facts of what happened that recuperates the mother's presence for Naomi, who regards the letters that have been read as "skeletons. Bones only" (292). Rather, as Sato observes, it is the silent attentiveness associated with the Momotaro story that enables Naomi to hear her mother. "Naomi realizes," writes Sato, "that she has comprehended neither her mother's suffering nor her love which tried to hide that suffering through silence. When self-centeredness is replaced by attendance, Naomi is able to recall her lost mother, and lost self" (255–56). I would add, however, that it is not only the act of attendance itself that recalls the mother. Naomi's direct appeal to her mother signals the possibility for maternal subjectivity that is both identified with and responsive to the daughter's presence. In her acknowledgment that "we were lost together in our silences. Our wordlessness was our mutual destruction" (291), she addresses herself to and aligns herself with her mother. Through Naomi's own silent speech, the mother becomes the listening presence: "I am thinking that for a child there is no presence without flesh. But perhaps it is because I am no longer a child I can know your presence though you are not here" (292).

While recognizing that to remain in a child's world where presence is always and only physical, and absence is always and only loss, Naomi is nevertheless still unable to reconcile herself to the finality of death:

After the rotting of the flesh, what is the song that is left? Is it the strange gnashing sound of insects with their mandibles moving through the bone marrow? Up through the earth come tiny cries of betrayal. There are so many betrayals — departures, deaths, absences — there are all the many absences within which we who live are left. (294)

Naomi questions whether, in the face of death's absences, it is "enough that we were once together briefly in our early Vancouver days," whether it is enough that through long years Obasan and Uncle "attended one another." She concludes, "Dead hands can no longer touch our outstretched hands or move to heal" (294). Gripped by grief and by the pervasiveness of absence, Naomi fears there is only more loss, "deeper emptiness" (295).

Her final recognition that departure, death and absence are not all there is comes through a remarkable metaphor that encapsulates the thematics of absence and presence that structure the novel. Significantly, the metaphor is based on a figure that simulates human presence:

Grief wails like a scarecrow in the wild night, beckoning the wind to clothe his gaunt shell. With his outstretched arms he is gathering eyes for his disguise. I had not known that Grief had such gentle eyes — eyes reflecting my uncle's eyes, my mother's eyes, all the familiar lost eyes of Love that are not his and that he dons as a mask and a mockery. (295)

The simile that connects grief to the scarecrow evokes the functional simile that connects the scarecrow to human presence. Unclothed and empty (a "gaunt shell"), it is merely a poor simulacrum for the subjectivity of those whom it would represent. Grief "personified" as such can only ever be the marker for what is not there. That this figure of loss is "gathering eyes for his disguise" references the many ways that eyes and the gaze are associated with subjectivity throughout the text and suggests that what most signifies her loved ones is appropriated by grief.[22] They are symbolically erased by a grief for that which is permanently lost. Naomi realizes that to identify her mother, father and uncle with such a figure makes a mockery of their acts of love and the lives they lived. To identify them with such absence is, in a sense, to absent them from Naomi's life as though they never were, as though the fact of their lives, finally, signifies nothing.

In a remarkable and beautiful passage that reverses Naomi's earlier dissociation from the physical, a sensate world holds the promise of the attendant language of silence, embodiment and recuperable absence:

This body of grief is not fit for human habitation. Let there be flesh. The song of mourning is not a lifelong song.

Father, Mother, my relatives, my ancestors, we have come to the forest tonight, to the place where the colours all meet — red and yellow and blue. We have turned and returned to your arms as you turn to earth and form the forest floor. Tonight we picked berries with the help of your sighted hands. Tonight we read the forest braille. See how our stained fingers have read the seasons, and how our serving hands serve you still. (295)

Significantly, as Naomi brings her parents into the present and out of a static past whose boundary is marked by death, Obasan sits near "her chocolate box of photographs . . . looking at the pictures one by one" (293). As Naomi readies to go to the coulee, Obasan sits in the dark: "in the palm of her open hand is Uncle's ID card" (296).

Walking silently down the coulee, Naomi heads to where "the underground stream seeps through the earth. . . . Above the trees, the moon is a pure white stone. The reflection is rippling in the river—water and stone dancing. It's a quiet ballet, soundless as breath" (296). Unlike the earlier stilted, oppressive silence, this silence is one that dances, lives, speaks. The underground stream that soaks Naomi's coat hem signals the presence of the maternal, the "amniotic deep" invoked at the novel's opening, and that presence is embodied, sensate.[23] Having found her absent mother through entering her abandonment and listening to her silences, Naomi is able to affirm her mother's subjectivity as well as her own, an affirmation suggested by the final words of the novel, the last two words of which reverse Naomi's previous state of nonbeing: "Between the river and Uncle's spot are the wild roses and the tiny wildflowers that grow along the trickling stream. The perfume in the air is sweet and faint. If I hold my head a certain way, I can smell them from where I am" (296).

Naomi, like the daughters in Yamamoto, Sasaki and Kadohata's stories, must recuperate maternal silence and absence in order to construct a viable subjectivity. In contrast to models that eclipse maternality and maternal narratives as the necessary condition for daughterly subjectivity to emerge, the writings by these Japanese American women suggest that, in fact, the daughter as subject must identify and align herself with, not against, the mother. Defined by both gender and race, the mother is a crucial agent of both enculturation and resistance whose silences, in particular, must be read within a context that recognizes both gender and culturally marked silences as "articulate" (Cheung). Only then can a space be created in which maternal subjectivity is represented and representable; ultimately, that space holds the possibility for the daughter's own subjectivity.

CHAPTER 5

Embodied Language

The Poetics of Mitsuye Yamada,
Janice Mirikitani and Kimiko Hahn

I've taken years to imagine an Asian American aesthetic. I think
it's a combination of many elements—a reflection of Asian form,
an engagement with content that may have roots in historical
identity, together with a problematic, and even psychological,
relationship to language.

Kimiko Hahn, "Writing over Borders"

Although there is a tendency to think of Asian American poetry as a relatively recent phenomenon, its beginnings reach back to the 1890s.[1] Japanese American poetic history started before the turn of the century with the publication of poems written in English by Sadakichi Hartmann and Yone Noguchi and grew during the 1920s and 1930s with the many unpublished poems in Japanese by Issei who formed groups to write haiku and senryu.[2]

With the maturation of the first American-born generation, the Nisei, in the 1930s, poetry and prose written in English, though mostly unpublished, signaled the beginnings of a collective and self-conscious Japanese American literary presence. There were at least two Nisei-operated literary magazines, *Reimei* and *Leaves,* and short story writer Toshio Mori produced a volume of short stories set for publication by a mainstream press in 1942 but postponed, owing to the war and anti-Japanese sentiment, until 1949. Elaine Kim notes that, according to Mori, between thirty and fifty Nisei were active in the burgeoning West Coast literary community (141). Although the war's aftermath resulted in the dispersal of that community, Nisei writers nevertheless continued practicing their craft, often publishing stories and poems in the English sections of the Japanese-language newspapers.

Little of this writing, particularly the poetry, circulated in the wider public sphere. Much of it remains buried within the pages of various literary camp publications, such as *Trek*, the Poston *Chronicle,* and *All Aboard*. It was not until the climate of ethnic revival in the 1970s, "a fervent time for Asian American writing" (Hongo, xxvii), that earlier work began to be recovered and new work began to find an audience. In conjunction with the feminist project of finding and encouraging writing by women, previously denied venues for Asian American women's voices began to open up.

Prepoetics and Politics

Although Nikkei women had been writing poetry since the early part of this century, it was not until the 1970s that their poetry began to be published in book-length form.[3] As Mitsuye Yamada hints in her dedication to *Camp Notes,* finally published in 1976 but written during and directly following the internment, the manuscript very nearly did not make it out of the "mothballs" to which Yamada had consigned it. For every volume like Yamada's, one can surmise that there were at least several others—written, unpublished and mothballed.[4]

In her discussion of Nisei women's poetry during the war, Susan Schweik reveals an established and active tradition of poems by women written during and about the internment. Marginalized and denied access to mainstream publication, however, this body of work has been, and largely remains, unknown and unrecognized.[5] Schweik recovers the poetry of Toyo Suyemoto, whose poems appeared regularly in internment publications, as well as in the *Yale Review*. In addition, Schweik lists several other women poets whose works are scattered throughout various in-camp papers—Taro Katayama, Chiye Mori, Ruth Tanaka, Miko Tamura, Taro Suzuki—who together comprise what she identifies as "a general prepoetics of Japanese American (or Nikkei) women's writing in internment" (1991, 178).[6]

These literary precursors provide an important context for and a crucial contrast with later Japanese American women poets. Schweik argues for recognition of their work:

the project which Nikkei, and especially Nisei, women writers undertook in the war years with grace and with distinction as well as with difficulty: defining differences—from Japan, from dominant U.S. culture, from their parents, from men, from each other, within themselves. . . . The making of differences in and through poetry could be, for Japanese American women, a significant means of resistance. (1991, 176)

The delineation of difference undertaken by earlier Japanese American women poets anticipates poststructuralist articulations of the subject's multiple positionalities, suggesting that the internment years, in particular, necessitated articulations of subjectivity that resisted dominant culture models. The social and historical circumstances under which wartime poetry was written mark two crucial distinctions from contemporary writing. First, as Schweik observes in her discussion of Toyo Suyemoto, the racist climate before and especially during the war years resulted in "poems [that] simply assume, rather than assert, an identity without the imprint of 'ethnicity,' aligning themselves inconspicuously with white European American literary tradition" (187). Second, because all published writing during the internment was subject to camp censors, articulations of resistance, particularly those that aligned the writer with her Japanese identity, were heavily encoded. Poems were inflected "with undertones of a Japanese poetic tradition" (191) through which the seemingly private concerns of the poet could be used to comment on the situation of the interned Japanese American community.

The thematics and strategies of wartime Japanese American women poets are both taken up and reversed by contemporary writers. For them, the articulation of differences remains central, but it is much more overt, often openly polemical. And unlike writers such as Suyemoto, these contemporary poets both assume and assert a self aligned with Japanese/American identity and culture. In addition, they struggle with issues of raced and gendered subjectivity, political resistance and nationalism, and the recuperation of Japanese American history and identity. Mitsuye Yamada, Janice Mirikitani and Kimiko Hahn, in particular, link the body and its various forms of markedness to issues of language. The twinned issues of language and the body are central for these three poets, and each struggles with the attempt to re-gender the Nikkei subject without acceding to either the essentialism of the body or the over-determinations of language.

If, as I argue in the preceding chapters, Japanese American women's relationships to their bodies are always problematized by the appropriative structures of race and gender as they circulate within discourses of national identity, it is also true that the body, nevertheless, is a primary source of identity. The body's recuperation is, in a very basic sense, the recuperation of the self as subject. Through various forms of masking, Japanese American women writers both reject reductive readings of the body that deny interiority and reclaim the body *as* body. Such acts of reclamation, however, cannot in any simple way be looked to as grand gestures of self-affirmation and resistance. Rather, the status of the Asian female body necessitates confronting the history that has dictated the terms and context within which that body has been constructed in order to rehistoricize, and thus renarrate, the particulars of the corporeal subject.

Perhaps more than any other historical event, war foregrounds in particularly stark fashion the ways in which the body is marked by the intersection of race and gender.[7] In her discussion of gender, sexuality and war narratives, Katherine Kinney notes that war, "as a privileged site of cultural and particularly literary representation . . . claims the position of ultimate reality and inscribes its bodily truth on men as soldiers. Within this logic, women can only know war through men." Denied the experiential, and thus narrative, authority of war, women are inscribed as those who are " 'protected' from the real site of struggle."[8]

The Second World War, however, positioned Japanese American women in a distinctive, and contradictory, space. Like other American women, they were not subject to the draft and did not participate in military combat. But *un*like other American women, Japanese American women were forcibly removed from their homes, relocated, and incarcerated for the duration of World War II. This experience, as Schweik notes, "brought to bear on their wartime writing a traumatic, undeniable 'authority of experience' " (1991, 174). Further, the experience of internment—and the humiliation, violence and upheaval it wrought—rendered almost meaningless the distinctions between war zone and home place, ally and enemy, protected and aggressor, through which the war could be understood as a national project binding citizens together as an identifiable "us" against an identifiable "them." Thus, one of the characteristic functions of wartime, the inscription of gender roles, similarly falters when we turn to Japanese American women and their experience of war. While the infamous "loyalty oath" functionally split

Japanese American men and women along traditional gender lines, it also ideologically split the Nikkei community along a number of other significant trajectories that served to destabilize rather than reinforce gender distinctions. That is, the oath's insistence on mutually exclusive categories of Japanese national or American citizen—cultural Japaneseness or political Americanness, loyal subject of the emperor or loyal citizen of the United States—overrode the relatively simple question of whether one was male or female, as is suggested by the fact that all Nikkei adults, men and women, citizens and Japanese-born, those of draft age and the elderly, were required to fill out the questionnaire.[9]

The point here is not that gender difference did not matter during the war, but rather that it did not register as a significant identificatory category in a war so overwhelmingly informed by and constructed along the lines of race. Obviously, young Japanese American men were required to stake their lives on their answers to the loyalty questionnaire in a way that women were not. Nevertheless, because of their particular identity as both Japanese American and female, Japanese American women inhabited a space wherein their identities as women were invoked primarily within, but not outside, the Nikkei community.[10] The historical moment of the Second World War thus provides a peculiar and ironic exception to the hyperfeminization and hypersexualization of the Japanese American female that exposes the constructed and therefore arbitrary nature of gender itself. In the face of perceived threat to the national body, the Japanese/American female body was de-gendered and de-sexed. As the subjects of national war discourse, Japanese American women registered as neither Americans nor women, but as alien "Japs."

Denied the various axes of identity that would secure their space as differentiated national subjects, Japanese American women poets faced the task of, in Schweik's terms, defining differences as they registered and constructed the terms of their experience of war and internment. Yet in the attempt to do so, these writers invariably encountered the problematics of language intensified by the distortions of war. Paul Fussell suggests that the most important project of twentieth-century literature has been to remake language, whose ability to represent transparently the realm of experience had been pushed beyond its limits by the Great War.[11] For Japanese Americans during the Second World War, the inherent limitations of discursivity dovetailed with the deliberate use of language for duplicitous purposes. Wartime rhetoric positioned Japanese Americans as sites of hostile national difference that had to be contained but simultaneously implied that they cheerfully and willingly submitted to their incarceration. Thus, language not only demarcated the otherness of the Nikkei but implied their consent to such demarcations.

Language, then, becomes a crucial, if problematic, territory of reappropriation for Japanese Americans writing during, in the aftermath of, and in reference to the war. For Nikkei women, war represents the moment at which the gendered subject is elided, but the memory of war and its renarrativization provides the possibility for discursively recuperating the gendered subject. The site of utterance is, in a profound sense, the site where the simultaneity of the subject's invisibility and the marked body's hypervisibility renders the speaking subject both extant and vulnerable.

Mitsuye Yamada: The Relocation of Identity

Mitsuye Yamada's two collections, *Camp Notes* ([1976] 1992) and *Desert Run* (1988), explore the possibilities and problematics of a subjectivity defined by both race and gender, and the complex relations between language, power and agency. But at their most basic level, these poems witness moments of national and personal history, often locating themselves in the space where the two histories collide. Interned at Minidoka, Yamada experienced firsthand the attempted erasure of Nikkei society, culture and language. In her work, the internment functions as a crucial site of both historical memory and the (re)construction of Nikkei subjectivity. Thus, the recovery of history is inextricably tied to the recovery of the voice that recovers history. Because the issue of reclaiming denied subjectivity is so central to Yamada's work, the poems often resist the critical convention of making clear distinctions between "the poet" and "the speaker." At various points throughout the following discussion of *Camp Notes,* therefore, I forego the awkwardness of this convention, since constantly foregrounding the disjunction between the writing and written selves would undermine Yamada's project of collective recovery through personal experience, as well as imply that such a clearly experientially based poetic is less legitimate than one that relies on clear demarcations between personal experience and aesthetic expression. Moreover, because many of

Yamada's poems assume the reader's knowledge of authorial identity, thus relying on an implicitly noted rather than explicitly stated speaker's subject-position, strictly new critical approaches to her work would result in inappropriate readings of several of the poems.

That said, however, it must also be noted that Yamada does not simply collapse the self into the landscape of things that happen to that self. The subject is not completely contained within or limited by its history; voice is not simply contingent on event. In a form of masking that parallels the use of tone in Nisei women's autobiographies, Yamada employs irony and ironic distance to suggest a self that exists outside the boundaries of the poetry, a self that, in a sense, precedes and exceeds the fact of its own utterance. In this sense, the poems' invitation to identify poet and speaker as one and the same is precisely that which lends many of the poems their curious air of guardedness, as though, for all their seeming candor, reservation—a reserved self—lingers beneath the poetic surface.

One such example is the short poem "Looking Out" ([1976] 1992, 39):

It must be odd
to be a minority
he was saying.
I looked around
and didn't see any.
So I said
Yeah
it must be.

The casual diction within the poem is echoed by the tonal irony that connects poet and reader in a moment of wry knowing. In the absence of any direct self-naming within the poem, the reader must infer the identity of the poem's "I" in a move that paradoxically relies on mainstream cultural knowledge of just who or what constitutes "minority" status to undermine the unspoken assumptions that support such identificatory declensions. But the poem also relies on the reader's knowledge of authorial identity and encourages the collapse of author and speaker: Yamada's identity as a Japanese American woman circulates both within and beyond the borders of the poem itself. Yamada's ironic use of what to the male speaker is an innocuously descriptive term, "minority," problematizes not only what we think we "know" but how we come to that knowledge. Thus, one of the striking elements of the

poem is that Yamada does not clarify whether the male speaker is identifying her as "a minority" because of her race or because of her gender,
instead rejecting the term of identification by reducing it to a ludicrous
statement about something that doesn't exist. The title, "Looking Out,"
suggests that she is protecting herself from the potential dangers of allowing herself to be named, and it also subverts the male speaker's assumption of normative centrality by placing Yamada in a central position from which she looks out. It is significant that she does not,
however, simply reverse the positions of center and margin, majority
and minority; thus, she claims the legitimacy of her particular position-
ing(s) without relegating anyone else, including the male speaker, to the
marginalized status of a "minority."

In her move from the relegated margin, that space in which she is
spoken for, Yamada might be said to enact a re-location of subjectivity.
But where "Looking Out" suggests that such moments are motivated
by another's ignorance and powered by a sly, if somewhat distanced,
irony, "Thirty Years Under" ([1976] 1992, 32) reveals the underpinning
difficulty:

I had packed up
my wounds in a cast
iron box
sealed it
labeled it
do not open . . .
ever . . .

and traveled blind
for thirty years

until one day I heard
a black man with huge bulbous eyes
say
there is nothing more
humiliating
more than beatings
more than curses
than being spat on

like a dog.

As in "Looking Out," Yamada does not specify the identity of the
speaker in this poem, once again inviting the identification of poet with
speaker. The poem refers to the psychological aftermath of the internment, and Yamada makes a direct connection between historical/

personal memory and the restoration of one's denied humanity. Thus, interpretive moves that attempt to place authorial identity under erasure in the interest of a purely formal reading replicate the denial of subjectivity central to the poem as well as obscure the recognition of a shared history of marginalization amongst people of color.

The poem is also a comment on the production, and near nonproduction, of *Camp Notes* itself: thirty years of denial, silence and packing up wounds have done nothing to reverse the treatment of Japanese/Americans during the war. In fact, through its clever use of allusion, the poem suggests that Japanese Americans in their silence have become like so many dogs licking their wounds. Admittedly, the poem also relies on an implicit contrast represented by the awkward and somewhat problematic image of the "huge bulbous eyes" of an African American man. This contrast functions in multiple registers: on the one hand, the African American man suggests a voice of empathy, sorrow, and compassion that conveys a sense of shared struggle, thus prompting the Japanese American poet to speech. On the other, or simultaneously, the man may also be offering an assessment of the depth and duration of systemic and social racism experienced by African Americans, in comparison to which "nothing is more humiliating." In this sense, the poet's decision to speak the wounds suffered by Japanese Americans follows from her realization that silence has placed the Asian American experience of U.S. racism under erasure.[12] In both cases, it is through this figure's voice that the poet comes to terms with her own blindness and unwillingness to bear witness to the humiliations of the internment and its devaluation of the Nikkei—who were forced to live in horse stalls still reeking with animal waste—to the status of animals. *Camp Notes'* very existence as a volume of poems thus attests to Yamada's unwillingness to remain blind and silent: the poems, like the wounds, are to be brought out of mothballs, out of the "cast iron box."

These poems exemplify two interrelated themes in Yamada's work: the need to document Nikkei experience, particularly, but not limited to, the internment; and the necessity of recuperating the self as subject from beneath racist and/or sexist constructions. Resisting the ways in which the raced body has been negatively marked and in contrast to earlier Nikkei women poets whose connection to Japanese identity was coded, Yamada makes overt connections to and reclaims Japanese/American identity. Several of Yamada's poems include words or lines in Japanese and direct allusions to Japanese culture. Yet far from merely providing exotic spice, the fairy tales, holidays and traditions clearly function as the means through which Yamada asserts identity.

Yamada's search for and recovery of her own identity is also the recovery of Issei culture, as is indicated by the title of the first section of
Camp Notes: "My Issei Parents, Twice Pioneers, Now I Hear Them."
In some of these poems, as in others included in *Desert Run* ("I Learned
to Sew," "Prayer for Change"), Yamada takes on the voices of Issei
women, a gesture that acknowledges the connections between her own
life and theirs. (Yamada's tendency to trace her ancestry through maternal figures follows the practice of identifying raced subjectivity with
maternality that I discuss in chapters three and four.) Like Yoshiko Uchida, who incorporates her mother's haiku within the pages of her autobiography, Yamada includes her father's senryu in her collection.
However, the intersubjective relationship between generations does not
elide differences. "A Bedtime Story" and "Enryo" ([1976] 1992, 6, 9),
for instance, focus on the Nisei daughter's misunderstanding or puzzlement about certain aspects of Japanese culture. Generational differences
between Issei and Nisei, of course, emblematize cultural distinctions
between the Japanese- and American-born.

Such distinctions, however, collapse in the syntax and lexicon of
American nativist racism, thus rendering the establishment of a specifically Japanese American identity difficult. A set of paired poems in *Camp
Notes,* "Here" (42) and "There" (43), points to the ways in which categories of national identity based on simplistic criteria of "blood" and/
or birth foreclose the possibility of Japanese American subjectivity. In
each poem, Yamada recounts being teased by other children because she
does not fit in. In "Here," a group of neighbor boys make fun of her
name ("Mit suey chop suey"), identifying her with an undifferentiated
Asian mass. "There" begins with the lines, "Once when I went back /
to where I came from." The irony in this line is doubled because Yamada refers not only to a common nativist epithet, but to the literal fact
of her own birth in Kyushu (Yamada was, however, raised in Seattle,
Washington). Despite the racist assumption that in Japan she is "with
her own kind" and despite Japan being the land of her birth, Yamada is
identified by the Japanese children who tease her as "America no ojo-o
san," an American girl. Yamada picks up the theme of conflated/dis-
placed identity in a later poem, "Guilty on Both Counts" (1988, 20),
where she is blamed for the bombing of Pearl Harbor *and* for the atomic
bombing of Hiroshima.

Beyond being alternately identified as Japanese by white Americans
and as American by Japanese, these poems comment on what happens
when one is named by the other, when one is denied a subjectivity that
is both Japanese and American. This is the textual context within which

we must read the eponymous "Camp Notes" section of Yamada's book. If it is true that these poems, like the reclamation of identity, must emerge from collective, historical silence, Yamada is also always conscious of how marginalized subjects cannot in any simple way assume empowerment through language. Nowhere is this clearer than in the sequence of internment-era poems in *Camp Notes* ("notes" itself indicating the limited powers of discursivity). For Japanese Americans, the internment illustrates with terrible clarity that the power of language to define and name is not equally applicable to all who use it. Racist rhetoric capitalizes on the unequal power relations between the "us" who uses speech and the "them" to whom speech is applied. If the very existence of Yamada's internment poetry attests to the ways in which language can document and recover Nikkei experience, the experience about which she writes brings in complex issues about the transparency of language, the contestability of documentation and the ruptures between experience and representation. Significantly, Yamada opens the sequence on the internment with a poem that demonstrates her uneasy relations to language:

> *Evacuation*
> As we boarded the bus
> bags on both sides
> (I had never packed
> two bags before
> on a vacation
> lasting forever)
> the *Seattle Times*
> photographer said
> Smile!
> so obediently I smiled
> and the caption the next day
> read:
>
> Note smiling faces
> a lesson to Tokyo.
>
> ([1976] 1992, 13)

The poem centers on the widespread practice by American magazines and newspapers, which regularly ran photos of the internees with captions that represented their subjects as happily acquiescent or willingly laboring in appalling conditions (Kogawa's *Obasan* includes a passage in which Naomi's memories of absolute misery compete with a Canadian newspaper's photo caption, "Grinning and Happy" [231]). "Evacuation" functions as a corrective to representations that allowed and encouraged non-Japanese Americans to sustain the fiction of a beneficent democracy. The newspaper caption frames (in all senses of the word) its photographic subject, denying even the representation of resistance.

Language can serve even more manipulative purposes, however. Apparently not content to misrepresent the internment to the outside world through the disjunction between representation and reality, camp authorities sought to regulate Nikkei subjectivity by renaming the reality of the internment through a kind of Orwellian doublespeak; thus "This was   not / im / prison / ment. / This   was / re / location" ("Desert Storm" [(1976) 1992, 19]). Yoshiko Uchida recalls a similar attempt to assert control through language. Newly arrived internees were handed instruction sheets, which read, "You are now in Topaz, Utah. . . . Here we say Dining Hall and not Mess Hall; Safety Council, not Internal Police; Residents, not Evacuees; and last but not least, Mental Climate, not Morale" (109). Yamada and Uchida recontextualize this language of duplicity within narratives that undermine its discursive authority and foreground its disruptive power. Yamada's strategic line-breaks call attention to the artifice of language as they mimic a tone of insistent coercion.

If the language of hegemony subjugates those whom it marginalizes, it is not always obvious that it also delimits the subjectivity of those who dominate. Yamada recognizes that the interaction between oppressor and oppressed always circulates within a realm defined by the former's need to control the latter and that this need ultimately, though not equally, constrains both. The opening stanza of "The Watchtower" ([1976] 1992, 22) is a subtle critique of nationalism and the self/other constructs it relies on: "The watchtower / with one uniformed / guard / in solitary / confined in the middle / of his land." Yamada's choice of words evoke the ironic image of the guard imprisoned, isolated in watchful vigil over "his land." Her use of awkward line-breaks and grammatical fragmentation reinforces the way in which the guard is cut off, contrasting with the images of community and the repetition of "we" in the last lines of the poem. This same sense of irony is evident in "Harmony at the Fair Grounds" ([1976] 1992, 15), which begins with a child wondering why "the soldier boy [is] in a cage / like that?" But Yamada is careful not to allow the irony of perceptual reversal to obscure the actual situation. Although "In the freedom of the child's / universe / the uniformed guard / stood trapped in his outside cage," the material, bodily reality of living in a constricted universe of "sawdusted grounds / where millions trod once / to view prize cows" brings into sharp relief who is free and who is not.

The child's perception and the way it is contrasted to the reality of the interned body is interestingly reversed in "The Trick Was" (27), where physical activity serves as a mask that is nevertheless unable to deny what the mind knows to be true:

> The trick was
> keep the body busy
> be a teacher
> be a nurse
> be a typist
> read some write some
> poems
> write Papa in prison
> write to schools
> (one hundred thirty-three colleges
> in the whole United States in the back
> of my Webster's dictionary
> answered: no admittance
> THEY were afraid of ME)
> But the mind was not fooled.

Like the accounts of interment in the autobiographies of Monica Sone, Jeanne Wakatsuki Houston and Yoshiko Uchida, Yamada's "The Trick Was" attests to the ways in which activity could function as a mask to cope with the reality of the Nikkei war experience. But the last line of the poem makes blatantly clear that while such strategies may function to preserve emotional equilibrium, they can only ultimately fail as strategies of denial.

Read in conjunction with "Evacuation," "The Trick Was" points to the manipulability of the body. That is, the same body whose seemingly quiescent surface can be employed as proof of acquiescence can also be temporarily deployed to distract the mind from its anguish—but only temporarily. There is no denying that the orientalized body, already incarcerated within the camps, is also that which bars legitimate entrance into the nation-state, symbolized by the lexical authority of the dictionary and its list of American colleges.

Recognition of the manipulation and disciplining of the Japanese/ American body is nowhere clearer than in internment writing. That race was the primary operating term during the war is reinforced by the relative absence of gender identification in Yamada's internment poems. As noted earlier in this discussion, Nikkei women were, in a sense, de-gendered by and in internment. Significantly, gender emerges as a subject-positioning in those poems that recount Yamada's exit from the camps and her resettlement in the Midwest. "The Night Before Good-Bye" (31) indexes a family separated by age, gender and ideological divisions: the father has been taken from the family by the FBI (as were many Issei men during the early months of the war), an older son has volunteered for the U.S. Army, a younger son sleeps while the mother helps ready her older daughter for relocation outside the camps to the Midwest. It is here that gender reemerges in the mother's admonishment to the daughter: "Remember / keep your underwear / in good repair / in case of accident / don't bring shame / on us" (31).

The mother's advice to her daughter not only gestures toward a familial and gendered bonding that contrasts with the surrounding fragmentation and the imminent departure of the daughter but also marks the moment at which the social conditioning of the female body reemerges. The underlying irony of the mother's words lies in their almost pathetic inappropriateness, as though one could simply revert to the proprieties of traditionally scripted (white) femininity in the face of wartime and postwar anti-Japanese sentiment. If the exit from camp is the exit from an ideologically degendered, race-defined space and reentry into the realm of socialized femininity, it is also a move into a space of vulnerability defined by race as well as gender.

It is therefore significant that the last poem in the section on the internment directly addresses this state of vulnerability. "Cincinnati" ([1976] 1992, 33) suggests that freedom from the literal confines of Minidoka is circumscribed by the threat of violence to the Asian female body:

Freedom at last
in this town aimless
I walked against the rush
hour traffic
My first day
in a real city
where

no one knew me.

No one except one
hissing voice that said
dirty jap

warm spittle on my right cheek.
I turned and faced
the shop window
and my spittled face
spilled onto a hill
of books.
Words on display.

In Government Square
people criss-crossed
like the spokes of
a giant wheel.

I lifted my right hand
but it would not obey me.
My other hand fumbled
for a hankie.

My tears would not
wash it. They stopped
and parted.
My hankie brushed
the forked
tears and spittle
together.
I edged toward the curb
loosened my fisthold
and the bleached laced
mother-ironed hankie blossomed in
the gutter atop teeth marked
gum wads and heeled candy wrappers.

Everyone knew me.

This poem brings together several themes in Yamada's work: the ways in which dominant culture can use language to name the other (here with a single phrase, "dirty jap") and the potential failure of language for those who are named. The imagery of the "criss-crossed" street and its comparison to "spokes" suggests continued social imprisonment. But race is not the only operative here: the focus on the "mother-ironed hankie" marks this experience as one in which gender intersects with race. As Schweik points out, this poem "entails a specific crisis of femininity": "Being squeaky-clean, bleached and lacy, does not protect her from the taunt 'dirty jap'; and being womanly, simply being a woman, increases the ways in which she is vulnerable to the barely deflected violence represented by 'teeth-marks' and 'heels.' The threat of rape for the young woman relocated by herself, muted but real, haunts the end of this poem" (1991, 206).

The feeling of freedom that begins the poem is thus completely gone by the poem's end. Freed from the literal imprisonment of the camps, this Japanese American woman is, in fact, not free from the ways in which she is deprived of comfortable anonymity ("no one knew me") because of her race and gender ("Everyone knew me"). In such a context, "freedom" means little, is reduced to mere "words on display," and signifies far less than the reflection of one's spat-upon Japanese face. The image of the Japanese face reflected in the window, literally facing the young woman with her difference, is also significant for its allusion to the Japanese face as mask: the shop window divides the young woman from the displayed books, symbols of discursive power, thus contrasting the silent subject with the "hissing voice" of white society; it also reflects the Japanese face whose racial markedness becomes a highly visible target (contrasting with the young woman's initial sense of "aimless" freedom), compounding the threat of danger faced by the female subject.

If one of the rationales for war is that "home" must be secured in order to protect "woman," the heart of this poem is the realization that such ideological categories do not apply to Japanese American women. Thus, the "crisis of femininity" may be located at the point where the Japanese body is degendered (that is, debarred from the category of Woman) but nevertheless remains sexed as a female, and therefore vulnerable, body.

Though several poems in both *Camp Notes* and the subsequent *Desert Run* attest to gender-based oppression, Yamada is clearly skeptical about any romanticized solidarity based on a shared experience of gender. Like many women of color, Yamada resists the liberal feminist tendency to privilege gender as the primary (or only) meaningful category of identity and to ignore the power differentials amongst women. The experience of the war and internment also suggests that Yamada's resistance to easy assumptions of gender solidarity is rooted in her understanding of the vexed relation between race and gender in this country.

This relation is most clearly addressed in "To the Lady" ([1976] 1992, 40), which is a reply to a white woman's inquiry as to why Japanese Americans "let" themselves be put into the camps "without protest."

Come to think of it I
    should've run off to Canada
    should've hijacked a plane to Algeria
    should've pulled myself up from my

       bra straps
       and kicked'm in the groin
       should've bombed a bank
       should've tried self-immolation
       should've holed myself up in a
       woodframe house
       and let you watch me
       burn up on the six o'clock news
       should've run howling down the street
       naked and assaulted you at breakfast
       by AP wirephoto
       should've screamed bloody murder
       like Kitty Genovese

    Then

    YOU would've
       come to my aid in shining armor
       laid yourself across the railroad track
       marched on Washington
       tattooed a Star of David on your arm
       written six million enraged
       letters to Congress

Yamada employs a tone of heavy sarcasm to highlight the woman's ignorance on two counts: many white Americans do not realize that, in
fact, Japanese Americans did protest their incarceration (among them a
young Nisei woman); second, sixties-style forms of activist protest cannot be retroactively prescribed to a period during which the politics of
race would have rendered such acts futile gestures of "self-immolation."
Yamada cuts across temporal and geographical boundaries to highlight
the parallels between the past and present, and, as the references to the
Holocaust and the war in Vietnam suggest, sharpens those parallels by
foregrounding issues of nationalism. "The lady" is thus indirectly implicated, through her privilege of ignorance, in the nationalist aggression
that has victimized Japanese Americans and the Vietnamese, as well as
in the collective apathy that did nothing to prevent the murderous anti-
Semitism in Europe. The reference to Kitty Genovese alludes to a more
local instance of social apathy as well as registers Yamada's critique of
simplistic forms of liberating rhetoric that assume social protest, like
cries for help, will be answered by knights "in shining armor."

    But the Genovese murder symbolizes what is undeniably common
to women: the threat of male violence. However, inasmuch as Yamada
rejects the problematic solidarity that follows from collapsing all women
within the rubric of "woman," she also rejects the easy solidarity of

victimhood. Though most of the poem is structured by an opposing "I" and "you," its final two stanzas join addresser and addressee in similar, though not identical, spaces of social responsibility.

> But we didn't draw the line
> anywhere
> law and order Executive Order 9066
> social order moral order internal order
>
> YOU let'm
> I let'm
> All are punished.

Yamada's earlier insistence on the positional differences between the "I" and "you" crucially modifies the parallel use of "let" in the last stanza, and it would be a mistake to read these lines as implicitly acceding to the assumptions of the opening query. Rather, the structure of these closing lines insists on an understanding of domination, oppression, collusion and implication that goes beyond reductive assignations of who is "good" and therefore innocent, and who is "bad" and therefore responsible.[13]

Yamada further explores the complexities of race, gender and discursive power in her second volume, *Desert Run* (1988). Perhaps the greatest difference between the two collections is that whereas *Camp Notes* depends on and develops what Schweik perceptively calls "a poetics of the gag, punch lines which reveal how language buffets and muffles" (1991, 201), the later book more or less leaves this tactic behind, no longer attempting to mask anger with tonal irony. One of the strongest pieces in *Desert Run* (which includes short fiction) is "The Club" (76), a powerful poem that addresses issues of domestic violence and male power, the intersection of gender and race for Japanese American women, and the possibility for an alliance between women that does not obscure raced subjectivity. Most striking in this poem is Yamada's use of the figure of the Japanese woman, particularly in relation to the author's and the speaker's identities:

> He beat me with the hem of a kimono
> worn by a Japanese woman
> this prized
> painted
> wooden statue
> carved to perfection
> in Japan or maybe Hong Kong.

She was usually on display
in our living room atop his bookshelf
among his other overseas treasures
I was never to touch.

Yamada indirectly associates the doll with the Second World War, when
American soldiers brought home the image of the servile and delicate
Japanese woman among their other "overseas treasures." Placed beyond
reach, the doll's wooden perfection whose impossible ideality is an instrument of violence: "That hem / made fluted red marks / on these
freckled arms / my shoulders / and back. / That head / inside his fist /
made camel / bumps / on his knuckles." Significantly, there is no desire
to destroy the doll; rather, the doll's indestructibility becomes a point
of identification and connection:

One day, we were talking
as we often did the morning after.
Well, my sloe-eyed beauty, I said
have you served him enough?
I dared to pick her up with one hand
I held her gently by the flowing robe
around her slender legs.
She felt lighter than I had imagined.
I stroked her cold thighs
with the tips of my fingers
and felt a slight tremor.

The phrase "sloe-eyed beauty" and the question "have you served him
enough?" ironically refer to dominant culture constructions of Japanese
women; leaving with the doll is an act of claiming that comes to terms
with Japanese womanhood by symbolically removing it from a discursive field that has perverted and reduced it to an oppressive stereotype.
Yamada refuses to disavow the Japanese woman with whom Japanese
American women have been identified; instead, she reappropriates that
figure as one of silent, unbreakable strength and forges an alliance in
resistance to male violence ("I prayed for her / that her pencil thin neck /
would not snap / or his rage would be unendurable. / She held fast for
me"). Yamada pushes the act of reappropriation even further through
the image of the woman stroking the doll's "cold thighs." This symbolic
act of autoeroticism reclaims the sexed body from the realm in which it
is untouchable for the female subject, but violently handled by others.
The poem ends as the speaker whispers, "We're leaving . . . you and I /

together," delicately wraps up the doll, places it in her packed suitcase and leaves "forever."

What is most remarkable about this poem, however, is its suggestion that the image of the Japanese woman threatens not only Japanese American women, but potentially any woman. Although many of Yamada's earlier poems employ a first-person voice that is often autobiographical, the poems in *Desert Run* put more distance between the writing and written selves. It is therefore possible, in the absence of any overt identification of the poem's speaker, to read this poem as spoken by a non-Asian woman. Thus, Yamada's poem explores how sexist and racist constructions threaten, among others, white women and indirectly comments on white feminism's ultimately self-defeating ignorance of race.

Although silence in "The Club" is associated with resistance, Yamada never forgets that language can inflict modes of violence whose power lies in its ability to impose silence on the other. Elsewhere, Yamada cautions against reliance on strategies of silence and forms of nonverbal resistance. In her essay "Invisibility is an Unnatural Disaster," she points out that such modes, particularly when deployed by Asian American women, are always vulnerable to misinterpretation. Recalling an instance in which she had actively ignored a racist remark and responded with silence, Yamada writes, "I had supposed that I was practicing passive resistance while being stereotyped, but it was so passive no one noticed I was resisting; it was so much my expected role that it ultimately rendered me invisible" (36). Yamada's recollection is a prime example of what Trinh Minh-ha identifies as being spoken: "silence as a will not to say or will to unsay and as a language of its own has barely been explored" (1990, 373), and in the face of that perceived absence of speech, others "will not fail to fill in the blanks on your behalf, and you will be said" (1989, 80).

"Enough" (1988, 79), which directly follows "The Club," explores the ways in which language may be used to colonize the body through "sympathetic" metaphoricity. "Being said" is experienced as a bodily assault:

I see my body metaphored by
peace-loving
young-blooded
eco-minded
oversexed
male poets.
They protest that

a forest of my pubic hair
prolific, fertile, enticing
is cut down
mercilessly macheted.
They wail that I
an ocean hiding huge
reservoirs of active oil
am pumped, drummed, depleted.

Yamada focuses on the atomizing metonymic constructions of "male poets," revealing through her own choice of words—fertile, enticing, pumped, ravaged—the latent desire for sexual domination. The racialization, sexualization and conflation of woman and country, though supposedly inflected through the politics of the Left, insidiously participate in the violence supposedly being decried: "They groan that I / a small Asian nation . . . is ravaged over / and over." The agency of the male speakers is predicated on the erasure of Asian/female agency, but Yamada resists this erasure through her own uses of language, piling on adjectives that define those who speak and closing the poem with a metaphor whose use suggests the potential for reappropriating language but which also provides an image of enraged, self-destructive silence:

I sit in this privileged circle
a lone woman
a lone Asian
with literal fingernails
digging into my palms
yellow blood oozing
to the floor.

This is one of the few poems in which the speaker clearly identifies herself as an Asian woman; significantly, that identification comes in a moment of powerless silence.

Discursive violence is also evident in "Lethe" (1988, 82), where a student/veteran (presumably of the Vietnam war) invokes the experiential, if solipsistic, authority of sight: "With my own eyes / I have seen them. / . . . / I knew then / I know now / they are not like us / who care / about life / liberty / and happiness." Through the student's identity as a veteran, and especially through his jingoistic mouthing of the Constitutional principle most identified with the idea of America, Yamada draws out the close relations between white masculinity and ideological citizenship. Confronted by the implacability of the student's racist nationalism, the teacher feels "pinned / against the blackboard wall / a broken piece of chalk / in the palm of my hand." At the end of the poem, this image is repeated, but with an important modification: "broken piece of chalk" is specified as "a broken piece of white chalk."

> Because I was silent then
> those metal-rimmed glasses
> hang pinned to the cork wall
> his grey eyes fixed
> while I stand before him
> a broken piece of white chalk
> in the palm of my hand.

The closing image of the white chalk reaches back to an earlier description of the male student's "tight pink skin. . . . / his lips a white line," identifying language with race, gender and national privilege. Additionally, discursivity is linked to the power of the gaze that underwrites the authority of what he "knew" and what he "know[s] now."

In contrast to "Enough," Yamada does not specify the race or gender of the speaker in "Lethe." The unmarked space of gender and race enacts within the poem the silencing of identity and subjectivity. The "I" cannot identify itself; instead, the twice-repeated line "because I was silent then" substitutes itself for the identifications of race and gender. Here, the absence of signifying agency, symbolized by the broken piece of chalk, divests silence of its potential to define subjectivity through resistance.

Yamada does not, however, abandon silence any more than she abandons speech. *Desert Run*'s title poem claims representation and discursivity, creating a space for Japanese American female subjectivity at its historical site of denial. Yamada returns to the desert where she was interned as a young woman. Strikingly, that act of return is marked by silence:

> Everything is done in silence here:
> the wind fingers fluted stripes
> over mounds and mounds of sand
> the swinging grasses sweep
> patterns on the slopes
> the sidewinder passes out of sight.
> I was too young to hear silence before. (1)

In dominant culture constructions, silence is often configured in visual and spatial terms; in such an equation, silence equals invisibility or the position of outsider. But in these lines Yamada's descriptions of the silence around her are rendered in visual, not auditory, terms. She realigns silence with visibility, reclaiming it from absence. Here, silence heals; it signifies not the absence of self but the complete presence of it. The dominating power of the addressed "you" is destabilized, its autonomy denied.

> I cannot stay in the desert
> where you will have me nor
> will I be brought back in a cage
> to grace your need for exotica.
> I write these words at night
> for I am still a night creature
> but I will not keep a discreet distance.

The recuperation of silence is tied to the reappropriation of written language and the body on the speaker's own terms. By refusing to satisfy the "need for exotica," Yamada regenders the body by refusing its sexualization, and it is significant that she does so at the site of the Japanese American subject's degenderization and complete racialization—on the grounds of the former Minidoka relocation camp. However, even here, Yamada is wary of the ways in which the Japanese American female subject can extricate the body completely from the hegemonic orientalist constructs. The poem ends on an uneasy note of mutual détente underscored by mutual threat: "If you must fit me to your needs / I will die / and so will you." The contingency registered by the "if" here recalls the similarly contingent freedom of the female body in "Cincinnati," and serves to remind us that the body is never a neutral site. Rather, it is a site of contestation, the terms of which continually shift. As Yamada suggests in "Masks of Woman" (1988, 89), it is through the manipulation and conscious deployment of the bodily surface that the writer sunders the forced identification between mask and self.

Refusing Masks, Refusing Silence: Janice Mirikitani and the Poetic Politics of Resistance

Unlike Yamada's early poetic of irony, Mirikitani's poetic tone from the outset has been one of rage pointedly expressed in a

polemical and militant politics of resistance. Though bot
on the difficult intersections of race, gender and nationalism; wt
vulnerability to male violence; and the desire to connect with ethnic
identity and Issei culture through maternal figures, Mirikitani deals
much more directly with the problems of the essentialized Asian female
body and its vulnerability to violent intrusion, at once ideological and
physical. If the body is a site of contestation for Mitsuye Yamada, it is
an all-out war zone for Janice Mirikitani. The internment is not only a
crucial experience of racial marking that must be witnessed but a foun-
dational metaphor for the violation of the raced body. As I discuss below, because all bodies are penetrable and thus vulnerable, internment
does not so much degender Nikkei women as feminize Nikkei men.

In many ways, Mirikitani is an important exception among the writers discussed in this book. For her, dominant culture readings of the
Asian body, male or female, reduce the Asian/American subject to an
opaque, inhuman mask. Strategies of resistance do not include reappropriating and strategically deploying that mask as a way to protect the
masked/masking self. Within Mirikitani's poetic, one deeply rooted in
oppositional politics, to reappropriate the Asian face as mask is to essentially accept the terms of its imposition. More important, that mask
serves only to distort and render completely nonexistent the subject
trapped beneath. "Doreen" (1987, 17) and "Recipe" (20), both clearly
articulate a belief in the truth of the body. In the first poem, a Japanese
girl attempts to escape the fact of her Asianness, "round face," and "narrow" eyes by "paint[ing] her eyes round" and covering her face with
white powder. Literally turning her face into a more acceptable mask
emblematizes Doreen's rejection of other Asians and her attempt to gain
acceptance through exploiting her own sexuality. The poem's end is a
deep indictment of the self-destruction that results:

One day,
Doreen riding fast
with her friend
went through the windshield
and tore off
her skin
from scalp to chin.

And we were sad.

Because
no one could remember
Doreen's face.

ıs the site of its own truth, anything that compromises that participates in the body's destruction; reconstructing the body in any way is to participate in a life-denying lie. In this poem, Doreen's mask of cosmetics and easy sex destroys her face, her person. Similarly, "Recipe" suggests that manipulation of the bodily surface is a perversion of bodily truth. Written in the imperative form characteristic of cookbooks, the poem directs its reader in the mechanics of eye-taping.[14] The poem begins with a list of "ingredients: scissors, Scotch magic transparent tape, / eyeliner—water based, black. / Optional: false eyelashes," explains the process step by step, then ends with the finishing touch: "Do not cry." Again, Mirikitani suggests the inseparability of visible body and interiority. The injunction not to cry (so as not to ruin the results of the process) disciplines and constricts emotional expression just as the eye-taping itself disciplines the Asian body. What on the surface might seem an example of "self-improvement" is, the poem makes clear, an act of self-silencing.

In all of her work, *Awake in the River* (1978), *Shedding Silence* (1987) and *We, the Dangerous: Selected and New Poems* (1995), and more than any other writer I discuss, Mirikitani is aware and wary of the ways in which silence has been used to dominate, oppress and deny the subjectivities of the marginalized. Several of her pieces—"Shedding Silence," "Prisons of Silence," "Breaking Silence" (1987, 125, 5, 33)—explicitly associate silence with the erasure of self, the appropriation and denial of agency, fragmentation and death. Mirikitani's work positions the subject squarely within the matrix of political, racial and sexual power, within which the subtleties and interrelatedness of speech and silence give way to one overarching reality: language is power, silence is powerlessness and helpless rage.

"Jungle Rot and Open Arms," an early poem in Mirikitani's first book, *Awake in the River*,[15] and dedicated to "a Vietnam Veteran brother, ex-prisoner," marks out the territories of speech and silence within a narrative context that directly associates the latter with violence enacted on the body. In the poem, the speaker's brother, drunk and filled with rage, tells her about his relationship with a Vietnamese woman. "Her hair / was long and dark—like yours," he begins. One morning, after a raid about which he was not informed, he awakes to discover the woman has been killed. Her body has been dismembered; all that remains is her arm, "still clasping" her lover. The sister's response is one of horrified silence:

We sat in a silence
that mocks fools
that lifts us to the final language.
. . . .
i stood amidst
his wreckage
and wept for myself.

so where is my
political education? my
rhetoric answers to everything? my
theory into practice? my
intensification of life in art?

words
are
like
the stone,
the gravemarker
over an arm
in Vietnam.

In some ways, this poem recalls the ambivalence toward language evident in several other pieces we have seen. In the face of the brother's
grief and fury, rhetoric and theory are reduced to facile ineffectiveness.
But Mirikitani does not offer silence as an alternative. The silence that
follows the brother's story parallels the silencing through violent death
and links it with the dismembered body of the Vietnamese woman.
Physically identified with the murdered woman, the speaker casts about
for a language of power different from that represented by the disembodied language of rhetoric and theory, the romanticized notion of the
"intensification of life in art." The "final language" to which this silence
leads, I believe, is not the language of silence but the language of rage.
The stone marks, as words do, a space defined by the force of political/
national rhetoric and its power to kill, but also by the brother's narrative
and the rage associated with it. Words of witness, like a gravestone,
mark the site of death, remember its happening and witness its facticity.[16] The gravestones that attest to silencing also serve as the catalyst
for a language of resistance born of anger. Speech wielded as the source
and tool of violence evokes speech reappropriated as a source and tool
of survival.

The linking of the body and language, represented by the speaker's
identification with the Vietnamese woman in the poem, are deeply im-
bedded in issues of appropriation. Throughout Mirikitani's work, the

violence of appropriation is associated with repression and murderous-ness. One of the primary ways in which Asian American women are denied identificatory power and therefore discursive power, is through the conflation of raciality with sexuality. Given the long history of the complete sexualization and exoticization of Asian/American women, the body's appropriation is synonymous with the appropriation of sexuality.

In "The Question Is" (1978), Mirikitani details ways in which Asian/Asian American women are sexually objectified. While the Asian woman who speaks in this poem thinks of yellow as "the color of lemons, / sun, / early morning on water," the white male speaker associates it with es-sentialized difference:

> You are so
> exotic
> so curiously pale
>
> Your Kind
> has always attracted me
>
> Your slanted eyes
> hold mysteries of the orient
>
> Give me
> your novelty body.
>
> But before you do
> the Question
> Is
> it true
> your cunt is slanted too?

Mirikitani suggests that the man's question, preceded by three declara-tive assertions and a command, "Give me / your novelty body," is less a query than a rhetorical question to which he already assumes the an-swer and for which he seeks titillating confirmation. More than idle curiosity, it is a fascination with the exotic configured as alien otherness. Mirikitani connects this sexual othering with exclusion in "American Geisha" (1987, 21). Here, physiological/sexual difference is directly re-lated to the assumption of foreignness: "My daughter / was called / F.O.B. // at the beach // bosomed in her swimsuit. // Shake it baby, does it slide sideways?" (23). Mirikitani surrounds this section with sev-eral others in which the conflation of Japanese American women with Japanese women draws on the same assumptions that motivate ques-tions about their national origin and ability to speak English.

In a monologue of Mirikitani's prose/verse play, "Shedding Silence"

(1987, 125), the sexuality of the Japanese American woman who speaks has been used against her and becomes a source of degradation and shame:

I had a crush on this white guy, see? He was a track star. Drove a blue convertible and had gray eyes. . . . One day the track star calls up. . . . Me and gray eyes in his blue convertible. He parks near the tennis courts, deserted and dark. Starts kissing me. The night sounds stopped. The air started smelling of jasmine and silver starts. It was really something. His hands start up my sweater and he kisses my breasts. My sweater comes up over my head. Suddenly all the white lights go on. It was crazy, like a bomb had dropped and I just didn't hear it. I look at him and he's smiling like nothing's happening. I grab for my sweater and bra and I hear the laughter now like red rain. Three of his friends from the track team turned on all the big tennis court lights and he is laughing too. Said they never made it before with a yellow chick and couldn't I take a joke? (131)

Later, she says that she is "a river. / Frozen on its surface" (133). For Japanese American women, "Lotus Blossom" and "Geisha" are not simply a relatively benign form of sexualized name-calling. As several of Mirikitani's poems attest, in a racist and sexist society sexuality is vulnerability. Discursive forms of appropriation—sexualization and exoticization—are inherently threatening because they are inextricably tied to other forms of appropriation—sexual exploitation, sexual humiliation and rape.

Several of Mirikitani's poems, like Yamada's, focus on the doubled threat of violence that faces Asian American women. While a few of her poems deal with the physical violence to which all women are potential victims, Mirikitani draws clear lines of difference between white women and women of color. In "Ms." (1978/1995, 95), she suggests that race and class privilege not only protects white women from the violence experienced by people of color but places them in a position in which they themselves are the perpetrators of that violence. The poem begins with a white woman's objection to being addressed as "Miss" instead of "Ms.":

Her lips pressed white
thinning words like pins
pricking me—a victim of sexism.
. . . .
I said,
        white lace & satin was never soiled by sexism
        sheltered as you are by mansions built on Indian land

your diamonds shipped with slaves from Africa
your underwear washed by Chinese laundries
your house cleaned by my grandmother
so do not push me any further.

And when you quit
killing us
for democracy
and stop calling ME *gook,*

I will call you
whatever you like.

While Mirikitani's elision of class differences is somewhat problematic, as is her assertion that "white lace & satin was never soiled by / sexism," this poem locates the greatest vulnerability to systemic oppression at the site of race. The phallic imagery of the white woman's words "like pins / pricking me" constructs her racial privilege as male-gendered. The poem lays out in no uncertain terms the high cost people of color have paid to maintain such privilege and focuses squarely on the reality against which any gesture toward self-definition must inevitably fight—against which it often loses with consequences much more serious than "Miss" feeling twitted over issues of nomenclature. While white women are also vulnerable to and all too often the victims of domestic battery and sexual brutality, Mirikitani points out that Asian American women are not only vulnerable to the sexist discourse that endorses and causes such violence, but that they are also potentially the victims of racial/nationalist discourses underwritten by structures of systemic oppression that, in effect, protect white women.

Indeed, for Mirikitani, the power conferred by whiteness supersedes differences of gender, at times erasing them altogether. "Japs" (1978), for instance, completely reverses the gendered identities of the white woman and the Japanese man who works for her. While the feminized "midget jap" works in the field, the "wife rapist / lurks behind [her] window shade." In "American Geisha" (1987, 21) the geisha image through which Japanese American women are constructed collapses both gender and ethnic distinctions:

Mr. Wong
went to Washington, D.C.
served on a Commission
for Small Businesses.

Was asked
if he was familiar
with the system of free enterprise?

and how come
he didn't speak
with an accent?

The inclusion of a Chinese American man in a poem entitled "American Geisha" comments on the ways in which gross outlines of racial caricature and assumptions of essential foreignness obliterate significant ethnic differences between Asians. Second, the emasculation to which Asian American men are subject is a symptom of a more generalized gendering of Asianness as female, much as in the poem "Japs." Mirikitani directly parallels the sexualization of Asian American women with the feminization of race and national identity.

Indeed, Mirikitani draws this equivalence out explicitly in her poems dealing with the internment. "Prisons of Silence" (1987, 5) uses gender-specific images that construct the internment as a metaphorical act of rape that collapses distinctions of gender:

Jap!
Filthy Jap!
. . . .
Hands in our hair,
hands that spread our legs
and searched our thighs for secret weapons,
hands that knit barbed wire
to cripple our flight.

Giant hot hands flung me,
fluttering, speechless into
barbed wire, thorns in a broken wing.

The strongest prisons are built
with walls of silence.

The internment, configured as sexual violation, also associates silence with violent acts of feminization and forced imprisonment. Several of Mirikitani's internment poems concentrate on silence or the loss of speech's signifying powers and a denial of subjectivity that tie silence to sexual brutality. The imagery of violent surveillance suggests that speech is the "secret weapon" whose forced removal renders the speaking subject a silent object of state control. In "Crazy Alice" (1978), for instance, Aunt Alice, who has been driven insane by her wartime experience, thinks of "invasions / and prison camps / and open[s] her legs / to the white boss man." Her loss of self is further indicated by the lower case "i" that suggests her namelessness in an internal refrain that runs throughout the poem: "life's so strange / before the war / i had a name."

Because the internment for Mirikitani is a powerful instance of the erasure of subjectivity, defined by race and by gender, nearly all of Mirikitani's poems about internment tend to focus on women's experiences. While she is specifically concerned with the doubled vulnerability of Japanese American women, Mirikitani also reads their compounded victimization as emblematic of the experience of Japanese American men in a racist, emasculating society.[17]

Problematizing the Truth of the Body: "Spoils of War" and Its Revisions

Mirikitani's identification of whiteness with power and sexual violence and the metaphor of rape in relation to discursive, social power are explicitly joined with the violence of nationalism in her first version of a combined prose and poetry piece entitled "Spoils of War" (1978/1995, 186–201).[18] In one striking passage, a Japanese American woman listens to the news as her white lover "mount[s] her again, pressing breath from her. . . . Between gasps of the fucking, T.V. droning": "Nixon, nose skiing to the corners of his jaws, *fingering* long stems of microphones, *pumping* with fists for emphasis . . . 'it is necessary to *escalate penetration* into enemy harbors. These communists stop at nothing . . . spread like maggots in a democracy [*sic*] clean world' " (Wong 1996, 196; emphasis mine, ellipses in original).

Nixon goes on to justify Lieutenant Calley's atrocities at My Lai as necessary actions "in the line of duty . . . to show we mean business" (Wong 1996, 196). Mirikitani's word choice and the way in which she cuts between Nixon's news conference and the Japanese American woman and her lover figure nationalism as a gendered enterprise that expresses itself through the paradigm of sexual violation; conversely, the poem also suggests that the sexual relationship between the unnamed Japanese American woman and her white lover, Gerald, cannot be separated from the context of, and functions as a metaphor for, nationalist aggression. It is, in fact, her lover who smilingly defends the massacre at My Lai as "a means to an end," which he compares to the dropping of the atomic bomb during World War II. He further asserts that the bomb prevented the United States from having "to share the spoils of war with Russia" (Wong 1996, 190).

The poem cuts between the past and present, as well as between the Japanese American woman's relationship with her white American lover and various scenarios of injustice: the internment, her family's fight against the injustice of a drunken white driver who was never charged for running over a fourteen-year-old cousin, the protagonist's molestation by an uncle and her mother's refusal to believe her. In all instances, there is a truth denied or obscured. Just as the truth is distorted for duplicitous purposes, so is the woman in the poem distorted by her white lover's desire, which is indistinguishable from the desire to dominate. She has little sense of identity as either a woman or a Japanese American apart from the ways in which both have been constructed through dominant discourse. Her sense of disconnection is so great, in fact, that she thinks of herself as nonexistent: "As long as she could remember, she did not exist. There was a physical body, thin legs and arms, small torso, flat hips, and a face that changed as often as the reactions to it" (188).

The piece resolves itself through an unconvincing reliance on a long-buried and mystical identification with Japan. The woman stands near the sea, identified earlier as "a magic place . . . where she played like a mermaid, singing in the sun . . . speaking strange tongues" (191), and listens/sings herself into connectedness with what seems to be a mythical Japaneseness (indicated by haiku-like fragments prefaced by words in Japanese) associated with grandmothers, home, song and embodiment. "Spoils of War," for all the litany of abuses it catalogues, ends on a celebratory note of possibility and healing. The truth of the body is locatable and recoverable, and it is at the point of recuperation that the woman calls out her name, "contrapuntal to the water's cry, My Name is Hatsuko" (Wong 1996, 201).

In her second book, *Shedding Silence,* published nine years after *Awake in the River,* Mirikitani reworks "Spoils of War," once again combining prose and poetry, but to a much different effect. The later version of "Spoils of War" (1987, 57) explicitly connects sexual brutality with racial/gender positioning and with the conflation of national and racial identities. But where the earlier "Spoils of War" suggests a recovery of self, identity and agency through the reclamation of Japanese womanhood, the later version refuses all possibility that the connection to ethnic and gender identity results in self-defined, resistant agency. The body is not recoverable, cannot be claimed and is always under the threat of erasure through a physical violence that is the logical outcome of white masculinist nationalism.

Indeed, Mirikitani seems to completely abandon the belief that the discursive power of self-naming is any kind of power at all. The piece again focuses on a Japanese American woman whose name, Violet, is the first word in the piece. Significantly, she is jogging through the park, so confident in her body that she has promised herself a five-mile run. The strength of her "sturdy thighs and sleek runner's calves" (1987, 57) is matched by the slogan of empowerment emblazoned across her sweatshirt: "Lotus Blossom Doesn't Live Here." She has recently decided, over her parents' objections, to move in with her African American lover. But Violet is meanwhile being watched by a white Vietnam veteran who has made a decision of his own: "Of all the joggers he saw, this was the one he wanted" (57). Mirikitani points to the uselessness and tragic irony of the statement on Violet's sweatshirt through a narrative strategy that alternates between the third-person prose description and first-person verse lines that run through the man's head:

> They all had Vietnamese women
> None like mine.
> . . . .
> She never withheld her warm thighs,
> even when gorged with woman blood,
> hot blood
> sucking me deeper into her.
> . . . .
> Swelling within her,
> my blade, gleaming in the moonlight
> exits flesh, flashes in her eyes.
> She licks the blood from the shaft.
> Deep, I thrust it past her teeth.
> She took it all
> her throat tightening on it
> blood bubbling from the edges
> . . . .
> My blade cuts the arm away,
> splits her womb
> that spumes hot blood.

This brutal and paranoid narrative inserts itself between Violet's thoughts and determination to reject her parent's devaluation of her as a female child. For the first time, she feels "free as the wind in her face. . . . She would leave this week. Run free of them. . . . She'd live her own life" (1987, 59, 61). Violet's sense of freedom, however, is set up in ironic counterpoint to the man circling closer and closer. When he attacks Violet, the man unsheathes a knife and silences her by saying "he will cut her throat if she screams" (61). He beats her unconscious, pulls off her shorts and "gently. Gently. Caressing, kisses her slightly open mouth, her neck, her still arms. Inserts his blade in her womb and makes her bleed" (61–62). Then he severs Violet's arm, "gently" wraps it and "carries it like a child to his van" (62). His brutal act of silencing is paralleled by his internal narrative, which ends the piece:

> Spirit of the bayonet.
> red / march
> white / hup
> blue / eyes front
> Square your piece
> left / right
> kill 'em
> thrust / jab
> jab
> jab / kill 'em
> "hey mamasan
> joto mate ichiban"
> poontang one / two
> poontang three / four
> when we're done
> we'll kill some more.

What is most disturbing about this reworked version of "Spoils" is its suggestion that Asian American women's attempts to construct their own subjectivity always have the potential to be reduced to a mere sweatshirt slogan, and that freedom and agency are always contingent, hanging in the balances of someone else's projections or paranoia.

In many ways, this reworked version is a dark commentary and critique of the earlier "Spoils." Where the unnamed Japanese American woman is able to claim her name through mystically connecting to the truth of her own female, Japanese body, Violet never escapes the body's construction by the alienating gaze of the white veteran, and any gestures toward self-proclaimed agency are always already futile.[19] Where the effects of the Second World War and the internment are ultimately escapable in the earlier piece, the 1987 version is unrelenting in its insistence that war, figured here through the war in Vietnam, is merely the historical emblem for the symbolic war within which Asian/American female bodies are the "spoils." Constructed in terms that elide both particularity and subjectivity, the body cannot be recast as the source and site of a truth that awaits rediscovery. A possible reading of the shift that takes place between the first and second versions of "Spoils" is that the piece's development traces Mirikitani's recognition that essentializing and dehistoricizing the Asian female body is highly problematic in that, in many ways, it replicates the structures of orientalism. Yet the version of the piece in *Shedding Silence* can imagine no place outside those structures. These two poems, then, map out the problematic within which Mirikitani rethinks the body and its relations to gender and race.

Historicizing the Body

The silence of the murdered woman that closes "Spoils of War" reminds us that for Mirikitani to be silent is to be silenced. Silence here, as in many of her poems, is identified with frustrated repression, racism and powerlessness configured through the trope of sexual violation. For Mirikitani, in a society that recognizes only speech as power, the language of silence is no language at all. Silence does not protest but enables rape, systemic racism and imperialist aggression. As in "Jungle Rot and Open Arms," where the severed arm of the Vietnamese woman symbolizes the severing of subject from speech, the relation between embodiment and language runs deep throughout Mirikitani's work. Yet, the poems come to resist easy formulations that would allow the voicing of rage and disempowerment itself to reclaim the body. As the poems progress, re-membering the body is enacted through remembering history and raising one's voice in witness.

A central poem in *Shedding Silence*, "Breaking Silence" (33) turns on the doubleness of the tongue-as-body and the tongue-as-speech. The poem is a tribute to Mirikitani's mother, who testified during the reparation hearings held in the late 1970s and early 1980s:

From the silences
in the glass caves of our ears,
from the crippled tongue,
from the mute, wet eyelash,
testimonies waiting like winter.
We were told

that silence was better
golden like our skin,
. . . .
We were made to believe our faces
betrayed us.
Our bodies were loud
with yellow screaming flesh
needing to be silenced
behind barbed wire.

(33, 34)

Through the image of the "crippled tongue," silence is synonymous with
the repression of racial identity. The mother's testimony bears witness
to and reverses the internment's erasure and silencing of the "yellow
screaming flesh." Unlike Yamada, who in "Desert Run" realigns silence
with visibility and reclaims the desert as a site of subjectivity, Mirikitani
constructs the testimonial act as a transformative one that claims visibility through language that grounds itself firmly in history:

I kill this,
the silence . . .
There are miracles that happen
[my mother] said,
and everything is made visible.
    We see the cracks and fissures in our soil:
We speak of suicides and intimacies,
of longings lush like wet furrows,
of oceans bearing us toward imagined riches,
of burning humiliations and
crimes by the government.
Of self hate and of love that breaks
through silences.
    We are lightning and justice.
    Our souls become transparent like glass
revealing tears for war-dead sons
red ashes of Hiroshima
jagged wounds from barbed wire.

Speaking through her mother's voice, Mirikitani transforms the desert
of internment to "a rainforest of color / and noise" in which "we must
recognize ourselves at last," in which raced subjectivity is neither silent
nor invisible. Significantly, Mirikitani reclaims both Japanese American
and Japanese subjectivity through her identification with the victims of
the atomic bomb. She extends this identification to all Asians in "We,

the Dangerous" (1978/1995, 26), in which "we" refers to an Asian diaspora that includes the exoticized Asian woman, the Chinese Americans who labored in sweat shops and laundries, the Japanese *hibakusha* (survivors of the atomic bombing), the Vietnamese, the internees at Tule Lake. This inclusion enacts a reversal of the ways in which the conflation of Asian Americans with Asians has been used to exclude and silence.

Mirikitani most strikingly employs the strategy of reversal and reappropriation in the poem "Slaying Dragon Ladies" (1987, 43). As the ambiguity of the title suggests, Mirikitani both undermines (slays) the Dragon Lady stereotype and appropriates it (Dragon Ladies themselves slay those who perpetuate the stereotype). The sexual fascination that constructs Asian American women as a "geisha girl / China Doll / slant cunt whore" who "shuffle[s] to you / . . . / and bow[s] / to your growing / fantasy" is turned against itself through the reimagining of the body mapped in and by history:

> You don't know me.
> . . . .
> You cannot see me.
> > my breasts are Manzanar's desert
> > my thighs an Arkansas swamp
> > my veins are California's railroads
> > my feet a Chicago postwar ghetto.
> I prepare slowly
> with the memory
> of my mother who is
> civilized,
> my father who
> fought a war for you,
> my grandmother, compassionate,
> who forgave you.
> My hands are steady.
> Pentipped fingers
> drenched in ink.
> Ready for the slaying.
> > You will know me.

Mirkitani employs the traditional association between woman's body and nation but undermines it by identifying the Asian body not with Asia but with the United States, as well as by rejecting the assumed link of passivity between female body and landscape. "You don't know me" is neither helpless complaint nor plaintive request, but a veiled threat. The Asian female body, so often used to obscure Asian American subjectivity, is rewritten with the histories of the oppressed and becomes an agent of retaliation. The stereotypical long, red fingernails of the Dragon Lady, "ready for the slaying," scratch out a language of protest rooted in a self-defined, but historically contextualized, Japanese American female identity.

It is this identification that pushes Mirikitani's poetic into the field of history and into an alliance of resistance with other oppressed peoples. "Who is Singing This Song?" (1987, 102) is structured in a call-and-response form that mirrors Mirikitani's call for an intersubjective relationship with international communities and communities of color that forges a solidarity of resistance:

> Who is singing this song?
>
>   I am
>
> a river of hands that reach
> to the suffering, the suppressed in
> South Africa,
> the paralyzed in El Salvador,
> the starving of Ethiopia, the dying Hibakusha.
>
> a wreath of hands
> woven from blossoms shaped from
> whispers for justice
> over the grave of Vincent Chin.
>
> a sea of beating hands
> that persuade patriarchies that
> strength is not force
> and real power is not oppressing
> nor patronizing,
> but shared power
> among people free, working,
> creating, passionate.
>
> Who is singing this song?
>
>   I am
>
> We survive by hearing.
> We speak to each other.
>
>   (107–8)

Firmly rooted in the identity and protest movements of the 1960s and 1970s, Mitsuye Yamada and Janice Mirikitani write out of a passionate conviction that language, that poetry, can act as witness to the wrongs of history. In speaking out of and for an identity defined by race, gender and national identity, their poetry reappropriates the figure of the Japanese woman and redefines Japanese American female subjectivity, confronting issues of nationalism, essentialism and sexuality and struggling with the problematics of power, language and silence.

Other contemporary Japanese American women poets also work with these issues, though in ways that suggest a shift in their poetic strategy — a shift that the poetics of advocacy and identity politics of writers like Yamada and Mirikitani made possible. Although the poetry of witness and protest is by no means abandoned, a much more self-conscious poetic emerges, one that is overtly concerned with its own status *as* a poetic and extends the interrogations into the nature of language found in Yamada's and Mirikitani's work. Of these poets, Kimiko Hahn foregrounds the complexities of the speaking subject and increasingly destabilizes the very structures of history through which that subject becomes "known."

Translating Subjectivity: Kimiko Hahn's Poetics of Fragrance

Kimiko Hahn's poetry encompasses a wide range, from oppositional politics to the complexities of sexual relationships, from childhood memories of Japanese fairy tales to the experience of being a mother. But one of the most persistent and interesting themes in Hahn's work—*Air Pocket* (1989), *Earshot* (1992) and *The Unbearable Heart* (1995)—revolves around language and its relation to subjectivity. As in the work of Mitsuye Yamada, many of Hahn's poems resist the strict separation of poet from speaker. But where Yamada's poetic is one comfortable with frequently assuming an autobiographical "I," Hahn's is much more ambivalent about positioning the poet's own voice in a seamless relationship with the speaker's voice within the poem. She interrogates the critical convention of separating the writer's own subjectivity and voice from that of the poem's "speaker," recognizing the ways in which this potentially hides the traces and particular investments of the writer, but she is equally wary of collapsing the two voices in ways that ignore the problematics of language and assume its transparency. Hahn's exploration of the writerly persona foregrounds a number of issues relating to the subjectivity, or subjectivities, that inform any text. Thus, she does not bracket her own subjectivity and its constructions of, by and within language. Because of that engagement, my discussion of several of Hahn's poems refer to Hahn herself, in a manner that remaps the possibilities between the extremes of a reductive autobiographical reading on the one hand and a disembodied textualism on the other.[20]

Indeed, finding a critical language with which to discuss Hahn's work mirrors Hahn's own poetic, which is in many ways about the search for a poetic, one that is grounded in the body understood as the site of both materiality and history. The complexities of embodied subjectivity, which have traditionally been negatively race- and gender-marked, find their corollary in Hahn's trope of translation, which returns to the body through the trope of fragrance.

Hahn's is no simplistic poetic of the body, as though the latter were merely the passive repository of an always locatable ur-language. "Going Inside to Write" (1992, 15), for instance, locates the possibilities of language in the body but also locates the body itself:

> She finds the only place to write
> is the *ote arai* [water closet].
> So she takes in her notebook
> and retells the story of the peach boy:
> . . . .
> [who] stepped out and said
> *chichiue hahaue domo arigato gozaimashita*
> (thank you).
> He was a baby
> but he could speak.
> In the half-light
> she finishes her version.
>
> Here the mind deregulates language.

Hahn shrewdly and comically references Virginia Woolf's room of one's own by placing the woman writer in the bathroom, a private space, as well as the site of the body's most basic and necessary functions. Clearing a space is "warranty toward tending oneself / in the onslaught of others" and is thus an escape from the constant demands of "an infant's bowel movements / stacks of dishes, / international economies or classical literature." It is also a "deregulat[ion]" of language, dissociating it from its male-centeredness and the father's voice that "calls from the far room" and, as implied by the allusion to Woolf, from Eurocentricity. Thus, what is given voice "in the half-light" of the bathroom is what usually is not accorded discursive power: babies, Japanese subjectivity (in the half-translated line), the female, the woman who writes "her version" of the Japanese children's tale, "Momotaro."

Hahn refuses the romanticized metaphoricity of the body and does not allow discursivity to empty out the body *as* body. Thus, the body is coded, not just through the socially saturated locus of maternality, but through the physicality of birthing:

> To know the body
> from the inside—
>
> the lining of the uterus, the muscles
> that squeeze blood out,
>
> the Braxton-Hicks contractions
>
> labor
>
> crisis
>
> C-section—
>
> to know the body from the inside
> is warranty against fear
>
> ("baby look what you've done to me")—
>
> against the fear
>
> of one's own body.
>
> (15–16)

Hahn's association of writing with the female body in labor and with Japaneseness in this poem might seem to evoke an essentialist poetic of "writing the body," but the complex syntax and structure resist that characterization. The abrupt phrasal breaks, parenthetical lines and convoluted sentences suggest that, in fact, these utterances are highly aware of their linguistic constructedness. Structurally, the poem shifts between what and how "she" is writing. Her poem is intercut with reflective passages about the process of writing, spoken by a depersonalized first-person narrator. The effect of this strategy is that the language self-consciously foregrounds its location in the body, which is itself constructed contextually by its own maternal and necessary functions. Thus, the ambiguity of the title, in which "going inside" refers equally to going inside the body and going into the bathroom, contests the idea that the body is an assumed locus of articulation, from which issues a latent, ready-made language.

The ways in which women must cobble together a language, as opposed to merely finding it, is more apparent in "Revolutions" (1992, 17). In this poem, Hahn explicitly identifies her own poetic as springing from the tradition of Heian women writers, who themselves had to fashion a language in which they could speak:

> Forbidden to learn Chinese
> the women wrote in the language
> of their islands
> and so Japanese
> became the currency of high aesthetics
> for centuries
> as did the female persona: the pine
> the longing. This is the truth.
>
> (We can rise above those needles.)

For Hahn, the Japanese female literary tradition begins with a gesture of resistance, a refusal to be relegated to non-expressivity because of their sex. Here, as in the poem above, Hahn avoids essentializing a historical necessity by focusing not on "a women's language," but on a "female persona" that was subsequently adopted by Japanese male writers. The image of the pine tree (*matsu* means both "pine" and "wait") as a symbol for woman further suggests the constructedness of language. The parenthetical assertion that "We can rise above those needles" rejects the metaphorical conflation of woman with passive longing, reaffirming the agency of the women writers.

Though Hahn writes that she too "didn't learn poetic diction from the Classics, / rather, transistor radios. Confidence in my body also," she lays no simple claims to the Heian tradition. Even as she invokes (literary) history, she refers to historical specificities that disallow an ahistorical nostalgia. "Anywhere else," she writes in another parenthetical line, "girls of mixed marriages would be prostitutes or courtesans." (In an earlier poem, "Resistance: A Poem on Ikat Cloth" [1989, 59], Hahn notes, "Centuries earlier / you'd have been courted / or sold . . . / For a Eurasian, sold.") Hahn's self-identification as Eurasian, a social identity instantiated at the site/sight of the body, complicates her construction of raced subjectivity and, in turn, informs her inquiry into the nature of language and the search for a viable poetic. In saying this, I do not intend to imply that Hahn's poetic is the inevitable outcome of her identity, an essentializing move that Hahn's own poetry contests;[21] rather, she points out that mixed-race identity precludes any easy alignment with the Japanese literary tradition, however much Hahn identifies it through its female line. While Heian women writers provide a model of writerly resistance, Hahn calls attention to her difference from them, a difference that would have barred her from the courtly ranks of the women whom she credits with the birth of the Japanese literary tradition and that prevents a romanticized, nostalgic identification with that tradition.

The several allusions to Japanese culture throughout her work, then, do not function as a taproot to an originary racial self. In fact, through the trope of translation, Hahn consistently calls attention to the difficulties of forging a poetic based in Japanese cultural and literary sources. Hahn's claim on the linguistic power of Japanese women's literature ("I want those words that gave women de facto power") immediately gives rise to the problematics of translation:

> I connect to that century
> as after breath is knocked out
> we suck it back in.
>
> The words the men stole after all
> to write about a daughter's death
> or their own (soft) thigh
> belongs to us—to me—
> though translation is a border
> we look over or into;
> sometimes a familiar noise
> ('elegant confusion'). But can *meaning*
> travel
> the way capital moves
> like oil in the Alaskan pipeline
> or in tanker in the Straits of Hormuz?
> Can those sounds move like that?
> Yes. But we don't understand
>
> . . . .
>
> If I could translate the culture
> women cultivate
> I would admit to plum
> and plumb.

Translation here is not only linguistic but cultural; transmission is never direct but is always inflected through the temporal and historical. Hahn figures her relation to this literary past as an act of translation, as a connection that comes only after a break: as when the "breath is knocked out," there is not undifferentiated breathing, but the breath that precedes and the breath that comes after. Moreover, the body—the instrument and site of respiration—marks a permeable border that transforms air to breath. Thus, translation, "a border / we look over or into," similarly marks a space of transformation. Nevertheless, the poem asserts that the words claimed by these writers—the language that "men stole after all . . . belongs to us—to me," and the search for "older sisters" of whom "there are never enough" leads "with the desperation of a root" to the literary tradition of the Heian women writers. Focusing on the body evokes a connection of identification through gender, and partly through race, but Hahn balances identification through the body with identification through the act of revolution:

> Revolution for example is the soft
> exact
> orbit of planet, moon, seed.
> Also seizing the means of production
> for our class.
> Where does that come from?
> *It all begins with women,* she said.

Identifying women as a class reinforces the anti-nostalgic strain set up by Hahn's insistence on her racial identity and suggests a solidarity conferred by a shared status, not simply shared biology. In this context, the poet's own act of cultural translation is not an isomorphic transposition that collapses difference but is analogous to the way in which Japanese women writers precipitated a literary revolution in trying to find a language through which to give their subjectivity voice.

In an earlier poem, "Daughter" (1989, 26), Hahn directly associates translation with historicity, exploring the problematics and possibilities of translation understood as a mode of cultural transmission. The poem implicitly relies on an understanding of a specific history to ground its central tension between representation and translation:

> Although I'm oldest I can't
> be the one who paints
>
> or speaks grandmother's language
> like a picture-bride marriage
>
> to a still life: a plate
> of oranges, plums and grapes

one takes care to arrange
precise as syntax—as a passage

one must translate
for someone else. That

is the greater danger
than waking with a stranger.

Hahn's reference to picture-bride marriages is a complex one: the language difference implicitly marks a generational difference between the speaker and the grandmother who, as an Issei, is of a generation in which many women were married as "picture-brides." Women and men, often having seen only photographs of their prospective partner until the day of the wedding, married virtual strangers. Hahn thus calls into question the nature of representation: like the marriage photographs that gave no hint of the subject behind the image, a carefully arranged still life is flat—a unidimensional rendering of its subject. In both cases, the fixity of the picture fails to articulate complexity; its convention of artifice only alludes to representational authenticity by assuming a fixed subject. In a similar way, translating the grandmother's language to satisfy the expectation of a seamless transmission of culture presupposes culture as inert. The translating subject herself then becomes, like a still life, a flat representation that elides subjectivity. In other words, one becomes a stranger to oneself, a "greater danger" than a picture-bride "waking with a stranger."

But the gap between representation and translation, as well as the gaps within any act of translation (here, between person and image), also references a particular practice by which prospective grooms and brides alike could capitalize on the absence of the photograph's referents. Those who feared they were too old, unattractive or otherwise not potentially desirable often sent pictures of subjects other than themselves. While duplicitous, the practice suggests a space for agency that complicates what at first might seem to be a poem wholly based on the assumption of female passivity and "acted-uponness." Once again, Hahn alludes to history while destabilizing its interpretive hegemony through specificity. The poem formally parallels this move through its rhetorical dependence on simile ("like a picture-bride marriage," "as a passage one must translate"), which invokes comparison but only through an implicit understanding of difference.[22]

Translation as a trope for the complex construction of subjectivity, implicit in "Daughter," is more explicitly explored in "Comp. Lit."

(1992, 81), an intertextual, multisectioned poem in which Hahn interrogates the ways that a translated text both resists and is subsumed by the subjectivity of the translator. "The translator's subjectivity," notes Hahn, "makes the parts whole: a saucer and cup. / Hot water" (sec. iv). That is, the interpretive element in translation shapes not only the form of the text but its content. In the face of this truth, Hahn suggests that, faced with two translations of the same text, the reader must negotiate between two wholly different subjectivities. Hahn thus plays with the abbreviation "comp. lit.," referring to the comparison between translation and original as well as to competing interpretive acts:

> You barely remember Japanese.
> ....
> What happens when there are two texts
> in translation?
> Who can we trust
> when our *bungo* [literary language] has deteriorated
> to elementary tables
> for *beshi, kemu, gotoshi* [archaicisms].
> How can we compare
> without the original.
>
>   (sec. 1)

Brief passages from *The Tale of Genji,* translated by Arthur Waley and Edward Seidensticker, immediately follow this stanza. Hahn complicates the issue of interpretation by employing paired translations throughout "Comp. Lit." which, removed from the context of Lady Murasaki's novel—yet depending on her story line—creates a subtextual, or intertextual, narrative that serves as an analogue for the real concerns of the poem. For, finally, this poem is not just about the necessary and revealing choices that shape a translated narrative: it is ultimately concerned with what happens to female subjectivity in the process of translation.

Hahn parallels the linguistic translation of *Genji* with the psychological relationships within *Genji* itself.[23] Cutting between paired translated passages and her own retelling of the story, she concentrates on Prince Genji's discovery of a little girl whom he adopts and later marries because she reminds him of "his second wife, Murasaki, / [who] resembled his stepmother who he loved / and who it is said resembled his real mother" (sec. vii).[24] For Hahn, this emblematizes the way in which male narratives of desire interpolate female subjectivity, female narratives: "He [Genji] wanted to be her father / but did not know what it meant /

to be in trust of her adoration and anger, / the one opening her narrative" (sec. ii). That opening for Hahn becomes a rewriting that erases female subjectivity:

> What would she like from him?
> A container of fireflies.
> He smiled. Of course.
> And had kimonos and dolls sewn anyway.
> Father. Brother.
> Husband.
> ....
> *She became the translation*
> and so did he.
>
> (sec. iv)

Genji's desire to form the girl into the woman he desires begins with gestures that do not merely *mis*interpret but *re*interpret her desires. In "Resistance: A Poem on Ikat Cloth" (1989, 59), which also alludes to *Genji*, "The Shining Prince realized / he could form her / into the one forbidden him. For that / he would persist / into old age." The girl herself becomes a text that is translated, indeed, who becomes the translation, in Genji's search "for the one who resembled his mother." Although Genji himself becomes the translation, a figure in his own fantasy, his control over the discursive or subjective field confers to him an agency denied the girl whom he translates. What he does not understand is that

> the mother would always be dead
> and always be someone he'd adore
> with a passion reserved for lovers;
> that he would annotate each woman
> like a chapter returned to again and again.
>
> (sec. vii)

Hahn suggests elsewhere that the act of annotation is a vivisection that destroys what it seeks to bring to light: "Though practical / you hate annotations / to the *kokinshu;* / each note vivisects / a *waka* [poem] / like so many petals / off a stem / until your lap / is full of blossoms. / How many you destroyed!" ("Resistance: A Poem on Ikat Cloth [1989, 59]). Genji's desire to find/reconstitute his dead mother in other women is a destructive one: woman as text precludes the possibility of subjectivity and, in fact, erases it.

For Hahn, this erasure is compounded by the translators of the text whose own subjectivities are not invested in the figure of the girl. In a move that foregrounds even more sharply the status of her own poem as translation, she asks "Why my interest in Genji?" (sec. ii), a question that is followed by a stanza in which Hahn inserts her own narrative into Murasaki's story line. Significantly, Hahn's rewriting creates the possibility of the girl seeing herself, instead of being seen by and through the male gaze:

The little girl makes advances on the quilt.
He gently pushes her away
and presents a lacquered handmirror
from a bed stand.
She still has it
though cannot recall the rewarded moment.
And he still recalls its other uses,
framing genitals or complexions.
The reader will not find this in any text.

Hahn thus positions herself as one who, like Genji, opens the girl's narrative. If Genji essentially erases the girl's subjectivity through his psychological translation that "locks her into womanhood" (sec. v), does the poet herself enact something similar in her attempt to release the girl from the narrative of womanhood? In a sense, the poet and Genji each participate in competing narratives centered around the figure of the young girl. But Hahn's narrative also competes with those of *Genji*'s translators, whose own subjectivity she attempts literally to locate:

Chirp, chirp, chirp, she said.
Translation?
Where do the translators translate?
New York? Tokyo? Kyoto?
At their desk? tatami? longhand?
Can we go from stroke to scribble?
And who are *they*?
When you turn your back
will they laugh[?]

(sec. iii)

Through the comparison of her own identification with the girl, Hahn aligns the Genji within the text with the translators of the text. Her final stanza, like the one in which she re-imagines and rewrites *Genji*'s narrative, imagines a narrative for the translator, inserting him as a character in her own poetic text:

> The translator puts the pen down
> and stretches his arms and neck.
> *Genji* is complete.
> He's completed the text
> in time for the fall semester.
> The students call him professor and bore him
> but bring a salary, medical benefits, an office.
> The volumes of translation are exact.
> Exactly right.
> He walks in to the bathroom,
> turns off the light and sits down.

Through the figure of the professor/translator, Hahn critiques any enterprise of translation based on the assumption of a determinate text. Much in the way that Genji attempts to force a "reading" on the women through whom he looks for his mother, textual translation that aspires to being "exact. / Exactly right" involves solipsistic motives that obliterate complexity in the search for vivisecting accuracy. The closing image, which echoes "Going Inside to Write," suggests that such acts of translation occur in the realm of regulated language disengaged from the fact of the body, which locates subjectivity in a matrix of contextual forces. Thus, the translator, wholly unaware of his own interpretive positioning, replicates the actions of the character whose story he has been translating.

What opens this poem up, however, is that Hahn questions her own attempts to recuperate female subjectivity. In a move that recalls her focus on the agency of female writers in "Revolutions," she raises the possibility that in her reading of *Genji* she herself has "examine[d] [it] from the male persona" (sec. v), thereby placing Murasaki, the author, under erasure:

> To make her his.
> What would this mean:
> wait a few years and put aside her toys,
> replace them with strips of paper,
> feel her crushed beneath him.
> *Why did a woman write this?*
> Did she speak from the small heart . . .
> . . . .
> He locks her into womanhood.
> She grows to need him,
> tolerate him and become the enemy
> of all other women.

Is this the translation:
the way women who need one another
are placed at odds for men.
Is this one of the lessons
that scrolls out from the many days on her knees
writing and rewriting.
Do I examine from the male persona?

(sec. v)

Hahn's indignation that a woman should have written a narrative of female erasure reverses itself and becomes a question of whether Murasaki, in fact, identified with the girl and spoke "from the small heart." The possibility that Murasaki uncritically endorsed Genji's agency at the expense of female agency is, like the translated passages throughout "Comp. Lit.," paired with the possibility that *Genji* was a coded protest against the ways in which women were separated from one another and denied the hand mirror through which to see themselves. Hahn becomes herself a metatranslator of Murasaki's text, but one who recognizes that "without the original" (sec. 1), her act of translation is, finally, inexact and ambiguous at best. However, given the model of translation presented throughout the poem, this alternative model, because it remains in the balances of ambiguity, is one that opens a space for the female subject. For Hahn, "the translation of figures became a fragrance, / *kaoru* — / as the author, Murasaki, designed — / so distinct one could taste it in one's throat" (sec. iv). She thus accords Murasaki linguistic agency; though her text is shaped by the male translators cited throughout "Comp. Lit.," Hahn reads it, to an extent, as resistant to complete appropriation through what she calls its "fragrance."

As an inquiry into the nature of subjectivity, "Comp. Lit." proposes that subjectivity, like written texts, is permeable and malleable. But the indeterminacy this suggests is problematic in its implication that agency is always contingent and subject to appropriation and rewriting by the other. In terms of a poetic, such indeterminacy implies that any text is merely a container—a saucer and cup—whose fluid content is perpetually changeable. The problem for Hahn, who conceives of language as located in the body, is that its contingency undercuts both text's and woman writer's integrity of agency. Further, the instability and indeterminacy of all categories make any self-positioning in terms of race (or gender) irrelevant. The body itself becomes an irrelevant signifier.

However, the alternative cannot be to propose that the appropriative possibilities of translation point to the essentially untranslatable nature of any given text, which would contradict Hahn's own literary identification with the Japanese literary tradition. More significantly, the correlative in terms of subjectivity would be that subjects are fixed, impermeable entities. For Hahn, as a woman, such a model would "lock her into womanhood," an entity much like the young girl in *Genji*. And, as one who identifies herself as biracial, this notion of raced subjectivity would suggest her own impossibility as anything other than a physiological and psychological schizophrenic.

The reversal Hahn enacts near the end of "Comp. Lit"—in which she examines the possibility of *Genji* as a resistant text, grounded in Murasaki's identification with the erased female subject—anticipates her development of the translation motif in "The Izu Dancer" (1992, 87), a poem that, an intertext like the previous poem, draws heavily from material in Yasunari Kawabata's *Izu no odoriko*. While this poem includes and extends the thematic of translation in "Comp. Lit.," it focuses in particular on the problematic of retaining the integrity of the originary text without locking it into a realm in which it becomes untranslatable. In many ways, "The Izu Dancer" is the obverse of "Comp. Lit." If, in the latter, Hahn attempts to clear a space for the recuperation of female agency, figured through the women writers of the Heian period, "The Izu Dancer" explores the question of subjectivity from the position of the translator. Hahn's investment here lies not only in her own capacity as textual translator, but also in how translation tropically implies the ways in which raced subjectivity is constructed.

As though wanting to avoid the problematic her own translated lines present, Hahn accompanies each with the original line from Kawabata. She subtly suggests both the accessibility and inaccessibility of Kawabata's text by including not romanized Japanese, but lines of Japanese script. Depending on the reader's ability or inability to read Japanese, the inclusion of Kawabata's lines either offers an opportunity for the reader to challenge the authority of Hahn's translation or literally lays out before the reader's eyes the difficulty of translation. But for Hahn, the purpose of translation is not the transposition of words from one language to another but the journey into and through words:

> Though not a difficult text
> every few words I was stuck
> flipping through water radicals[25]
> so I could resume the journey inside words
> . . . .
> I did not know

I did not want to know Japanese
so much as a way back to, say, salt
and to him in his heaven.
(Or to him, in such a rush to pick me up
he forgot his shoes, stood at my door in red woolen socks.)

It is not proficiency in Japanese that the poet wants, but something more elemental, salt or, perhaps, God. The ambiguity of the pronoun "him" in these lines refers variously to God, Kawabata himself or a male acquaintance; the deliberate vagueness foregrounds Hahn's subjective motivations of her translation. The poet counterposes the potential intrusion of her own intentions with a few lines of Kawabata's original text, which follows her own lines of translation: "Yet from the fragrance of his lines I struggled to raise: / 'I thought for a moment of running out barefoot to look for her. / It was after two.' " The "struggle" of translation is not simply linguistic difficulty; rather, it is getting to "the information locked in ink — / each stroke, a signal; each kanji a panorama. / And barbed fence." The frustration of feeling that what is most difficult to translate — the tenor and shades of words — surfaces in what at first seems to be a non sequitur directly following these lines:

There are over 2,000 species of fireflies,
each with its own mating signal
so as not to crossover.
If you catch one they will not burn a hole in your hand
or explode in your face.
They call out: hey baby. They say: wait up, girl.

Hahn closes this sequence with the Japanese script for *matte*, wait. The image of the fireflies implies a species-specific coding that prevents crossbreeding. The biological implications are deliberate and introduce the connection between language and raced subjectivity with which the poem closes. Here, the fireflies represent that which is not human. But Hahn cuts through species difference by suggesting linguistic fluidity in the humorous image of fireflies who speak both American slang and informal Japanese.

This image reaches back to the preceding lines and modifies the "barbed fence" of language: it does not, despite the difficulty of translation it presents, completely bar one from the "panorama" behind it. What comes through is "the fragrance of [the] line." Much as in "Comp. Lit.," Hahn uses the metaphor of fragrance to evoke that which resists

the literalizing tendencies of translation; it is that which is inexplicable —
not to be explicated or annotated. It is what resists appropriation:

> In time we belong to what the objects mean.
> Then around 2 am the stomach sours from all the coffee.
> The strokes blur into the mess of lines and noises they really are.
> Though in some respects the characters are astonishingly simple
> . . . .
> But the complex unfolding of a single sentence
> with whole sentences modifying a noun
> at the end of the line baffled, humiliated
> and toughened my spirit.
> I persevered in my search for the fragrance of words.

"To write," says Hahn, "and never discover the scent / is to signal a
firefly behind a wall." In cruder and fixed form, "fragrance" might approximate something like "essence." But fragrance, unlike essence, is at
once there and not there, resistant and permeable. Hahn implies the
relation between language and the body in the image of kanji dissolving
into a "mess" that will not signify while the translator's stomach "sours
from all the coffee." But Hahn offers the converse possibility: that it is
through the body that one plumbs beneath the "mess of lines and
noises." Hahn writes out a line from Kawabata, wondering "where . . .
he unearthed it." Her translation, wrested from sentences that baffle and
humiliate, tellingly gives way to a passage that links her own physical
experience to the woman in Kawabata's text:

> Where did he unearth
> . . . .
> ("Her hair, so rich it seemed unreal, almost brushed against my
>   chest.")
> Where did I find the hands on my shoulders, sliding down my arms
> then up under my t-shirt, into my bra,
> squeezing my breasts, pinching my nipples so hard
> I blinked to hold back tears.
> He watched my expression as a meteorologist reads delicate
>   instruments.
> If the body is a map, a weathermap, summer vacations or winter
>   holidays
> all begin here. Something a student may not realize.

The translation and what follows dovetail so that the initial description
of "hands on my shoulders" is an empathetic displacement of subjectiv-

ity that reimagines Kawabata's passage from the woman's point of view, as well as a memory prompted by the act of translation. Through the body and the way in which it deregulates language, the subjectivity of the (female) translator connects to "the fragrance of words," to what is fluid and shifting beneath the words themselves.

Yet, as in "Going Inside to Write," Hahn does not construct the body as an overarching site of authority that somehow simply cuts to the heart of things. Her conflation of empathetic response and personal memory suggests that the map of the body is not necessarily a fixed one. The body, like language, is always mediated by its own metaphors. For Hahn, Japanese written characters illustrate this most clearly because they can be broken down into pictograms that reveal their elements (in one of Hahn's examples, the character for "woman" in triplicate is the character for "mischief; noisy; assault"). Hahn notes that "in the kanji for mother," whose strokes are a pictogram of female breasts,

> the two nipples reduce it to a primitive symbol.
> I reach to touch a lover with the confidence
> of a child burying into a breast;
> a tangible connection but also the perfume
> or stench that is language. Ah,
> the irregular verbs. Oh, the conditional.
> An occasional classical phrase
> nestled into the vernacular.
> The lullabies: should, would, could.

The character for "mother" suggests that the body both implies and is implied by language. But if the translation of language is a trope for the construction of subjectivity through the body, then even where words rely on the essentials of biology, that which remains unaccounted for itself becomes a trope for the ways in which the body resists and is never fully contained by categories of articulation.

Hahn's earlier image of the coding boundaries between firefly species reverberates in the closing lines of the poem as a metaphor for translation: like "the information locked in ink" in the kanji characters, the firefly's mating signals are locked within its species' coding. But as Hahn illustrates through this image, the body, no less than language, can and does "crossover," contesting boundaries. Hahn closes the poem with an intriguing metaphor that directly addresses the issue of subjectivity that has been implicit throughout. As she sits in a restaurant where she has

presumably been translating the Kawabata and drinking the coffee that
sours the stomach, she looks over

> to catch the back of a man's neck,
> his heavy black hair in a severe razor-cut style.
> I imagine he is B.D. Wong
> the incredibly handsome actor in *M. Butterfly.*
> His moist white cotton shirt
> hangs a bit off his shoulders
> and he holds a cup of cappuccino in one hand
> and a slim hard-cover book in the other.
> I imagine he turns around to ask for—
> an ashtray
> and ends up at my table
> talking about contemporary poetry, mutual friends
> and international affairs.
> But as the man gathers his belongings he turns
> and instead of the aristocratic profile and rakish glow
> it's an older Italian man, moustached and serious.
> But briefly that fragrance!

Although she has misread the physical markers of identity, mistaking an
unidentified Italian man for Chinese American actor B. D. Wong,
through her imagined scenario "that fragrance" is briefly present. Fil-
tered through her own subjective gaze, the translation of the man's black
hair and white shirt, while literally inaccurate, nevertheless momentarily
evokes what is not defined by the facticity of the Italian man. But the
reference to race suggests that Hahn's image of de-essentialized, fluid
subjectivity specifically addresses and destabilizes the fixity of race as a
constitutive element of subjectivity. That is, she does not deny raced
subjectivity, as her deliberate identification of the man as Italian indicates, but explores the ways in which racial identity, like language, might
circulate in ways that do not lock subjectivity within the limited lexicon
of biology.

Hahn engages complex issues of language, agency, and raced and
gendered subjectivity in her search for a poetic. Grounded in the body
but not essentialized by the body, crossing over and between boundaries, and self-reflexively attentive to the difficulties of its own status as
translation in literal and metaphorical senses, Hahn's poetics claim both
the power and inexplicable fragrance of words.

The Hemisphere: Kuchuk Hanem

And now that she's gone how do we find her—
especially my small daughters who will eventually recall their
   grandmother
not as a snapshot in the faults of the mind
but as the incense in their hair long after the reading of the
   Lotus Sutra.

Kimiko Hahn, "The Unbearable Heart"

By way of a conclusion, I want to examine a multisectioned prose poem from Hahn's most recent volume, *The Unbearable Heart* (1995). "The Hemisphere: Kuchuk Hanem" extends many of the thematics I have been discussing, and in many ways it brings the central concerns of this study together in a poem whose power is inextricably tied to its formal difficulty. Hahn examines the orientalized Asian female body (ch. 1), the difficulties of representation and agency (ch. 2), the uses of autobiography and strategic masking, particularly its textual forms (ch. 3), and the thematics of maternality and absence (ch. 4)—and in doing so suggests a direction for a postmodern poetics that does not obscure or elide the specificities of the marked subject in a jumble of textual play.

"The Hemisphere: Kuchuk Hanem" focuses on the essentialized and orientialized body, but its center is constituted by the powerful presence and then absence of the maternal body. The poem is written as a series of seeming fragments, many of them taken directly from Edward Said's *Orientalism* and from the letters of Gustave Flaubert, concerning Flaubert's travels in Egypt and his affair with a dancer/courtesan named Kuchuk Hanem.[26] Other segments take on various other voices, indicated by different typographical styles; however, as the poem progresses, the distinctions between the poet, first- and third-person speakers, Kuchuk Hanem, and Flaubert become less determinate, less identifiable as distinct personae. Despite the poem's reliance on pastiche as the principle of composition, the poem resists the deferral and indeterminacy of meaning. At the same time, it resists summarization and the mastery of narrative containment. At stake in this poem is not only the recuperation of the Asian female body, but more specifically the reclamation of the absent mother. Indeed, the presence/absence of the mother is deeply personal—the writing of the poems in this volume welled up from the sudden death of Hahn's mother—and Hahn self-consciously blurs the lines between speaker and poet, persona and person.

This grounding of the poem in personal grief also foregrounds the way Hahn/the speaker "trespass[es] the boundaries of fiction and non-fiction" (53), as well as the ways in which any narrative act—whether "autobiographical" or "fictional"—always, consciously and unconsciously, elides such artificial boundaries. Additionally, one of the central concerns of the poem is the writer's assumption of power to speak for the absent subject of its meditations. Thus, there is a crucial parallel drawn between Hahn's childhood memories of her mother in the bath, which open the poem, and Flaubert's narrativizing of Kuchuk Hanem's body:

The female body as imperialist's colony is not a new symbol. Sexual impulse as revolutionary impulse? Do women depend on the sexual metaphor for identity, an ironic figure of speech? Will I fall into the trap of writing from the imperialists' point of view? From a patriarchal one? How can we write erotica and not? What would an anti-imperialistic framework look like? Are not women the original keepers of narrative? Of lineage? (51)

That parallel becomes outright identification between Hahn and Flaubert: as writers, both seek to claim through narration. The way in which orientalist thinking atemporally connects any Asian female body with any and every other Asian female body suggests a problematic parallel to the way in which the poet seeks generational connection to the women in her family: "The need to belong overwhelms—to hold my own sister, hold her hand or link arms. Rest a cheek against her neck. To feel in my daughter, my sister. To feel in my mother, my sister. To feel in my sister, my self." This section is immediately followed by its orientalist counterpart, which distorts the desire for connection and identification: " 'You know you want it and it's big' . . . 'Sit on my face, China' . . . 'Nice titties' . . . 'Do you want me to teach you some English?' . . . 'Are you from Saigon?' " (60; ellipses in original). This uneasy parallel confronts the poet who seeks to recuperate memory, find her way back to the mother's body and claim a tradition of storytelling ("narrative") and connectedness ("lineage") without replicating an orientalist narrative that locks her into "oriental womanhood." She grounds herself instead in the "wish [for] mother to speak up so I can become a woman" (53). The paucity of the primary operative narrative—the sexualizing orientalism represented by Flaubert—not only reinforces the absence of the mother's body in its inability to acknowledge noneroticized relations between women but also alienates the Asian/American woman from her own body and sexuality.

Hahn opens "The Hemisphere" with a memory of her mother: "I am four. It is a summer midafternoon, my nap finished. I cannot find her. I hear the water in the bathroom. . . . I stand outside the white door. Reflected in the brass knob I see my face framed by a black pixie-cut" (45). Hahn's shaping of her poetic narrative within the framework of this memory is echoed in the several images of framing in these lines: the door frame, the brass knob that frames the child's reflection, the hair that frames her face. The recollection of the mother's nakedness dominates the daughter's memory, obscuring what either might have said: "What did she say to me? Did she scold? Laugh? Just smile or ignore me?" (45). In a sense, the site of memory—the mother's body—is unnarrated, marked by visuality and the intensity of the mother's physical presence. Significantly, this initial memory yields to passages from Said's *Orientalism*, in which he notes that Flaubert's privilege "allowed him not only to possess Kuchuk Hanem physically but to speak for her" (46). After these passages comes the first of Kuchuk Hanem's first-person addresses.

As the poem presents her, Kuchuk Hanem is well aware of the way in which she is read as the paradigmatic "oriental" woman, and she understands that "I have made a name for myself that will, Flaubert boasts on his own behalf, not mine, that will cover the globe. Know that. That the image is not my own. My image does not entirely belong to me. And neither does yours, master or slave" (47). Still, this must compete with the blunt reality, that "Flaubert fucked her and wrote about her. His words. His worlds" (53). This recognition again reinforces the identification between Flaubert, who writes about Kuchuk Hanem, and the poet/speaker who "allows" Kuchuk Hanem to speak through an act of narration that nevertheless speaks "for" her: "Can I speak for her? For the Turkish, the Nubian, the—brown, black, blacker?" (51). The question lingering in the background is not only whether the poet reenacts the very narrative domination she resists, but whether the narratives of memory obscure the maternal presence whose recuperation is the emotional center of the poem. It is perhaps for this reason that the poem does not follow either a linear narrative model or an easily identifiable emotional trajectory, as might be expected in the elegiac tradition.

The surface identification between Flaubert and Hahn/the speaker, however, is complicated in a number of ways: Asian/American women are generally identified not with Flaubert, the Western male writer, but with Kuchuk Hanem, the Eastern female other. The same voice that comments on the social politics of Flaubert's discursive domination of Kuchuk Hanem ("His words. His worlds"), as well as attempts to flesh the memory of the maternal body, is also the voice that recalls the process of her own sexualization and the ways in which she has been subject to the same orientalist modes she critiques. Memories of being approached as a young adolescent by a Portuguese sailor who, "by way of conversation . . . pointed to a large tattoo on his arm; an intricately designed geisha after Utamaro. He smiled as if somehow I identified with this. I did a little. He asked if I'd like to board his ship" (57) are interwoven with the angry recognition that "three wars have taught military men 'about' Asian women. Orientals. Extended by the classifieds" (54). If it is true, in Simone de Beauvoir's formulation, that "women are made, not born," it is also true that "oriental" women are made, not born, and that Asian/American women are made not born.[27] This is the crux of the poem's insistent questioning. In the absence of mothers, sisters and others who "teach" one to become a woman, an Asian/American woman, there is little to compete with the narratives, as Trinh Minh-ha puts it, that will "say you," that will lock one into the structure of orientalism.

Hahn poetically exploits and parallels the orientalist conflation of Asian women through an increasing conflation of voices. Fairly early on in the poem, the typography that identifies the poet's first-person voice seems suddenly to be identified with Kuchuk Hanem's first-person voice:

He wanted someone who did not resemble his mother or his friends' sisters or wives. The mistress he had dumped before departure. He wanted license. The kind available not even in one's own imagination—but in geographic departure. . . . He will think that I am one thing, even as he learns about me. He will believe those things and make them true even while he remembers my eyes, organs no different from his own. Yet what he witnesses on tour and what I see daily are experienced differently. Does no one bugger animals in France? Does not one martyr himself? Is that why he adores prostitutes and monks. Adores. (48)

In confusing narrative voices, Hahn mimics the atemporal sweep that refuses to differentiate between the "geisha girl," "the Egyptian prostitute," and the contemporary Asian/American woman by conflating the voices of dancer and poet. Over the stretch of more than a century, they are joined by the orientalist gaze that reads their bodies as exotic surfaces onto which are projected the desires through which they are then "understood." The power of the Western male gaze fixes the eyes of the Eastern other with a kohl-ringed haze of fantasy sustainable only by refusing to "see" that those eyes are simply "organs no different from his own."

Increasingly, the several voices that segment the poem reveal themselves to be both the framework and content of the poem, as well as a series of narrative forms through which Hahn explores the mask of "the oriental woman." However, it would be singularly inaccurate to read the poem as simply enacting a reversal of the narrative power that Western masculinity has heretofore claimed. Whoever the agent, the narrative act itself is always, at least partly, an act of artifice that continually forestalls all attempts to decide whether it is "the story or the story of the story" (54). Hahn further interrogates the authority of her position by commenting on her own process of poetic critique, in which she "cannot subvert a category without being engaged" (54). Almost as a reply, she then notes that "I am so hungry. I consume Said's text. // My questions strike a different facet: what does Desire seek? It must become a radical question" (55).

It is this process of radicalization that prevents an overidentification with the figure of Kuchuk Hanem, as though she were a recovered symbol of essential Asian womanhood—which would only replicate in seemingly more "positive" inflections Flaubert's own narrative appropriation. The romanticizing tendencies of orientalism, which must mark the other as a site of absolute difference, are no less appropriative, finally, than the potentially romanticizing tendencies of recuperation, which must mark the other as a site of imagined sameness. Thus, Hahn imagines what might happen were she to find herself in Kuchuk Hanem's presence:

What would [she] say if I were to sit beside her in the predawn, tobacco wafting into our hair like the memory of my first husband studying for exams. The fragrance of a coffee as rich as the mud from the Nile that must flood the fields to award farmers a relatively easy season, or predict irrigating with buckets haled from the same, circa 1840. The thick silt coating the land, the throat, the tongue. Sheer caffeine heightening the blue tiles as we turn towards one another. . . . Would she offer me figs and ask me to stay or tell me to get the hell out, what's a married woman doing here—curious? You want lessons? You want me? You looking for someone? (58)

The historical specificity here indexes the specificity with which Hahn attempts to imagine Kuchuk Hanem, not presuming a reciprocated or acknowledged connection. Though both may be able to claim "I have become a continent. I have become half the globe" (49), a statement whose speaker is unidentified, lines of difference are nevertheless present, and Hahn allows for the possibility that those differences would not be inert, that they might, in fact, be the ground for antagonism. But even more crucially, the structure of the poem suggests that to identify unproblematically with/as Kuchuk Hanem is to court an impossibility: the poet herself is no more Kuchuk Hanem than memory can render the poet's mother, now dead, literally present. The task at this point, then, is somehow to allow for recuperation without literalization, to allow for the possibility of presence in absence.

Significantly, this passage is marked, through the waft of tobacco and the rich smells of coffee, by Hahn's hallmark trope of fragrance. In this poem, as in others in *The Unbearable Heart,* what previously was a poetic of fragrance develops into something of an ontology of fragrance. In the earlier poems, as I pointed out, metaphorizing language as scent allows for the slippage between words and their translation, between word and world. In these later poems, and particularly in "The Hemisphere," Hahn more deeply explores the possibility that subjectivity figured as fragrance poetically creates a space in which the subjectivity of Kuchuk Hanem might escape the constricting formulation of "His words. His worlds." In doing so, Hahn also ruptures the assumed connection between all "oriental women" yet still allows for a sense of connection able to move between the confinements imposed by orientalist constructions.

Hahn's use of this trope is particularly striking in its reappropriation of a key element of orientalia: the waft of incense, the heavy scents of musk and oil, the cloying smells of perfume and opium. For Flaubert, the "nauseating odor [of bedbugs] mingled with the scent of [Kuchuk Hanem's] skin which was dripping with sandalwood oil" is "the most enchanting touch of all" (61). Unlike Flaubert's almost literal association between scent and subject—an association that leads him to a sensory parallel between Kuchuk Hanem and the bedbugs—Hahn's description joins speaker and dancer in an imaginative space, the room through which the smells of cigarettes and coffee waft and weave.

The passage above also plays on the almost physical relation between smell and memory, the way in which scent accesses the past in a way both indefinable and particular. "Tobacco wafting into our hair like the memory of my first husband studying for exams" blurs temporal boundaries, the demarcation between imagined scenario (the poet meeting Kuchuk Hanem) and recalled past (a husband studying). Hahn does not, however, rely on an olfactory version of Proust's memory-soaked madeleine. Fragrance does not then become a direct, if attenuated, line to the mother: there are no sense memories of lilac-scented handkerchiefs or face powder that evoke the mother's presence. A closer look at the image of the tobacco smoke reveals that Hahn associates the way the smoke moves not so much with the husband studying, but with memory: "tobacco wafting . . . like the memory." The relation set up through simile suggests a deliteralization of the way memories, and thus remembered presences, move through us. Smell moves *like* the memory of; it is not the memory itself. At the same time, fragrance partakes of memory; it is memory's most irreducible prompt.

Beginning fairly early on in "The Hemisphere," Hahn intercuts her segmented narrative with lines that clearly foreground a sensate presence: "The air smells of garlic" (49) is shortly followed by a third-person segment whose acting subject is unclear, "She will read from Grimm's Fairy Tales where the youngest daughter is always the prettiest and the stepmother murderous. Her hands smell of garlic from our dinner" (49). These "images" of a lingering presence persist throughout the poem, formally enacting the way that the smell of garlic remains long after its use. Like a scent that one catches on the edge of consciousness, brief fragments occasionally appear as entire lines: "Or the garlic she sliced" (56), which is repeated twice, and "Even after washing my hands for dinner, after rinsing the dishes—" (58).

It is not until the closing sections of the poem that these fragments begin to constitute a kind of narrative, which alternate with sections taken directly from Flaubert's letters:

After I cook garlic, chop it, dice it, sliver it up, spread it over the crackling oil, I can smell it on my fingers even after I have washed my hands for dinner. Even while I am eating the pasta. Even after eating chocolates.

"[Dear Louise,] The oriental woman is no more than a machine: she makes no distinction between one man and another man. Smoking, going to the baths, painting her eyelids and drinking coffee—such is the circle of occupations within which. . . ."

Even after having washed the children. Even after drinking coffee and throwing out the grounds. Even after cutting my finger on the dog food can. Sucking it. Bandaging my finger. Showering outdoors in the twilight.

". . . within which her existence is confined. As for physical pleasure, it must be very light, since the well known button, the seat of same, is sliced off at an early age. . . ."

Even after television and a bowl of popcorn. After washing the dishes in hot sudsy water. After reading Said's *Orientalism*. After touching every crease and crevice of my husband's body. (60–61)

The insistence on detail—cooking, feeding the dog, showering, snacking, making love—resists Flaubert's assumption of "the oriental woman's" homogeneity and unconsciousness. The ironic counterpoint of narratives highlights the way in which Hahn employs fragrance as that which is of the body but is not the body itself. The scent of garlic persists; its lingering is the trace of its strongest characteristic. The garlic is there and/but not there. As a trope, fragrance does not "stand for" a particular memory or a particular presence; rather, it signals the process of memory and the way that memory evokes presence but is not itself presence. This distinction is crucial, and it is one that Flaubert, for whom the act of writing about Kuchuk Hanem was to create her, did not make, thus eliding whatever subjectivity she might claim for herself. This distinction also suggests that in being "given" a voice by the poet, there is yet something uncontained and unaccounted for that irreducibly but not essentially "is" Kuchuk Hanem. What slips out in any account of the subject is similar to what slips out in any act of translation.

This slippage of the subject is indicated by the inability to identify the subject in the initial garlic fragments earlier in the poem, as well as by the gradual shift to the first-person speaker. The possibilities of identification are numerous: is it the mother? A generalized first-person speaker? Kuchuk Hanem? Hahn herself? Hahn's imagining of her mother's first-person voice? In fact, any and all are possible, suggesting the ways in which subjectivity itself shifts and is mobile, like scent itself. The speaking persona as mask resists definite and reductive identification. Yet particularity remains: the lingering scent is identifiable and specific. In a similar way, the mother's presence pervades the entire poem, lingering in the daughter/poet's consciousness and heart long after the mother's death. But what is most crucial in the distinction between imaginative memory and literal presence is that it does not allow the poem to sentimentalize death as that which merely interrupts a presence that can then be simply reconstituted through memory. For Hahn, the fact of her mother's death is not changeable through poetic imagination. In refusing to recuperate the subjectivity of Kuchuk Hanem through the same essentialist thinking by which Flaubert denied it, in acknowledging that something eludes any narration, Hahn also refuses the easy and illusory comfort of her mother's presence. The limits of Hahn's own words as worlds reveal themselves in the poem's abrupt closure, "My mother might have told me this story but she died suddenly a few months ago" (61).

Yet this moment, where poetic imagination thuds against reality, follows one that allows for the recuperation of something that persists nevertheless: "Even after drifting into sleep my fingers smell of the garlic I sliced for dinner. I am hungry when I wake to the baby's cries at 2 am. My breasts are leaking as well. The milk may also taste of garlic. I drink a glass of water" (61). This section is rich with associations: the trace of garlic that permeates the body and mother's milk reinforces the image of connection between mother and child; the act of breastfeeding contrasts with the completely sexualized body of Kuchuk Hanem and the imaginary "oriental woman"; and the speaker's memory of awkward surprise at seeing her mother's breasts, a memory that begins the poem, becomes an image that links the two through maternality.

It is this connection to the mother that links the daughter-poet to the power of narrative: "Woman's role as storyteller included creator and healer. My mother knew this, unconsciously" (60). In the absence of the mother and the story she "might have told," the daughter pieces together her narrative. Through exploring, interrogating, undermining and finally claiming both the power and failure of narrative, Hahn recognizes that just as there is no narrative that can contain Kuchuk Hanem or Hahn's own particularity as an Asian American woman, so also there is no memory that can completely recall the mother's presence, no narrative that can contain and no story that prepares one for grief. Paradoxically, it is in their ability to evoke but not re-present the mother that the limits of language gesture toward the fullness of being.

Conclusion

Without writers, the risks they take and the books they write, there could be no literary criticism or theory. I would like to acknowledge them here and express my appreciation and admiration for the women whose works I discuss. With the exception of Yoshiko Uchida, who died in 1992, the writers in this study continue to explore and complicate their relationship to experience turned into language. I thank all of them for what their work has meant to me both personally and professionally.

Through formal experimentation and narrative complexity, the autobiographies, short stories, novels and poems I examine here represent the ways in which Japanese American women grapple with the complex intersections of race, gender, sexuality and national identity. Taken together, these writers constitute a tradition in which they write the self as subject, refusing to be spoken or spoken for, a tradition in which they insist on their singularity of perception as well as their ties to community and shared experience. Identified as both racial and sexual others, they reject and dismantle those constructions through complex explorations of what it means to be an embodied subject, and their writing evidences the ways in which the articulation of subjectivity cannot be decontextualized from social and political positionings within the cultural dominant. In that process, these writers reappropriate the infantilized and hyperfeminized figure of the Japanese/American woman and claim their connection to Japanese identity through Issei culture, through their mothers, through their bodies.

But these writers also insist on the ways in which the subject constructed by cultural, social, discursive and representational forces is not wholly contained by those structures. Through various forms of masking they create a space for a self that resists appropriation and subjection. In "Masks of Woman," Mitsuye Yamada articulates how the vision of the other is always a projection that can be turned against the gazer:

> Over my mask
> is your mask
> of me
> an Asian woman
> grateful
> gentle
> in the pupils of your eyes
> as I gesture with each
> new play of
> light
> and shadow
> this mask be
> comes you.
>   (1988, 89)

With the condensed intensity of poetic language, Yamada suggests that masking is a complex presentation whose surfaces are both constructed and deployed by a self that understands itself to exceed the boundaries that would denote its totality. This poem foregrounds the questions of subjectivity and agency I pursue in these pages, which are a criticism of and challenge to the persistent construction of Japanese American women as the subordinate and passive inheritors of the enticing difference, inarticulate invisibility and sexual subservience of "the Orient."

And yet the representational and theoretical issues that comprise the focus of this book do not encompass or completely define Japanese American women's writing, which is as varied and contradictory as subjectivity itself. The multivalence of language can only begin to approximate the complexity and richness of being. So for the writer: so for the critic. It is in that space between the discursive and the experiential that the possibilities of each reside.

Notes

Introduction

1. Since the publication of Elaine H. Kim's *Asian American Literature: An Introduction to the Writings and Their Social Context* (Philadelphia, 1982), only five book-length studies of Asian American literature have been published: Amy Ling, *Between Worlds: Women Writers of Chinese Ancestry* (New York, 1990); Stephen H. Sumida, *And the View from the Shore: Literary Traditions of Hawai'i* (Seattle, 1991); Sau-ling Cynthia Wong, *Reading Asian American Literature: From Necessity to Extravagance* (Princeton, 1993); King-Kok Cheung, *Articulate Silences: Hisaye Yamamoto, Maxine Hong Kingston, Joy Kogawa* (Ithaca, 1993); and Josephine Lee, *Performing Asian America: Race and Ethnicity on the Contemporary Stage* (Philadelphia, 1997).

2. The necessity of a limited focus has resulted in at least one obvious area of omission: I include no Japanese American women of the Hawai'ian literary tradition. Because Hawai'i occupies a very particular space in U.S. history and culture, because Japanese Americans in Hawai'i stand in a significantly different relationship to white Americans and other Asian American ethnic groups, and because complex issues of colonialism are essential to any examination of Hawai'ian literature, I have found it necessary to concentrate only on mainland Japanese American women in order to avoid generalizations that would distort or erase the complexity and richness of, the Hawai'ian female literary tradition. Readers should consult Sumida's *And the View from the Shore*. For works by Hawai'ian Japanese American women writers see Juliet S. Kono and Cathy Song, eds., *Sister Stew: Fiction and Poetry by Women* (Honolulu, 1991); Marie Hara, *Bananaheart and Other Stories* (Honolulu, 1994); Jessica Saiki; *From the Lanai and Other Hawai'i Stories* (Minneapolis, 1991); Juliet S. Kono, *Hilo Rains* (Honolulu, 1988); Sylvia Watanabe, *Talking to the Dead* (New York, 1992); and Lois-Ann Yamanaka, *Saturday Night at the Pahala Theatre* (New York, 1993), *Wild Meat and the Bully Burgers* (Honolulu, 1996), *Blu's Hanging* (New York, 1997).

The thematic content of works, and in some cases their availability, guided my choice of writers for this book, but it is not offered as an exhaustive study of Japanese American women writers on the mainland. Many authors whose work I could not include certainly merit discussion: Mine Okubo, *Citizen 13660* (1946; Seattle, 1983); Ai, *Cruelty* (Boston, 1973), *Greed* (New York, 1993), and several works in between; Velina Hasu Houston, *Tea* (1987; published in *Unbroken Thread: An Anthology of Plays by Asian American Women*, ed. Roberta Uno [Amherst, 1993]) and other plays; Yuri Kageyama, *Peeling* (Berkeley, 1988); Karen Tei Yamashita, *Through the Arc of the Rain Forest* (Minneapolis, 1990) and *Brazil Maru* (Minneapolis, 1992); Amy Uyematsu, *30 Miles from J-Town* (Brownsville, 1992); Kyoko Mori, *Fallout* (Chicago, 1994) and *The Dream of Water* (New York, 1995); and Julie Shigekuni, *A Bridge Between Us* (New York, 1995).

Chapter 1: "As natural as the partnership of sun and moon"

1. I am indebted to Professor Haruko Moriyasu of the University of Utah for directing my attention to the following passage: "By the West's own estimation, railways meant progress. This fact had been hinted at in the very beginning of its dealings with Japan, when a 'Lilliputian locomotive' (as well as a telegraph) was among the gifts brought by Perry in 1854. According to his report on the formal presentation, the train was an instant hit. Indeed, some of the Bakufu officials, 'not to be cheated out of a ride . . . betook themselves to the roof' of the miniature carriage, so that the ceremonial was enlivened by the sight of 'a dignified mandarin whirling around the circular road at the rate of twenty miles an hour, with his loose robes flying in the wind' " (Hawks, quoted in W. G. Beasley, *The Meiji Restoration* [Stanford, 1972], 1:357–58]). See also Edward Yorke McCauley, *With Perry in Japan: The Diary of Edward Yorke McCauley,* ed. Allan B. Cole (Princeton, 1942), 98–99.

2. I am here adapting Edward Said's notion of "orientalization" as articulated in his much-referenced study *Orientalism* (New York, 1978).

3. Indeed, Harry D. Harootunian argues in his article "America's Japan / Japan's Japan" (in *Japan in the World,* ed. Masao Miyoshi and H. D. Harootunian [Durham, N.C., 1993]) that the Occupation narrative of "modernization was simply a transformation of imperialism and colonialism. . . . I would like to propose that this Occupation narrative and its subsequent articulation in countless studies devoted to demonstrating the modernization of Japan combined to establish the terms for constituting America's Japan and to mark the place of a new stage of imperialism and colonialism without territorialization" (200).

4. There is a crucial distinction to be made between traditional, area-studies Japanologists, many of whom came to prominence in the 1950s and 1960s, and more recent, progressive Japan scholars, such as Harootunian, Masao Miyoshi, Miriam Silverberg and John Treat, among others. The distinction is more than simply a temporal one, as there are presently plenty of individual scholars and area studies programs around the country whose stance in relation to Japan—a combination of assumed mastery and intellectual orientalism—is indistinguish-

able from that of their predecessors in the postwar period. In contrast, progressive Japan studies positions Japan as a dynamic site of ideological production and contestation, as well as self-reflexively acknowledges that Japan's representations in the West are powerfully shaped within a field of power relations whose discourse is neither neutral nor objective.

5. This is not to say that there are no books on Japan prior to this period. Writing on Japan dates back to at least the middle of the sixteenth century. Basil Hall Chamberlain's *Japanese Things* (1905; reprint, Boston, 1971) includes mention of several earlier sources. However, after Japan closed its borders in 1640, until Perry's 1854 landing, the writing of books about Japan and the Japanese decreased considerably. In the United States, one of the earliest publications to appear was *Manners and Customs of the Japanese in the Nineteenth Century* (1841; ed. Terence Barrow [Tokyo, 1973]), whose information was largely gleaned from Dutch sources and thus entirely secondhand. I have chosen to begin with the period just preceding and following the turn of the century, for it is then that the number of eyewitness narratives intended for popular consumption, as opposed to strictly scholarly endeavors, noticeably increases.

6. According to Sandra C. Taylor's biography, *Advocate of Understanding: Sidney Gulick and the Search for Peace with Japan* (Kent, Ohio, 1984), Gulick's *Evolution of the Japanese* (New York, 1905) established his reputation as a recognized Japan scholar. The book eventually went through five editions and earned its author substantial royalties. During his lifetime, Gulick was a well known, widely recognized authority on matters Japanese who argued that cultural understanding would promote positive relations between the United States and Japan. Taylor points out that Gulick believed in two types of evolution: biological and social. In terms of the former, the "innate abilities [of the Japanese] were the same as those of any other race" (46), suggesting that in terms of the latter, the Japanese need only continue their move toward modernization in order to reach the same socially evolutionary level as Westerners. However, the rhetorical line between biological and social evolution becomes considerably blurred in passages such as the one quoted above, despite Gulick's stated intentions or his professed "love for the Japanese people" (45). If we are to believe such sentiments—and I see no reason why we should not, however problematic such a love may ultimately prove—it is all the more ironic that Gulick, who was at one time wrongly suspected of being an agent for Japan, should himself seemingly recirculate and reify much of the anti-Japanese rhetoric of the time.

7. This passage illustrates one of the greatest ironies in much Japan scholarship of this period. While insisting on the backwardness of the Japanese—which could be read as simultaneously evincing their lower developmental level as a nation and their charming child-like innocence—many so-called Japan experts conveniently neglected to mention what had made Japan, at the turn of the century, an object of intense interest in the first place. The Meiji Restoration, which took place between 1868–1912, was a period of rapid modernization and represented a break from the feudal society of the Tokugawa period. What the West found both stunning and disturbing was the fact that the industrialization of Japan took place in roughly thirty years. Such rapid development was not easily explainable by recourse to the backward innocence of the Japanese. It is

thus around this period that the rhetoric of simianlike imitation comes to the fore.

8. Barthes reiterates a standard stereotypical association between "the Orient" and highly refined surfaces that exude a mystical nothingness. This pairing is also deployed in relation to Asian Americans, as Fatimah Tobing Rony notes: "The Asian American, whether male or female, is consistently allied with Art: with costume, surface, design, detail and artifice. The 'Oriental' is thus made akin to the 'Ornamental.' But like other people of color, whether African American or Inuit, the Asian American is also pathologized, hence the use of 'Yellow Peril' and other metaphors that portray Asian Americans as virulent" (221 n.25). See Rony, *The Third Eye: Race, Cinema, and Ethnographic Spectacle* (Durham, N.C., 1996).

9. I believe this oversight is deliberate, and here I am speaking less of a personal deliberateness on Hearn's part and more of an unconscious, cultural trend that involves repression, displacement, substitution and projection. This rhetorical absenting of Japan's threatening, distinctly unchildlike militarism would later be compensated for by gross exaggerations of the threat posed by the Japanese. In saying this, I do not mean to imply that Japan's aggressive militarism was wholly imagined. The atrocities of the Japanese Imperial Army are well documented and incontrovertible. What I speak of here has more to do with the construction of the Japanese as monolithically and monstrously desirous of the West's demise.

10. The connection between perversity and Japanese maternal practices may be found in even what are otherwise sympathetic accounts of Japan and Japanese culture. In Cathy N. Davidson's *36 Views of Mount Fuji: On Finding Myself in Japan* (New York, 1994), one finds the following: "Like it or not, the typical Japanese mother falls into the role of the *kyoiku mama*, the much maligned 'education mom' whose life is focused on the academic success of her children. Not surprisingly, family violence is rising. Newspapers recount incidents of teenage boys beating up mothers who put pressure on them to do well in school. There are also grim reports (perhaps apocryphal) of an increase in mother-son incest, rapes, as well as mothers having sex with their sons to help relieve the boys' tension. Such lurid stories are no doubt exaggerated, yet their prevalence in the popular media suggests the depth of Japanese misgivings about the present situation" (36–37). Despite the fact that such stories are "perhaps apocryphal," Davidson nevertheless serves them up in a manner that once again connects Japanese maternal practices with deviance.

11. A book with related intentions, though much better researched and written, is Nicholas Bornoff's *Pink Samurai: Love, Marriage and Sex in Contemporary Japan* (New York, 1991).

12. In conversation, Susan Jeffords has pointed out that the U.S. has often relied on similar proof-by-absence arguments in reference to other countries, most notably the (former) Soviet Union. This same no-win logic was used effectively and, for Japanese Americans, with disastrous consequences during WW II. Despite its possession of what has come to be known as the Munson Report, in which it was stated that there was absolutely no proof or indication of sabotage or treachery on the part of Nikkei, the army stated that "the very fact that no

sabotage has taken place to date is a disturbing and confirming indication that such action will be taken" (Michi Weglyn, *Years of Infamy: The Untold Story of America's Concentration Camps* [New York, 1976], 38). Thus stated, the internment of Japanese nationals (who were legally barred from U.S. citizenship) and Japanese Americans was justified as a preventative measure, a preemptive strike against certain fifth-column activity.

13. Christopher's logic, in which difference may manifest itself in uncontrollable, and thus dangerous, outbursts is not original. The foreword to Helen Mears's *Year of the Wild Boar: An American Woman in Japan* (Philadelphia, 1942) makes a similar move. Published shortly following the bombing of Pearl Harbor, the logic of threatening difference seemed not only incontrovertible but inevitable. Thus, Mears implies that violence is the teleological end of difference: "It is difficult for an American to write intelligibly of Japan. Everything about the Japanese civilization is almost precisely opposite from ours; their institutions, customs, and the ways of looking at everything are peculiar to them, so that even when they speak English they seem to be talking in a code, or some kind of double talk, which the American has difficulty in translating into sensible American. Yet it is necessary today, as perhaps never before, to understand something of what has been going on in Japan. It is no longer wise or possible to ignore the special civilizations of our neighbors, especially those aspects of their civilizations that seem to us merely 'quaint and old-fashioned.' For one of the things Japan teaches us is that such 'backward' civilizations can develop, under the spur of a partial industrialization, with almost fantastic rapidity. It teaches us also that, in a competitive world, such development is likely to take the direction, not toward liberal democratic regimes, but toward totalitarian New Orders" (8).

14. Marjorie Garber ("The Occidental Tourist," in *Nationalisms and Sexualities,* ed. Andrew Parker, Mary Russo, Doris Sommer, and Patricia Yaeger [New York, 1992]) comments that *M. Butterfly* illustrates how "racism and sexism . . . intersect with one another, and with imperialist and colonialist fantasies" (124). But where Garber seems to see the discourses of racism and sexism as to some extent separable from imperialism and colonialism, Bhabha's contention that colonialism requires formulations of racial and sexual difference suggests that such differences are instantiated at the inaugural moment of colonial discourse

15. See also, for instance, John C. Condon's *With Respect to the Japanese: A Guide for Americans* (Yarmouth, 1984). The primary point of ch. 1, entitled "The Odd Couple: America and Japan," is to illustrate the numerous ways in which "no nation is more different from America than Japan" (2).

16. See Caroline Chung Simpson's discussion on the symbolism of MacArthur's surrender ceremonies in "American Orientalisms: The Cultural and Gender Politics of America's Postwar Relationship with Japan" (Ph.D. diss., University of Texas, 1994).

17. My phrasing references Gayatri Spivak's contention that the colonial abolition of *sati* must be understood "as a case of 'White men saving brown women from brown men' " ("Can the Subaltern Speak?" in *Marxism and the Interpretation of Culture,* ed. Cary Nelson and Lawrence Grossberg [Urbana, 1988], 297).

18. In a similar vein, the author of *The Three Bamboos,* published in 1942,

dedicates his novel "to the gentle, self-effacing and long-suffering mothers of the cruellest, most arrogant and treacherous sons who walk the earth" (quoted in D. N. Lammers, "Taking Japan Seriously," in *Asia in Western Fiction,* ed. Robin W. Winks and James R. Rush [Honolulu, 1991], 206).

19. The connection between missionary zeal and imperialist impulses has been articulated by numerous critics of imperialism. In the history of Japan, this connection has resonances dating to the sixteenth century when Jesuit priests sought to convert the Japanese "heathens" by exposing them to the culture and language of the West (the Japanese language was referred to by St. Francis Xavier as "the Devil's own tongue"), and this was directly responsible for Japan's sealing itself off from Western influences—a condition that obtained until 1854.

20. There are a few curious departures from the general habit of representing the Japanese woman as the sweet, all-suffering helpmate. "It is evident," claims one writer, "that in a nation where the women cannot in normal society become overtly aggressive, violence on the part of a woman might be regarded by the Japanese as a manifestation of mental illness or antisocial behavior. . . . Murder— by some such secret methods as poisoning—has long been almost the only outlet for the pent-up hostility of Japanese women" (James Clark Moloney, *Understanding the Japanese Mind* [New York, 1954], 34–35).

21. I refer here to white women of the middle class. Women of color and working-class white women had already been working outside the home prior to the war.

22. As I note in the following chapter, the rhetoric of Japanese/Asian women as more feminine, compliant and obedient has experienced a new surge in the mid-1980s through mid-1990s. The conservative, sexist perception that American women of nearly all ethnic backgrounds are no longer "womanly" has led to a booming, "mail-order bride" business whose customers are attracted to the notion that Asian women have somehow retained the female virtues supposedly embodied by white American women in the nineteenth century and the Eisenhower fifties.

23. In the discussion that follows I use both the film (1957) and novel (1953) versions of *Sayonara.* Although I recognize that filmic and textual narratives differ in their use of representation and, most notably, in their positioning of the audience, I nevertheless see both versions of *Sayonara* as employing the same rhetorical strategy in relation to issues of nationalism and the articulation of national identity.

24. See both Simpson and William Manchester, *American Caesar: Douglas MacArthur, 1880–1964* (Boston, 1978).

25. So popular, in fact, that in addition to its success in novel and film versions, *Sayonara*'s latest incarnation, in the 1990s, is as a musical (as it turned out, extremely short-lived). This situation is similar to that of *Teahouse of the August Moon,* which was a highly successful Broadway show before its filmed version of 1956.

26. The War Brides Act of 1945 primarily affected the Chinese wives of Chinese American servicemen. The 1952 McCarran-Walter Act allowed the entry of Japanese, Korean and Filipina wives of primarily non-Asian men. The women were categorized as non-quota immigrants—that is, as the wives of U.S. citi-

zens—instead of as "war brides." In addition, under the terms of the McCarren-Walter Act, "aliens" previously ineligible for citizenship were allowed naturalization rights. See Sucheng Chan, *Asian Americans: An Interpretive History* (San Francisco, 1991a), 140.

27. The immensely popular television miniseries *Shogun* provides an excellent example of the depiction of Japanese men as savagely brutal and Japanese women as exotically sensual and willing to serve. More recently, *Rising Sun*, portrays Japanese men as so many economic kamikazes. This representational strategy is not limited only to the Japanese. See, for instance, Michael Cimino's notorious *Year of the Dragon* (1986), *Harry's Hong Kong* (1987), *Rambo: First Blood, Part II* (1985), *Walk Like a Dragon* (1961).

28. J. D. Bisignani, *Japan Handbook* (Chico, 1983). Subsequent references in the text will be cited parenthetically. According to a representative at Moon Publications, the *Handbook* has sold well over 100,000 copies. It is one of Moon Publication's top best-sellers. On an anecdotal level, several travelers to Japan have told me that they either used the guide themselves because they had been told it was a standard guide or saw fellow travelers using it.

29. Inspired by an attitude similar to that displayed in Bisignani's book, there exists a subgenre of travel books on Japan that might all be classified as "how to get laid" guides. The best known of these is *Bachelor's Japan* (Rutland, 1967) by Boye DeMente, now in its thirteenth printing. Among the chapter headings may be found the following: "The Pleasure Capital of the World," "The Girls Say 'Ah So,' " "How to be a Gigolo" and "Just Tell Them You're Married."

30. In *The Rhetoric of Empire: Colonial Discourse in Journalism, Travel Writing, and Imperial Administration* (Durham, N.C., 1993), David Spurr notes a similar move in the context of British colonial culture in Africa: "Charles Allen's glossary of Anglo-African slang tells us that among British colonial officers the euphemism for an African mistress was 'sleeping dictionary' (164). Colonial officers were required to learn native languages, and native mistresses could provide a relatively painless form of language instruction. Beyond this prosaic etymology, however, the metaphor suggests an entire series of unstated connections between the sexual and the lexical. It suggests, for example, that the African woman is a text to be opened and closed at will, and whose contents allow entry into the mysteries of African language; that this language, and by extension, African culture, is itself both contained within and revealed by the female body; that sexual knowledge of her body is knowledge of Africa itself" (170–71).

31. Although the publisher for Morley's book would not divulge its sales figures, a representative did say that it had sold "very, very well." Iyer's book sold 8,000 copies in hardcover and, two years into its life in paperback, 15,000 trade editions. *The Lady and the Monk* also received extremely favorable reviews in the *Los Angeles Times Book Review* (Alex Gibney, "Kimono Lisa," 13 October 1991) and the *New York Times Book Review* (Lesley Downer, "Zen and the Art of Flirtation," 29 September 1991).

32. In his discussion of the role of surveillance in imperialist writing, Spurr notes: "When it descends from the heights of mountain ranges and hotel rooms, the gaze of the Western writer penetrates the interiors of human habitation, and it explores the bodies and faces of people with the same freedom that it brings

to the survey of a landscape. . . . In these interiors the confrontation of cultures takes place face to face, or rather eye to eye, and it is here, at close range, that the gaze of the writer can have its most powerful effect" (*Rhetoric of Empire*, 19–20).

33. A similar example of this feminization and sexualization of Japanese cultural arts can be found in John Burnham Schwartz's stunningly juvenile novel *Bicycle Days* (New York, 1989), which received high praise. In it, the tea ceremony (*cha no yu*) is described as an art of sexual tension and the postponement, but eventual fulfillment, of sexual gratification.

Chapter 2: In/Visible Difference

1. I borrow this question from the title of one of the essays in Gary Okihiro's *Margins and Mainstreams: Asians in American History and Culture* (Seattle, 1994).

2. The phrase "racial formation" comes from Michael Omi and Howard Winant, *Racial Formation in the United States: From the 1960s to the 1980s* (New York, 1994).

3. The apparent motive for the 1995 murders in Seattle of Susana Remerata Blackwell, Veronica Laureta and Phoebe Dizon, all Filipinas, was the fury of Blackwell's white American husband at her failure to be the passive, submissive Asian wife he had expected. Consistently identified by the mainstream press as "a mail-order bride," Susana Remerata Blackwell was pregnant and had filed for divorce from her abusive husband. He shot her and her two friends outside the Seattle courtroom where the case was being heard. And as recent events near American military bases in Korea and Okinawa remind us, acts of violence against Asian American women mirror those against Asian women, especially— but not limited to—Asian sex workers who primarily service American military personnel. The sexualizing metaphors of American geopolitics combined with decades of representations of Asian women as delicate, sexually talented and subserviently obtuse by nature are the cause and context for largely unpunished acts of sexual violence enacted upon their bodies.

Given the pervasive, historical and contemporary failure to distinguish between Asians and Asian Americans (few Asian Americans have not been asked at one time or another where they came from or how they have learned to speak English so well), the latter learn early that their well-being in this country depends heavily on the political and economic relationship between the United States and Asia. Asian Americans, both male and female, have suffered violence by white Americans who see them as targets for "getting even" with an economically and ideologically threatening "Orient." I refer here not only to the internment of Japanese Americans during WW II, but to the highly publicized (within but not outside the Asian American community) murder of Vincent Chin, a Chinese American who was beaten to death in Detroit by two white unemployed autoworkers who mistook him for a Japanese American and thus considered him an appropriate target on which to vent their frustrations with the Japanese auto industry. Other incidents include the hanging of an eight-year-old Chinese girl in North Carolina, the murder of a Vietnamese American in Florida, and the murder of a Chinese American woman who was decapitated by a subway train in New York, after having been pushed by a white man who yelled, "Now we're even." In 1996 white supremacist skinheads looking for "fun" beat to death Ly Minh Thien, a twenty-four-year-old graduate student of UCLA, in what might be interpreted as an act of revenge by "dispossessed" white youth.

And in a tragic example of projected racialized fear on 28 April 1997, Kuanchung Kao, a thirty-three-year-old man, was shot to death by police in Rohnert Park, a northern California suburb. Police justified the shooting by claiming that Kao was poised to attack them, indicated by what they interpreted as a "ninja" martial-arts pose. At the time, Kao was intoxicated and wielding a wooden pole, six feet long and one inch thick. Witnessed by Kao's wife and six-year-old daughter, police shot Kao in his own driveway, handcuffed him as he lay bleeding and refused to allow Mrs. Kao, a registered nurse, to aid her husband. According to later reports, Kao was agitated and upset when he arrived home from the bar where he had been drinking, because some other patrons had decided it would be fun to harass an intoxicated Asian man. Throughout the evening, Kao had been continually taunted with racial epithets and several scuffles ensued, one resulting in his being stabbed over the eye with a dart. Police officers called to the scene by Kao had declined to arrest those who had assaulted him.

In the aftermath of Kao's death, police have reportedly gone to several martial-arts studios in the attempt to find someone who will affirm that he practiced the martial arts, but they have been unable to find anyone who will make such a claim. One of the first steps of the investigation into the shooting involved securing a search warrant to look for martial-arts weapons in the Kao family home. None were found.

4. My decision to focus on a specific ethnic Asian group also recognizes the larger debate as to the problematics, inaccuracies and/or political positionings of "Asian American" as an aggregate term.

5. The distinction I draw here between Asian nationals and Asian Americans is in many ways problematic, particularly given the recent immigration trends among various Asian/American ethnic groups and the rise of so-called 1.5 and parachute generations. I do not intend, implicitly or otherwise, to contribute to the racist discourse that pits (usually "colored") "foreigners" against (usually "white") "citizens." That I make a distinction at all is directly attributable to the fact that many non-Asians in the United States regularly fail to recognize Asian Americans as anything other than perpetual foreigners.

6. I am thinking here of films such as *The World of Suzi Wong* (1960), *Year of the Dragon* (1986) and *Golden Gate* (1994). In his book *Marginal Sights: Staging the Chinese in America* (Iowa City, 1993), James S. Moy discusses the prevalence of porn films that capitalize on the apparently insatiable market for depictions of sex between white men and Asian/Asian American women: *Asian Anal Girls, Banzai Ass, Asian Slut* and *Oriental Sexpress*, to name just a few.

7. This phrase is taken from the title of Mitsuye Yamada's essay, "Invisibility is an Unnatural Disaster: Reflections of an Asian American Woman," in *This Bridge Called My Back: Writings by Radical Women of Color*, ed. Cherríe Moraga and Gloria Anzaldua (Watertown, Conn., 1992).

8. See Richard Dyer, "White," *Screen*, autumn 1988; Ruth Frankenberg,

White Women, Race Matters: The Social Construction of Whiteness (Minneapolis, 1993); Vron Ware, *Beyond the Pale: White Women, Racism and History* (London, 1992); Earl Jackson, Jr., "Oxydol Poisoning," in *Names We Call Home: Autobiography and Racial Identity*, ed. Becky Thompson and Sangeeta Tyagi (New York, 1996).

9. I refer to theories of the postmodern subject similar to those articulated by Jean-François Lyotard in *The Postmodern Condition*, trans. Geoffrey Bennington and Brian Massumi (Minneapolis, 1984). Additionally, the problematics of difference are varyingly addressed (and not addressed) in the work, among others, of Linda Hutcheon, *A Poetics of Postmodernism: History, Theory, Fiction* (New York, 1988) and Paul Smith, *Discerning the Subject* (Minneapolis, 1988).

10. For a discussion of the discourse of spatiality, displacement and geography that characterizes so much recent feminist theory, see Caren Kaplan, *Questions of Travel: Postmodern Discourses of Displacement* (Durham, N.C., 1996).

11. In their discussion of stereotypical constructions of Latinas, Eliana Ortega and Nancy Saporta Sternbach describe the process of articulating the self as subject ("At the Threshold of the Unnamed: Latina Literary Discourse in the Eighties," in *Breaking Boundaries: Latina Writing and Critical Reading*, ed. Asuncion Horno-Delgado [Amherst, 1989], 14): "For a subject who is not part of the dominant ideology, construction of the self is a far more complex negotiation. In constructing herself as subject, a Latina must dismantle the representation of stereotypes of her Self constructed, framed, and projected by the dominant ideology."

12. Frankenberg addresses this point in *White Women, Race Matters,* 193: "Provocatively linking the status of such apparently diverse locations as the Chinatowns and American Indian reservations of the United States and the Bantustans of South Africa, Trinh points out that the status of some cultures as nameable and 'bounded' goes alongside their marginalization from the dominant culture. As she argues, 'bounded' cultures, while apparently valorized, are in fact relegated to 'reservations' (or Chinatowns) in the name of 'preservation,' a process that has the effect of reinforcing rather than dislodging the normativeness of the dominant culture."

13. The history of Asian Americans is rife with examples of how Asians were considered non- or subhuman. And the contemporary rhetoric of Asians and Asian Americans as "super brains" driven by the desire to achieve success supplies another variation: whether sub- or superhuman, the Asian/American subject is rarely perceived as simply "human."

14. In a 1994 national survey commissioned by the National Conference of Christians and Jews, the majority of white Americans were found to "feel most in common with African Americans, but least in common with Asian Americans" (Lynne Duke, "Ethnic Groups Divided over Opportunity," *Seattle Times,* 3 March 1994).

15. In *Modernism Relocated: Towards a Cultural Studies of Visual Modernity* (St. Leonards, Australia, 1995), 180–81, John C. Welchman notes in his discussion of Barthes's *Empire of Signs* that there is "a discourse of liberal intellectualism" in which "in a particular theoretical appropriation . . . the Japanese ('Oriental') face is colonized by the textualist metaphorics of the Western intellectual, such

that it is returned as a script to be written. . . . The reduction [in many of Barthes's passages] of Japanese faciality to *'un caractère idéographique'* ('an ideographic character'), the analagous [*sic*] *'reprise ici et là'* ('resumption here and there') or oriental 'beauty' from (Western) *'singularité'* ('singularity') to *'le grand* (eastern) *syntagme des corps'* ('the great [eastern] syntagm of bodies'), is an operation that literally in*scribes* the Other as a semi-arbitrary notational language articulated by an endless column ('syntagm') of partially legible faces. To the Western gaze, the 'Oriental' mass becomes an index of signs whose syntactical relation is the product of the West's classificatory imagination. The horde becomes a field of ideograms: the projection of military violence in numbers becomes an always replicating hermeneutic grid fixing (entrapping) the Other. The horde is hoarded (and held) as a dictionary of Others compiled by the West."

16. Since most non-Asians find the issue of "The Fold" a confusing one, it may therefore be useful to clarify the terminology used throughout this section. Terms that refer to so-called large non-Asian eyes include "double lid," "double fold," "double eyes," "The Fold," "natural crease" and "defined palpebral fold." Terms used to refer to so-called small Asian eyes include "single lid," "lidless," "single fold," "epicanthic fold," "epicanthic lid" and "creaseless." Though I attempt to lessen potential confusion by primarily using "lid" to refer to "Asian eyes" and "fold" to refer to "Caucasian eyes," the list above illustrates a slippage of terms that exemplifies the arbitrary construction of the relation between physiology and value.

17. Joanne Chen, "Before and After," *A. Magazine: The Asian American Quarterly* 2, no. 1 (1993): 15. Subsequent references in the text are noted parenthetically.

18. The glossy Asian American beauty magazine *Face,* for instance, featured an article on upper blepharoplastic procedures, "What You Should Know About Eyelid Surgery" (*Face* 2, no. 1 [November–December 1993]). Contrary to the title, in which it might be reasonably presumed that the reader will be warned of the potential failures or dangers of such procedures, the article is geared toward those who have decided to undergo eyelid surgery. Notwithstanding the argument I make in this section, the rhetoric of this article, which includes information on "the amount of fat to be removed" and "the amount of excess skin to be removed," implies that complete removal of the epicanthic fold, not its modification, is the primary procedural method required for Asian women's eyes. It is significant that the article was written by a plastic surgeon. Of the six issues published up to June 1994, over half feature covers in which the first byline under "Beauty and Fashion" refers to eyes and eye makeup.

19. See Chen, "Before and After"; and Eugenia Kaw, "Medicalization of Racial Features: Asian American Women and Cosmetic Surgery," *Medical Anthropology Quarterly* 7, no. 1 (1993): 74–89.

20. While I may seem to overstate the case in order to make my point, this is unfortunately not the case. I am familiar with several instances on at least three university campuses where small but vocal groups of Asian American undergraduates—rightly fed up with negative portrayals of Asians and flush with a newfound sense of ethnic empowerment—informally instituted a social hierarchy that equated greater "Asianness" in physical appearance with greater com-

mitment to and identification with Asian Americanness. Thus, those with darker hair and skin tone and more "Asian" eyes considered themselves to be "down for the cause" in a way that other Asian Americans were not. The rationale was that those who looked "more Asian" had experienced greater devaluation and oppression and were therefore more aware of racism and more radical in their opposition to it.

21. See, for instance, Kaja Silverman's discussion in "White Skin: Brown Mask; The Double Mimesis, or With Lawrence in Arabia," *differences* 1, no. 3 (1989): 48.

22. Discussing the uses of the mask in Anglo-American modernism, in *The Dialect of Modernism: Race, Language, and Twentieth-Century Literature* (New York, 1994), 67, Michael North notes that for many artists and writers of the period "the African mask is a particular case of rare power for Europeans, because it is so difficult for them to distinguish it from the African face. For a writer like Conrad, an African face *is* a mask because there is something essentially mysterious about it, something paradoxical and ambiguous. It is at once brutally repulsive, far *too* real, and mysteriously elusive, abstract, and distant. It is no accident that James Wait's name appears in the ship's log and thus in the novel as an indecipherable blot, an unreadable sign, because the character himself is an unreadable sign." North goes on to note that Paul Laurence Dunbar's poem "We Wear the Mask," written at roughly the same time as Conrad's *Nigger of the "Narcissus,"* speaks "from the other side, from behind the barrier of enforced unreadability" (67 n.44). North's analysis of the imposed unreadability of the African face works very well as a gloss of Barthes's similar move in relation to the Japanese face.

Chapter 3: "That other, private self"

1. Mine Okubo's *Citizen 13660* (Seattle, [1946] 1983) should rightly be considered the first Nisei autobiographical text. Okubo's book is a textual and visual account of her experience in camp. Significantly, she represents herself in almost every illustration, reminding the reader/viewer of the autobiographical nature of her text. Because the whole issue of visuality and visual representation takes up significant concerns beyond the scope of this chapter, I omit it from my discussion. See Kristine C. Kuramitsu's discussion of Okubo in her article, "Internment and Identity in Japanese American Art," *American Quarterly* 47, no. 4 (December 1995): 624–28.

For autobiographies by Nisei men, see *The Kikuchi Diary* (Urbana, 1973) by Charles Kikuchi, Daniel Okimoto's *American in Disguise* (New York, 1971), and Gene Oishi's *In Search of Hiroshi* (Rutland, 1988). The predominance and greater general knowledge of autobiographies by Nisei women reflect their publication by larger companies as well as traditional and cultural gender expectations: within the Nisei community, as in the dominant culture of the time, it was less acceptable for a man to spend time on what would have been considered a hobby—i.e., writing—instead of applying himself to building a "legitimate" career with which he could support a family.

A very recent addition is *Beyond Loyalty: The Story of a Kibei* (Honolulu, 1997), by Minoru Kiota. Unlike any of the other autobiographies written by Nisei, male or female, this one is written from the perspective of a Nisei who was born in the United States, spent four years of his childhood being educated in Japan, and renounced his American citizenship in protest over the treatment of Japanese Americans during World War II.

For those interested in autobiographical narratives written by Japanese immigrants, see Etsu Inagaki Sugimoto, *A Daughter of the Samurai* (New York, 1925), Haru Matsui, *Restless Wave* (New York, 1940), and Reiko Hatsumi, *Rain and the Feast of the Stars* (Boston, 1959). Unlike the vast majority of Issei, these women were born into the Japanese upper middle class and had opportunities for education and travel. A recent addition, Kyoko Mori's *The Dream of Water* (New York, 1995), should technically be included in this category, but its many differences—of class background, time period, content and narrative purpose—distinguish it from earlier Issei autobiographies.

2. Indeed, so little work has been done in this area that Bella Brodzki and Celeste Schenck, the editors of *Life/Lines: Theorizing Women's Autobiography* (Ithaca, 1988), state that "despite . . . strenuous efforts to include them . . . Asian women's autobiographies remain underrepresented in our collection" (13). In fact, Asian and Asian American women's autobiographies are not just underrepresented—they are not represented at all.

3. In his discussion of African American autobiography, Robert Sayre notes that unlike the autobiographies of white Americans whose conversion narratives of the "self-made man" were to provide an emulative ideal, African American autobiographers "hoped to deliver the white man from political ignorance to knowledge . . . to teach and persuade rather than to acquire white imitators. . . . [They] told a story that would change the national character or renew it by making it responsive to conditions it had previously ignored" ("Autobiography and the Making of America," in *Autobiography: Essays Theoretical and Critical*, ed. James Olney [Princeton, 1980], 166, 167).

4. The Nisei tendency to avoid calling attention to oneself reflects Japanese cultural behavior codes but results primarily from their Issei parents' experience of racism in the United States. Issei parents stressed the values of "fitting in" and self-effacement as a strategy for avoiding the kind of prejudice they themselves had experienced. The irony, of course, is that the assimilationist drive of the Nisei was used against them during World War II, when they were accused of attempting to carry out acts of sabotage by moving unnoticed in white American society. For more on Nisei cultural behavior, see Bill Hosokawa, *Nisei: The Quiet American* (New York, 1969); Harry H. Kitano, *Japanese Americans: The Evolution of a Subculture* (Englewood Cliffs, 1969); David O'Brien and Stephen S. Fugita, *The Japanese American Experience* (Bloomington, 1991); Paul R. Spickard, *Japanese Americans: The Formation and Transformations of an Ethnic Group* (New York, 1996).

5. Shirley Geok-lin Lim writes in her autobiographical memoir: "The self is paltry, phantasmagoric; it leaks and slips away. It is the family, parents, siblings, cousins, that signify the meaning of the self, and beyond the family, the extended community" (*Among the White Moon Faces: An Asian-American Memoir of Home-*

lands [New York, 1996], 164). However, it should be pointed out that this cultural tendency has often been misread and reduced to simplistic formulations of anti-individualism in Asian/American cultures. Such extreme culturalist readings, obviously, should be avoided.

6. Theorists in the fields of African American, Native American and Chicano autobiography repeatedly stress that for these communities, identity is understood as relational and group-defined, not individual-based. See, for instance, Selwyn R. Cudjoe, "Maya Angelou and the Autobiographical Statement," in *Black Women Writers (1950–1980),* ed. Mari Evans (Garden City, 1984); Doris Sommer, " 'Not Just a Personal Story': Women's Testimonios and the Plural Self," in *Life/Lines: Theorizing Women's Autobiography,* ed. Bella Brodzki and Celeste Schenck (Ithaca, 1988); and Ramón Saldívar, *Chicano Narrative: The Dialectics of Difference* (Madison, 1990). Feminist theorists of women's autobiography stress a similarly defined group or relational sense of identity. See Shari Benstock, ed., *The Private Self: Theory and Practice of Women's Autobiographical Writings* (Chapel Hill, 1988); and Mary Mason, "Autobiographies of Women Writers," in *Autobiography: Essays Theoretical and Critical,* ed. James Olney (Princeton, 1980).

7. Although I cite other critics' work dealing with Houston, Sone or Uchida, none focuses on the body of autobiography written by Nisei women. As far as I am aware, Rayson's article remains the only attempt to theorize these autobiographical narratives as a group. While Rayson's analysis, indicated by its title, uses the image of the mask, it does not develop the image as a narrative or writerly trope. Additionally, it discusses the mask in negative terms that reinscribe it as a barrier and sign of the failure to disclose the self in an act of assent that inaugurates the subject into full participation in "the larger culture."

8. Sau-ling Wong's analysis of the photographs included in Uchida's book suggests that they are "a graphic rendition" of the process of the "*undoing* of home-founding" (*Reading Asian American Literature,* 136–38).

9. To resolve feelings of fragmentation, some Nisei dissociated from Japanese culture and from any part of themselves they identified as Japanese. A saying within the Nikkei community was that Japanese Americans had to become not 100 percent but 200 percent American. To this extent, one could possibly argue that this response—isolating an identifiable "American" element and exaggerating it—is an instance of conversion; that is, conversion being understood as going beyond simply emphasizing "American" and instead emphatically not being "Japanese." But finally, that is less a conversion than an adaptive response—one that not cannot be said to generally characterize Japanese Americans of the Nisei generation.

10. The editors of *Aiiieeeee!* rightly, I believe, indict Okimoto for his acceptance of "white standards of objectivity, beauty, behavior, and achievement as being morally absolute, and his acknowledgment that, because he is not white, he can never fully measure up to white standards" (Frank Chin, Jeffery Paul Chan, Lawson Fusao Inada, and Shawn Wong, eds., *Aiiieeeee! An Anthology of Asian American Writers* [New York, (1974) 1991], 11). Okimoto's assessment of Japanese Americans crosses over the fine line from describing the effects of racism on the Japanese American subject to embodying and endorsing those stereo-

types. He is an example of the raced subject who, to use W. E. B. DuBois's term, has moved from the double consciousness marginalized subjects develop on entry into the dominant social order to a total acceptance of that order's construction of the other.

11. Mitsuye Yamada, herself an internee, describes a similar coping strategy in her poem "The Trick Was" (*Camp Notes* [New York, (1976) 1992], 27), which I discuss in chapter five.

In her article on the production of visual art in the internment camps, Kristine C. Kuramitsu notes that representational art that focused on the natural beauty of the surrounding landscape provided a means of distraction and spiritual empowerment. Kuramitsu includes part of an unpublished interview conducted by Rea Tajiri, whose mother remembered one woman having a complete breakdown in camp: "She [Rea's mother] felt like this woman had thought about why she was there [at Minidoka] too much and that if they all sat around and thought about why they were there, they would probably all have gone crazy" (quoted in "Internment and Identity in Japanese American Art," *American Quarterly* 47, no. 4 [December 1995]: 637; brackets in original).

12. See Lauren Berlant, *The Anatomy of National Fantasy: Hawthorne, Utopia, and Everyday Life* (Chicago, 1991a).

13. Sone's equation of being Japanese with being "freakish" echoes Daniel Okimoto's feeling of "racial freakishness" cited earlier in this discussion.

14. See also Sau-ling Wong's excellent analysis of this passage in *Reading Asian American Literature*, 93–95.

Chapter 4: Mothers, Daughters and the Trope of Maternal Absence in Japanese American Women's Fiction

1. Examples of novels that would seem to lend themselves to a generational model but whose complexity exceeds such a framework include John Okada, *No-No Boy* (Seattle, [1957] 1976); Louis Chu, *Eat a Bowl of Tea* (New York, [1961] 1990); Ronyoung Kim, *Clay Walls* (Seattle, 1987); Fae Myenne Ng, *Bone* (New York, 1993). Two Japanese American novels that deal specifically with mother-daughter relationships and generational differences, but which I do not discuss in this chapter, are Julie Shigekuni's *A Bridge Between Us* (New York, 1995) and Holly Uyemoto's *Go* (New York, 1995).

2. The following passage by Elizabeth Grosz typifies psychoanalytic models of the child's process of individuation: "The recognition of lack or absence, whether this is the absence of the mother, or an absence of gratification of needs . . . marks the first stage in the child's acquisition of an identity independent of the mother, the genesis of a sense of self or personal unity, the origin of the child's sexual drives and the first process of social acculturation" (*Jacques Lacan: A Feminist Introduction* [New York, 1990], 32).

3. In their discussion of black mother-daughter relationships, Gloria I. Joseph and Jill Lewis state that one cannot analyze "specific psychological mechanisms" (*Common Differences: Conflicts in Black and White Feminist Perspectives* [Boston, 1981], 75) apart from considerations of race; one must further consider

that "societal conditions intensified Black mother/daughter relationships . . . while social factors had a tendency to fracture the European mother/daughter relationships" (90).

4. Two highly influential studies, Nancy Chodorow's *The Reproduction of Mothering* (Berkeley, 1978) and Carol Gilligan's *In a Different Voice: Psychological Theory and Women's Development* (Cambridge, Mass., 1982), exemplify the way in which race, as well as class, is elided in focusing on gender as the primary category of theorization. Patricia Hill Collins cites a survey of the feminist literature on mother-daughter relationships conducted by Carol J. Boyd, who concludes that the two primary theories of motherhood—psychoanalytic and social learning—both fail to take issues of race and class into account. See Patricia Hill Collins, "Shifting the Center: Race, Class, and Feminist Theorizing about Motherhood," in *Mothering: Ideology, Experience, and Agency* (New York, 1994); and Carol J. Boyd, "Mothers and Daughters: A Discussion of Theory and Research," *Journal of Marriage and the Family* 51 (1989): 291–301. For examples of feminist work on mothers and daughters for which issues of race and class are central, see Evelyn Nakano Glenn, Grace Chang, and Linda Rennie Forcey, eds., *Mothering: Ideology, Experience, and Agency* (New York, 1994); and Joseph and Lewis, *Common Differences,* particularly chs. 3 and 4.

5. Both essays are included in Houston's work *Beyond Manzanar: Views of Asian-American Womanhood* (Santa Barbara, 1985). Parenthetical cites in the text include both the work's original date and the date of publication.

6. Many Japanese Americans, particularly of the Issei and Nisei generations, make this division of actions into Japanese and American categories as a kind of shorthand for the recognition of real and identifiable cultural differences but tend to perceive these categories as inherent markers of "Japaneseness" and "Americanness", assuming in both cases that "American" is synonymous with "white." See Sylvia Junko Yanagisako, *Transforming the Past: Tradition and Kinship Among Japanese Americans* (Stanford, 1985).

7. In *Obasan* (1981; reprint, New York, 1994), Joy Kogawa similarly associates the act of serving with considerate and loving attendance or "alert and accurate knowing" (68).

8. Many Issei women who might have preferred to work in a more circumscribed arena were unable to do so. In fact, the 1920 census report showed that 26 percent of Japanese women participated in paid labor, most of it domestic and agricultural. This represented the second-highest percentage of working women within any ethnic group during the same period. Almost 40 percent of African American women participated in the labor force. See Teresa L. Amott and Julie A Matthaei, *Race, Gender and Work: A Multicultural Economic History of Women in the United States* (Boston, 1991).

9. For the purposes of this discussion, I understand "individuate" to imply a level of autonomy from, and necessary rejection of, the mother that sets it apart from "differentiate." The latter allows for a level of identification with her that does not resonate in the former, whose connotations associate it strongly with ideologies of individualism.

10. Vivien E. Nice (*Mothers and Daughters: The Distortion of a Relationship* [New York, 1992]), to her credit, consciously sets out to study mother-daughter

relationships within the matrices of patriarchy, class structures and racism, taking issue with the prevalent notion, articulated by Signe Hammer, that "the basic psychological mechanisms in the mother-daughter relationship are common to almost all women" (*Mothers and Daughters: Daughters and Mothers* [London, 1976], xii). Nevertheless, in Nice's brief section on Asian women in Britain and North America (in which she does not differentiate between Asian-born and British- or American-born Asians), she bases her conclusions on the startling assumption that there "is a lack of concentration on the mother-daughter relationship within the literature" (*Mothers and Daughters: Distortion*, 192). As a result, her analysis is necessarily limited and ultimately inaccurate.

11. See Yanagisako, *Transforming the Past;* and Glenn et al., *Mothering.*

12. Zenobia Baxter Mistri (" 'Seventeen Syllables': A Symbolic Haiku," *Studies in Short Fiction* 27, no. 2 [1990]: 198) points out that Mrs. Hayashi's pen name foreshadows the events that take place in the story: "in Japanese, the name *Ume* stands for an exquisite flowering tree which blossoms in early spring and bears fruit by the end of spring—that is, in three months. *Hanazono* means 'a flower garden.' " Thus, Mrs. Hayashi's life as a poet, like the life span of this tree's blossoms, will be "very brief."

13. Sau-ling Wong provides an excellent analysis of the conflict between necessity and extravagance in "Seventeen Syllables": "In this tale of frustrated aspirations, the central conflict can be understood as Extravagance demanding a hearing in spite of the forces of Necessity, which are amassed in a formidable alliance against the individual woman" (*Reading Asian American Literature*, 167–68). For more on what Wong identifies as a central conflict in many Asian American literary works, see her study.

14. The short story "And the Soul Shall Dance" was originally published in the *Los Angeles Rafu Shimpo Holiday Supplement*, December 1966, but was not widely read until its 1974 publication in *Aiiieeeee!* The play was first performed in 1977.

15. *The Music Lessons* was first performed in 1980 but was not published previous to its inclusion in *Songs My Mother Taught Me: Stories, Plays, and Memoir* (New York, 1994). The play is based on a short story entitled "In Heaven and Earth," first published in the *Los Angeles Rafu Shimpo Holiday Supplement*, December 1968.

16. *Obasan* was published in Canada in 1981 and during the next year in the United States. Parenthetical cites in the text come from its 1994 edition.

17. See Cheung, *Articulate Silences*, ch. 4, especially 126–28.

18. Julia Kristeva asserts that "the unspoken doubtless weighs first on the maternal body: as no signifier can uplift it without leaving a remainder, for the signifier is always meaning, communication or structure, whereas a woman as mother would be, instead, a strange fold that changes culture into nature, the speaking into biology" ("Stabat Mater," in *Tales of Love,* trans. Leon S. Roudiez [New York, (1976) 1987], 259).

19. See Jacqueline Rose, "Julia Kristeva—Take Two," in *Sexuality in the Field of Vision* (London, 1986). Marianne Hirsch argues that Kristeva reiterates traditional representations by either idealizing or denigrating the maternal (*The Mother/Daughter Plot: Narrative, Psychoanalysis, Feminism* [Bloomington, 1989],

173). Hirsch cites others whose criticisms of the Kristevan maternal are similar to her own: see Domna Stanton, "Difference on Trial: A Critique of the Maternal Metaphor in Cixous, Irigaray and Kristeva," in *The Poetics of Gender*, ed. Nancy K. Miller (New York, 1986); and Jane Gallop, *The Daughter's Seduction: Feminism and Psychoanalysis* (Ithaca, 1982).

20. See Kristeva, *Desire in Language*, 195: "To rediscover the intonations, scansions, and jubilant rhythms preceding the signifier's position is to discover the voiced breath that fastens us to an undifferentiated mother, to a mother who later, at the mirror stage, is altered into a *maternal language*."

21. King-Kok Cheung discusses in detail the ways in which Kogawa represents language as both unreliable and destructive. Language "becomes especially treacherous when abusive slurs pass for news and oppressive edicts for laws. . . . More subtle are the racist lies embedded in institutional rhetoric. During the war the Canadian bureaucracy used words to camouflage the most offensive actions against people of Japanese ancestry" (*Articulate Silences*, 134–35). Kogawa also includes less threatening examples of the arbitrary nature of language and the ways in which it can be used to signify in multiple ways: "Some of the ripe pidgin English phrases we pick up are three-part inventions—part English, part Japanese, part Sasquatch. 'Sonuva bitch' becomes 'sakana fish,' 'sakana' meaning 'fish' in Japanese. On occasion the phrase is 'golden sakana fish' " (218).

22. Early on Kogawa identifies the manner in which one deploys one's gaze with respecting or disregarding another: Naomi recalls as a child being stared at by a white child and her own knowledge that "in the language of eyes a stare is an invasion and a reproach." Kogawa also calls Naomi, and the rest of her family, "visually bilingual" (*Obasan*, 58), connecting the gaze to ethnic cultural identity. Eyes and the gaze also link the subjectivity of mother and child in the episode where the hen pecks its chicks to death: the mother's calm reflects "the eyes of Japanese motherhood" (71).

23. In *Itsuka* (1992; reprint, New York, 1994), the sequel to *Obasan*, Aunt Emily becomes a mother-figure to Naomi, who becomes increasingly involved with the Japanese Canadian reparations movement. Like the earlier novel, *Itsuka* ends with an image suggesting the maternal amniotic as the source of connectedness and life:

I can hear the waves from childhood rippling outward to touch other children who wait for their lives. I can hear the voices, faint as the faraway sound of a distant, almost inaudible wind. It's the sound of the underground stream. It speaks through memory, through dream, through our hands, our words, our arms, our trusting. I can hear the sound of the voice that frees, a light, steady, endless breath. I can hear the breath of life. (331)

Chapter 5: Embodied Language

1. See Juliana Chang's very useful introduction to her edited anthology *Quiet Fire: A Historical Anthology of Asian American Poetry, 1892–1970* (New York, 1996).

2. See Elaine Kim, *Asian American Literature*, 137–40; Sachiko Honda, "Issei Senryu," in *Frontiers of Asian American Studies*, ed. Gail M. Nomura, Russell

Endo, Stephen H. Sumida, and Russell C. Leong (Pullman, Wash., 1989). Because of the Japanese education system, Japanese immigrants tended to have a high rate of literacy. According to Honda, "In 1910 the tradition of senryu [Japanese light verse that is related to, but different from, haiku] was transplanted to America by Kaho Honda, an immigrant farmer who settled in Yakima, Washington. He introduced it to his fellow laborers to help them cope with the loneliness and harsh working conditions. Up to that point, they had resorted to alcohol and gambling, but writing senryu provided them with an intellectual outlet. This new activity in Yakima later captivated issei in other parts of the States and became a literary tradition among them" (170). By the 1930s, senryu, haiku and tanka written by Issei were regularly published in U.S. Japanese language newspapers, and Issei literary groups were common, especially on the West Coast. Unfortunately, in the weeks following the bombing of Pearl Harbor, the Issei themselves destroyed much of the unpublished writing of their generation, fearful that anything Japanese — and particularly books or writing, which could not be read by the *hakujin* FBI agents — would be confiscated and used as proof of Nikkei disloyalty. In fact, such fears were not misplaced. Later, during the initial period of the internment, even Bibles written in Japanese were not allowed in the camps. For collections of translated Issei haiku and senryu, see Lucille M. Nixon and Tomoe Tana, eds. and trans., *Sounds from the Unknown: A Collection of Japanese-American Tanka* (Denver, 1963); Jun Fujita, *Tanka: Poems in Exile* (Chicago, 1923); and the haiku included in Kazuo Ito, *Issei: A History of Japanese Immigrants in North America,* trans. Shinichiro Nakamura and Jean S. Girard (Seattle, 1973).

The Chinese American literary tradition likewise begins with the immigrant generation, as is attested by the numerous and moving poems written on the walls of the Angel Island immigration detention center. These poems have been collected and translated by Marlon K. Hom in *Songs of Gold Mountain: Cantonese Rhymes from San Francisco Chinatown* (Berkeley, 1987).

3. This situation is true for Asian American writers generally, female and male. Lawson Fusao Inada's *Before the War: Poems as They Happened* (New York, 1971) was the first volume of poems by a Japanese American to be accepted by a major publishing house.

4. The copyright page begins, "My affectionate thanks to Alta and Angel who have coaxed *Camp Notes* out of mothballs."

5. I am aware that my emphasis here on writings by contemporary Nisei and Sansei poets — widely read, book-length works — potentially replicates the marginalization and erasure of earlier Nikkei women poets, whose works are unavailable. The project of recovering internment-era literature by Nikkei men and women is an important one that remains to be undertaken.

6. Because Susan Schweik's book, *A Gulf So Deeply Cut: American Women Poets and the Second World War* (Madison, 1991), concentrates on women's war poetry, she does not discuss the significant literary activity of Nikkei men both before and during the war. Like their female counterparts, male writers grappled with issues of identity, difference and resistance.

7. Though sexuality and class, like race and gender, are crucial factors in terms of how the subject is constructed and acted upon, neither structurally operates

in terms of a visual economy vis-à-vis the body in quite the same way as do race and gender.

8. Katherine Kinney, *Friendly Fire: American Identity and the Literature of the Vietnam War* (New York, forthcoming); see ch. 5, "Humping the Boonies: Women, Sexuality, and the Memory of War."

9. Sucheng Chan provides the following account of the so-called loyalty oath in *Asian Californians* (San Francisco, 1991b), 99: "the U.S. Army aroused the greatest controversy when it decided in February 1943 to allow Nisei to enlist in a segregated regiment. Before the internees could register, they had to answer a series of questions, two of which were most critical: 'Are you willing to serve in the armed forces of the United States on combat duty, whenever ordered?' and 'Will you swear unqualified allegiance to the United States of America and faithfully defend the United States from any or all attack by foreign or domestic forces, and forswear any form of allegiance or obedience to the Japanese emperor or any other foreign government, power or organization?' Nisei were told that those who answered no to either question, but especially the latter, would be classified as 'disloyal' and segregated at Tule Lake. The internees were caught in a double bind. Those who answered yes and were considered 'loyal' might be drafted—a possibility that caused many Issei parents great anxiety. Those who answered no and were branded as 'disloyal' would be removed to Tule Lake and possibly separated from their families. The second question was particularly troubling, for how could Nisei forswear allegiance to the Japanese emperor unless they had given such allegiance in the first place? To answer yes meant that they had offered such allegiance. Some insisted on giving conditional answers, while others refused to answer altogether. For the Issei, who were denied citizenship by U.S. law, a renunciation of their loyalty to Japan would make them stateless persons. WRA officials eventually reworded it for Issei only: 'Will you swear to abide by the laws of the United States and to take no action which would in any way interfere with the war effort of the United States?' "

10. In her essay "A Needle with Mama's Voice: Mitsuye Yamada's *Camp Notes* and the American Canon of War Poetry" (in *Arms and the Woman: War, Gender, and Literary Representation*, ed. Helen M. Cooper, Adrienne Auslander Munich, and Susan Merrill Squier [Chapel Hill, 1989], 225), Susan Schweik notes that "in accounts of the American canon of war literature, the enforced exile, imprisonment, economic losses, and dehumanizing treatment that Japanese-American civilians endured and recorded are, at best, relegated to footnotes. Experiences and responses specific to Japanese-American *women* disappear entirely."

11. Paul Fussell, *The Great War and Modern Memory* (New York, 1977).

12. I am indebted to Gregory Choy for sharing this insight with me in conversations about this chapter.

13. The ambivalent stance toward the white woman and liberal feminism in "To the Lady" is also apparent elsewhere in Yamada's work. In her essay "Asian Pacific American Women and Feminism" (in *This Bridge Called My Back: Writings by Radical Women of Color*, ed. Cherrie Moraga and Gloria Anzaldua [Watertown, Mass., 1981], 72) Yamada discusses the importance of feminism for Asian American women but refutes the perception among feminists that "Asian

women are of course traditionally not attuned to being political" and observes, as have many women of color, that much of white feminist thought ignores the particularities of race, privileging gender in ways that are detrimental to women who are defined and who define themselves in terms of race. More damaging than benign neglect, however, is the active erasure of Asian American women through stereotypes held by other women, as well as by men:

Every time I read or speak to a group of people about the condition of my life as an Asian Pacific woman, it is as if I had never spoken before, as if I were speaking to a brand new audience of people who had never known an Asian Pacific woman who is other than the passive, sweet, etc. stereotype of the "Oriental" woman. . . . We speak to audiences that sift out those [threatening] parts of our speech (if what we say does not fit the image they have of us), come up to shake our hands with "That was lovely my dear, just lovely," and go home with the same mind set they come in with. No matter what we say or do, the stereotype still hangs on. (71)

14. In Mirikitani's most recent volume, *We, the Dangerous,* this poem is included as the second section of the four-part "Beauty Contest" (5) and has been retitled "Recipe for Round Eyes."

15. *Awake in the River* (San Francisco, 1978) was unpaginated, but those of its poems that Mirikitani included with new work in *We, the Dangerous* (London, 1995) carry page citations from this later publication. Such poems are identified by the parenthetical citation "1978/1995."

16. A later poem, "Prisons of Silence" (*Shedding Silence* [Berkeley, 1987], 5), employs a similar image: "From this cell of history, / this mute grave, / we birth our rage. / We heal our tongues."

17. Although Mirikitani includes several references to the oppressive violence of Japanese American men, poems like "To My Father" (1978) strongly suggest that at least some of that violence is a consequence of their own powerlessness, which is directly identified with internment. In this poem, the father's frustration is doubled by an economic reality structured by racism: he is unable to protect his children from the racist taunts of the white children whose parents can afford to buy the berries his own children cannot taste but which he labors to pick. The silence of endurance, or *gaman,* is thus perverted to frustrated wordlessness, symbolized by the emptiness in his eyes as he whips his children.

18. This version of "Spoils of War" has been reprinted in *Asian American Literature: A Brief Introduction and Anthology,* ed. Shawn Wong (New York, 1996), 185–201. Again, because the volume in which the poem first appeared is not paginated, text citations follow the anthology.

19. Perhaps its denial of any possibilities for agency explains the absence of this later version of "Spoils" from Mirikitani's volume of selected poems; the earlier version appears in the 1996 anthology.

20. My decision to retain references to Hahn herself also stems from her most recent book, *The Unbearable Heart* (1995). While exploring many of the themes in her earlier poems, the poems in this volume do so in the context of the sudden death of the poet's mother, an event whose occurrence and aftermath are continually referenced in the poems. To insist on parsing the distinctions between poet and speaker, or between Kimiko Hahn (the person) and "Kimiko

Hahn" (the persona) would be to enact a particularly callous form of academicism, as well as undermine much of what Hahn is attempting in these poems.

21. I use the term "mixed race" hesitantly and unwillingly. Similar terms such as "racially mixed," "mixed blood," "biracial, "etc., carry within them the assumption that race is a fixed substance that can be "mixed" or quantitatively combined with other similarly fixed substances. Unfortunately, the terminology of race does not articulate the subjectivities and identities of those who are defined and define themselves by more than one racial category, if indeed such terminology can be assumed to do so for anyone.

22. The disjunction between image and person in the picture-bride transaction is put to comic effect in Yoji Yamaguchi's novel, *Face of a Stranger* (New York, 1995).

23. *Genji monogatari,* by Lady Murasaki Shikibu, is considered the first true novel in the Japanese tradition and is widely considered to be the first novel in any tradition. It appeared in the early eleventh century, and its narrative development and exploration of psychological, in addition to social, relationships set *Genji* apart from earlier court narratives.

24. Relationships that base feelings toward the beloved on a resemblance to someone else proliferate to a dizzying degree throughout the novel. As Japanese literary scholar Shuichi Kato writes in *A History of Japanese Literature: The First Thousand Years,* trans. David Chibbet (Tokyo, 1979), 187: "Impressions of characters from the past are overlapped with the impressions of present characters and operate in a special way on any given character. For example, the reason Emperor Kiritsubo loves Fujitsubo is that she reminds him of his dead wife, Lady Kiritsubo. Genji was captivated by Murasaki because she reminded him of Fujitsubo. The reason he was attracted by Tamakazuna was that she was a living image of her mother Yugao who died an untimely death. Kaoru loved Uji no Oigimi and when he met her step-sister Ukifune who put him in mind of her, he came to love Ukifune. In the case of these men, they found in one woman what they had loved in another, with echoes of the love past mingling with the anticipation of the love to start. Thus, by overlapping the past, present and future into the emotion of one moment the author demonstrates the flow of time vividly." For Hahn, what Kato describes would only reinforce her sense that male desire always translates or erases female subjectivity.

25. Japanese organizes Chinese-based kanji characters into formal categories by the primary individual element of the character, its radical. To look up a kanji in the dictionary, one must isolate the appropriate radical and turn to the corresponding section of the dictionary.

26. Hahn credits Francis Steegmuller's edition of Flaubert's letters, *Flaubert in Egypt,* and gives page citations from Steegmuller's and Said's work throughout the poem.

27. Simone de Beauvoir's now famous statement comes from her 1949 work, *The Second Sex.*

Works Cited

Ai. *Cruelty*. Boston: Houghton Mifflin, 1973.

———. *Greed*. New York: W. W. Norton, 1993.

Amott, Teresa L., and Julie A. Matthaei. *Race, Gender and Work: A Multicultural Economic History of Women in the United States*. Boston: South End Press, 1991.

Ancheta, Angelo. *Race, Rights, and the Asian American Experience*. New Brunswick, N.J.: Rutgers University Press, 1998.

Barrow, Terence, ed. *Manners and Customs of the Japanese in the Nineteenth Century*. 1841. Tokyo: Charles E. Tuttle, 1973.

Barthes, Roland. *Empire of Signs*. Trans. Richard Howard. New York: Hill and Wang-Farrar Strauss and Giroux, 1982.

Beasley, W. G. *The Meiji Restoration*. Stanford: Stanford University Press, 1972.

Benstock, Shari, ed. *The Private Self: Theory and Practice of Women's Autobiographical Writings*. Chapel Hill: University of North Carolina Press, 1988.

Berlant, Lauren. *The Anatomy of National Fantasy: Hawthorne, Utopia, and Everyday Life*. Chicago: University of Chicago Press, 1991a.

———. "National Brands/National Body." In *Comparative American Identities: Race, Sex, and Nationality in the Modern Text*, ed. Hortense J. Spillers, 110–40. New York: Routledge, 1991b.

Bhabha, Homi K. "The Other Question: Difference, Discrimination and the Discourse of Colonialism." In *Out There: Marginalization and Contemporary Cultures*, ed. Russell Ferguson, Martha Gever, Trinh T. Minh-ha, and Cornel West, 71–87. New York: New Museum of Contemporary Art, 1990.

Bisignani, J. D. *Japan Handbook*. Chico: Moon Publications, 1983.

Bornoff, Nicholas. *Pink Samurai: Love, Marriage and Sex in Contemporary Japan*. New York: Pocket Books-Simon and Schuster, 1991.

Boyd, Carol J. "Mothers and Daughters: A Discussion of Theory and Research." *Journal of Marriage and the Family* 51 (1989): 291–301.

Brodzki, Bella, and Celeste Schenck, eds. *Life/Lines: Theorizing Women's Auto-biography*. Ithaca: Cornell University Press, 1988.

Buck, Pearl S. *The People of Japan*. New York: Simon and Schuster, 1966.

Bumiller, Elisabeth. *The Secrets of Mariko: A Year in the Life of a Japanese Woman and Her Family*. New York: Vintage-Random House, 1995.

Buruma, Ian. *Behind the Mask: On Sexual Demons, Sacred Mothers, Transvestites, Gangsters and Other Japanese Cultural Heroes*. New York: New American Library-Dutton, 1984.

Butler, Judith. *Gender Trouble: Feminism and the Subversion of Identity*. New York: Routledge, 1990.

Chamberlain, Basil Hall. *Japanese Things: Being Notes on Various Subjects Connected with Japan*. 1905. Reprint, Boston: C. E. Tuttle, 1971.

Chan, Sucheng. *Asian Americans: An Interpretive History*. Boston: Twayne Publishers, 1991a.

———. *Asian Californians*. Golden State Series. San Francisco: MTL/Boyd and Fraser, 1991b.

Chang, Juliana, ed. *Quiet Fire: A Historical Anthology of Asian American Poetry, 1892–1970*. New York: Asian American Writers' Workshop/Rutgers University Press, 1996.

Chen, Joanne. "Before and After." *A. Magazine: The Asian American Quarterly* 2, no. 1 (1993): 15–18, 64–65.

Cheung, King-Kok. *Articulate Silences: Hisaye Yamamoto, Maxine Hong Kingston, Joy Kogawa*. Ithaca: Cornell University Press, 1993.

Cheung, King-Kok, and Stan Yogi. *Asian American Literature: An Annotated Bibliography*. New York: Modern Language Association of America, 1988.

Chiang, Fay, et al., eds. *American Born and Foreign: An Anthology of Asian American Poetry*. New York: Sunbury Press Books, 1979.

Chin, Frank, Jeffery Paul Chan, Lawson Fusao Inada, and Shawn Wong, eds. *Aiiieeeee! An Anthology of Asian American Writers*. 1974. Reprint, New York: Mentor-Penguin Books, 1991.

———. *The Big Aiiieeeee! An Anthology of Chinese American and Japanese American Literature*. New York: Meridian-Penguin Books, 1991.

Chodorow, Nancy. *The Reproduction of Mothering*. Berkeley: University of California Press, 1978.

Chow, Rey. *Woman and Chinese Modernity: The Politics of Reading Between West and East*. Theory and History of Literature 75. Minneapolis: University of Minnesota Press, 1991.

Christopher, Robert C. *The Japanese Mind*. New York: Fawcett Columbine, 1983.

Chu, Louis. *Eat a Bowl of Tea*. 1961. Reprint, New York: Citadel Press, 1990.

Collins, Patricia Hill. "Shifting the Center: Race, Class, and Feminist Theorizing about Motherhood." In *Mothering: Ideology, Experience, and Agency*, 45–65. New York: Routledge, 1994.

Condon, John C. *With Respect to the Japanese: A Guide for Americans*. Yarmouth: Intercultural Press, 1984.

Corliss, Richard. "Pacific Overtures." *Time*, 13 September 1993, 68–70.

Creef, Elena Tajima. "Notes from a Fragmented Daughter." In *Making Face, Making Soul: Haciendo Caras,* ed. Gloria Anzaldua, 82–84. San Francisco: Aunt Lute Foundation, 1990.

Cudjoe, Selwyn R. "Maya Angelou and the Autobiographical Statement." In *Black Women Writers (1950–1980),* ed. Mari Evans, 6–24. Garden City: Anchor Books, 1984.

Davidson, Cathy N. *36 Views of Mount Fuji: On Finding Myself in Japan.* New York: Plume-Penguin Books, 1994.

De Lauretis, Teresa. *Alice Doesn't: Feminism, Semiotics, Cinema.* Bloomington: Indiana University Press, 1984.

DeMente, Boye. *Bachelor's Japan.* Rutland: Charles E. Tuttle, 1967.

Doi, Takeo. *The Anatomy of Dependence.* Trans. John Bester. 1973. Tokyo: Kodansha International, 1982.

Dower, John W. *War Without Mercy.* New York: Pantheon Books, 1986.

Downer, Lesley. "Zen and the Art of Flirtation." Review of *The Lady and the Monk: Four Seasons in Kyoto,* by Pico Iyer. *New York Times Book Review,* 29 September 1991.

Duke, Lynne. "Ethnic Groups Divided over Opportunity." *Seattle Times,* 3 March 1994.

Dyer, Richard. "White." *Screen,* Autumn 1988.

Enloe, Cynthia. *Bananas, Beaches and Bases: Making Sense of International Politics.* London: Pandora, 1989.

Fanon, Frantz. *Black Skin, White Masks.* Trans. Charles Lam Markmann. New York: Grove Press, 1967.

Faust, Allen K. *The New Japanese Womanhood.* New York: George H. Doran, 1926.

Fong, Gisele. "Corrosion." In *Making Face, Making Soul: Haciendo Caras,* ed. Gloria Anzaldua, 117. San Francisco: Aunt Lute Foundation, 1990.

Fox-Genovese, Elizabeth. "My Statue, My Self: Autobiographical Writings of Afro-American Women." In *The Private Self: Theory and Practice of Women's Autobiographical Writings,* ed. Shari Benstock, 62–89. Chapel Hill: University of North Carolina Press, 1988.

Frankenberg, Ruth. " 'When We are Capable of Stopping, We Begin to See': Being White, Seeing Whiteness." In *Names We Call Home: Autobiography and Racial Identity,* ed. Becky Thompson and Sangeeta Tyagi, 3–18. New York: Routledge, 1996.

———. *White Women, Race Matters: The Social Construction of Whiteness.* Minneapolis: University of Minnesota Press, 1993.

Friedman, Susan Stanford. "Women's Autobiographical Selves: Theory and Practice." In *The Private Self: Theory and Practice of Women's Autobiographical Writings,* ed. Shari Benstock, 34–62. Chapel Hill: University of North Carolina Press, 1988.

Fujita, Gayle K. " 'To Attend the Sound of Stone': The Sensibility of Silence in *Obasan*." *MELUS* 12, no. 3 (1985): 33–42.

Fujita, Jun. *Tanka: Poems in Exile.* Chicago: Covici-McGee, 1923.

Fussell, Paul. *The Great War and Modern Memory.* New York: Oxford University Press, 1977.

Gallop, Jane. *The Daughter's Seduction: Feminism and Psychoanalysis.* Ithaca: Cornell University Press, 1982.

Garber, Marjorie. "The Occidental Tourist: *M. Butterfly* and the Scandal of Transvestism." In *Nationalisms and Sexualities,* ed. Andrew Parker, Mary Russo, Doris Sommer, and Patricia Yaeger, 121–46. New York: Routledge, Chapman and Hall, 1992.

Gibney, Alex. "Kimono Lisa." Review of *The Lady and the Monk: Four Seasons in Kyoto,* by Pico Iyer. *Los Angeles Times Book Review,* 13 October 1991.

Gilligan, Carol. *In a Different Voice: Psychological Theory and Women's Development.* Cambridge, Mass.: Harvard University Press, 1982.

Glenn, Evelyn Nakano. *Issei, Nisei, War Bride: Three Generations of Japanese American Women in Domestic Service.* Philadephia: Temple University Press, 1986.

Glenn, Evelyn Nakano, Grace Chang, and Linda Rennie Forcey, eds. *Mothering: Ideology, Experience, and Agency.* New York: Routledge, 1994.

Goellnicht, Donald C. "Father Land and/or Mother Tongue: The Divided Female Subject in Kogawa's *Obasan* and Hong Kingston's *The Woman Warrior.*" In *Redefining Autobiography in Twentieth-Century Women's Fiction: An Essay Collection,* ed. Janice Morgan and Colette T. Hall, 119–34. New York: Garland Publishing, 1991.

Grosz, Elizabeth. *Jacques Lacan: A Feminist Introduction.* New York: Routledge, 1990.

Gulick, Sidney L. *Evolution of the Japanese.* 1903. 5th ed., rev. New York: Fleming H. Revell, 1905.

Gusdorf, Georges. "Conditions and Limits of Autobiography." Trans. James Olney. In *Autobiography: Essays Theoretical and Critical,* ed. James Olney, 28–48. Princeton: Princeton University Press, 1980.

Hahn, Kimiko. *Air Pocket.* Brooklyn: Hanging Loose Press, 1989.

———. *Earshot.* Brooklyn: Hanging Loose Press, 1992.

———. *The Unbearable Heart.* New York: Kaya Production, 1995.

———. "Writing Over Borders: A Conversation with Kimiko Hahn." With Terry Hong. *A. Magazine: The Asian American Quarterly* 2, no. 1 (1993): 51.

Hammer, Signe. *Mothers and Daughters: Daughters and Mothers.* London: Hutchinson, 1976.

Hara, Marie. *Bananaheart and Other Stories.* Honolulu: Bamboo Ridge Press, 1994.

Harootunian, Harry D. "America's Japan/Japan's Japan." In *Japan in the World,* ed. Masao Miyoshi and H. D. Harootunian, 196–221. Durham, N.C.: Duke University Press, 1993.

Hatsumi, Reiko. *Rain and the Feast of the Stars.* Boston: Houghton Mifflin, 1959.

Hawks, F. L. *Narrative of an Expedition of an American Squadron to the China Seas and Japan, Performed in the Years 1852, 1853, and 1854, Under the Command of Commodore M. C. Perry.* 3 vols. Washington, D.C., 1856.

Hearn, Lafcadio. *Glimpses of Unfamiliar Japan.* 1894. Tokyo: Charles E. Tuttle, 1976.

————. *Japan: An Attempt at Interpretation*. New York: Grosset and Dunlap, 1904.

Hirsch, Marianne. *The Mother/Daughter Plot: Narrative, Psychoanalysis, Feminism*. Bloomington: Indiana University Press, 1989.

Holte, James Craig. "The Representative Voice: Autobiography and the Ethnic Experience." *MELUS* 9, no. 2 (1982): 25–46.

Hom, Marlon K. *Songs of Gold Mountain: Cantonese Rhymes from San Francisco Chinatown*. Berkeley: University of California Press, 1987.

Honda, Sachiko. "Issei Senryu." In *Frontiers of Asian American Studies*, ed. Gail M. Nomura, Russell Endo, Stephen H. Sumida, and Russell C. Leong, 169–78. Pullman: Washington State University Press, 1989.

Hongo, Garrett. Introduction to *The Open Boat: Poems from Asian America*. Ed. Garrett Hongo. New York: Anchor-Doubleday, 1993.

Hosokawa, Bill. *Nisei: The Quiet American*. New York: William Morrow, 1969.

Houston, Jeanne Wakatsuki. *Beyond Manzanar: Views of Asian-American Womanhood*. Santa Barbara: Capra Press, 1985.

————. *Farewell to Manzanar*. New York: Bantam Books, 1973.

Houston, Velina Hasu. *Tea* (1987). In *Unbroken Thread: An Anthology of Plays by Asian American Women*, ed. Roberta Uno, 155–200. Amherst: University of Massachusetts Press, 1993.

————, ed. *But Still, Like Air, I Rise: New Asian American Plays*. Philadelphia: Temple University Press, 1997.

Hsu, Kai-yu, and Helen Palubinskas, eds. *Asian-American Authors*. 1972. Boston: Houghton, 1976.

Hutcheon, Linda. *A Poetics of Postmodernism: History, Theory, Fiction*. New York: Routledge, 1988.

Hwang, David Henry. *M. Butterfly*. New York: Plume-Penguin Books, 1989.

Inada, Lawson. *Before the War: Poems as They Happened*. New York: Morrow, 1971.

Ito, Kazuo. *Issei: A History of Japanese Immigrants in North America*. Trans. Shinichiro Nakamura and Jean S. Girard. Seattle: Executive Committee for Publication of *Issei*, 1973.

Iyer, Pico. *The Lady and the Monk: Four Seasons in Kyoto*. New York: Alfred A. Knopf, 1991.

Jackson, Earl, Jr. "Oxydol Poisoning." In *Names We Call Home: Autobiography and Racial Identity*, ed. Becky Thompson and Sangeeta Tyagi, 171–96. New York: Routledge, 1996.

Joseph, Gloria I., and Jill Lewis. *Common Differences: Conflicts in Black and White Feminist Perspectives*. Boston: South End Press, 1981.

Kadohata, Cynthia. *The Floating World*. New York: Viking Penguin, 1989.

Kageyama, Yuri. *Peeling*. Berkeley: I. Reed Books, 1988.

Kaplan, Caren. *Questions of Travel: Postmodern Discourses of Displacement*. Durham, N.C.: Duke University Press, 1996.

Kato, Shuichi. *A History of Japanese Literature: The First Thousand Years*. Trans. David Chibbet. Tokyo: Kodansha International, 1979.

Kaw, Eugenia. "Medicalization of Racial Features: Asian American Women and Cosmetic Surgery." *Medical Anthropology Quarterly* 7, no. 1 (1993): 74–89.

Kikuchi, Charles. *The Kikuchi Diary*. Ed. John Modell. Urbana: University of Illinois Press, 1973.

Kim, Elaine H. *Asian American Literature: An Introduction to the Writings and Their Social Context*. Philadelphia: Temple University Press, 1982.

Kim, Ronyoung. *Clay Walls*. Seattle: University of Washington Press, 1987.

Kincaid, Jamaica. *Lucy*. New York: Plume Penguin, 1991.

Kingston, Maxine Hong. *The Woman Warrior: Memoirs of a Girlhood Among Ghosts*. 1975. New York: Vintage International, 1989.

Kinney, Katherine. *Friendly Fire: American Identity and the Literature of the Vietnam War*. New York: Oxford University Press, forthcoming.

Kitano, Harry H. *Japanese Americans: The Evolution of a Subculture*. Englewood Cliffs, N.J.: Prentice-Hall, 1969.

Kiyota, Minoru. *Beyond Loyalty: The Story of a Kibei*. Trans. Linda Klepinger Keenan. Honolulu: University of Hawai'i Press, 1997.

Kogawa, Joy. *Itsuka*. 1992. Reprint, New York: Anchor-Bantam Doubleday Dell Publishing Group, 1994.

———. *Obasan*. 1981. Reprint, New York: Anchor-Bantam-Doubleday Dell Publishing Group, 1994.

Kondo, Dorinne K. *Crafting Selves: Power, Gender, and Discourses of Identity in a Japanese Workplace*. Chicago: University of Chicago Press, 1990.

Kono, Juliet S. *Hilo Rains*. Honolulu: Bamboo Ridge Press, 1988.

Kono, Juliet S., and Cathy Song, eds. *Sister Stew: Fiction and Poetry by Women*. Honolulu: Bamboo Ridge Press, 1991.

Kristeva, Julia. *Desire in Language: A Semiotic Approach to Literature and Art*. Ed. Leon S. Rudiez, trans. Thomas Gora, Alice Jardine, and Leon S. Roudiez. New York: Columbia University Press, 1980.

———. *Powers of Horror: An Essay on Abjection*. Trans. Leon S. Roudiez. New York: Columbia University Press, 1982.

———. "Stabat Mater." In *Tales of Love*, trans. Leon S. Roudiez. 1976. New York: Columbia University Press, 1987.

Kuramitsu, Kristine C. "Internment and Identity in Japanese American Art." *American Quarterly* 47, no. 4 (December 1995): 619–58.

Kuzuma, Yoshi. "Images of Japanese Women in U.S. Writings and Scholarly Works, 1860–1990: Formation and Transformation of Stereotypes." *U.S.-Japan Women's Journal*, English Supplement, no. 1 (August 1991): 6–50.

Lai, Tracy. "Asian American Women: Not For Sale." In *Race, Class, and Gender*, ed. Margaret L. Andersen and Patricia Hill Collins, 163–71. Belmont, Calif.: Belmont Publishing, 1992.

Lammers, D. N. "Taking Japan Seriously." In *Asia in Western Fiction*, ed. Robin W. Winks and James R. Rush, 195–214. Honolulu: University of Hawai'i Press, 1991.

Lee, Josephine. *Performing Asian America: Race and Ethnicity on the Contemporary Stage*. Philadelphia: Temple University Press, 1997.

Lim, Shirley Geok-lin. "Japanese American Women's Life Stories: Maternality in Monica Sone's *Nisei Daughter* and Joy Kogawa's *Obasan*." *Feminist Studies* 16, no. 2 (summer 1990): 288–312.

———. *Among the White Moon Faces: An Asian-American Memoir of Homelands*. New York: Feminist Press, 1996.

Lim, Shirley Geok-lin, and Amy Ling, eds. *Reading the Literatures of Asian America*. Philadelphia: Temple University Press, 1992.

Ling, Amy. *Between Worlds: Women Writers of Chinese Ancestry*. New York: Pergamon Press, 1990.

Lott, Eric. *Love and Theft: Blackface Minstrelsy and the American Working Class*. New York: Oxford University Press, 1993.

Lowe, Lisa. *Critical Terrains: French and British Orientalisms*. Ithaca: Cornell University Press, 1991a.

———. Heterogeneity, Hybridity, Multiplicity: Marking Asian American Differences." *Diaspora* 1, no. 1 (spring 1991b): 24–44.

———. *Immigrant Acts: On Asian American Cultural Politics*. Durham, N.C.: Duke University Press, 1996.

Lyotard, Jean-François. *The Postmodern Condition*. Trans. Geoffrey Bennington and Brian Massumi. Minneapolis: University of Minnesota Press, 1984.

Ma, Karen. *The Modern Madame Butterfly: Fantasy and Reality in Japanese Cross-Cultural Relationships*. Rutland: Charles E. Tuttle, 1996.

Magnusson, A. Lynne. "Language and Longing in Joy Kogawa's *Obasan*." *Canadian Literature/Littérature canadienne* 116 (spring 1988): 58–66.

Manchester, William. *American Caesar: Douglas MacArthur, 1880–1964*. Boston: Little, Brown, 1978.

Marchetti, Gina. *Romance and the 'Yellow Peril': Race, Sex, and Discursive Strategies in Hollywood Fiction*. Berkeley: University of California Press, 1993.

Mason, Mary G. "Autobiographies of Women Writers." In *Autobiography: Essays Theoretical and Critical,* ed. James Olney, 207–35. Princeton: Princeton University Press, 1980.

Matsui, Haru. *Restless Wave: An Autobiography*. New York: Modern Age Books, 1940.

McCauley, Edward Yorke. *With Perry in Japan: The Diary of Edward Yorke McCauley*. Ed. Allan B. Cole. Princeton: Princeton University Press, 1942.

Mears, Helen. *Year of the Wild Boar: An American Woman in Japan*. Philadelphia: J. B. Lippincott, 1942.

Mercer, Kobena. "Black Hair/Style Politics." In *Out There: Marginalization and Contemporary Culture,* ed. Russell Ferguson, Martha Gever, Trinh T. Minh-ha, and Cornel West, 247–64. New York: New Museum of Contemporary Art, 1990.

Michener, James A. *Sayonara*. 1953. New York: Bantam Books, 1955.

Miller, Nancy. K. "Writing Fictions: Women's Autobiography in France." In *Life/Lines: Theorizing Women's Autobiography,* ed. Bella Brodzki and Celeste Schenck, 45–61. Ithaca: Cornell University Press, 1988.

Minatoya, Lydia Yuri. *Talking to High Monks in the Snow: An Asian American Odyssey*. 1992. Reprint, New York: Harper Perennial, 1993.

Mirikitani, Janice. *Awake in the River*. San Francisco: Isthmus Press, 1978.

———. *Shedding Silence*. Berkeley: Celestial Arts, 1987.

———. *We, the Dangerous: New and Selected Poems*. London: Virago Press, 1995.

Mistri, Zenobia Baxter. " 'Seventeen Syllables': A Symbolic Haiku." *Studies in Short Fiction* 27, no. 2 (1990): 197–202.

Miyamoto, S. Frank. "Problems of Interpersonal Style Among the Nisei." *Amerasia* 13, no. 2 (1986–87): 39–45.

Mohanty, Chandra Talpade. "Under Western Eyes: Feminist Scholarship and Colonial Discourses." In *Third World Women and the Politics of Feminism,* ed. Chandra Talpade Mohanty, Ann Russo, and Lourdes Torres, 51–80. Bloomington: Indiana University Press, 1991.

Moloney, James Clark. *Understanding the Japanese Mind*. New York: Philosophical Library, 1954.

Mori, Kyoko. *The Dream of Water*. New York: Fawcett Columbine-Random House, 1995.

———. *Fallout*. Chicago: Tía Chucha Press, 1994.

Morley, John David. *Pictures from the Water Trade: Adventures of a Westerner in Japan*. New York: Perennial Library-Harper and Row, 1985.

Moy, James S. *Marginal Sights: Staging the Chinese in America*. Iowa City: University of Iowa Press, 1993.

Mura, David. *Turning Japanese: Memoirs of a Sansei*. New York: Atlantic Monthly Press, 1991.

Nakano, Mei. *Japanese American Women: Three Generations 1890–1990*. Berkeley: Mina Press Publishing, 1990.

Ng, Fae Myenne. *Bone*. New York: Hyperion, 1993.

Nice, Vivien E. *Mothers and Daughters: The Distortion of a Relationship*. New York: St. Martin's Press, 1992.

Nixon, Lucille M., and Tomoe Tana, eds. and trans. *Sounds from the Unknown: A Collection of Japanese-American Tanka*. Denver: A. Swallow, 1963.

Noda, Kesaya E. "Growing Up Asian in America." In *Making Waves: An Anthology of Writings by and about Asian American Women,* ed. Asian Women United of California, 243–51. Boston: Beacon Press, 1989.

North, Michael. *The Dialect of Modernism: Race, Language, and Twentieth-Century Literature*. New York: Oxford University Press, 1994.

O'Brien, David, and Stephen S. Fugita. *The Japanese American Experience*. Bloomington: Indiana University Press, 1991.

Oishi, Gene. *In Search of Hiroshi*. Rutland: Charles E. Tuttle, 1988.

Okada, John. *No-No Boy*. 1957. Seattle: University of Washington Press, 1976.

Okihiro, Gary Y. *Margins and Mainstreams: Asians in American History and Culture*. Seattle: University of Washington Press, 1994.

Okimoto, Daniel I. *American in Disguise*. Foreword by James A. Michener. New York: Walker/Weatherhill, 1971.

Okubo, Mine. *Citizen 13660*. 1946. Reprint, Seattle: University of Washington Press, 1983.

Olney, James, ed. *Autobiography: Essays Theoretical and Critical*. Princeton: Princeton University Press, 1980.

———. "Some Versions of Memory/Some Versions of *Bios:* The Ontology of

Autobiography." In *Autobiography: Essays Theoretical and Critical,* ed. James Olney, 236–67. Princeton: Princeton University Press, 1980.

Omi, Michael, and Howard Winant. *Racial Formation in the United States: 1960–1990.* 2d ed. New York: Routledge, 1994.

Ortega, Eliana, and Nancy Saporta Sternbach. "At the Threshold of the Unnamed: Latina Literary Discourse in the Eighties." In *Breaking Boundaries: Latina Writing and Critical Reading,* ed. Asuncion Horno-Delgado, 2–23. Amherst: University of Massachusetts Press, 1989.

Pratt, Mary Louise. *Imperial Eyes: Travel Writing and Transculturation.* London: Routledge, 1992.

Rayson, Anne. "Beneath the Mask: Autobiographies of Japanese-American Women." *MELUS* 14, no. 1 (1987): 43–57.

Rhodes, Richard. *Making Love: An Erotic Odyssey.* New York: Simon and Schuster, 1992.

Rony, Fatimah Tobing. *The Third Eye: Race, Cinema, and Ethnographic Spectacle.* Durham, N.C.: Duke University Press, 1996.

Rose, Jacqueline. *Sexuality in the Field of Vision.* London: Verso, 1986.

Rowbotham, Sheila. *Woman's Consciousness, Man's World.* London: Penguin, 1973.

Said, Edward W. *Culture and Imperialism.* New York: Alfred A. Knopf, 1993.

———. *Orientalism.* New York: Vintage Books-Random House, 1978.

Saiki, Jessica. *From the Lanai and Other Hawai'i Stories.* Minneapolis: New Rivers Press, 1991.

Saldívar, Ramón. *Chicano Narrative: The Dialectics of Difference.* Madison: University of Wisconsin Press, 1990.

Sasaki, R. A. *The Loom.* Minnesota: Graywolf Press, 1991.

Sato, Gayle K. Fujita. "Momotaro's Exile: John Okada's *No-No Boy.*" In *Reading the Literatures of Asian America,* ed. Shirley Geok-lin Lim and Amy Ling, 239–58. Philadelphia: Temple University Press, 1992.

Sayre, Robert F. "Autobiography and the Making of America." In *Autobiography: Essays Theoretical and Critical,* ed. James Olney, 146–68. Princeton: Princeton University Press, 1980.

Schwartz, John Burnham. *Bicycle Days.* New York: Summit Books, 1989.

Schweik, Susan. *A Gulf So Deeply Cut: American Women Poets and the Second World War.* Madison: University of Wisconsin Press, 1991.

———. "A Needle with Mama's Voice: Mitsuye Yamada's *Camp Notes* and the American Canon of War Poetry." In *Arms and the Woman: War, Gender, and Literary Representation,* ed. Helen M. Cooper, Adrienne Auslander Munich, and Susan Merrill Squier, 225–43. Chapel Hill: University of North Carolina Press, 1989.

Sechi, Joanne Harumi. "Being Japanese-American Doesn't Mean 'Made in Japan.'" In *The Third Woman: Minority Women Writers of the United States,* ed. Dexter Fisher, 442–49. Boston: Houghton Mifflin, 1980.

Shigekuni, Julie. *A Bridge Between Us.* New York: Anchor Books-Doubleday, 1995.

Silverman, Kaja. "White Skin, Brown Masks: The Double Mimesis, or With Lawrence in Arabia." *differences* 1, no. 3 (1989): 3–54.

Simpson, Caroline Chung. "American Orientalisms: The Cultural and Gender Politics of America's Postwar Relationship with Japan." Ph.D. dissertation, University of Texas, Austin, 1994.

Smith, Paul. *Discerning the Subject.* Minneapolis: University of Minnesota Press, 1988.

Smith, Sidonie. *A Poetics of Women's Autobiography.* Bloomington: Indiana University Press, 1987.

Sommer, Doris. " 'Not Just a Personal Story': Women's Testimonios and the Plural Self." In *Life/Lines: Theorizing Women's Autobiography,* ed. Bella Brodzki and Celeste Schenck, 107–30. Ithaca: Cornell University Press, 1988.

Sone, Monica. *Nisei Daughter.* 1953. Seattle: University of Washington Press, 1979.

Spickard, Paul R. *Japanese Americans: The Formation and Transformations of an Ethnic Group.* New York: Twayne Publishers-Simon and Schuster Macmillan, 1996.

Spillers, Hortense J. "Interstices: A Small Drama of Words." In *Pleasure and Danger,* ed. Carole Vance, 73–100. New York: Routledge, 1984.

———. "Mama's Baby, Papa's Maybe: An American Grammar Book." *Diacritics* (summer 1987): 65–81.

Spivak, Gayatri. "Can the Subaltern Speak?" In *Marxism and the Interpretation of Culture,* ed. Cary Nelson and Lawrence Grossberg, 271–313. Urbana: University of Illinois Press, 1988.

Spurr, David. *The Rhetoric of Empire: Colonial Discourse in Journalism, Travel Writing, and Imperial Administration.* Durham, N.C.: Duke University Press, 1993.

Stanton, Domna C. "Autogynography: Is the Subject Different?" In *The Female Autograph,* ed. Domna C. Stanton. New York: New York Literary Forum, 1984.

———. "Difference on Trial: A Critique of the Maternal Metaphor in Cixous, Irigaray and Kristeva." In *The Poetics of Gender,* ed. Nancy K. Miller. New York: Columbia University Press, 1986.

Steedman, Carolyn Kay. *Landscape for a Good Woman: A Story of Two Lives.* New Brunswick, N.J.: Rutgers University Press, 1987.

Sugimoto, Etsu Inagaki. *A Daughter of the Samurai.* New York: Doubleday Page, 1925.

Sumida, Stephen H. *And the View from the Shore: Literary Traditions of Hawai'i.* Seattle: University of Washington Press, 1991.

Tan, Amy. *Joy Luck Club.* New York: Putnam, 1989.

Taylor, Sandra C. *Advocate of Understanding: Sidney Gulick and the Search for Peace with Japan.* Kent, Ohio: Kent State University Press, 1984.

Trinh, Minh-ha T. "Not You/Like You: Post-Colonial Women and the Interlocking Questions of Identity and Difference." In *Making Face, Making Soul: Haciendo Caras,* ed. Gloria Anzaldua, 371–75. San Francisco: Aunt Lute Foundation, 1990.

———. *Woman, Native, Other: Writing Post-Coloniality and Feminism.* Bloomington: Indiana University Press, 1989.

Ty, Eleanor. "Struggling with the Powerful M(Other): Identity and Sexuality in Kogawa's *Obasan* and Kincaid's *Lucy*." *International Fiction Review* 20, no. 2(1993): 120–26.

Uchida, Yoshiko. *Desert Exile: The Uprooting of a Japanese-American Family*. 1982. Seattle: University of Washington Press, 1984.

Uyematsu, Amy. *30 Miles from J-Town*. Brownsville: Story Line Press, 1992.

Uyemoto, Holly. *Go*. New York: Dutton, 1995.

Wand, David Hsin-Fu, ed. *Asian-American Heritage: An Anthology of Prose and Poetry*. New York: Washington Square Press, 1974.

Ware, Vron. *Beyond the Pale: White Women, Racism and History*. London: Verso, 1992.

Watanabe, Sylvia. *Talking to the Dead*. New York: Doubleday, 1992.

Weglyn, Michi. *Years of Infamy: The Untold Story of America's Concentration Camps*. New York: Morrow Quill Paperbacks, 1976.

Welchman, John C. *Modernism Relocated: Towards a Cultural Studies of Visual Modernity*. St. Leonards, Australia: Allen and Unwin, 1995.

Wiegman, Robyn. *American Anatomies: Theorizing Race and Gender*. Durham, N.C.: Duke University Press, 1995.

Wong, Sau-ling Cynthia. *Reading Asian American Literature: From Necessity to Extravagance*. Princeton: Princeton University Press, 1993.

Wong, Shawn, ed. *Asian American Literature: A Brief Introduction and Anthology*. New York: Harper Collins, 1996.

Yamada, Mitsuye. "Asian Pacific American Women and Feminism." In *This Bridge Called My Back: Writings by Radical Women of Color*, ed. Cherrie Moraga and Gloria Anzaldua, 71–75. Watertown, Conn.: Persephone Press, 1981.

———. *Camp Notes*. 1976. Reprint, Latham, N.Y.: Kitchen Table / Women of Color Press, 1992.

———. *Desert Run: Poems and Stories*. Latham, N.Y.: Kitchen Table / Women of Color Press, 1988.

———. "Invisibility is an Unnatural Disaster: Reflections of an Asian American Woman." In *This Bridge Called My Back: Writings by Radical Women of Color,* ed. Cherrie Moraga and Gloria Anzaldua, 35–40. Watertown, Conn.: Persephone Press, 1981.

Yamaguchi, Yoji. *Face of a Stranger*. New York: Harper Perennial, 1995.

Yamamoto, Hisaye. *Seventeen Syllables and Other Stories*. Latham, N.Y.: Kitchen Table / Women of Color Press, 1988.

Yamanaka, Lois-Ann. *Blu's Hanging*. New York: Farrar Straus and Giroux, 1997.

———. *Saturday Night at the Pahala Theatre*. Honolulu: Bamboo Ridge Press, 1993.

———. *Wild Meat and the Bully Burgers*. New York: Farrar Straus and Giroux, 1996.

Yamashita, Karen Tei. *Brazil Maru*. Minneapolis: Coffee House Press, 1992.

———. *Through the Arc of the Rain Forest*. Minneapolis: Coffee House Press, 1990.

Yamauchi, Wakako. *Songs My Mother Taught Me: Stories, Plays, and Memoir*. New York: The Feminist Press, 1994.

Yanagisako, Sylvia Junko. *Transforming the Past: Tradition and Kinship Among Japanese Americans.* Stanford: Stanford University Press, 1985.

Yogi, Stan. "Rebels and Heroines: Subversive Narratives in the Stories of Wakako Yamauchi and Hisaye Yamamoto." In *Reading the Literatures of Asian America,* ed. Shirley Geok-lin Lim and Amy Ling, 131–50. Philadelphia: Temple University Press, 1992.

Index

abjection, 133–135, 137. *See also* disavowal
agency: of daughters, 144, 152, 156; denial
of, 95, 112–113, 134; and discursivity, 103–
105, 111, 112–113, 114–115, 189, 203, 252;
and masking, 107, 117; problematized
strategies of, 96–98, 130–131, 138–139,
242; and silence, 187, 190; and subjectivity, 76–77, 78, 79–81, 90–91, 97–99,
100, 128, 143. *See also* appropriated
agency; maternal agency
Aiiieeeee!, 128. *See also* dual personality
Ancheta, Angelo, 64
antimiscegenation, 33–34, 39. *See also* interracial marriage
Anzaldúa, Gloria, 92
appropriated agency, 48, 50, 56, 60, 71,
74, 93, 218, 219, 222, 229–231, 244, 246–
247
Asian Americans: invisibility of, 63–65, 67,
72–75; violence against, 272n3
Asian American women, 64–68; comparison with white American women, 66;
invisibility of, 64, 74; sexualization of,
65–67, 73–74, 81, 224–225. *See also* Japanese American women
authenticity, 82, 99
autobiography, 88–89, 102–140; for African Americans, 7, 105, 106, 277n3; for
Americans, 107–109; as conversion narrative, 108–110, 125; for Nisei, 105–107,
112–114, 122; traditional theories of, 108–

109, 112–113; of women, 102–103, 108–
109, 113. *See also* slave narrative

Barthes, Roland, 14–15, 93–95. *See also* face;
eyes
Behind the Mask (Buruma), 17–19
Berlant, Lauren, 72–73, 126
Beyond Manzanar (Houston), 146–151
Bhabha, Homi K., 15, 20–21, 36, 44
black-white paradigm, 62–64
body: as contested site, 77, 81, 90–92, 200–
201, 233–235; as country, 22–23, 33–34,
38, 41, 60, 67, 217–218, 234–235; and
language, 237–239, 251; and visuality, 3,
4–5, 6, 62–65, 71–74, 87–88, 91–92; vul-
nerability of, 231–232. *See also* Asian
American women; Japanese American
women; Japanese women
Brando, Marlon: in *Teahouse of the August
Moon*, 28–32; in *Sayonara*, 34–44
Buck, Pearl S., 14
Bumiller, Elisabeth, 14
Buruma, Ian, 17–19.
Butler, Judith, 30–31, 146

Cheung, King-Kok, 6, 169, 174–175, 187,
197
Chow, Rey, 47, 48
Christopher, Robert C., 9, 14, 19–20, 22
citizenship, 7, 72–73, 109, 113, 122–126, 135
Collins, Patricia Hill, 145, 149–150

299